Program Planning
for the Training and
Continuing Education of Adults:
North American Perspectives

Edited by Peter S. Cookson

KRIEGER PUBLISHNG COMPANY
MALABAR, FLORIDA
1998

Original Edition 1998

Printed and Published by
KRIEGER PUBISHING COMPANY
KRIEGER DRIVE
MALABAR, FLORIDA 32950

Library of Congress Cataloging-in-Publication Data

Program planning for the training and continuing education of adults:
    North American perspectives/edited by Peter S. Cookson.—
    Original ed.
        p.   cm.
    Includes bibliographical references and index.
    ISBN 0-89464-767-9 (hardcover: alk. paper)
    1. Continuing education—United States—Planning.   2. Adult education—United States—Planning.   3. Continuing education—Canada—Planning.   4. Adult education—Canada—Planning.
I. Cookson, Peter S., 1944–   .
LC5251.P686   1998
374.12—dc21   97-35031
                                                                   CIP

10   9   8   7   6   5   4   3   2

This book is dedicated to three distinguished leaders
in the field of lifelong education whose lives,
leadership, and scholarship, during the second half
of the twentieth century, have profoundly influenced,
instructed, and inspired training and continuing
education program planners
throughout North America and worldwide:

Professor Emeritus Cyril O. Houle
and two of his most outstanding students
at the University of Chicago,
Malcolm S. Knowles and William S. Griffith.

Contents

Introduction

It is widely accepted that the effectiveness of training and education programs for men and women is somehow related to the economic productivity and social and cultural vitality of organizations and nations. It is therefore ironic that the systematic learning activities of men and women are generally fragmented, uncoordinated, and often given a low priority in both organizations and nations. Those who are responsible for the planning, implementation, and evaluation of training and education programs often work in isolation from their counterparts in other organizations. As a consequence, the planning process often tends to be circumscribed by the internal politics of organizational leaders and other stakeholders, leaving program planners to discover for themselves the what, how, and why of their training and education responsibilities.

A central premise of this book is that training and education program planners can strengthen their competence and, as a result, enable the men and women learners within their respective organizations or served by their organizations to optimize their participation in education or training programs. By expanding their consciousness and commitment beyond their organizations to the broader field of practice, program planners can come to share with their counterparts across a wide spectrum of organizational settings a sense of professional responsibility that embodies a commitment to excellence and ethical rightness. They thus can be in a much better position to fortify the education and training enterprise in which they are involved. Of course, the improvement in the competence levels of training and education program planners within an entire society implies a long and protracted trajectory. Even the longest trip begins with the first step.

Perhaps an initial step towards the forging of a professional identity is the recognition that program planning involves a generic process. As such, it can be described, analyzed, and learned—as well as implemented. As the authors of the 19 chapters that follow explain, the program planning process touches on *all* forms of organized learning for men and women, regardless of the institutional or program context. The ways in which that process applies to different settings, however, can vary greatly. To enable practitioners from a variety of organizational backgrounds to relate to different aspects of the process, the authors provide examples from different fields of practice: training and human resource development, distance education, agricultural extension and nonformal education, university continuing education, continuing professional education, and adult education for individual, organizational, and community development. These fields of practice are played out in such organizational settings as hospitals, labor unions, voluntary and nonprofit organizations, professional associations, business and industrial organizations, government agencies, universities, colleges, institutes, and schools.

The authors intend this book to serve as a resource for practitioners across the entire length and breadth of education and training for men and women. Accordingly, the contents of this book reflect the literature and practice of what has been referred to in Canada and the United States as *adult education*. Although it is possible that many of the principles discussed in this book will apply to organized learning in cultural contexts outside of Anglophone North America, no claims to universality are made. The extent to which they may be applicable must be left for practitioners in such cultural contexts to determine.

The order of the chapters reflects an underlying structure. The first four chapters present a conceptual frame of reference for examination of the phenomenon and practice of program planning. In Chapter 1, Cookson presents a conceptual basis for the study of the organizational, technological, and programmatic contexts for education and training programs as well as a comprehensive and synthetic approach to the implementation of planning such programs across the adult education spectrum. In Chapter 2, several authors describe what might be called conventional program planning models that have had a profound impact on the field: Houle's Fundamental System, Knowles's Andragogical Model, and Nadler's Critical Events Model. In Chapter 3, Long reviews several alternative and lesser known models.

Chapters 4 through 6 address personal and professional antecedents that affect the program planning enterprise but are usually overlooked. In Chapter 4 Shipp addresses the various roles that planners occupy. In Chapter 5, Brockett and Hiemstra address philosophical and ethical issues programmers must deal with but often ignore. In Chapter 6, Cervero and Wilson present a detailed case study that enables us to view program planning as an unavoidable intermeshing and negotiation of competing interests within an organization. Consideration of these antecedents can preclude any tendency to perceive the practice of program planning as a merely mechanical, by-the-numbers exercise.

Chapters 7 through 9 encompass program planners' efforts to address the various contexts that influence and shape their work. In Chapter 7, Cookson outlines how program planners can identify and respond to conditions external to the sponsoring organization. In Chapter 8, Donaldson identifies ways in which planners can come to grips, both intellectually and interpersonally, with various dimensions of the organizational sponsor. In Chapter 9, Ross-Gordon explains what planners should keep in mind about program participants. All of the elements detailed in Chapters 7 through 9 underlie the planner's efforts to identify the learning needs their programs should address. In Chapter 10, Pearce reviews different approaches planners may employ to conduct what is commonly termed a "needs assessment."

Having engaged the relevant contexts enables planners to design specific education and training programs. Chapters 11 through 14 describe the strategies to design the program. In Chapter 11, Sork explains various options for prioritizing needs from which purposes and objectives can be derived and delineated. In Chapter 12, Deshler explains how planners might ascertain the extent to which their programs are successful. In Chapter 13, Sisco and Cochenour discuss principles of the instructional design component of program planning. In Chapter 14, Fellenz discusses how planners might wish to think about and select formats for learning that include appropriate methods, techniques, and devices.

Besides design of the program, planners must also turn their attention to administrative concerns, the common thread of Chapters 15 through 18. In Chapter 15, Havercamp reviews a variety of ways to promote education and training programs. In Chapter 16, Quigley explains the theoretical and practical bases for recruitment and retention of program participants. In Chapter 17, Watkins and Sechrest offer guidelines for financial and budget arrangements. In Chapter 18, Flannery discusses specific procedures for hiring, supervising, and training instructional and other program-related staff members.

In Chapter 19, the editor provides an analytical review of the overall program planning process. He also discusses some of the implications of increased awareness for the improvement of program planning practice across the training and continuing education spectrum.

Program Planning for the Training and Continuing Education of Adults: North American Perspectives has three central objectives:

1. To increase the familiarity of readers with the conceptual and theoretical underpinnings of the program planning process
2. To examine particular tools for the systematic design of learning activities for men and women
3. To explore options for specific steps in the process of planning education or training programs

The intended readers for this guide are those professionals, managers, educators, and trainers who attempt to understand and increase their skills and knowledge with respect to the training or educational design for adults. For those who have recently entered this field, the guide can serve as an introduction to this exciting and challenging line of work. For readers already familiar with many of the themes discussed, the book can serve as a review of the skills and knowledge they have already mastered. For those who consider themselves to be seasoned program planners, the guide will provide an opportunity to consider in broad terms the numerous elements of their practice. The chapters present points for reflection for all program planners, regardless of the depth and breadth of experience. Through such reflection, they can expand the horizons of their performance possibilities and thus contribute to a higher quality of life for the men and women who participate in their programs.

Peter S. Cookson

The Authors

Ralph G. Brockett is an associate professor of adult education at the University of Tennessee, Knoxville. He received his B.A. in psychology and his M.Ed. and Ph.D. in adult education from Syracuse University. Previously, he held faculty positions at Montana State University (1984-88) and Syracuse University (1982-84) and has worked in continuing education program development for health and human services professionals. He is past chair of the Commission of Professors of Adult Education and has served on the board of the American Association for Adult and Continuing Education. In addition, he has held positions on the editorial boards of three different adult education journals and currently is coeditor-in-chief of *New Directions for Adult and Continuing Education*. His previous books include *Overcoming Resistance to Self-direction in Adult Learning* (co-editor with R. Hiemstra, 1994), *Self-direction in Adult Learning: Perspectives on Theory, Research, and Practice* (with R. Hiemstra, 1991), *Professional Development for Educators of Adults* (editor, 1991), *Ethical Issues in Adult Education* (1988), *Adult and Continuing Education* (co-editor with S. E. Easton and J. O. Picton, 1988), and *Continuing Education in the Year 2000* (editor, 1987). His major scholarly interests are in the areas of professional ethics for adult education, self-direction in adult learning, and the study of the adult education field.

Ronald M. Cervero is a professor in the Department of Adult Education at the University of Georgia. He has published extensively in adult education, with particular emphasis in the area of continuing education for the professions. His three books on the topic have won several national awards, including the 1989 Cyril O. Houle World Award for Literature in Adult Education (*Effective Continuing Education for Professionals*). His recent book co-authored with Arthur Wilson, *Planning Responsibly for Adult Education: A Guide* *to Negotiating Power and Interests,* offers a theory of program planning practice. He has served in a variety of leadership positions in adult education including the editorship of *Adult Education Quarterly,* the Commission of Professors of Adult Education, and the Adult Education Research Conference. He has been a visiting faculty member at the University of Tennessee, the University of Wisconsin-Madison, the University of British Columbia, and Pennsylvania State University.

John Cochenour is associate professor of instructional technology in the Adult Learning and Technology Unit at the University of Wyoming. He received his Ph.D. in educational technology at the University of Oklahoma, Norman and served in that university's School of Library and Information Studies. He has extensive experience in the application of communication technologies for distance instruction and has taught numerous courses in information technology, distance education, visual literacy, and instructional technology. He serves on the board of directors of the International Visual Literacy Association and was recently elected vice president. His research interests include symbols and their interpretation, information access and use, and distance education at the adult level. His coedited book, *Compressed Video: Operations and Applications* was recently revised and updated.

Peter S. Cookson is associate vice president, academic and professor of distance education at Athabasca University, the open university of Canada. Prior to his present appointment in Athabasca, Alberta, he taught at what is now Texas A&M at Kingsville, the University of British Columbia, and Pennsylvania State University (where he was professor-in-charge of the Adult Education Program). A native of England and now a citizen of Canada and the United States, he received his Ph.D. in adult education at the University of Chicago and his B.Sc. and M.Sc. in sociology and Latin American Studies at Brigham Young University. He has taught university courses for educators and trainers of adults in Nicaragua, Costa Rica, Panama, Venezuela, Mexico, and Sudan. He serves on the editorial boards of *Revista Iberoamericana de Educación a Distancia* (Spain) and *Educación y Ciencias Humanas* (Venezuela). His professional interests include distance and continuing education programming and evaluation, continuing higher education administration, and national development. He has conducted research on the role of education and training on development in Third World societies, participation in organized learning, and various topics related to the study of interaction in distance education. He edited *Recruiting and Retaining Adult Students* and coauthored *Beyond Instruction: Comprehensive Program Planning for Business and Education.*

David Deshler is associate professor of agriculture, extension, and adult education in the Department of Education, Cornell University, Ithaca, New York. He received his Ed.D. degree in adult education from the University of California, Los Angeles. His scholarly interests and publications have focused on program evaluation, futures research and participatory action research approaches, extension education, community development, and critical reflective learning in adulthood.

Joe F. Donaldson is associate professor in the University of Missouri-Columbia's program in higher and adult education, a program in the Department of Educational Leadership and Policy Analysis. He is responsible for teaching courses on the adult learner, organization and administration of continuing education, program planning, continuing education for the professions, and educational leadership. His research and writing focus on continuing education for the professions and the organization and administration of continuing higher education. From 1987 to 1991 Donaldson served on the adult education faculty at Pennsylvania State University. Prior to that, he was head of the Division of Extramural Courses at the University of Illinois at Urbana-Champaign. He has chaired the National University Continuing Education Association's (NUCEA) Council for Continuing Education Management and Administration and served on NUCEA's Board of Directors. He currently serves on the editorial boards of the *Continuing Higher Education Review*, the *Journal of Continuing Higher Education*, and the *International Journal of Continuing Education Practice*. He chairs the University Continuing Education Association's (UCEA, formerly NUCEA) Advisory Committee for its publication series on organizational issues in continuing higher education. Donaldson is the author of *Managing Credit Programs in Continuing Higher Education* and UCEA's publication, *Continuing Education Reviews: Principles, Practices and Strategies*. He holds a B.S. and M.S. from the University of Tennessee-Knoxville and a Ph.D. in continuing education from the University of Wisconsin-Madison.

Robert A. Fellenz recently retired as professor of adult education at Montana State University. He began his career working with adults in community and church programs in the Green Bay area of Wisconsin. His Ed.D. in adult education was earned at the University of Wyoming. With Don Seaman he built a graduate program at Texas A&M that became one of the largest in the country. He taught there for fifteen and a half years, moving to Montana State University in 1987 to assume the position of principal investigator of a W. K. Kellogg Foundation grant. The project concentrated on research on adult learning and sponsored summer institutes for adult education professors. This led to the publication of a series of monographs on adult learning and a Self-Knowledge Inventory of Lifelong Learning Strategies (SKILLS). He is also the coauthor with Don Seaman of *Effective Strategies for Teaching Adults.*

Daniele D. Flannery is assistant professor and coordinator of the D.Ed. Adult Education Program at Pennsylvania State University-Harrisburg. Her professional interests include learning, particularly of women and minorities, and the assessment of learning in business and other-than-profit agencies. She currently serves on the editorial boards of *Adult Education Quarterly* and the *Pennsylvania Adult and Continuing Education Journal* and is writing a book on women's learning.

Michael J. Havercamp has over fifteen years of experience in community and organizational development, group facilitation, and mediation. As an associate professor in human development and family studies at the University of Nevada in Reno, he provides training to university faculty, staff, community leaders, and international groups in conflict management and group facilitation. He received a Ph.D. in education and community development from the University of Michigan and an M.A. in adult education from the University of Chicago. In 1993, he was awarded the Thornton Peace Prize by the University of Nevada for his work mediating community disputes.

Roger Hiemstra is a consultant in professional planning, training, and writing, in Syracuse, New York. He obtained his Ph.D. in adult community education from the University of Michigan, his M.S. in extension education from Iowa State University, and his B.S. in rural sociology and agricultural economics from Michigan State University. From 1980–1992 he chaired the adult education program at Syracuse University, directed the Kellogg Project on the dissemination of adult education information at Syracuse from 1986–1992, and was a professor on the School of Education faculty there until 1996. He is past president of the Commission of Professors of Adult Education and former editor of *Lifelong Learning and the Adult Education Quarterly*. He has focused much of his scholarship on the identification of teaching implications and resources related to adult self-directed learning. Author of numerous articles and book chapters, he also has authored or coauthored several books, including *Overcoming Resistance to Self-Direction in Adult Learning, Professional Writing: Processes, Strategies, and Tips for Publishing in Educational Journals, The Educative Community, Creating Effective Learning Environments, Self-Direction in Adult Learning,* and *Individualizing Instruction*.

Malcolm S. Knowles before his death on Thanksgiving Day in 1997 was Professor Emeritus of Adult and Community College Education at North Carolina State University, where he served from 1974 to 1979. Previously he was professor of education at Boston University, 1960–1974; executive director, Adult Education Association of the USA, 1951–1959; executive secretary, Central YMCA, Boston, 1940–1943; director of training, National Youth Administration of Massachusetts, 1935–1940. He received his A.B. from Harvard in 1934, and his M.A. and Ph.D. in adult education from the University of Chicago in 1949 and 1960 respectively. Following his retirement in 1979 he was actively engaged in consulting and conducting workshops with education institutions, business and industry, government agencies, religious institutions, voluntary agencies, and American Society for Training and Development chapters and conferences, in North America, Europe, South America, Australia, Japan, South Korea, Singapore, and Bangkok. He was author of eighteen books, the most recent being *The Modern Practice of Adult Education, The Adult Learner: A Neglected Species, Andragogy in Action, Using Learning Contracts, The Making of an Adult Educator*, and over 230 articles.

Huey B. Long is Kellogg Professor of Continuing Professional and Higher Education at the University of Oklahoma. He has been a tenured faculty member at Florida State University and the University of Georgia. In addition he has served as visiting professor at universities in Canada, China, England, Germany, South Korea, Sweden, and the United States. He has published more than 600 articles, books, and chapters on a variety of adult education topics including program planning. In recognition for his book *Adult Learning: Research and Practice* he was awarded the Houle

World Literature Award. He has held a variety of leadership positions including that of president of what is now known as the American Association of Adult and Continuing Education, and other positions in the Community Development Society of America, International Council for Adult Education, and the University Continuing Education Association. He has received awards from the AAACE, Georgia Adult Education Association, NUEA (now UCEA), and the Oklahoma Lifelong Learning Association.

Leonard Nadler is Professor Emeritus, School of Education and Human Development, George Washington University where he developed the first full M.A. and Ed.D. programs in human resource development as well as the graduate program in adult education. He also worked with a wide variety of clients in the field of adult learning, both in the United States and in many other countries. He has written more than ten books and over 150 articles in the field of adult learning. He is a partner in Nadler Associates.

Zeace Nadler is president of Nadler Associates, a company that has provided assistance in various forms of adult learning to organizations in the United States and 33 foreign countries. She has also been active in planning and conducting conferences and meetings. She has coauthored five books (with Leonard Nadler) and numerous professional articles. She has been an adjunct member of the George Washington University faculty in human resource development and adult education.

Sandra Pearce is an associate professor in the School of Human Justice at the University of Regina, where she provides an adult education perspective to the academic and professional education programs. A continuing higher education practitioner for many years (she was formerly the head of the Professional and Social Development Division of University Extension) her programs have been recognized with national awards. She has a B.A. in French from Simon Fraser University, an M.A. in community development from the University of Alberta, and a D.Ed. in adult education from Pennsylvania State University. She is the cofounder and editor of *The International Journal of Continuing Education Practice*—an electronic refereed journal—and her writing and research focus on leadership, professional education, and the administration of higher and continuing education. She is a partner in *Innova Learning International*, a group which specializes in program evaluation, training needs assessments, and training audits.

B. Allan Quigley is associate professor in the Adult Education Department at St. Francis Xavier University in Antigonish, Nova Scotia. He was formerly an associate professor and regional director of adult education in the College of Education, Pennsylvania State University. He has more than twenty-five years of experience in teaching, administering, developing policy, and researching adult education in North America. His doctorate is in adult and continuing education from Northern Illinois University. His M.A. and B.A. degrees are from the University of Regina. He helped found the Saskatchewan community college system and later directed Saskatchewan's university sector with the Government of Saskatchewan. He helped found Saskatchewan community college system. He has published over 100 articles, book chapters, edited books, monographs, and sponsored research studies. He has chaired the GED Advisory Committee and the Research Unit of the American Association for Adult and Continuing Education, has been a member of the steering committee of the Adult Education Research Conference, and serves as a consulting editor for several adult education and literacy journals. He was named Outstanding Educator of the Year in Pennsylvania in 1994.

Jovita M. Ross-Gordon is associate professor of education and director of the Center for Adult Learning Services in New College at St. Edwards University, Austin, Texas. From 1985-1995 she was a member of the faculty in the Adult Education Program at Pennsylvania State University where she served as Professor-in-Charge from 1991-1993. She earned her B.S. in speech and language pathology and M.A. in learning disabilities at Northwestern University in Evanston, Illinois, and her Ed.D. in adult education at the University of Georgia in Athens, Georgia. Her professional leadership in the field of adult education includes service as co-chair of the Adult Education Research Conference in 1993, as chair-elect and later chair of the Publications Standing Service Unit of the American Association for Adult and Continuing Education from 1991–1993, and as a member of the Executive Committee of the Commission of Professors of Adult Education from 1987 to 1989. Her scholarly honors include selection by the Kellogg Foundation as one of the most promising young scholars in adult education in 1987, receipt of the National University Continuing Education Association Research Award in 1993, and receipt of a research fellowship from the National Center on Adult Learning in 1995.

She has published extensively on teaching and learning of adults with a primary focus in three areas: learning disabilities, continuing higher education, and multiculturalism/diversity.

Thomas L. Sechrest is a senior learning and development specialist for Leadership/Management Development Programs at Advanced Micro Devices, Austin, Texas. He was formerly the training manager for the U.S. Department of Labor's Occupational Safety and Health Administration in Atlanta, and also worked for several years as an educational and industrial television producer and as a consultant in management assessment and development. More recently, he worked as a conference coordinator in the Continuing Education Program of the College of Education at the University of Texas at Austin. He received his B.A. in psychology and his M.S. in instructional design from Florida State University in Tallahassee. He is coauthor, with George L. Morrisey, of *Effective Business and Technical Presentations.* He is a member of the American Society for Training and Development, the American Association for Adult and Continuing Education, and Phi Kappa Phi.

Travis Shipp is associate professor of continuing studies and chair of the Department of Adult Education at Indiana University. He earned his doctorate at the University of Georgia and his M.B.A. and B.S. in engineering at Auburn University. He has written more than sixty articles and chapters and several books, fiction and nonfiction. He has edited books, presented research papers, and held national office in several professional organizations. He has developed two graduate programs in adult education and is currently developing a distance learning graduate program in adult education.

Burton Sisco is associate dean for graduate studies and research professor of adult education at the University of Wyoming. He received his doctorate in adult education from Syracuse University. Sisco teaches courses on adult learning and lifespan development, historical foundations of adult education, administration, program planning and evaluation, and teaching adults. He has held numerous leadership positions with the American Association for Adult and Continuing Education. He is past editor of the Mountain Plains Adult Education Association's *Journal of Adult Education,* and has served as book review editor of *Adult Literacy and Basic Education,* and on the editorial board of the *Adult Education Quarterly.* His primary research interests lie in the areas of adult cognition, self-directed learning, and teaching effectiveness. Among his books are *Individualizing Instruction: Making Learning Personal, Empowering, and Successful* with Roger Hiemstra, *Confronting Controversies in Challenging Times: A Call for Action* with Michael Galbraith, and *Administering Successful Programs for Adults: Promoting Excellence in Adult, Community, and Continuing Education* with Michael Galbraith and Lucy Guiglielmino.

Thomas J. Sork is associate professor and coordinator of adult education in the Department of Educational Studies at the University of British Columbia. He has worked in university continuing education and community development and has taught courses and led workshops on program planning, needs assessment and evaluation in the United States, Canada, Hong Kong, and Singapore. His current research interests focus on the human dynamics of planning, the process of resource allocation, and professional ethics in adult education. He has served on the editorial boards of *Adult Education Quarterly* and the *Journal of the Canadian Association for the Study of Adult Education* and on the executive boards of the Adult and Continuing Education Association of Nebraska, the Pacific Association for Continuing Education, the Commission of Professors of Adult Education, and the Adult Education Research Conference. His recent experience with the human dynamics of planning includes chairing the program committee of the Pacific Association for Continuing Education and serving on a committee given the task of developing and receiving approval for policies and procedures for a newly formed university department. He received his Ph.D. in adult education from Florida State University.

Karen E. Watkins is associate professor of adult education and director of graduate programs in human resource and organizational development at the University of Georgia. She received her Ph.D. in educational administration from the University of Texas at Austin. Dr. Watkins has published over fifty articles, chapters, and monographs. She is author or coauthor of six books, including *Sculpting the Learning Organization* and *In Action: The Learning Organization,* both coauthored with Victoria Marsick. She conducts research in the areas of organizational change and in trends and issues affecting the field of human resource development. She is president of the Academy of Human Resource Development.

Arthur L. Wilson is assistant professor in the Department of Adult and Community College Education at North Carolina State

University in Raleigh. His teaching and planning experience includes literacy (ABE/GED) work, design and instruction of literacy
staff development projects, continuing education in the professions, and graduate adult education programs. He is coauthor,
with Ronald M. Cervero, of *Planning Responsibly for Adult Education*
as well as consulting editor for the *Adult Education Quarterly* and the
Journal of Adult Basic Education. His research interests include program planning practice in adult education, the history and philosophy of adult education, and the social context of adult learning.

A Conceptual Context for Program Planning

Peter S. Cookson

ABSTRACT

Sponsored education and training occur not only within specific organizational settings but also within a context of shared meanings and assumptions. The central aim of this chapter is to explicate those assumptions and meanings that comprise the conceptual context that underlies the overall structure of this book. The term *adult education* as an inclusive term is defined. To permit classification and analysis of organizational, technological, and programmatic contexts of broadly defined adult education activities, a multidimensional scheme is then presented. With specific reference to the program planning steps detailed in succeeding chapters, the final part of the chapter highlights a specific program planning framework that guided the selection and sequencing of those steps.

ASSESSMENT

1. What does the term *adult education* mean to you? What is the relevance of the term for your own education and/or training practice?

2. Describe *program planning* as it is practiced within your own organization. What elements might that process share in common with program planning in other organizations that are different from your own?

3. What importance does training or education have in your organization with respect to its impact on the organization itself, members of the organization, and others outside your organization?

INTRODUCTION

Upon completion of your study of this chapter, it is anticipated that you will be able to achieve the following objectives:

* Identify the diversity of training and education activities encompassed by the term *adult education.*
* Distinguish among organizational, technological, and programmatic aspects of adult education activities that occur within your own and other organizations.
* Outline a comprehensive approach to the selection and sequencing of education and training program planning steps.

WHAT IS MEANT BY THE TERM *ADULT EDUCATION*?

The program planning principles and practices presented in this book have their origin in the literature of adult education. Because the term *adult education* means different things to different people, it is important to begin with a clear definition.

When the term first appeared in a book title in 1810 in England, it had reference exclusively to adult literacy. A century later when it was the subject of a widely circulated post-World War I statement of British government policy, it had reference almost exclusively to liberal and nonoccupational education. For the representatives of a wide variety of organizations on this side of the Atlantic who attended the founding meeting of the American Association for Adult Education in 1926, however, the term had a much broader meaning. The same was true of the Canadian Adult Education Association that was founded in 1933.

Since the first graduate programs and courses in adult education were begun in the United States and Canada in the 1930s, the number of masters and doctoral programs in the field has grown to more than 100 in the 1990s. With few exceptions, these graduate programs have retained a comprehensive orientation toward the spectrum of education and training programs in an infinite variety of organizational settings. Unfortunately, this broad orientation is not shared by practitioners responsible for the design, delivery, and evaluation of education and training programs in a myriad of organizational settings. Indeed, the term *adult education* has become problematic; since the mid-1960s the federal government-financed and state-administered programs for men and women who had not completed their primary or secondary schooling have monopolized the term. In the public's mind, the meaning of adult education is often restricted to adult literacy, adult basic education, or other forms of compensatory and remedial education for adults. It is not surprising, therefore, that many practitioners are unaware of the comprehensiveness of the term.

Educators and trainers who work with men and women who typically engage in learning outside of school settings prefer to associate themselves with such terms as continuing education, continuing professional education, staff development, inservice training, training, human resource development, workers' education, university extension, agricultural extension, and distance education. Unaware of the comprehensive orientation of the discipline of adult education, those who work in these specific fields look increasingly for their professional preparation and/or continuing professional development to such disciplines as curriculum and instruction, vocational education, instructional systems design, and higher education. While such disciplines address specific sectors of the universe of organized learning, they lack the comprehensive and broad orientation that has been a part of the field of adult education for the last seven decades. None of these fields claims to take into its scope the full spectrum of organized learning. Yet this has been and continues to be the claim of adult education.

Although this issue of an overly restrictive definition of adult education is avoided in the title of this book, *Program Planning for the Training and Continuing Education of Adults*, a clear understanding of the perspective of the editor of this book may be helpful to readers unfamiliar with that term. While many meanings may be attributed to the term *adult education*, one meaning that is clearly not subscribed to in this work is that of publicly funded adult basic education and literacy. While such programs represent important examples of adult education, they constitute only a part of what might be referred to as adult education practice. As used in this book, *adult education* refers to much, much more than remedial education for people who did not successfully complete primary or secondary schooling during their childhood or adolescence. My general orientation in assembling the chapters in this book has been to take the definition of adult education offered by Professor Cyril O. Houle at the University of Chicago some 25 years ago:

> the process by which men and women (alone, in groups, or in institutional settings) seek to improve themselves or their society by increasing their skills, knowledge, or sensitiveness; or it is any process by which individuals, groups, or institutions try to help men and women improve in these ways. (Houle, 1972, p. 26)

This comprehensive definition contains four elements:

1. Adult education refers to a *process* of systematic, organized, and intentional learning.
2. That process involves people who act on the basis of *a priori* acceptance of adult social roles.
3. Men and women participate in that process as individuals or as members of groups, communities, or institutions.
4. The result of such participation (ideally) is development of the person or society.

Although a poll of the authors of this work would suggest a preference for specific definitions, I suspect that few of these authors would disagree with this general orientation. Although some contemporary writers in the academic discipline of adult education are critical of such broad comprehensiveness of adult education, one of the strengths of this definition, as originally intended by Houle, is that, as an integrating concept, it encompasses distinctive activities which otherwise would not be included. Note that it does not distinguish education from training. Nor does it discriminate among learning activities organized by community based organizations to foment specific community or societal change on the one hand and learning activities calculated to reinforce existing patterns of relationships on the other. This definition permits us to recognize that, regardless of innumerable differences of institutional and organizational context, all instances of organized education and training have in common what Houle (1972, p. 26) refers to as a "basic unity of process."

With its central focus on that "basic unity of process," the term *adult education* can be thus considered as a comprehensive "umbrella" term which includes all forms of training and education for adults. Recognition by those who are engaged in divergent forms of education and training for men and women that they share a common process can permit mutual identification, sharing of ideas and practices, and collaborative professional development activities otherwise unimaginable. Evidence for the veracity of this assertion of direct benefits derived from a shared perception of the "basic unity of process" may be cited in the experience I had while serving as a Fulbright researcher in two Central American countries in 1991. Besides being useful as an organizing framework for my study of the entire adult education spectrum in Nicaragua and Costa Rica, the comparative analytical scheme described in the next section facilitated dissemination of the resulting reports (1991a, 1991b) to practitioners. In September 1991, the first national seminar on lifelong (adult) education in Nicaragua was conducted in Managua. In December of that same year, the first national seminar on lifelong (adult) education in Costa Rica was conducted in San José. A second national seminar was conducted in March 1992 and further activities involving educators and trainers across the entire education and training spectrum were planned. It is notable that prior to dissemination of the comprehensive definition offered by Houle (1972), education and training practitioners from all societal sectors had been unaware that they belonged to the same field and that they were engaged in the same "unity of process." Out of such meetings emerged what might be regarded as the beginnings of a shared professional identity and a collective commitment to continue meeting as fellow professionals.

What occurred in both of these societies may be regarded as suggestive of experiences which may be replicated in other nations and regions of the world. If practitioners across the spectrum were to share the perspective of a common field of practice, such recognition could serve as a powerful catalyst for mutual identification, collaborative professional activities, and the formation of a shared professional consciousness and commitment. Even in the face of diminution of funding and other resources directed to the expansion of training and education for men and women, such efforts could strengthen the capacity of educators and trainers to respond to the economic and technological challenges accompanying organizational and societal growth and development.

Another implication of adult education as a process common

to all forms of education and training is the possibility of classification and analysis of the program planning process. It is possible to think of program planning in terms of clusters of related activities that comprise distinctive steps or phases that may be employed by educators and trainers in a wide diversity of organizational contexts. Indeed, most of the chapters in this book focus on specific program planning steps.

The authors of these chapters illustrate program planning principles and practices, drawing on examples from a variety of education and training contexts. The underlying premise is that because of the "basic unity of process," to some degree the program planning process described applies to *all* education and training contexts. Of course, the points of application of that process are as diverse as the different purposes, methods, and contexts associated with the myriad forms of adult education. In deepening our understanding of adult education program planning, however, it is important to go beyond mere recognition of this basic unity of process. We also need some conceptual tools to understand the various contexts in which adult education activities take place. The next section presents an analytical scheme to help classify and hence compare the many contexts in which the spectrum of adult education programs occur.

AN ANALYTICAL SCHEME FOR CLASSIFYING
PROGRAM PLANNING CONTEXTS

Instances of adult education cover a wide range:

- A worker studying alone in order to improve job performance
- Rural peasants participating in a literacy campaign
- A school teacher enrolling adults in evening classes for their secondary school diploma
- A lay religious leader teaching mothers how to guide their children's moral development
- Retired citizens inviting a registered nurse to teach them how to increase their bone mass and muscle tone through regular exercise
- Physicians teaching each other how to work more effectively within the changing landscape of managed health care
- A social worker helping a group of abused women learn more effective coping strategies

- An organizational development specialist facilitating a working conference for business executives and union leaders to explore ways to work together to capitalize on changing international market conditions

Even to those acquainted with the notion of "basic unity of process" whereby such programs are planned and implemented, the settings for adult education programs present a bewildering diversity. What then, other than case-by-case descriptions, can enable us to recognize the commonalities and similarities?

This section presents an analytical scheme that can permit detailed description of contexts in which adult education programs occur. The premise is that it is possible to identify certain elements of the contexts in which adult education programs take place. Although these contexts are not always apparent, they are always present. Three types of contexts are particularly important: *organizational, technological,* and *programmatic.* Each comprises a set of attributes of adult education activities that can be examined and analyzed. These attributes can serve as standards for measurement and comparison across the spectrum of adult education programs.

While it is possible to think of the *field* of adult education as *the sum total of organized training and education opportunities for men and women within a society,* there are also benefits to being able to distinguish distinctive organizations within that field. Attempts have been made to typify the universe of adult education within a society, but such attempts have not permitted detailed comparative analyses of programs with similar ends or of programs across the entire spectrum of the field. A comprehensive comparative analytical scheme is now proposed in terms of organizational, technological, and programmatic sets of attributes or rating criteria.

Attributes of the Organizational Context

The first set of attributes in this conceptual scheme concern aspects of the organizational context. For the purposes of our discussion, *organizations* may be defined as administrative and functional structures established by collections of people working together to accomplish certain shared objectives. Some of those objectives may include education or training in systematic pursuit of "knowledge, skill, or sensitiveness" (Houle, 1972, p. 26). To say this book's focus is on organized learning in organizational contexts is not to discount self-directed education activities planned by individuals outside of organizational contexts. Such activities are important but they involve different contexts than those planned within organizations. The conceptual scheme includes eight organizational attributes.

1. Structural Type. With Houle's definition of *adult education* as process in mind, our attention now turns to the organizations which provide the structural context for that process. Apps (1989) conceptualized that structure within a society to be coterminous with the sum total of that society's associations and institutions. Institutions have a hierarchical structure, operate within traditional purposes, enjoy resources often assigned by legal mandate, and have employees who play formally defined roles. Associations are organizations to which members belong by choice, control rests with the members more than the executive officers, and workers at the local level are generally volunteers with more immediate and specific concerns than those which might be established by mandate for institutions. Taking into account the different manifestations of adult education offered by institutions and associations, Apps proposes the "structure of providers" as described below:

- *Type I* organizations constitute those which are partially or fully supported by taxes. Such organizations would include government ministries and state-financed universities.
- *Type II* organizations constitute nonprofit associations and institutions. They include associations and private foundations, nongovernmental organizations, unions, professional societies, and private nonprofit educational organizations.
- *Type III* organizations constitute state-run and private for-profit organizations. They include private business and technical schools, business and industrial associations, and businesses— both those operated by the state (as para-statal institutions) and the private sector.

Apps (1989) explains that this structure

> ... is based on the assumption that adult learners have choices for learning opportunities—a long-standing characteristic of the adult [lifelong] education field. It should be noted, however, that although almost all adult learners have some element of choice, some adults are mandated by their professions, or by governmental units, to participate in learning activities. (p. 279)

It is useful to consider that perhaps most learning is something that is experienced rather than systematically planned by human beings. It is also important to recognize that learning can be self-planned outside of specific organizational contexts. Nevertheless, the principal focus in this guide is the invocation of the planning process within the three major categories of organizational settings specified in Apps's typology. Accordingly, this typology serves as a guide to the identification of organizations that offer adult education programs irrespective of the labels such programs carry.

For example, in my study of the national profiles of education and training programs for adults in the countries of Nicaragua and Costa Rica, I used Apps's typology as a guide to construct a comprehensive list of institutions and associations offering education and training programs for men and women. I then drew samples of organizations from which data were collected to form the basis of two national reports (Cookson, 1991a and 1991b) and a comparative report (Cookson, 1992). My listing of adult education organizational categories, ordered according to Apps's typology, is presented as follows.

- Organizations and agencies completely or partially supported by taxes:
  National institutions
  —Ministry of Education
  —Programs for workers and employees
  —Inter-institutional organizational units
  —Intra-institutional organizational units
  —Universities
  —Agricultural extension
  —Armed forces
  —Health institutions
  —Libraries and museums
  International organizations

- Nonprofit organizations which sponsor programs:
  —International organizations
  —Religious institutions
  —Health institutions
  —Community-based organizations
  —Volunteer organizations

—Professional organizations
—Nongovernmental organizations
—Political organizations
—Private foundations
—Private nonprofit schools
—Private higher education institutions
• For profit organizations:
—Private schools
—Private higher education institutions
—Programs sponsored by business or industrial associations
—Enterprises which sponsor programs of human resource development

2.   Scope. In terms of geographical distribution, the program may serve a local community, a region, or an entire nation.

3.   Sector. Organizations may be characterized in terms of the sector of the economy or the society which they serve, e.g., agriculture, industry, religious, rural-urban.

4.   Mission. The mission of the training or education program will reflect the overall mission of the sponsoring organization.

5.   Extensiveness of Organizational Infrastructure. The organizational context for education and training programs may range from relatively simple to relatively comprehensive.

6.   Ideological Awareness. While it may be argued that ideology plays a role in the operation of all organizations, the extent to which particular ideological positions are consciously promoted and implemented may vary from low to high.

7.   Priority of Adult Learning Functions. Knowles (1964) devised a scheme based on the way in which the function of training or education relates to "other purposes of the agencies in which it takes place" (p. 42). It may be the *sole* or *primary* function of the organization, e.g., a proprietary school or a residential learning organization.

• It may serve the *secondary* function, e.g., an education or training agency, such as a ministry of education or labor, a vocational-technical school or university.
• It may serve a *complementary* function, e.g., a community service agency, such as the Red Cross or professional association.
• It may serve a *supplementary* and *supportive* function, such as a business or religious organization.

8. **Strength of Organizational Commitment**. The degree of priority afforded education and training within an organization may range from low to high.

Attributes of the Technological Context

The second part of this analytical scheme involves *technologies*. Although *technology* usually refers to "hardware (or artifacts) ... [and a] ... sociotechnical system of manufacture" (Kline, 1985, pp. 215–216), for the purpose of this analytical scheme, *technology* refers to "a sociotechnical system of use ... using combinations of hardware, people (and usually other elements) to accomplish tasks that humans cannot perform unaided by such systems—to extend human capacities" (Kline, 1985, p. 216). For this text, *technology* is defined as the organizational and didactical processes utilized by an organization to transform training or education ideas into output or planned training or education programs. This definition is similar to the one utilized by Burnham (1988) who indicated that organizational technologies include such program planning activities as: (1) originating program ideas, (2) developing ideas, (3) establishing objectives, (4) designing programs, (5) ensuring participation, (6) securing resources, and (7) evaluating programs. Didactical technologies may include the teaching methods, techniques, and devices used in the delivery of education and training programs. Technological aspects of adult education may be thought of as comprising at least five sets of attributes.

1. **Program Planning Technologies**. Burnham (1988) drew on the work of Thompson (1967) to categorize program planning activities of three adult education institutions as examples of (1) *long-linked technology*, (2) *mediating technology*, or (3) *intensive technology*.

- Organizations which deploy *long-linked technology* "may be expected to plan programs in a lock step manner, offer the same or very similar programs on a cyclical basis, maintain a stable number of programs, and [offer programs] ... in a standardized format" (Burnham, 1988, p. 213).
- Programs which deploy *mediating technology* "could be expected to plan programs by brokering between teachers and learners (both considered as clients), and by involving multiple clients" (Burnham, 1988, p. 213).
- Programs which deploy *intensive technology* "could be expected

to plan differently from one program to another, use information about a program to help determine needed planning steps, and modify the emerging program based upon information about the program" (Burnham, 1988, p. 213).

2. Planning Orientation. Boyle (1981) typified three sets of planning orientations: (1) *developmental,* (2) *institutional,* and (3) *informational.* The activities engaged in by the organization to effect both program design and program implementation will vary systematically according to the particular program planning orientation:

- *Developmental planning* is directed toward the definition and solution of individual, group, or community problems with the educational agent acting as a facilitator of the learning process in cooperation with learners. The technologies that are employed are identified and operationalized in the course of interactions between the educational agent and learner client systems. The technology applied to activities with this orientation may be referred to as *program development.*
- *Institutional planning* is directed toward growth and improvement of an individual's basic abilities, skills, knowledge, and competencies, with the educational agent system originating objectives primarily on the basis of the discipline or field of knowledge rather than on emerging patterns of relationships with client systems. The technology applied to activities with this orientation may be referred to as *curriculum development.*
- *Informational planning* is directed toward the exchange or dissemination of information, with the agent system designating objectives and procedures in accordance with predetermined objectives for information dissemination, usually independent of any interactions with target audiences. The technology applied to activities with this orientation may be referred to as *information dissemination.*

3. Predominant Methods, Techniques, and Devices. These terms, as defined by Verner (1964) are not synonymous.

- *Methods* refer to the ways in which the organization establishes a learning relationship with a prospective body of participants. As such it represents an administrative decision.
- *Techniques* refer to ways in which the individual education or training agent establishes a learning relationship between the

learner and the learning task. As such it represents an operational rather than an administrative task.

- *Devices* refer to mechanical instruments, audio-visual aids, physical arrangements, and materials which augment the methods and techniques employed for a particular program.

4. Variety of Technology Used. The education and communications technologies used by education and training programs may range from a predominant reliance on one or two communications technologies to a predominant reliance on multiple communications media.

- *Limited technology utilization* refers to use, at any one time, of few methods and techniques.
- *Multiple technology utilization* refers to simultaneous use of multiple methods and techniques.

5. Sophistication of Technology Used. The education and communications technologies used by education and training programs may range from *simple* to *complex*.

- *Simple technology* refers to traditional and nonmediated forms of educational and training technologies, e.g., face-to-face lecture, presentation, group discussion, "chalk-talk," print.
- *Complex technology* refers to electronically mediated technologies that increase the effectiveness of traditional forms of education and training delivery, as well as the technologies that permit bridging of spatial and temporal distances between learners and instructors.

Attributes of the Programmatic Context

The third set of attributes concern the nature of the *program*, defined as the constellation of organized learning activities systematically planned to achieve, in a specified period of time, certain learning outcomes for one or more adults. Programs result from a process of setting objectives and identifying the actions needed to obtain those objectives involving an education or training planner, sometimes in collaboration with one or more learners. In this conceptual scheme, nine attributes have been identified.

1. Type of Program. In connection with an international project called *Comparative Analysis of Educational Programs for Adults*, Knox and Savicevic (Knox, 1987) collected descriptions of some 175 programs in 32 countries. In their analysis of the different forms of training and education, these authors presented the following classification of programs:

- *Literacy.* Programs of practical literacy and basic education for adults (however they might be defined in each country), paying especial attention to literacy campaigns, local community groups, the role of the schools, and efforts made to include groups of adults many times marginalized such as ethnic minorities, refugees, and prisoners.
- *Agriculture.* Extension programs to help farmers and peasants to improve their productivity (subsistence and cash) and the quality of rural life, giving special attention to initiatives of local community groups, the ministry of agriculture, and agricultural schools and universities.
- *Workers.* Educational programs to increase productivity and changes in the jobs of the workers in every kind of business or industry (apart from professional workers), with special attention to the initiatives on the part of businesses, employers, workers' universities, labor unions, and commercial associations.
- *Professional, Technical.* Every kind of professional development and inservice training program for scientific and technical occupations, such as engineering and medicine, with special attention to the initiatives of universities, professional associations, and businesses (factories, hospitals).
- *Professional, Others.* Activities with the purpose of continuing professional education in other kinds of occupations which tend to be influenced less by new results of scientific research (such as law, social work, teaching).
- *Secondary.* Programs to complete secondary school via part-time participation, with special attention to the initiatives of the schools operated by the ministry of education.
- *Advanced.* Programs to complete university studies via part-time for adults who work, paying attention to the ministry of education and advanced educational institutions. In some countries this category may include formal part-time programs for awarding degrees and diplomas.
- *Health.* Programs for curative and preventive health for adults

in rural and urban areas, paying attention to the initiatives of the ministry of health, clinics, and local hospitals.

- *Family.* Education in family life and home economics (including preparation of meals, nutrition, child development, and family relations), paying attention to local providers.
- *Personal.* Every kind of educational activity related to recreation, entertainment, arts, cultural activities, personal enrichment, and general education, paying attention to the initiatives of the ministry of culture, local libraries, and museums.
- *Citizenship.* Educational activities related to forming community organizational leaders, solving problems, and enabling the adult population to become better informed and actively participating citizens. This type of program may include the study of international affairs.

2. Learning Category. Houle (1972, p. 44) identified the following 11 categories of adult learning situations (Copyright 1972 by Jossey-Bass. Reprinted with permission.).

INDIVIDUAL
C-1   An individual designs an activity for himself.
C-2   An individual or a group designs an activity for another individual.

GROUP
C-3   A group (with or without a continuing leader) designs an activity for another individual.
C-4   A teacher or a group of teachers designs an activity for, and often with, a group of students.
C-5   A committee designs an activity for a larger group.
C-6   Two or more groups design an activity which will enhance their combined programs of service.

INSTITUTION
C-7   A new institution is designed.
C-8   An institution designs an activity in a new format.
C-9   An institution designs a new activity in an established format.
C-10   Two or more institutions design an activity which will enhance their combined programs of service.

MASS

C-11   An individual, group, or institution designs an activity for a mass audience.

3.   Client System. Schroeder (1980) distinguished program participants according to whether they belonged to the organization offering the training or education.

- *Internal agent membership systems* are those in which the leader originates from within the organization.
- *External agent membership systems* are those in which the leader originates from outside the organization.
- *Nonmembership client systems* are those in which clients come together from outside the organization hosting the education or training. Clients come together to learn on the basis of (a) geographic criteria, (b) demographic criteria, (c) social role criteria, (d) interest criteria, or (e) individual and social needs.

4.   Locus of Authority to Make Program Planning Decisions. Adapting a conceptual framework proposed by Blaney (1974), it is possible to distinguish three modalities of program planning on the basis of who determines the education or training objectives:

- *Modality I.* The education or training agent assumes full responsibility for setting the objectives and designating the activities required to achieve those objectives. Program planning in this modality can be more precise and systematic than the other two modalities.
- *Modality II.* The education or training agent shares responsibility with the learner(s) for planning education and training programs.
- *Modality III.* The education or training agent assumes no direct planning responsibility for the education or training of the learner(s).

5.   Financial Support.

- *Source.* Financial support for training or education activities may originate from one or more of the following:
  Parent organization subsidy
  Participant fees
  Auxiliary enterprises and sales

Private grants and contracts
Government funds

- *Availability*. The level of financial support may vary not only from organization to organization but also for any one organization from year to year. The values assigned to this characteristic are *unavailable, inadequate, barely adequate, adequate,* or *abundant*.

6. Availability of Instructional Resources. Instructional resources available to an organization may or may not be independent of the availability of financial support. This criterion refers to the extent to which materials essential to achievement of declared learning outcomes are available. The range of availability varies from *not available, inadequate, barely adequate, adequate,* to *abundant*.

7. Formality of Training and Education Leaders' Preparation. The range of leaders' preparation *in the technology of training and education* may range from *informal* to *nonformal* to *formal*.

- *Informal preparation* is limited to on-the-job experience which may or may not be reflected upon.
- *Nonformal preparation* comprises participation in workshops, courses or systematic study of books and manuals and/or other activities which focus on training and education technologies relevant to the systematic learning of men and women.
- *Formal preparation* comprises preparation in a formal (certificate or degree) program of study of education or training technology relevant to the systematic learning of men and women.

8. Differentiation of Staff. The number of staff assigned to education and training functions within an organization can range from a mere fraction of a full time equivalent person to numerous persons. In larger staffs, division of labor and differentiation of functions become operative principles. Differentiation values include *high, mid,* and *low*.

9. Prognosis for Achievement of Program Objectives. This criterion refers to the investigator's assessment of the likelihood that the program—at least in the short term—will meet intended outcomes. Prognosis values include *high, mid,* and *low*.

The above conceptual scheme, with its three sets of attributes, may be applied to the study of adult education programs at both micro and macro levels of analysis. At the micro level, practitioners may begin to look at their own program planning practice and the nature of adult education provision within their own organization. At the macro level, a matrix may be constructed which lists the organizational sponsors of education and training for men and women in the left margin and the attributes across the top. Notations can then be made and duly noted in each cell, thus forming the basis for comparisons among organizations, technologies, and programs. Although the authors of the chapters that follow do not necessarily subscribe to this conceptual scheme, they do refer to many of the concepts included in the scheme. It is important to realize these terms permit distinctions that may differ from meanings normally attributed to them in common parlance. Together they may enable program planners across the spectrum of adult education organizations and programs to develop further toward a shared vocabulary and resultant understanding of what Houle (1972) refers to as "a basic unity of process."

A COMPREHENSIVE APPROACH
TO PROGRAM PLANNING

The purpose of this third section is to delineate the comprehensive approach to program planning that underlies the selection and order of the chapters that follow. With reference to education or training, program planning usually refers to the process of setting objectives and designating the activities required to achieve those objectives. As Brookfield (1986) has aptly pointed out, many of the program planning models that have been advanced in the past have described that process with the context or its occurrence as a given that somehow falls outside of the process. Such is the case for the models that are described in the next two chapters. Because they form part of the familiar literature of the field of adult education, the models described and discussed in Chapters 2 and 3 collectively have contributed to the general orientation to program planning shared by the authors of the chapters that follow. The structure of the book, as manifested by the table of contents, however, suggests a more developed approach to program planning.

Just as the maxim for qualitative research that the researcher is the instrument, program planners themselves can also be regarded as an integral part of the program planning process. In this light, how program planners perceive themselves in relation to the multiple and varied tasks involved with planning education and training programs can affect how that process is played out. Part of that self-reflection can profitably focus on the nature of the multiple roles they play within the organization and how those roles impact the planning process. Examination of the sometimes varying sets of expectations surrounding their program planning duties can lead to a more realistic sense of current programming potentialities. It may also enable identification of areas of strength as well as areas requiring further attention. Clarification for themselves of the distinctive and sometimes conflicting expectations may increase their ability to convey a more realistic sense of the nature of their programming roles to others within the organization, thus raising the level of support for the education or training functions within the organization.

In addition to examination and clarification of the programming-related roles, planners can perform self-examination that focuses on their philosophical orientation toward education and training. Self-examination, together with thoughtful reflection, can be helpful in the formation of what Apps (1973) refers to as "a working philosophy" of adult education practice. Although knowledge and skill contribute to planners' abilities to plan programs, a "working philosophy" can help those same planners to determine why some programs are to be valued while others ought to be avoided. A working philosophy can also provide the *why* for the myriad of decisions implicit in the program planning enterprise. Unless program planners arrive at an understanding of what is good, better, and best, planners can be at the mercy of whatever policy or fashion happens to be current at the time. As with the self-examination of their planning roles, identification and articulation of their working philosophy help planners to form a stance toward the program planning process. Both steps precede and underlie the specific tasks that comprise the planning of discrete education or training programs.

A sense of professional responsibility can enable program planners to transcend the organization of employment to encompass a sense of responsibility to both learners and to the broad adult education field of practice. One way planners can manifest a sense of professional responsibility is through continuing professional development. Participation in both formally and informally organized learning activities can result in an enhancement of both knowledge and skills relating to desired areas of competence. Yet another way in which continuing professional development may be pursued is through the collection and analysis of data relative to program planning activities. As planners strive to conceptualize the particulars of their day-to-day experience and then conduct research to further clarify and test their conceptual understanding of their experience, greater insights can be generated. Such insights can be expected to generalize to other program planning experiences in the future.

Although often dismissed by authors of most program planning models presented in the adult education literature, various contexts can be instrumental in fostering or inhibiting effective programming. Hence, planners who wish to ground their day-to-day practice in a more general conceptual understanding of their craft will benefit from obtaining a heightened awareness of the contextual elements that impact on their program planning practice in general and on specific programs in particular. Such elements include the situational context and the organizational context as well as the parameters set by the attributes of the learners likely to participate in the programs.

Before focusing on the particulars of any one education or training program, the planner needs to take into account the milieux in which the organization finds itself. Planners need to become aware of the conditions, relationships, and policies outside the organization that frequently find their echo in the conditions, relationships, and policies within the organization. As they conduct an inventory of the external or situational context of their organizations, they not only place themselves in a position to form a more realistic stance towards their various program planning roles, but they will also be better prepared to design specific education and training programs that are responsive to specific identified conditions.

Besides the external context, conditions internal to the organization in which programs are to be conducted also impact the planning process. The administrative structure represented by the table of organization and the patterns of exercise of power reinforced by the culture and the informal social organization significantly determine the definitions of what is appropriate and possible with respect to different forms of adult education. The policies, purposes, goals, objectives, restrictions, and problems that an organization faces can both encourage and retard the carrying out of effective training and education programs within an organization. Wise planners will inform themselves and stay abreast of these conditions internal to the organization, taking them into account in their planning, and seek to shape them for the advancement of their training and education programs.

An additional part of the "getting the lay of the land," so to speak, that precedes the discrete planning steps of specific education and training programs is gaining a working knowledge of the kinds of adults who typically participate in the kinds of education and training programs for which the planners are responsible. In addition to the physical, psychological, and mental characteristics that those participants will have in common with most adults, there will be characteristics that arise from different national, regional, local, cultural, and ethnic backgrounds. Education and training program planners who disregard such characteristics do so at the risk of planning programs that make unreasonable, unrealistic, or otherwise inappropriate demands of the participants.

The foregoing components of the program planning process constitute ways in which planners can develop a sense of their professional responsibility as well as an awareness of the general conditions impacting their program planning work in a particular organizational context. These components can be implemented independently of any given program planning project. The remaining components of the process, in contrast, focus on the precise strategies needed in specific education and training programs.

Using the foundation of knowledge and sensitivities formed during implementation of preceding components, planners will be well equipped to proceed with an assessment of specific sets of learning needs to which they will need to respond. Diagnosis of some sets of learning needs will disclose situations for which some form of education or training will constitute the most appropriate response. Other problem situations may call for responses other than training. Program planners will review the conditions defined as problems in order to determine whether or not they constitute learning needs. Such actions commonly are referred to as needs assessment. The outcomes of such analysis include the setting of learning objectives, one further step in the development of a program design.

Planners who have scanned the external and internal contexts of their planning circumstances and who are cognizant of the characteristics of adults as learners will be prepared to utilize their assessment of learning needs in the setting of appropriate goals and objectives. It is assumed that goals and objectives thus established will have greater practical value than those goals and objectives set in a vacuum unrelated to ongoing reality. The goals and objectives will illuminate all of the subsequent actions of program design.

The purposes and intents announced in the form of goals and objectives also become a basis for comparisons between participants' performance at the beginning of, during, at the end of, and following their participation in the program as well as comparisons between that which is intended and that which is achieved. These comparisons constitute evaluation, which enables planners to focus not only on the outcomes of the programs, but also on the processes used to accomplish such outcomes. Evaluation can impact the entire sequence, enabling planners to assume a critically reflective perspective by which to examine each of the distinctive components and subcomponents of the planning process.

The content and sequence of what is to be learned, consonant with the general goals and objectives, constitute the learning design. To elaborate an instructional design, the planner specifies the content to be learned and, in accordance with the principles of human learning and more especially of adult learning, specifies the content and order of engagement. The instructional design becomes a resource in the hands of the instructor or, in the absence of an instructor, for an individual or group of individuals who desire to learn in a self-directed way.

Together with the instructional design, it is necessary to specify the formats for learning. Besides designating the subject or skills, knowledge, and attitudes to be learned, planners must consider the particular ways in which participants are going to experience such learning. For that reason, it is important to think about the most appropriate methods, techniques, and devices. Besides face-to-face formats for learning, distance education modalities may be considered. Remembering Houle's (1972) schema of learning categories, we recognize that human beings can experience lasting changes in their performance as the result of self-directed learning; learning assisted by a tutor or coach; learning as members of groups, not always with a continuous leader; learning within organizational settings; and learning as part of a mass audience. Effective planners will seek to enlarge continually their repertoire of learning formats in accordance with innovative learning-teaching modalities.

Effective program planners will not be content with simply designing the elements related to the delivery of instruction. Programs for adults must also relate to patterns and rhythms of their settings. Promotion serves the purpose of encouraging acceptance of the legitimacy and credibility of the organization or the organizational unit that sponsors the education or training programs. The positive image thus generated by the promotional activities forms the basis for the subsequent marketing of specific programs, that is, activities designed to delineate and respond to individuals and groups whose opinions and perspectives are critical to the acceptance of the program.

One of the distinctive characteristics of adult education, in contrast to other forms of education, is that it is primarily a voluntary enterprise. Even in training situations where participants have been ordered to participate, their cooperation and willingness to contribute to and receive the instruction may be regarded as a voluntary act. For that reason, it is not enough for planners, once the program has been designed, to merely expect the people to appear. On the contrary, program planners must think about how to induce the target participants to participate actively in the programs they offer. At the same time, they must think about specific principles and practices that will increase the likelihood that participants will continue their participation in their programs.

If the organization or organizational unit responsible for education or training is to provide such programming and if it is to maintain its capacity to continue to provide such programming, certain administrative considerations must be addressed. Two such considerations are (1) program financing and (2) staffing. With respect to financing, program support can originate in the financial systems of the sponsoring institution, participant fees, fees paid by the participants' respective organizations, and contracts or agreements with businesses, government agencies, or nonprofit foundations. With respect to staffing, if planners are charged with delivering the education and training they themselves design, they may not be concerned with selecting, supervising, or training other instructors. However, if they plan and coordinate programs delivered by others, they will have general responsibility for contracting with instructors. In carrying out staffing responsibilities, adherence to certain rigorous and reliable standards can result in a significant improvement in the instructional performance and consequently in the performance of the entire organization.

To summarize the points presented in this section, program planning can be conceptualized as a multifaceted process. In addition to the program design steps most commonly mentioned in other models, the process outlined in this section suggests some additional elements. Before planning the discrete activities intended to respond to given problem situations, planners need first to examine themselves in order to identify their own particular education and training roles and their own philosophical and ethical stance toward their programming work. Such self-examination and self-orientation can enable planners to be more assertive, self-directive, and prepared to seek principled practice than would be the case if they were merely to react to the priorities of the moment. Self-examination is then followed by seeking a comprehensive understanding of the contexts, both internal and external to their organization, surrounding the program planning enterprise. That understanding is further enhanced by a sound grasp of the characteristics the likely program participants share in common with adult learners in general. Execution of these steps enables planners to build a foundation of general understanding of program planning work that underlies the specific strategies involved with the planning of any given instance of education or training.

SUMMARY

A serious deterrent to the expansion of training and education opportunities for men and women in industrialized as well as developing countries is the absence of any shared understanding of the term *adult education*. Those who plan education and training programs are generally unaware of their own counterparts in organizations different from their own. They do not know that they are involved in the identical *process*. They do not recognize that such programs frequently involve similar and overlapping technologies.

In this chapter we have presented a definition of adult education that focuses on the "basic unity of process" all education and training programs for men and women share in common. So defined, adult education is a broad enterprise without institutional or organizational boundaries. It covers all societal sectors and a multiplicity of purposes, methods, and technologies. It is hoped that you can place your own training or education activities for men and women within this lifelong education framework. This recognition can enable you to join forces with other trainers and educators in other areas of activity. Together you can forge a common professional identity and a shared commitment to raising the quality of your own educational work—not only in behalf of your organization of employment, but also to the men and women who participate in your programs and to the broader society of which you and they are a part.

Although the underlying structure of this book shares much with typical program planning models, there are some notable differences. Preceding and transcending any one instance of program planning, the program planner must first undertake some form of self-assessment and self-orientation. Thus, the planner is concerned with an examination of personal and professional philosophy, articulation of ethical principles, and an examination of the multiple roles performed in connection with planning education and training programs within a given organizational context. The basic idea is that the planner should avoid acting as a mere weather vane, pointing whichever way the wind is blowing at the time. Rather, the planner should have a strong sense of professional identity that permits a vision of what constitutes ideal programming practice. True enough, that vision will almost always be curtailed by constraints pertaining to the particular realities in which the planning must take place. But holding out a vision of the ideal can bring the real closer to the ideal than would otherwise be possible. The activities that enable the planner's self-awareness can then be buttressed by another set of activities deigned to form a comprehensive picture of the external context, the organizational context, and the general characteristics of adult learners. Having accomplished these planning activities that transcend any given program, the planner is then prepared to carry out the other planning steps mentioned by any number of models, including those referred to as *prototypical* and *alternative* program planning models in the next two chapters. Because of the breadth of meaning attached to the definition of adult education, the chapters in this book present each of the steps in the program planning process in such a way that they apply to both education and training programs across the entire spectrum of organizational, technological, and programmatic contexts.

QUESTIONS FOR STUDY AND DISCUSSION

1. To what degree are the programs of organized learning which occur in your own organization instances of adult education? Explain your answer.
2. What do you think about the definition of adult education proposed by Houle? To what extent do you agree with the implications of Houle's definition for education and training practice?
3. Comment on the value of mutual identification for those who work in different forms of adult education, as that term is defined in this chapter. What does it mean to you personally that there is such a variety of institutions and programs represented by the field of adult education, as defined in this guide?
4. What differences do you perceive between the terms *training* and *education*? Of what importance are these differences with respect to what you do within your organization?
5. Where does your organization lie with respect to Apps's framework of adult education provider organizations? What are the implications of that location?
6. Using the criteria presented in the chapter to compare organizations which sponsor training and education, technologies utilized, and programs, describe the functions of training and/or education as they are found within your own organization.
7. Critically analyze the program planning structure suggested in this chapter. Which elements of program planning have been omitted from the model? Which elements are nonessential? How might the model be strengthened?
8. How does the program planning structure suggested in this chapter relate to the approach to program planning typically adhered to within your own organization?

REFERENCES

Apps, J. W. (1973). *Toward a working philosophy of adult education.* Syracuse University: Publications in Continuing Education and ERIC Clearinghouse on Adult Education.

Apps, J. W. (1989). "Providers of adult and continuing education: A framework." In Sharan B. Merriam and Phyllis M. Cunningham (Eds.), *Handbook of adult and continuing education.* San Francisco: Jossey-Bass.

Blaney, J. (1974). Program development and curricular authority. In J. Blaney, I. Housego, and G. McIntosh (Eds.), *A monograph on program development in education.* Vancouver: University of British Columbia.

Boyle, P. G. (1981). *Planning better programs.* New York: McGraw-Hill.

Brookfield, S. (1986). *Understanding and facilitating adult learning.* San Francisco: Jossey-Bass.

Burnham, B. R. (1988). Program planning as technology in three adult education organizations. *Adult Education Quarterly, 38* (4), Summer, 211–223.

Cookson, P. S. (1991a). "Educación permanente en Nicaragua: Un resumen preliminar." Unpublished paper presented at the First National Seminar on Lifelong Education in Nicaragua: Forging a Professional Identity, Universidad Nacional Autónoma de Nicaragua - Managua, 26 September 1991.

Cookson, P. S. (1991b). "Educación permanente en Costa Rica: Un resumen preliminar." Unpublished paper presented at the First National Seminar on Lifelong Education in Costa Rica: Forging a Professional Identity, Colegio Federado de Ingenieros y de Arquitectos de Costa Rica, San José, 3 December.

Cookson, P. S. (1992). "Educación Permanente en Nicaragua y Costa Rica: Un vistazo de la actualidad." Unpublished paper presented in the Second National Seminar on Lifelong Education in Nicaragua, Instituto Nicaragüense de Administración Pública, Managua, 28 February 1992.

Houle, C. O. (1972). *The design of education.* San Francisco: Jossey-Bass.

Kline, S. J. (1985). "What is technology?" *Bulletin of Science, Technology, and Society,* Vol. 1, 215–216.

Knowles, M. S. (1964). "The field of operations in adult education," In G. Jensen, A. A. Liveright, and W. Hallenbeck (Eds.), *Adult education: Outlines of an emerging field of university study.* Chicago: Adult Education Association of the U.S.A.

Knox, A. B. (1986). "Project plan. A world perspective: International comparative analysis of selected educational programs for adults." Memorandum dated July 1986, pp. 7–10.

Knox, A. B. (1987). Puntos de importancia y pautas del plan del proyecto en Español. Unpublished memorandum, January.

Schroeder, W. L. (1980). A typology of adult learning systems. In J. M. Peters and Associates (Eds.), *Building an effective adult education enterprise.* San Francisco, Jossey-Bass.

Thompson, J. D. (1967). *Organizations in action.* New York: McGraw-Hill.

Verner, C. M. (1964). "Definitions." In G. Jensen, A. A. Liveright and W. Hallenbeck (eds.), *Adult education: Outlines of an emerging field of university study.* Washington, DC: Adult Education Association of the U.S.A.

## 2

Prototypical Program Planning Models

Peter S. Cookson, Malcolm S. Knowles,
Leonard Nadler, and Zeace Nadler

ABSTRACT

The aim of this and the next chapter is to inform the reader of various ways in which leading adult education theorists have conceptualized the process of program planning. Because of their widespread dissemination and influence on the broad field of practice, the three models profiled in this chapter are referred to as *prototypical* models. Houle's *fundamental system* attempts to provide an overarching conceptual framework capable of encompassing the entire spectrum of all organized forms of education for men and women. Knowles's *andragogical model* suggests a central focus on learning, rather than teaching, as well as a sensitive, caring, and collaborative relationship between the educational agent and the learner. The Nadlers's *critical events model* provides an open systems approach to the identification of critical decision points for the systematic design of programs primarily, but not exclusively, in the training arena.

ASSESSMENT

Imagine you are invited in each of the four situations that follow to consult with the organizational officer responsible for a specific educational or training program. Drawing on your knowledge and your previous program planning experience, decide how you would respond to each request for assistance.

1. The members of a professional association suddenly and unexpectedly find themselves needing to respond to new regulations that will come into force within the next six months. In response to requests from members who look to the association for assistance in preparing to comply with the regulations, the association's executive committee has decided to convene a conference three months from now to which all association members will be invited. The president of the association has invited you to outline the program planning decisions to be considered so that the conference will meet the needs of the members.

2. To lower the currently high rate of attrition among new students, the department heads of a business school have decided to conduct a 3-day seminar for the school's instructors. The professional development coordinator has decided to confer with you before the first meeting of the committee to plan the seminar. She wants you to help her to outline the general decision points to be considered in planning the proposed professional development program.

3. As the result of a technical breakthrough by the research and development department followed by some astute decisions on the part of upper management, a medium-sized company that fabricates agricultural machinery has decided to initiate production of a vehicle powered by a small, economical, and highly efficient hydrogen motor. The director of the project has made an appointment with you to discuss the implications of the project for training. His principal interest is that you outline the major components of the training program he will have to implement.

4. As a consequence of some revolutionary medical discoveries, the hospital director responsible for community outreach has received the assignment to organize a series of seminars for physicians about an experimental nutrition program for the prevention of cancer. Before she begins to detail the preparations for the seminar series, she decides to ask you to orient her with respect to the general decision points she needs to consider in planning the program.

Reflect on the four situations in which you were invited to contribute to the planning of a specific education or training program. Aside from the nuances and particulars of each, what features of the process you were recommending did they have in common? To what extent in your responses to the situations did you note evidence of that *basic unity of process* mentioned in Chapter 1?

THE NEED FOR SYSTEMATIC PLANNING

In each of these four scenarios you have been invited to consult with someone about a systematic approach to the planning of a training or education program. The fact that you are being asked to outline a complete design suggests that those who have the planning responsibility are not content to do it in an *ad hoc* way as do many of their counterparts in other organizations. Program planning models suggest a structured way of thinking through the process of planning education and training.

Despite the abundant opportunities to learn structured approaches to the design of education and training programs, there are still many situations in which the systematic design of programs is still the exception rather than the rule. Even where program planners have years of experience and educational preparation for their work, many programs are planned and conducted without setting precise goals and objectives. As a consequence, decisions taken one by one can cumulatively comprise a planning process that is uncertain and based on invalid criteria. All too frequently there is no awareness of either the costs or the impact of these programs. Focusing on the selection of instructional location, activities and schedules, numbers of enrollees, and their reactions, many education and training planners narrow their appraisal of program effects to unsystematic and *ad hoc* hunches and guesses. When such programs are successful, it is more by accident than design. Programs that turn out well are repeated; those that do not turn out well are not repeated.

Underlying the information provided in this and succeeding chapters is the assumption that recourse by planners to a clearly identified and articulated design can help them to plan more effective training and education programs. This assumption is consistent with the concept of *adult educationist* that Thurmon White (1970) invented to distinguish between those who only practice and those who commit themselves to the knowledgeable practice of adult education, critically aware of program alternatives as well as the "why's" and "why nots" of their decisions.

Although it may be argued that programming is more an art than a science, it is assumed that it involves skills that may be learned and perfected. Besides what one can learn by doing on-the-job, another way to increase one's knowledge and skills relative to program planning is by gaining familiarity with the way others have conceptualized the process. For that reason, the program planning process will be reviewed in this and the next chapter in terms of various training and/or education models. The term *model* is employed here in the sense that it represents an ideal design. The abstraction of a theoretically ideal program can provide practical reference points with which real programs may be compared. Such comparisons may serve to increase our sensitiveness to various decision alternatives.

The originators of the program planning models profiled in this chapter (Houle, Knowles, and Nadler) identify similar and dissimilar steps and activities in the program planning process. Although many other models could be used, these three were selected because together they cover the universe of possible situations of adult education and therefore contain many of the general features of the majority of models. They are viewed as *prototypical models* in the sense that they are among the first that were proposed that have had great influence in the study of training and education program planning processes in North America. The innumerable models that have followed, in the opinion of this author, have not had as great an influence.

The first model profiled in this chapter is referred to as the *fundamental system.* In proposing this "system of program planning or analysis" Houle (1972) attempted to conceptualize all organized and purposive learning of men and women. Some have criticized the model for not adequately accounting for certain kinds of adult education situations. Others have pointed to the model's datedness in not emphasizing certain kinds of adult education activities, namely those most readily associated with egalitarian and liberating social movements. Perhaps these critics would be less vocal if they were to recognize that Houle's intent in proposing the model was to unify all instances of organized learning, as opposed to a restricted number of segments on the broad spectrum of adult education practice. The model leaves program planners themselves to adapt different facets of the model, in accordance with their own particular philosophical and ideological preferences. While maintaining an all-inclusive orientation, Houle articulates his own value structure in stating his seven assumptions. Another notable contribution of the model is the classification of the full range of learning situations, from those that are self-designed by the learner as planner to those that are planned for a mass audience. Although almost a quarter of a century has passed since Houle first announced his fundamental system, it has never been surpassed in its inclusiveness with respect to either the range of educational situations from individual learners to a mass audience or to the entire society-wide spectrum of organized educational programs.

The second model is referred to as the *andragogical model*. In proposing this model, Knowles (1970) espouses philosophical positions that draw heavily on the philosophy of humanism and parallel many of the ideas of the humanistic psychologist Carl Rogers. In contrast to his former University of Chicago mentor, Cyril O. Houle, who sought to unify the existing disparate strands of adult education practice through a broader conceptualization of the field, Knowles sought to convince adult education practitioners to unite through adoption of a particular philosophical orientation. He urged adult educators to abandon the banner of *pedagogy*, which he defined as the art and science of teaching, in favor of the banner of *andragogy*, which he defined as the art and science of helping people learn. Central to his scheme is the notion that adult learners possess certain distinctive characteristics that dictate andragogical responses. These responses demonstrate respect for learners and their capacity, as adults, to accept responsibility for collaborating with other learners and with planners in designing their own learning activities. The andragogical model applies equally to teachers of specific groups of learners as well as administrators in organizations that involve many groups of instructors and learners.

The third model is referred to as the *critical events model* (CEM). Although, as originally conceptualized (Nadler, 1982), the CEM targeted training situations within the context of the workplace, it has features that can be adapted to accommodate other educational planning situations. Although the CEM is based on the idea of the program planning process as *an open system*, in the sense that factors outside of the model may influence the design process, Nadler and Nadler identify what they consider to be the most critical planning events. It is notable that as each of the critical events are played out, planners continuously evaluate and solicit feedback about the program.

It is important to keep in mind that, as with all models, each of these represents an exaggerated simplification of reality. To compile a listing of all the decisions and actions that might be taken in the planning process would be an endless task. Thus, each of the models constitutes the steps that their originators considered most important. Although written language dictates that the presentation of the steps be made according to a logical order, the sequence in which they are applied may vary in practice. An alternative way to regard these models, besides specific programming steps, is as "systems" that comprise inputs, processes, outcomes, and feedback. For both educators and trainers, a systems approach can be useful in discerning underlying facets of their work and in recognizing features common to planning across the entire adult education spectrum.

HOULE'S FUNDAMENTAL SYSTEM

Interpreted by Peter S. Cookson

Houle (1972, p. 26) posed his "educational framework" as part of his "system of program planning or analysis." This framework offers a systematic way to design, conduct, and evaluate education programs for adults. Building on his definition of education as a process intrinsic to innumerable forms of organized learning of men and women, it constitutes a comprehensive program planning model equally applicable to all instances of training and education. The model consists of four parts: (1) a definition of adult education as a purposive process of systematic learning, (2) seven suppositions about adult education, (3) 11 categories of educational situations, and (4) a framework which constitutes a "complex of related elements that do not necessarily constitute a sequence" (1972, p. 39).

A Definition of Adult Education

The first part of Houle's *fundamental system,* a definition of adult education, has already been presented in Chapter 1 as "the process by which men and women (alone, in groups, or in institutional settings) seek to improve themselves or their society by increasing their skills, knowledge, or sensitiveness; or it is any process by which individuals, groups, or institutions try to help men and women improve in these ways" (1972, p. 26). This process constitutes that which every manifestation of training and education comprising the concept of adult education has in common. As affirmed by Houle, "The fundamental system of practice of the field, if it has one, must be discerned by probing beneath different surface realities to identify a basic unity of process" (1972, p. 32). Without a recognition of such basic unity of process, it would be impossible to perceive the similarities between dissimilar education and training programs.

Seven Assumptions

The second part of Houle's model comprises seven assumptions (1972, pp. 32–40). These assumptions involve important implications for the ways in which education and training programs are carried out. Let us examine briefly the implications of each one.

1. *Any episode of learning occurs in a specific situation and is profoundly influenced by that fact.* No program occurs in a vacuum. The majority of training and education programs occur within the boundaries of some organization with its own particular set of limitations and possibilities. The situation includes multiple aspects of the organization as well as aspects of the principal actors: someone who is to learn and someone to help the learner to master certain knowledge or skills. Characteristics of the internal or organization context, including the norms, values, and prevailing traditions, constitute elements of a specific situation that exercise a distinctive influence. For example, an educational program about total quality management, even with many aspects in common—such as learning objectives, duration, methods and techniques, and even with the same instructors—will have a substantially different form when delivered in the different contexts of a governmental ministry and a for-profit firm.

2. *The analysis or planning of educational activities should be based on the realities of human experience and upon their constant change.* Taking into account this assumption, along with the previous

one, emphasizes the analysis of the situation as a step which
ideally precedes the program design. Having discovered the
distinctive dimensions of the reality which surround the person or unit in charge of the program planning, it is possible to
prepare the plans which coincide with the possibilities and
necessities that arise from that same reality. Therefore, a training director cannot simply take a program which has been
successful in one business and transfer it to another business
without checking first that it is in accordance with the particulars of the second organization. By learning the similarities and
dissimilarities of the two businesses, the manager will be able to
adapt the plan before adopting the program.

3. *Education is a practical art.* The essence of education is the
    action of learning. It is something which occurs. It is certain
    that the designs and plans which guide the distinctive mani-
    festations of the process of systematic learning, separated from
    the implementation of such designs and plans, do not make
    any sense. It is possible to treat education as if it were a science,
    that is, to analyze and dissect the process in a systematic way.
    However, the implementation of the process requires more
    than a systematic application of intellectually internalized
    principles. Incorporating the precepts related to the inten-
    tional learning process, those who practice the *art* of education
    also develop a devoted and careful attitude toward their educa-
    tional labors with an eye to the greater effectiveness and bene-
    fits for the organization as well as for the individuals who learn.

4. *Education is a cooperative art.* In education the term *cooperative*
    is used in two senses:

    a. In the most profound sense, it signifies action by the
        learner as well as by the educator in accordance with the
        dictates of nature. The designer of training and education
        programs must act in accordance with the possibilities that
        arise from the ability and disposition of those who learn as
        well as of the instructors. An example demonstrates the
        difference in time required to learn simple or difficult
        skills. For the employees, it will be fairly easy to learn new
        procedures for submission of reports to superiors. For the
        same employees, it will not be so easy to learn new com-
        puter applications to project future needs for human re-
        sources.

b. In the second sense, it signifies voluntary interaction among individuals during the learning. Although in every instance of adult education, participation is not a voluntary matter, the will of those who learn is a strong impulse in the interaction that constitutes education or training. Adults do not usually assume docile positions of children. For that reason it is necessary to gain not only their attention but also to persuade them to take advantage of the opportunity to involve themselves.

5. *The planning or analysis of an educational activity is usually undertaken in terms of some period which the mind abstracts for analytical purposes from complicated reality.* Adult education is something we experience all our lives. However, for specific determined goals, it is possible to think of sets of events which together comprise programs with temporal limits. For the purpose of learning to utilize the process effectively, it is possible to think about planning programs which in given moments in time, begin, continue, and end. Abstracting the programming process it is possible to examine one's own educational activities with an eye to improving them. It is also possible to learn more about the process by examining the educational activities of others. This assumption underlies the existence of this guide.

6. *The planning or analysis of an educational activity may be undertaken by an educator, a learner, an independent analyst, or a combination of the three.* This assumption implies that planning is not an activity carried out without previous preparation. Certainly the actions can constitute in part an extension of one's personality but at the same time planning requires the obtaining of specialized knowledge and skills—not only in the subject to be learned but also in the processes whereby the learners come to the subject. It is possible that some people exhibit the knowledge and skills of planning naturally as an extension of their personality without any preparation. Whether a novice or expert, the assumption is that all can improve the skills required to carry out the role of the planner.

7. *Any educational design can be best understood as a complex of interacting elements, not as a sequence of events.* The means by which the nature of the planning process is communicated—printed letters on paper—dictates that the planning steps are presented in a certain order. However, it is important to note that

the order can differ substantially from the reality. Some steps may be accomplished simultaneously. Some steps will begin before others and will continue throughout the duration of the preparations for the design. The circumstances which attend each situation and the personal taste of the planners will dictate the sequence that finally will be manifest in connection with any program.

Major Categories of Educational Design Situations

The third component of Houle's model is his typology of major categories of educational design situations (1972, pp. 40–46). This typology is presented in Figure 2.1 and was presented in Chapter 1 as *learning categories*, one of the attributes of programs that permit us to classify organizations that sponsor adult education programs.

It is noteworthy that according to this classification scheme, learners may be organized in one of four ways: as individuals,

INDIVIDUAL
C-1   An individual designs an activity for himself.
C-2   An individual or a group designs an activity for another individual.

GROUP
C-3   A group (with or without a continuing leader) designs an activity for another individual.
C-4   A teacher or a group of teachers designs an activity for, and often with, a group of students.
C-5   A committee designs an activity for a larger group.
C-6   Two or more groups design an activity which will enhance their combined programs of service.

INSTITUTION
C-7   A new institution is designed.
C-8   An institution designs an activity in a new format.
C-9   An institution designs a new activity in an established format.
C-10   Two or more institutions design an activity which will enhance their combined programs of service.

MASS
C-11   An individual, group, or institution designs an activity for a mass audience.

Figure 2.1 Major Categories of Educational Design Situations (Houle, 1972, p. 44). Copyright 1972 by Jossey-Bass. Reprinted by permission.

groups, institutions, or as a mass. The majority of trainers and educators concentrate on the group forms and many times omit alternative forms. In contrast, Houle's model suggests consideration of 11 ways to organize learners.

Decision Points and Components of an Educational Framework for Adults

In accordance with the definition of adult education, the seven assumptions, and the 11 categories of educational situations described above, the fourth component of Houle's model (1972, pp. 46–57) focuses on the decisions involved in planning adult educational activities. As was already mentioned, these should not be thought of as a linear sequence of steps from which there can be no variation. On the contrary, they are points which cover the necessary elements to accomplish successful programs for which there is not a fixed order. The decision points shown in Figure 2.2 are detailed as follows:

1. *A possible educational activity is identified.* The need to offer a particular educational activity is recognized. It may be an additional course offered by a division of an organization such as a university. It may be a new activity offered to employees located in local centers of a government ministry, a private enterprise, or a professional association. The activity may be regarded as an organizational response to one of the following kinds of needs: *normative need, felt need, expressed need,* or *comparative need* (Bradshaw, 1974, pp. 184–185) which may be identified via a needs assessment or it may merely be a function of a decision maker's choice to conduct a program irrespective of any documented need. The selection of the activity may well reflect the philosophy of the organization, as well as its goals and objectives.
2. *A decision is made to proceed.* Once the feasibility and practicality of conducting a particular activity have been determined, the planning of that activity may proceed.
3. *Objectives are identified and refined.* The objectives are formulated in accordance with the results of identified needs. Such objectives must be specific enough to be practical yet broad enough to cover all the sessions in the program.

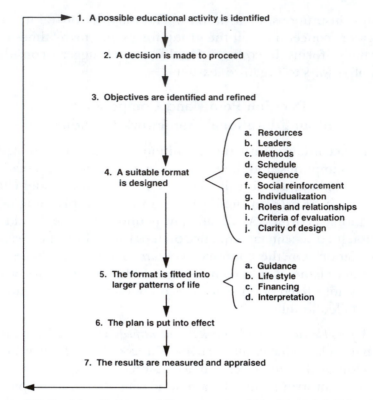

Figure 2.2 Decision Points and Components of Houle's Adult Educational Framework (Houle, 1972, p. 47). Copyright 1972 by Jossey-Bass. Reprinted by permission.

4. *A suitable format is designed.* The set of distinctive components that make up the program should constitute a coherent and significant whole. A suitable form is that which accomplishes the following criteria:

    a. *Resources.* The learning resources are selected in accordance with the capacity of the educational sponsor. Resources may include instructional material, different electronic media, and human resources such as the previous experience and knowledge of the participants.

    b. *Leaders.* In the design stage and the following stage of program implementation, leadership is a critical criterion to determine the adequacy of the format. In the design stage of specific activities, one or more representatives of the participants may constitute part of the program development team. Someone has to assume decision-making responsibility for the design and execution of the activity. In contrast to the orientation that has been referred to as *banking education* (Freire, 1970) at the primary, secondary, and tertiary levels of formal schooling in which knowledge is poured into the heads of submissive and passive students, one of the foundations of much, though not all, adult education is that participants tend to be more actively involved in the leadership in the learning activities. Therefore, education or training which conforms to an *andragogical mode* (Knowles, 1980) probably incorporates some form of participative leadership. The program designers who conceive of education or training as a "cooperative art more than an operative art" (Houle, 1972, p. 32) will seek more aggressively the inputs of their participants with an eye not only to accomplish the learning objectives, but also the utilization of a certain kind of process. Advisory committees, learning-teaching teams, and flexible learning contracts can be part of education and training (Knowles, 1986). Even in programs oriented to the assimilation of psychomotor skills, objectives, assignments, and alternative means of evaluation can offer certain options to participants.

c. *Methods.* In designing learning activities, methods must be designated as ways to organize participants relative to the sponsoring organization and the learning tasks. The nature of any method will vary according to the nature of the educational category selected for the program. Methods for C-1 could include self-directed learning projects, direct observation, and learning by doing. Methods for C-2 could include an individually tailored coaching, tutorial, apprenticeship, correspondence instruction, or a course delivered to noninteracting individuals via computer-mediated communication. Methods for group categories could include group-directed study circles, courses, seminars, and forums. Institutional categories could include a course formerly taught face to face but now offered via satellite, or a certificate program offered by one or more institutions. A mass method might include a program of instruction delivered via public television, dissemination of print-based materials, or a public awareness campaign waged by an army of volunteers to whole sections of a given population, or a public exposition or fair. Verner (1964) preferred a more comprehensive term of *processes* to include three additional terms: *methods, techniques,* and *devices:*

    i. *Methods,* according to Verner (1964), refer to the different arrangements whereby participants are organized in relation to the organization under whose auspices the program is offered and may be classified as (a) individual, (b) group, or (c) community methods.

    ii. *Techniques* refer to the arrangements whereby, within the context of particular method, the participants are organized in relation to the learning task.

    iii. *Devices* refer to tools that increase the effectiveness of the methods or techniques.

d. *Schedule.* Each program requires sufficient time for its design and implementation. Some activities, such as using self-teaching guides and audio or videocassettes, are designed so that participants may use them at different times, often of their own choosing. Other types of programs, such as a course in a given site or in multiple remote sites via audio teleconferencing originating in one central site, may be planned to occur in only one determined period of time.

e. *Sequence.* Once desired outcomes have been identified, then it is possible to specify the sequence of activities that will lead to those outcomes. In accordance with the nature of the activity, the organizing principles that determine the sequence may be chronology, simple to complex, from the parts to the whole or the whole to the parts. In some cases, the principle may be determined by the participants themselves. In any case, participants should become informed of the existence of the sequence at the time they are notified of the activity.

f. *Social reinforcement.* All aspects of a learning activity should be planned in such a way that a satisfactory experience for the participants can be assured. If the learning activities incur higher costs than the anticipated rewards, future participation will be considered punishing and probably will not be carried out. On the other hand, if the symbolic, material, or other rewards are more positive than negative, the probability will increase that participation will be repeated. The participants should experience success in their learning and that success should be considered positive and significant. Examples of reinforcement in training or education may include: preparation of learning tasks within a unit of instruction that are manageable and achievable, encouraging comments by the instructor and/or by other students, correction and rapid return of participants' assignments in a correspondence course, and a reasonable orientation for participants enrolled for the first time in an audio or computer teleconferencing course.

g. *Individualization.* In spite of the need in many training or education programs to permit the learning of large groups of people, it is essential to take measures to prevent individual participant isolation. At the same time, it is important to provide opportunities for participants to apply in a personal way those parts of what is learned that appear to be most relevant.

h. *Roles and relationships.* Because much of human conduct is determined on the basis of expectations and because education and training differ a great deal from child and youth schooling, it is necessary to create new sets of expectations for adults. If from the beginning of the program the roles and responsibilities are different and the acceptable and anticipated patterns of interaction are clear, then the expectations of the participants will tend to be more realistic and more likely to be fulfilled. With respect to the training and education programs for adults, the relevant roles include those of designer, producer, content specialist, tutor or instructor, advisor, and co-learner.

i. *Criteria of evaluation.* When they are aware of the criteria whereby their final performance will be judged, participants can more easily calibrate their own progress through the process of learning-teaching. Clearly written objectives include not only the desirable learning outcomes, but also the conditions under which those outcomes will be accomplished and the criteria for their evaluation. Specification of these criteria signals to the designer of the program how much practice will be needed to attain the final desired performance.

j. *Clarity of design.* When the design for the dimensions of the learning activity are clear to all those involved, the possibility of confusion and miscommunication can be significantly diminished. Because their participation in an education or training activity may constitute the first involvement with formal learning since adolescence, many adults may feel apprehensive about returning to study. A clear idea of the learning design can therefore assure and motivate participants. Also important is the clarity with which the education or training agent communicate expectations of participants' responses to the different learning units as well as participants' interactions with the sponsoring institution.

5. *The format is fitted into larger patterns of life.* Those who plan education or training programs must remember that their target learners are adults first and participants second. Thus, participants do not fit so easily the patterns and structures of conventional schooling as is the case for younger students. Participation in learning programs should be linked with other requirements of adult life, such as occupation, family life, and civic duties. For this to be possible, the following decision points need to be addressed:

a. *Guidance.* Because education or training represents a contrast to normal life activities of the adults, programs should include the means to help adults to incorporate the educational activity and the to-be-learned performance within their respective life situations.

b. *Life style.* If what is learned is to endure, those who plan programs will have to take into account the necessity of helping participants to incorporate what is learned in their other life routines—whether in the workplace or elsewhere.

c. *Financing.* The costs associated with the program must be accounted for in some way. Sometimes the costs are raised on the basis of the fees charged participants. For other programs, the sponsoring organization or another agency subsidizes the costs.

d. *Interpretation.* Because so many factors affect the results of participation in the program, support for the participant is essential. Participants need to be assisted in interpreting their own progress. Their participation must be understood and appreciated by those who surround them, including family members, work companions, and their supervisors.

6. *The plan is put into effect.* Once the plan is outlined and the necessary plans have been made, it can be put into effect. This step often implies orchestration of the planner's efforts, the independent analyst, and the participant, in addition to other persons whose collaboration is essential for effective implementation. The unforeseen events which always seem to occur may oblige additional planning.

7. *The results are measured and appraised.* Some form of evaluation is essential if the desired efficacy of the program is to be determined and future iterations of the training or education are to be improved. Formative evaluation can provide information about how participants are experiencing the program while it is still in process. Certain aspects of the activity can then be adjusted to more closely reach the objectives. Summative evaluation can provide feedback on how well the objectives were attained. Follow-up or impact evaluation can provide information about the persistence over time of the desired performances once the program has concluded. Obtaining measurements of the results is insufficient. These need to be judged with respect to their significance for other iterations of the same or similar programs in the future.

Houle's theoretical educational framework represents the decision-making points and components of a way to improve people and society through systematic learning. Although it was presented more than 25 years ago as a *descriptive* model—and not necessarily as a *prescriptive* model—it has yet to be empirically corroborated that exemplary educational and training programs employ these decision points and other components as naturally and unconsciously as Houle affirms. However, it does offer a way of categorizing and analyzing exemplary training and education program planning practices. It also offers a guide for rational planning, on the basis of experience, through which educators and trainers can interact with the design of effective programs. As Houle states,

The mastery of this system of planning and analysis, like that of any other complex process, is initially tedious since it requires close attention and application. One must examine many cases, looking beneath the specifics of each activity to discover the basic structure which gives a common design to all of them…. But the major way by which anyone can learn the system is by the analysis of his own practice. In time, the ability to identify categories and construct designs is greatly facilitated. Experience provides not only skill but speed, particularly in the delicate art of balancing components. (Houle, 1972, p. 57)

THE ANDRAGOGICAL MODEL:
THE EVOLUTION OF A MODEL OF LEARNING

Malcolm S. Knowles

When I first started conceptualizing a model of adult learning in the late 1960s, based on my own experience with adult learners and recent research findings regarding the unique characteristics of adult learners (Houle, 1961: Tough, 1967), I perceived that there were two entirely separate, dichotomous models of learning. Pedagogy (from the Greek *paid*, meaning "child," and *agogus*, meaning "leader") referred to the teaching of children, while andragogy (from the Greek *aner*, meaning "adult") referred to the art of helping adults learn.

The Pedagogical Model

Pedagogy evolved between the ninth and the twelfth centuries from the descriptions of teachers in the monastic and cathedral schools of their experience in teaching young boys primarily in preparation for the priesthood. It was based on several assumptions about learners:

1. Learners are, by definition, dependent personalities, so teachers are responsible for making all the decisions about what should be learned, when it should be learned, how it should be learned, and if it has been learned.
2. Learners have only limited experience that is of little value as a resource for learning; the experiences of the teachers and textbook writers are the resources that really matter—hence, the lecture and assigned readings are the primary methods of education.

3. Learners are subject-centered in their orientation to learning; they perceive that learning is a process of accumulating trans-mitted subject matter content. So educational programs are organized by subjects.

4. Learners become ready to learn something when they are told by the teacher or the system that they have to learn it if they want to be promoted to the next level of grade or job; readiness to learn is the result of external forces.

5. Learners are motivated to learn by external motivators, such as grades, eligibility for promotion, and pressures from teachers, peers, family, and supervisors.

Since this was the only model of learning known to educators from the Middle Ages until the late 1960s, it was the model on which our national educational system—elementary, secondary, and higher—was founded in the late eighteenth and early nineteenth centuries, and which dominated the adult education movement from its inception in the early twentieth century.

The Early Andragogical Model

My early conceptualization of the andragogical model was based on a very different set of assumptions:

1. Adults have a deep need to be self-directing; they resent and resist being controlled by others; they see it as a symbol of their maturity that they are able to take responsibility for their own lives, to make their own decisions about what should be learned, when it should be learned, how it should be learned, and if it has been learned.

2. Adults have accumulated a body of experience that is itself a rich resource for their own learning and that of others, and educational programs should make use of it.

3. Adults are life-centered and task-centered in their orientation to learning; they perceive that the acquisition of new knowledge and skills is worthwhile to the extent that it enhances their ability to perform real tasks that are relevant to their life situations.

4. Adults become ready to learn something when they perceive that it will contribute toward their achieving some life goal; readiness to learn is a function of desire to learn.

5. Adults are motivated primarily by intrinsic motivators, such as

the desire for greater self-confidence, self-esteem, responsibility, opportunity, and the like; external motivators, such as grades, have a low potency for them.

The Current Andragogical Model

After I published my first conceptualization of an andragogical model in *The Modern Practice of Adult Education* (with the subtitle "Andragogy *versus* Pedagogy") in 1970, I began receiving communications from teachers in elementary and secondary schools saying that they had been exposed to the andragogical model, had been experimenting with applying it to their classes, and had found that "children and youth learn better, too, when they are treated like people." And I received an even greater volume of communications from trainers and managers in corporations and government agencies saying that they had been experimenting with the andragogical model and finding that in some situations—especially where the subject matter was totally new and strange to the learners—it didn't work very well. As a result of this feedback I came to perceive the pedagogical and andragogical models as parallel or complementary, rather than as separate and antithetical. This revised model was presented in the second edition of *The Modern Practice of Adult Education* (with the subtitle "From Pedagogy to Andragogy") (Knowles, 1980) and in *The Adult Learner: A Neglected Species* (Knowles, 1984a).

The assumptions about learners in this new model are different from those in either the pedagogical or original andragogical model:

1. Human beings move from a state of total dependency at birth toward increasing self-directedness. Since self-directedness is an ultimate condition of maturity, this movement should be nurtured throughout childhood and youth, so that when they reach adulthood they are highly competent self-directed learners. However, until this state of nirvana is reached in our educational system, many (if not most) adults will enter into adult educational programs conditioned to perceive the role of "student" as a dependent role and will be disoriented if they are suddenly expected to take responsibility for their own learning. Accordingly, many programs that are based on the andragogical model provide a preparatory experience to en-

tering learners that orients them to the concept of self-directed learning and offers them "safe" opportunities to practice some of the basic skills of self-directed learning. My little paperback book, *Self-Directed Learning: A Guide for Learners and Teachers* (1975), is used as a tool in many of the programs.

However, even highly skilled self-directed learners occasionally find themselves wanting to learn new knowledge or skills totally beyond their previous experience; they are, indeed, dependent learners. In these situations, the new andragogical model proposes that it is appropriate for the "teacher" to use pedagogical strategies (such as lectures, assigned readings, tests, etc.) at least up to the point that the learners have accumulated sufficient basic content for them to be able to start planning their own learning projects.

2. Human beings enter into a learning situation with a varied background of experience. In some situations their previous experience may qualify them to serve as resources for less experienced learners, in which case mentoring relationships with individuals or small groups may be called for. In any situation in which there are learners who are deficient in experience, experiential techniques—such as simulations, demonstrations, field experiences, and the like—may overcome the deficiency.

3. Human beings vary in their orientation to learning; some are more subject-centered and others are more task-centered in regard to particular kinds of learning. These differences can be respected through the use of individualized learning plans as proposed in my *Using Learning Contracts* (1986), but the learning will be enhanced if some provision is made for helping the learners identify the relevance of the subject matter to their own life situations.

4. Human beings become ready to learn those things that they perceive will be useful to them. I remember resisting learning anything in a required course in poetry as an undergraduate, for example, until I got the insight that it could make me a more interesting speaker and writer by increasing my ability to use rhythm, similes, metaphors, and the like. It seems to me that this assumption places on the "teacher" a responsibility to make it clear how a given learning would be useful in one's life.

5. Human beings are motivated by both external and internal

motivators, but the latter are often the more potent. The most obvious implication of this assumption for adult educators is that in publicizing their programs both kinds of rewards should be specified. I am impressed, for example, with how university continuing education programs in recent years have been emphasizing how participation in their programs could lead both to better jobs and higher salaries and how it could help to increase self-confidence and self-esteem.

Implications for Teaching and Program Design and Operation

The pedagogical and andragogical models result in two very different approaches to teaching and program design and operation. The basic format of the pedagogical model is a *content plan,* which requires the educator to answer only four questions:

1. What content needs to be covered?
2. How can this content be organized into manageable units (e.g., courses, lessons)?
3. What would be the most logical sequence in which to present these units?
4. What would be the most efficient means of transmitting this content?

In contrast, the basic format of the andragogical model is a *process design* which consists of seven elements:

1. *Creating the climate setting.* The andragogical model proposes that a climate conducive to learning is a prerequisite for effective learning to take place. As I see it, there are two aspects to a learning climate: physical and psychological.

    In regard to physical climate, the typical classroom setup, with chairs in rows and a lectern in front, is probably the least conducive to learning that the fertile human brain could invent. It announces to anyone entering the room that the name of the game here is one-way transmission, that the proper role of the learner is to sit and listen to transmissions from the lectern. I make a point of getting to a meeting room before the participants and put the chairs in one large circle or several small circles. My preference is to have the participants sitting around tables, five or six to a table. I also prefer meeting rooms that are bright and cheerful.

Important as physical climate is, psychological climate is even more important. The characteristics of a psychological climate that is conducive to learning, as I see it, are:

- *A climate of mutual respect.* People are more open to learning when they feel that they are respected. If they feel that they are being talked down to or ignored and that their experience is not valued, their energy is spent dealing with that feeling more than with learning. Among the techniques I use to create a climate of mutual respect are: providing friendly greeters at the door of an opening session, having the participants fill out name tags with their names in large letters, and putting them in small groups as the first activity to have them introduce themselves to one another, share their interests and resources, and pool their goals for the program.

- *A climate of collaboration.* Because of their conditioning in their earlier school experience, in which competition for grades and teachers' favor was the norm, adults often tend to enter into any educational activity with a rivalrous attitude toward fellow participants. Since, for many kinds of learning, peers are the richest resources, this competitiveness interferes with learning. Accordingly, an opening exercise in which participants in small groups are put into a sharing relationship improves the quality of learning.

- *A climate of mutual trust.* People learn more from people they trust than from those they don't trust. In general, people in an authority-figure role, such as teachers and trainers, are mistrusted—at least until their trustworthiness is tested. One way to minimize this problem, I have found, is to introduce myself (or have myself introduced) as a fellow learner, with emphasis on who I am as a person rather than what my credentials as an expert are.

- *A climate of pleasure.* Learning should be one of the most pleasurable and gratifying experiences in life; it should be an adventure, spiced with the excitement of discovery. It is likely to be such for the participants if the teacher or trainer displays enjoyment in what is happening.

- *A climate of humanness.* Learning is a human activity; training is for dogs and horses. The more people feel that they are being treated as human beings, the more they are likely to learn. Among other things, this means providing for human comfort—good lighting and ventilation, comfortable chairs, availability of refreshments, frequent breaks, and the like. It also means providing a caring, accepting, respecting, helping social atmosphere.

2. *Involving learners in mutual planning.* What procedures can be used to get the participants to share in the planning? At the minimum, a representative group of participants—preferably selected by them—can work with the teacher or trainer in the planning process. I prefer, when it is possible, to outline several optional activities and ask small groups to discuss them and report their preferences. There is a basic law of human nature at work here: people tend to feel committed to any decision to the extent that they have participated in making it; the reverse is even more true—people tend to feel uncommitted to any decision to the extent that they feel others are making it and imposing it on them.

3. *Involving participants in diagnosing their own needs for learning.* One of the pervasive problems in this process is meshing the needs the learners are aware of (felt needs) with the needs their organizations or society has for them (ascribed needs). A variety of strategies are available for this process, ranging from simple interest-finding checklists to elaborate performance assessment systems, with a balance between felt needs and ascribed needs being negotiated between the facilitator and the learners. I frequently use a model of competencies which reflects both personal and organizational needs, so that learners can identify the gaps between where they are now and where the model specifies they need to be.

4. *Involving learners in formulating their learning objectives.* Most educational programs have broadly stated general objectives, but learning will be enhanced if each participant has formulated specific objectives within this broad framework. This result is accomplished most easily by the use of learning contracts, with each diagnosed learning need being translated into a learning objective.

5. *Involving learners in designing learning plans.* This step is also

most easily accomplished with a learning contract, in which the learner identifies—with the facilitator's guidance—the most effective resources (teacher or trainer, fellow students, outside experts, printed materials, field experiences) and strategies for accomplishing each objective.

6. *Helping learners carry out their learning plans.* Ideally, this step involves providing the learners with a combination of classroom activities, one-on-one consultations, field experiences, and individual projects.

7. *Involving learners in evaluating their learning.* A learning contract specifies what evidence a learner will collect to show the extent to which objectives have been accomplished and how that evidence will be judged or validated. The final validator, of course, is the teacher or trainer—but in a supportive rather than a chastening spirit.

So this is my current thinking about the andragogical model. I find that I keep emphasizing, particularly with new converts, that it is not an ideological entity to which one must be faithful and apply obediently, but a system of concepts, principles, and strategies that are responsive to the realities of particular situations. Andragogy is not antithetical to pedagogy; it incorporates it into its system. Other terms have attempted to supplant it—methetics, humanagogy, pedandragogy—but it has survived.

Andragogy's Record to Date

The andragogical model has been applied or adapted in a number of educational settings during its first quarter of a century of existence. In my *Andragogy in Action* (Knowles, 1984b) I pulled together case descriptions that were prepared by their leaders in the following categories:

Business and Industry
- The Master of Management Program of the American Management Associations
- The Management Skills Development Program at the General Electric Company in Cincinnati
- Technical skills training at Price Waterhouse Company, DuPont Corporation, and the World Bank

- Training line managers as learning facilitators at Joy Manufacturing Company, Pittsburgh
- Self-directed learning on the job at Lloyds Bank of California
- Introducing data processing at a large insurance company
- Product use training for customers at the Clinical Systems Division of DuPont Company, Wilmington, Delaware
- A management development program at The Queensland Public Service Board, Brisbane, Australia

Colleges and Universities
- Self-directed undergraduate study at Alverno College, Milwaukee
- The Adult Entry Program at the Center for Lifelong Learning, Mercy College, Dobbs Ferry, New York
- The Seminar in Process Education, University Without Walls, University of Minnesota
- Faculty orientation and in-service development, School for Lifelong Learning, University System of New Hampshire
- Faculty development through growth contracts, Gordon College, Wenham, Massachusetts
- Internships for improving academic administration in Brazilian universities, Center for Interdisciplinary Studies for the Public Sector, Federal University of Bahia, Salvador, Brazil
- Training college lecturers in Africa, International Cooperative Alliance, Moshi, Tanzania
- Sharing responsibility for learning in a science course—staff-student cooperation, Center for the Advancement of Learning and Teaching, Griffith University, United Kingdom
- Using andragogy in a public speaking course in a community college, Winston-Salem, North Carolina
- The Eco-Action Project at Kansas State University, Manhattan, Kansas
- Delivering adult education to distant communities: a cost-effective model, Georgian College of Applied Arts and Technology, Barrie, Ontario, Canada

Education for the Professions
- Preparing medical students for lifelong learning, McMaster University Faculty of Health Sciences, Hamilton, Ontario, Canada

- Clinical legal education at Vanderbilt University School of Law, Nashville, Tennessee
- Social work education at the University of Georgia School of Social Work, Athens, Georgia
- Learning through teaching among undergraduate social work students, School of Social Work, University of Victoria, British Columbia, Canada
- A baccalaureate degree program in nursing for adult students, Franklin University School of Nursing, Columbus, Ohio
- Teaching school administration at Cleveland State University, Cleveland, Ohio

Continuing Education for the Health Professions
- Self-directed learning for physicians at the Health Science Campus, University of Southern California, Los Angeles
- Self-directed continuing education for nurses, American Nurses Association
- Teaching nurses advanced skills at a metropolitan hospital, Cardiovascular Nursing Program, Doctors Hospital, Little Rock, Arkansas
- In-service nursing education through clinical units, Department of Nursing, St. Mary's Hospital, Waterbury, Connecticut

Religious Education
- The Biblical Andragogy Clinic, Mississauga, Ontario, Canada
- Adult education in the Archdiocese of Detroit, Institute for Continuing Education, Archdiocese of Detroit

Elementary and Secondary Education
- The Challenge Education Program, Simon Fraser University, Vancouver, British Columbia, Canada
- Involving the community as a resource for learning, Jefferson Elementary School, Rochester, Minnesota
- Individualized education at a Catholic high school, Bishop Carroll High School, Calgary, Alberta, Canada

Remedial Education
- Developing basic competencies at Department of Defense Schools, Pacific

- Teaching English as a second language to immigrant community college students, Piedmont Community College, Charlotte, North Carolina

Since the publication of this book I have received communications from scores of other people reporting their experience in applying the andragogical model in a wide variety of settings. One setting not represented in this collection is graduate programs in adult education in universities around the world. Although no systematic survey of these programs has been taken, I know from conversations with many professors of adult education that most, if not all, expose their students to the andragogical model and that many have adapted their programs to it—so that their students *experience* andragogy, rather than just study it. Another major development has been the founding of free-standing external degree programs offering graduate degrees that proudly proclaim their andragogical roots. I have been associated as an adjunct professor or mentor with three of the most notable: Empire State College in Saratoga Springs, New York; the Fielding Institute in Santa Barbara, California; and the Union Institute in Cincinnati, Ohio. Another development that especially warms my heart is the increasing number of research studies probing into various aspects of the andragogical model that have appeared in our scholarly literature. On the whole, their findings have been highly supportive.

The Future of Andragogy

I see no reason at this point to doubt that the application of the andragogical model will continue to spread, especially in higher education, business and industry, government agencies, and myriad voluntary organizations. My deepest hope is that it will continue to influence the elementary and secondary levels, so that before too long our entire educational enterprise will be organized around the concept of learning as a lifelong self-directed process.

THE CRITICAL EVENTS MODEL

Leonard Nadler and Zeace Nadler

In 1982 we wrote *Designing Training Programs: The Critical Events Model* (Nadler, 1982). Perhaps we should start with first qualifying the "we." For many years we have worked together professionally, but generally only Len's name appeared on the written material. We won't go into details, but more recently Zeace's name has also appeared. So, for purposes of this chapter, the "we" refers to both of us.

We had been using the critical events model (CEM) for almost 20 years before the first edition of the book was published. The comments in this chapter are based on using the book in a wide variety of situations. We have used the CEM in working with clients in the United States as well as in other countries. We have used it in teaching human resource development (HRD) practitioners how to design training programs. We have received feedback on the model from our students and from our clients. We have received feedback from people who bought the book, used the model, and told us about it when we met them at conferences or at other activities. And, of course, we have also received feedback from professional colleagues.

There have been situations where people did not ask Len questions, perhaps because he was the author and they might have felt intimidated. But, no such hesitation was experienced when it came to questioning Zeace. So, what follows is truly material from both.

What have we learned about using this model? First—it works! It works best when people realize that it is a model, and not a prescription. It does not have to be followed in exact detail. Rather, it highlights the "critical events" which must take place if an effective design is to result.

One of the newer trends in HRD is concerned with organization learning. Without going into depth on that, it should be noted that this model is part of what many mean when they talk or write about organizational learning. As this model indicates, a good part of the organization must be involved in the design. It is not possible to use the CEM by just sitting behind a desk and working alone. In going through the model, people in the organization will learn from each other, even though the model itself is not presented as a learning experience.

Every model is based on some assumptions. First and foremost, the assumption underlying the CEM is that the learners are adults. Also, the learning is being provided by the employer though it may be delivered by an outside organization (such as a community college) or a supplier (organization or individual providing materials and services in the area of HRD). Another assumption is that a problem or opportunity creates the need for the learning. (In this discussion, "problem" will include opportunities.)

It is also necessary to define some basic terms. The following (presented in detail in Nadler and Nadler, 1989) are essential in understanding the CEM:

- *Training*—learning related to the present job of the learner
- *Education*—learning related to a future job of the learner

The CEM, as presented here, is focused essentially on training, although it can also be used for education. The events would remain the same, but what is done within each event is different. In the second edition of *Designing Training Programs: The Critical Events Model* there is specific material on this.

The term *designer* will be used to indicate that there is a person responsible for the design process. In some situations, more than one person may take a leadership role. Similarly, the term *employee* will generally be used as if the designer was just concerned with one individual, although usually in an organization, training needs will exist for a group. When only one individual is concerned, the CEM can still be used, but might result in something different than designing a training program. To simplify the grammar in this chapter, employee will be used though it is obvious that in most cases it refers to a group of employees.

The model is shown in Figure 2.3, but it must be recognized that this is not an absolute flow chart or any similar limiting structure. These are the *critical events* that must take place when designing training, and generally they will take place in this sequence. However, there are times when it becomes necessary to use a different sequence, though still cover all the events.

Identify the Needs of the Organization

Some people want to skip this event and go right to the next one. Yet, this is probably the most important event in the entire model. Until agreement has been reached on the identification of the problem, and the determination that training is a possible response, nothing further should be done in the design process.

The wrong people may be involved in this first event. One reason is that there has not been agreement within the organization as to the problem—even in general terms. Until that is clari-

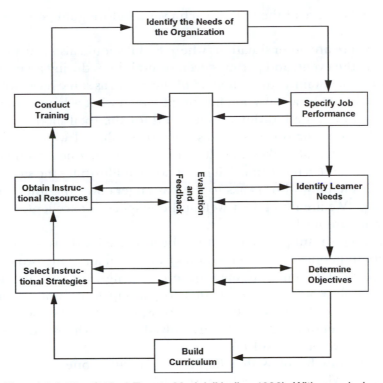

Figure 2.3 The Critical Events Model (Nadler, 1982). With permission.

fied, it is virtually impossible to even start a design process, whether with the CEM or any other model.

Although much has been written and spoken about customers and customer service, it is only infrequently that customers are involved in this first event, but they should be! This is sometimes done, when the customer is an internal part of the organization. It is rarely done when the customer is external, and there are effective ways of doing this through focus groups, video interviews, etc.

Evaluation and Feedback

Figure 2.3 does not fully illustrate what is intended in this activity of Evaluation and Feedback (E&FB). We even hesitated to call it an event, for that may contribute to the confusion. Rather, it is an activity that needs to be built into each event. Placing it as we did, and with arrows going two ways, we are emphasizing that it must take place at the end of each event, before going on to the next event.

There are other situations where E&FB should also take place during the event, and perhaps even several times during an event. Rather than waiting until the end of the event, as some have done, there should be a constant checking to see if what is happening is on target for the individual event, and for the total model.

Reasons for not doing this have been shared with us. The major one is that it takes time. It certainly does, but one can end up spending much more time if it is not done. It illustrates the story of the airline pilot who speaks to the passengers over the intercom, saying, "We are doing very well and our speed is excellent. However, we are lost!"

A significant problem that has been shared with us is getting the right people to attend meetings when evaluating the progress of a particular event. This suggests several things. For one, perhaps the people who are being invited to participate do not see any advantage to themselves. In other words, they are not concerned with whether or not the problem is solved. If so, perhaps the wrong people have been involved.

Another factor is that E&FB is generally done in a group meeting. Why? Sometimes because of a low level of trust. There are certainly times when consensus is desirable, but it is not always needed. The designer must be able to differentiate between those items that need a group decision, and those which can just as effectively be made by a single individual with whom the designer communicates.

Specify Job Performance

Once the problem has been identified, it is necessary to look at the job and at how it is performed. The emphasis here is on the job, not on the individual doing that job. That will be important for the next part of the CEM.

The difficulty that may arise is in really defining the "job"— what is being done by an individual when the job is actually performed. Since an organization is the result of individuals and groups working together, a system, it is important to analyze that system and recognize the interdependency of jobs. In a job, something is done at an agreed upon level of standards related to quantity and quality. Over time, those standards may not have changed sufficiently to reflect what the organization needs now. Or, the standards may have changed, but other parts of the organization are not aware of the changes.

Also, because of interdependency, a job has to be viewed as part of the system. This can be shown as: input → job → output. Therefore, the designer should encourage looking at the input, or what comes in from places outside of the job unit. It may be from other units in the organization, or from external sources such as customers in a retail establishment. It may be that the input must be changed, or accommodated in some way different from what is now the pattern, in order for the job to be done appropriately.

The output must also be analyzed, and that becomes very obvious. The problem may have arisen because the output was not what was expected. Or, the output might be going to the wrong part of the organization.

There may also be differing perceptions in the organization of the contribution that the job is making to the organization. When agreement has been reached about the job, there may be several alternatives to explore. This may be done before the E&FB is activated for this event. It can take place anytime during the event when it appears appropriate.

At the end of this event it may be decided that training is not the solution to the problem. There may be other alternatives such as: redesign the job, change either the input or output, or select different employees.

The designer should not see this as criticism or negative feedback. Quite the contrary, the designer will have avoided the waste of designing a program and having it conducted, only to find that it did not solve the problem. With E&FB effectively completed, it is possible to move on to the next event.

Identify Learner Needs

On the other hand, if it is determined that training might be the solution, the designer must determine what is expected from the output of a job. It is time then to look at who is performing that job. Here is where a match or fit must be explored.

If the job has not been changed as a result of the previous event, then another variable to be considered is the employee doing the job. One approach is to share the results of the previous event with the employee and determine if that is what the employee thinks the job is meant to do. A possible result could be the employee saying, "Why didn't somebody tell me that was the way to do the job? I can do it!" In other words, the solution is not that the employee needed training, but what the employee needed was better information and supervision on how to do the job.

Another reaction might be, "If that is the way you want me to do the job, I don't want it." This does not mean that the employee should be fired, but consideration should be given to the need for job counseling and a transfer to a different job. Once again, no training program is needed, but the designer will have helped solve a problem in the organization.

Frequently, however, it is probable that training is the appropriate response. Therefore, it becomes necessary to determine the learning needs of the employee.

Too many organizations try to determine this by sending out questionnaires to employees, asking them what they think they need. Actually, they are not determining *needs*, but they are surfacing *wants*. It is possible to design a learning program for wants, but that is not training, and will not fulfill a need, and not solve a problem.

The needs can be determined by comparing, the following:

$$JP - AK = LN$$

where JP = Job performance
 AK = Already knows
 LN = Needs to learn

The result of this kind of investigation should lead to the specific learning needs of the employee.

As part of E&FB, this result should now be tested by asking (1) If the employee accomplishes this learning, will performance then be as determined by the Specify Job Performance event? (2) If the employee accomplishes this learning, will the problem have been solved? When the answers to those questions are "yes," it is time to go to the next event.

Determine Objectives

After the learning needs of the employee have been identified, objectives need to be determined. An objective is seen as a statement of what is to be accomplished by the training program.

It is possible that the needs identified in the previous CEM event will have resulted in a long list. If so, it becomes necessary to establish some kind of priority, given many limitations. Among the major limitations are:

- *Urgency*—How soon must the training be completed?
- *Availability of learner*—When can the learner be released from the job? The assumption here is that the learning will take place away from the job.
- *Duration*—For how long can the learner be away from the job?

The answers to these questions will contribute to program objectives. From these, the next step is to develop learning objectives.

There are many ways to state learning objectives ranging from the specific behavioral to the general philosophical. The designer should choose the approach that best suits the style of the organization. It is also important for the designer to choose the type of learning objective with which that designer will feel comfortable.

An undue emphasis has been put on writing learning objectives, rather than on understanding them. One technique a designer can use is to first write learning objectives based on the data gathered.

Then, the learning objectives should be shared with the learner, supervisor, and other concerned parties. Have them read the objectives and comment. They can be asked to restate the objectives in any way that would be more meaningful for them, or to write different objectives based on the data gathered. It is important that the designer avoid the trap of "pride of ownership" or be in any way defensive about the objectives that have already been written. What is important is that the objectives should be very clear, and accepted by the people who are expected to benefit from the training program.

When everybody is comfortable with the objectives, the designer should move to E&FB. At this point, if not earlier, the designer should first determine if the program objectives are acceptable. When agreement is reached on them, then the designer should determine if the learning objectives are acceptable.

The next determination is how the objectives relate to the Specify Job Behavior event. Particularly, are there any objectives which do not relate to the job?

The question that needs to be asked is: If these program and learning objectives are met, will the problem be solved? It is important to ask this question repeatedly. Designing takes time and from the time the first event of the CEM was completed, until nearing the completion of this event, conditions may have changed.

Even if there is a decision to proceed, the designer should stop at this point and not go on to the next event—yet. First, the question should be asked: Should these learning needs be met by an internal or an external program? That is, should the design process continue, or are there packaged programs available? Packaged programs are available from a wide variety of sources including academic institutions, HRD companies, or suppliers of HRD materials.

For some programs, it may be less expensive and more convenient to purchase the learning from an external source. That decision, however, should not be made until after the learning objectives have been agreed on.

If it is determined to continue the design process internally, then the designer should move to the next event of the CEM.

Build Curriculum

As used in the CEM, curriculum is defined as the material that has to be learned and the sequence of that learning. There are many learning theories that can be utilized by the designer, and this emphasizes that an essential competence a designer must have is in the field of adult learning.

In building the curriculum, the designer must consider factors which at first appear to have little to do with learning. One of these is *geography*, or the relative distance between the instructors and the designer. In large organizations, multisite and multinational, the designer may have to design training programs without having any direct contact with the instructors.

A core activity in this event is *selecting content*. Here is where the designer must recognize that there will probably be the need for others to help, people commonly called subject matter specialists (SMS). They can come from within the organization or from external sources such as academia, suppliers, and other designers. An SMS does not have to know anything about how adults learn, since that is the specialty of the designer. The SMS should be able to tell the designer what content needs to be learned to meet the learning objectives determined in the previous event of the CEM.

One way to look at the curriculum content is in terms of the following categories:

1. Essential
2. Helpful
3. Peripheral
4. Unrelated

The "essential" content is the absolute minimum that must be learned for the learner to reach the projected objectives. For many designs, that is all that is actually required. Beyond that, the other three content possibilities must be viewed in terms of the question: Will the learning objectives be met, and performance changed, without this content? Even if the answer is "yes," there may be other reasons to include that content, within the restrictions of limited time and resources.

The "helpful" content supplements the essential. Although not required, there may be situations where it can provide additional insight into the job for which training is being designed.

The "peripheral" is in the "good to know" category, but is not necessary to accomplish the goals of the learning program. This content usually arises from an SMS comment: "When I learned this material, I also learned ... [the peripheral]."

The "unrelated" content has little or nothing to do with the learning objectives. It does not arise too often, but may, when somebody higher up in the organization than the designer, communicates either directly or indirectly that certain content should be included. There are times when the designer may find it more judicious to include that unrelated content, rather than fight the higher authority or the system. It is important, however, that the designer not engage in self-delusion and try to rationalize that content as belonging under the essential.

Once the content has been determined, the designer must consider the *sequence* in which the learning should take place. This requires, once again, that the designer be competent in the area of adult learning theory.

There are many possibilities, but one way to consider organizing the sequence is from the general to the specific, while another is from the specific to the general. Within those two parameters, many options are available. It is, however, more than just choosing one or the other. The choice will be influenced by several factors.

One of these is the nature of the subject matter. In some areas, general theory comes first, and then application. In others, it may be more beneficial to start with the application and then build the theory base.

The learner must also be considered. Some do quite well going from the total picture (the gestalt) to the specifics. Other learners need to start with the specifics before they can effectively deal with the general picture.

The sequencing must also reflect the time available for the learning. The designer may want to consider "spaced learning"—providing the learning in small curriculum units. After each unit, the learner returns to the job and is given the opportunity to apply the new learning on the job. Then, the learner returns to the learning for the next unit, which starts with the processing of what happened on the job before going on to the next curriculum unit.

There are many variations possible, but it is more than just creating different curriculum/learning sequences. There must be a reason underlying the choices that the designer makes in sequencing the curriculum units.

Once again, the designer may want to consider the *make* or *buy* alternatives. This was done during an earlier event of the CEM, and in this event it might be helpful to reexamine that decision. As the curriculum is now determined, the designer is in a better position to examine what is available from suppliers (buy) before proceeding in the design process (make).

Let us continue with the "make" alternative. After the content and the sequence have been determined, the curriculum will be divided into units. The length of each unit will depend on the amount of time available for each session, and the number of sessions in all.

From that, it is necessary to develop lesson plans. Here, the designer must consider who will be doing the instruction. If it is to be machine-oriented (for example, computer), the lesson plans are actually built into the program.

Where there is a person-oriented program (instructor or facilitator), the lesson plans are crucial. In some cases, the designer may be doing the instruction, though this trend is decreasing. Even when the designer will also be the instructor, lessons plans should be developed and committed to writing.

Even if the instructor is a professional (either internal or external), the designer must still write lesson plans. They will not have to be as detailed as might be necessary for a nonprofessional instructor, but the lesson plan is essentially the major way that the designer communicates the objectives, content, and operation of the curriculum to others.

There has been an increasing trend in work organizations to utilize nonprofessional personnel for instruction. There are many good reasons for that. The designer must recognize that writing a lesson plan for a nonprofessional will be much different than writing one for a professional.

Whatever the lesson plan, the designer must be sure to build in evaluation as part of the lesson plan. There can be a formative evaluation, which takes place during the conduct of the training. The designer may not be able to react to that data, but provision should be made for the instructor to make some changes, if necessary, in the remainder of the training based on the formative evaluation.

Summative evaluation takes place at the end of the program, but before the learner returns to the job. There should also be an evaluation after the learner has been back on the job and had the opportunity to apply the learning. Both of these evaluations should be available to the designer. That data may change future iterations of the program and be helpful in those design efforts.

The activity of E&FB should not be ignored. Although it may be time consuming, the designer must check the curriculum and see how it relates to the decisions made in all of the previous events. With that agreement, the designer can move on to the next event.

Select Instructional Strategies

In this event the designer is concerned with selecting the appropriate learning strategies to implement the curriculum. Let us pause and look at the word *strategies*. It is meant to include all the methods, techniques, and devices available to facilitate the learning process.

The designer should also consider an important possibility in this event, namely, returning to the previous event. As the designer goes through the process of selecting instructional strategies related to the curriculum, it may be necessary to make some adjustments to the results of the previous event. Different instructional strategies can have some influence on the curriculum, but they should not drive it. It may even require bringing together some of the people who participated in the successful completion of the previous event.

During this event, the designer may want to call on the services of another kind of specialist—in this case an instructional design specialist. The designer is expected to be competent in learning theory, but not necessarily in the myriad of instructional strategies that are available, particularly those utilizing technology (for example, computer, interactive video). This does not mean that the designer does not know what they can contribute to the learning process, but it is not essential for the designer to know how to write a computer program.

The designer may also have to utilize the SMS again, to ascertain some of the instructional strategies that are common in the particular field, but with which the instructional designer may not be familiar.

One of the most important factors for the designer to consider is the *learner*. Different learners have different learning styles, and are comfortable with some strategies, and antagonistic towards others. If possible, the designer should have determined something about learning styles in the earlier Identify Learner Needs event. If not, it becomes important to get that data in this event.

That does not mean that learners cannot change, but that the provision for change must be built into the curriculum. That means that the designer may have to return to the previous event and make necessary adjustments.

Consideration must certainly be given to the management practices in the organization. For example, the availability of *budget*. Some instructional strategies require money to either write them (cases, for example) or acquire them (interactive video). Who controls the budget for this training program is an important consideration.

Facilities must also be taken into account when selecting instructional strategies. Some organizations have their own facilities, frequently called conference centers. Other organizations rely on rented facilities in hotel and motels. Whatever the pattern, the facilities must be considered when selecting instructional strategies. For example, the strategy chosen may require breakout rooms, perhaps four small rooms to facilitate small group discussion. In some facilities, that may not be available. In others, it might significantly increase the expense of the program.

The *culture of the organization* is also a factor. There may be some kinds of strategies that are expected to be used in most programs, at certain levels. For example, it may be the culture to use case studies with upper level employees, but not with those at lower levels of the organization. It may have little to do with the objectives and/or curriculum, but more to do with what is expected in that organization (the culture). Organization cultures change, but it is not suggested that a designer attempt to do that while designing a training program.

The designer must consider the *instructor,* or whoever will be in direct contact with the learner. If a machine-oriented strategy will be used, the instructor will become a coach rather than a presenter. If the potential instructor is experienced in using certain strategies, this must be known to the designer, as well as which strategies the instructor does not know or may be uncomfortable with. The designer can provide instruction for the instructor on how to use some strategies not previously used, but plans for that must be built into the design process.

There are a wide range of instructional strategies available to the designer, and the list grows constantly. Suffice it to say, however, that after the instructional strategies have been selected, the designer must once again consider E&FB. The major question is: Will the instructional strategies implement the curriculum? If not, then it will be necessary to reexamine both the strategies selected and the curriculum. The lesson plans will need to be examined to see that they reflect the application of the strategies to the curriculum.

Obtain Instructional Resources

The training program has now been designed, so the designer must move to the next event, to assure that there are resources for implementation. In some situations, this will be a management responsibility rather than a designer one. However, it is part of the design process and within the scope of the CEM, so it is included here.

It is now possible for the designer to determine the *physical* resources that will be necessary to implement the program. That includes the equipment, materials, and facilities needed based on the program that has thus far been designed.

Equipment is generally comprised of those items that will be used over and over again, such as a VCR. Some of this may be available within the organization, or it may be necessary to purchase or rent from external sources.

By contrast, materials are those items which are anticipated to be expended during the conduct of the program. This would include items like workbooks, handouts, newsprint, and markers. There may be a stock of those items in the HRD unit, and the availability would depend on several factors. One of those relates to the financial aspects, whether materials will be charged to each program, or absorbed in the general budget.

The facilities will depend on many factors. For some training programs, it might be advantageous to have them "off the ranch," away from the workplace. For others, being as close to the workplace as possible might be part of the program design.

Training programs cost money, so there must be adequate *financial* resources. Some organizations start out by indicating the budget for the training program. If that is a constraint, then the designer must keep that in mind.

It is possible for the designer to get to this part of the CEM and be able to tell management what the program will cost. The designer should not assume that the organization wants the cheapest program possible. Cost is a relative matter. The training program cost can be compared to how much might be saved by improved performance.

The *human resource* must also be considered, for the effective implementation of a training program requires several different kinds of people. The discussion of human resources that follows does not signify any kind of hierarchy.

The learner, of course, is essential. The major purpose of a training program is to enable the learner to perform differently or better. Depending upon the time used to design the program, the designer may have to check to verify that the learner who was the focus of the earlier Identify Learner Needs event is still the same learner who will be involved in the program. There may have been changes, and it may be necessary to verify that the same learner is still in the job, or whether any new learner in that job has the same learning needs.

The supervisor is very important, for several reasons. For one, it is the supervisor who will make the learner available for the training program. It is also the supervisor who will want to know the results of the program, for those results should have a direct impact on performance for which the supervisor is responsible. The supervisor, who had the problem, also wants to make sure that the training program will contribute to solving that problem.

Then, there is the instructor (facilitator), the person who will have direct contact with the learner. The instructor may come from the HRD staff. In that case, it is relatively easy for the designer to relate to that individual and to obtain the services of that human resource. If the instructor will be coming from some other source, internal or external, it may be more complicated and require the assistance of somebody higher in the HRD unit or the organization.

As part of this event, the designer should also be considering the training program *schedule*. This is necessary, as the schedule will be influenced by the availability of the resources. Scheduling may have to be modified, depending upon the equipment and materials required for the program.

E&FB is extremely important for this event. When it is completed, the program has essentially been designed and moves to implementation. Of course, modifications can be made during the Conduct Training event, but any significant changes can disrupt or obviate the training.

The most important activity during E&FB is to once again relate the training program back to the original problem, as described in the Identify the Needs of the Organization event. Time and other factors may have created changes that need to be considered.

It may be that limitations on resources (physical, financial, human) will result in modifications in curriculum and objectives. The modified objectives will have to be examined to determine if a successful program would still solve the problem. In organizations where there is excessive concern with the bottom line or any form of cost-benefit ratio, this is the point at which all parties should agree, or at least those making the decisions should be in agreement.

This is also the time to verify the trainee (or list of trainees) and confirm availability for the training program.

When the designer feels that E&FB has been satisfactorily completed, it is possible to move to the next event.

Conduct Training

This is the payoff! This is where it all comes together.

It is possible that the designer will be only peripherally involved in this event as it moves into implementation. In a sense, the design is finished, and it now becomes an activity under the supervisor of HRD programs and/or learning facilitators (instructors, coaches, and similar delivery people).

Although the major activity will now be performed by others, the designer should still consider it part of the design process, for several reasons. Depending on how the program was designed, there may be the need for some fine tuning, modifications, or customization.

The designer must also know the outcomes of the training program in terms of reaching the goals, attitude of the learners, and experiences of the instructors. Some of that information will be necessary in helping to improve the present program, and can be extremely helpful to the designer when involved in designing future training programs.

E&FB may be much different from the other events. After the Conduct Training event, there can be several evaluations. Most will be conducted by learners, instructors, and supervisors. In addition, the Designer may want to gather the relevant data so as to close the loop, to report back to those who made the decision to design, at the end of the first event, Identify the Needs of the Organization.

SUMMARY

The three prototypical models differ with respect to many points but they also are similar in that they cover some of the same or at least parallel steps. Paralleling a systems approach to program planning, all three models called for the following steps: inputs of a learning needs assessment, process directed to those needs, outcomes that represent what is learned, and feedback in the form of evaluation that provides the information necessary to repeat the programming cycle.

Together these models present us with alternative strategies for planning education and training programs. As such, they increase our sensitiveness to different ways in which we can structure our activities in response to various conditions, problems, or deficiencies. With his seven assumptions that underlie education design, Houle offers significant insights about the deeper meaning of our program planning work. Houle's 11 categories of learning situations constitute a challenge to expand our horizons beyond the usual instructor-designed courses where so many planners by default find themselves. The components of Houle's design framework provide us with checkpoints with which to analyze education programs which have occurred as well as guidelines for programs still in the design stages.

From Knowles we can take into account the five assumptions—the nature of the learner, the role of experience, learning orientation, readiness to learn, and motivation—which differentiate pedagogy with its characteristic emphasis on instruction from adult education (andragogy) with its characteristic emphasis on learning. The notion that adults are capable of self-direction and self-development has significant implications for the design of programs that involve the defining and solving of problems arising from the business of living. The andragogical notion that part of the planner's role is to structure planning as a joint planner-learner activity is consonant with one of Houle's seven assumptions that learning is a shared enterprise between the planner and the learner.

From the Nadlers we can consider the value of adopting an open systems model that comprises a series of critical planning events integrally connected to the steps of evaluation and feedback. Lending itself to the design of planner-directed education and training, their model guides us in the design of training programs which respond to differences between what is done and what ought to be done within organizations.

One assumption underlying both this and the succeeding chapter is that examination of different program planning models can contribute to a comprehensive view of one's own program planning practice. What specific actions may be inferred from each step in each of these models for the planning of learning activities in your own organization? Which specific steps are not presently being addressed in your own program planning practice? What might be the likely consequences and/or benefits to be derived from adopting one or more of these steps in your own practice? Through such consideration, it may be possible to expand your vision of what is possible and thus improve the effectiveness of your craft as a program planner.

QUESTIONS FOR STUDY AND DISCUSSION

- Compare and contrast what you think are the stated and un-stated assumptions underlying each of the three prototypical models described in this chapter. What do they offer in common? How do they differ?
- What are the strengths and weaknesses of each model in relation to your own program planning context?
- Which, if any, of the models describes most accurately the programming practices adhered to in your organization?
- Suppose the authors of these prototypical models were invited to visit your own organization to advise you about your training and/or education programs. What advice can you imagine each author would give? Would you agree with their advice? Justify your response.
- If you were to prioritize each of these three models in terms of the degree to which they resemble your own concept of an ideal model, what would be the order you would propose? Justify your selection.

REFERENCES

Bradshaw, J. (1974). "The concept of social need," *Ekistics 220*, March, pp. 184–185.

Freire, P. (1970). *Pedagogy of the oppressed.* New York: Seabury Press.

Houle, C. O. (1961). *The inquiring mind.* Madison, WI: University of Wisconsin Press, 1961.

Houle, C. O. (1972). *Design of education.* San Francisco: Jossey-Bass. (Revised edition, 1996).

Knowles, M. S. (1970). *The modern practice of adult education: Pedagogy versus andragogy.* Chicago: Follett.

Knowles, M. S. (1975). *Self-directed learning: A guide for learners and teachers.* Englewood Cliffs, NJ: Prentice-Hall.

Knowles, M. S. (1980). *The modern practice of adult education: From pedagogy to andragogy.* New York: Cambridge.

Knowles, M. S. (1984a). *The adult learner: A neglected species.* Houston: Gulf Publishing Company.

Knowles, M. S. (1984b). *Andragogy in action.* San Francisco: Jossey-Bass.

Knowles, M. S. (1986). *Using learning contracts.* San Francisco: Jossey-Bass.

Nadler, L. (1982). *Designing training programs: The critical events model.* Reading, MA: Addison-Wesley.

Nadler, L. (1994). *Designing training programs: The critical events model.* (2nd ed.) Houston: Gulf.

Nadler, L., & Nadler, Z. (1989). *Developing human resources.* San Francisco: Jossey-Bass.

Tough, A. (1967). *Learning without a teacher.* Toronto: Ontario Institute for Studies in Education.

Verner, C. M. (1964). "Definitions." In G. Jensen, A. A. Liveright and W. Hallenbeck (eds.), *Adult education: Outlines of an emerging field of university study.* Washington, DC: Adult Education Association of the U.S.A.

White, T. (1970). Some philosophical consideration. In Robert Smith, George Aker, and J. Roby Kidd (Eds.), *Handbook of adult education.* Washington, DC: Adult Education Association of the U.S.A.

3

Alternative Program Planning Models

Huey B. Long

ABSTRACT

This chapter discusses six planning models that may serve as alternatives to the three prototypical models discussed in the previous chapter. The exact number of planning models available in the literature is unknown; however, Buskey and Sork (1982) identify more than 90. Therefore, in selecting the six models explicated in this chapter, several criteria were applied: existence of a theoretical base, potential for application in a range of institutional settings, empirical support, and use by different agencies. Most of the above considerations were met by all of the models discussed here except Simerly's model. His model was explicitly selected because of its association with continuing higher education program development and as such serves as an alternative to Houle's model as described in the previous chapter. The five others are models developed by Boone (1985), Burnham (1988), Long (1983a and 1983b), and Schroeder (1980). Similarities and differences among the six models are noted as well as implications for their application in organizations with unlike purposes, clients, and so forth.

ASSESSMENT

Instructions: Select the best answer from the options provided below.

1. Program planning in adult education and training is best described as:

_____ a. a haphazard process.

_____ b. something seldom discussed in the literature.

_____ c. a science.

_____ d. an art.

2. Program planning may be conducted at two levels:

_____ a. the university and the high school.

_____ b. business and education.

_____ c. micro and macro.

_____ d. international and national.

3. Edgar Boone's program planning model is best described as

_____ a. a cookbook model.

_____ b. a theoretical model.

_____ c. a practical model.

_____ d. a how-to-do-it model.

4. Program planning models are usually

_____ a. complex.

_____ b. simple.

_____ c. prescriptive.

_____ d. limited.

5. Which of the following is most usually found in program planning models?

_____ a. plans for historical analysis.

_____ b. organizational mission analysis.

_____ c. needs analysis.

_____ d. literature searches.

6. Program planning

_____ a. has nothing to do with organizational questions.

_____ b. is related to organization in all planning models.

_____ c. is frequently explicitly associated with organizational questions.

_____ d. is related to organization in no planning models.

7. List and briefly describe at least three program planning models, other than the models discussed in the previous chapter, found in the literature.

8. Provide a schematic containing at least five steps in a program planning model that you would expect to find in most of the models discussed in this chapter. Compare your schematic with the models after reading the chapter.

9. Why is it so difficult to briefly describe the procedures that may be used to conduct such common program planning steps as needs assessment? (Answers to items 1–6 are provided at the end of the chapter.)

INTRODUCTION

Program planning, sometimes referred to as program development or program building, is a fundamental adult education process (Long, 1996). Because of the numerous interacting variables involved in planning an adult education program, it may be described as more art than science. Discussion of the activity is further complicated by the different connotations reported in the literature. Program planning may refer to at least three different things or levels of activity. One use of the term is similar to curriculum. Another usage refers to the totality of educational opportunities provided by an organization. Yet another refers to all of the educational activities conducted within a community. Less frequently, a fourth use of the term equates program planning with organizational development. At least three of the program planning models to be discussed in this chapter also may be applied to organizational development tasks, and they all are concerned with curricula problems.

No recent effort to completely inventory the range of program planning has been identified. Buskey and Sork (1982) identified 90 program planning models. Later Sork and Buskey (1986) conducted an analysis of the program planning literature published between 1950 and 1983. Long (1983b) reveals that numerous approaches to program planning are reported in the adult and continuing education literature. As a result, analyses of the different approaches may be made from a variety of perspectives. The following analytic frameworks may be used (Long, 1996): (1) program elements, (2) conceptual bases, and (3) philosophical bases. As some of these topics are discussed in other chapters of this book, relative comments are purposely kept to a minimum here.

While the program models suggested by Cyril Houle, Malcolm Knowles, and Leonard Nadler are definitely well known, important, and useful models, they do not exclude alternative approaches from consideration. Long (1996) identifies a variety of planning models based on a range of conceptual bases used in diverse educational settings. These models have been used in continuing professional education (Mazmanian, 1980; Pennington and Green, 1976), reform or liberation education as espoused by Paulo Freire (DeVries, 1978; Spencer, 1980), and liberal education (Apps, 1979). Space limitations prevent a general discussion of all of the program planning models reported in the literature. Therefore, six models were selected for explication. These models were selected for several reasons such as the existence of a theoretical base, potential for application to a range of institutional settings, empirical support, and use by different agencies. The rest of this chapter provides a brief comment about the model developers and a description of the six models. In alphabetical order they are Boone (1985), Burnham (1988), Long (1983b), Morrison (1987), Schroeder (1980) and Simerly (1990). The detail provided on each model varies according to the detail available in the literature. Following the description some comparative comments are made. A summary and conclusion end the chapter.

MODEL DEVELOPERS

The developers of the models discussed in the following pages have been involved in higher education. Their total experience goes beyond the campus, however. Thus, their involvement in program planning is more heterogeneous than indicated by their employment positions. For example, Edgar Boone is noted for his leadership of an academic department of adult and community college education and his work in cooperative extension. His experience thus includes work with two different kinds of higher education providers. Huey Long has been engaged in academic administration and instruction, community development, governmental training, continuing higher education, and continuing professional education. The other developers' models of program planning are apparently influenced by their activities in higher continuing education, continuing professional education, and training.

Thus, the authors of the models discussed in the following pages reflect practical program planning experience in diverse settings as well as academic instruction in graduate degree programs. The varied practice is revealed in the individual approaches to program planning.

SELECTED MODELS

Boone's Model

Edgar Boone's (1985) model is based on three major conceptual divisions: (a) planning, (b) design and implementation, and (c) evaluation and accountability. Each major division contains subordinate activities, which, in turn, include additional minor steps for a total of 20 elements. The first three levels of activity are outlined in Table 3.1 (p. 59).

Boone's procedural model emerges from the rich theoretical developmental framework that he recommends and from a carefully crafted nomological net that facilitates an empirical testing. Yet, only one study has been identified that appears to directly test the model. Carpenter (1980) submitted a dissertation that was designed to determine how Boone's model is confirmed by articles appearing in five adult education periodicals between 1959 and 1979. Among other things, he reports a trend toward macro processes of program design. More is said about this in the discussion of Long (1983b), Morrison (1987), and Schroeder (1980).

Burnham's Model

Byron Burnham (1988) conceptualizes program planning as "technology." He defines technology in the words of Perrow (1967) as follows:

> … actions that an individual performs upon an object with or without
> the aid of tools or mechanical devices, in order to make some change
> in that object. (p. 212)

Burnham implies that thinking about program planning as technology should liberate the educator from assumptions concerning the universal application of a particular program planning model to all institutions. He also invokes Boone (1985) for support of maximizing of program planning to benefit the organization.

The relationship between program planning technology and program output is illustrated as follows: (1) Input → (2) Program Planning Technology → (3) Output. According to Burnham's scheme, inputs comprise needs, problems, and impulses to learn or teach. He draws from a variety of adult educators' ideas about program planning processes to arrive at seven operations that constitute the technology. They are originating program ideas,

Table 3.1. Boone's Program Planning Model. Reprinted by permission.

Primary Level Activities	Secondary Level Activities	Tertiary Level Activities
Planning	Organization renewal	1. Understanding of and commitment to the function of the organization: mission, philosophy, and objectives. 2. Understanding of and commitment to the organization's structure: roles and relationships. 3. Knowledgable about and skilled in organization's processes: supervision, staff development, evaluation, and accountability. 4. Understanding of and commitment to a tested conceptual framework for programming. 5. Understanding of and commitment to continuous organizational renewal.
	Organization/ public linkage	1. Study, analysis, and mapping of the organization's public. 2. Identifying target publics. 3. Identifying and interfacing with leaders of target publics. 4. Collaborative identification, assessment, and analysis of needs specific to target publics.
Design and implementation	Design of planned program	1. Translating expressed needs into macro needs. 2. Translating macro needs into macro objectives. 3. Specifying general educational strategies and learning activities. 4. Specifying macro outcomes of the planned program.
	Implementation of planned program	1. Developing plans of action: a. Translating needs into teaching objectives. b. Specifying learning experiences for each teaching objective.

Table 3.1. (*Continued*)

Primary Level Activities	Secondary Level Activities	Tertiary Level Activities
Design and implementation (*cont.*)	Implementation of planned program (*cont.*)	c. Developing plans for evaluating learner outcomes and assessing learning experiences. 2. Developing and implementing strategies and techniques for marketing the plans of action. 3. Developing and following through on plans to recruit and train leader-learner resources. 4. Monitoring and reinforcing the teacher-learner transaction.
Evaluation and accountability		1. Determining and measuring program outputs. 2. Assessing program outputs. 3. Using evaluation findings for program revisions, organizational renewal, and for accounting to publics, parent organization, funding sources, the profession and where appropriate the governance body.

developing ideas, establishing objectives, designing programs, ensuring participation, securing resources, and evaluating programs. Finally, the output includes the organized learning activities and involved learners.

While the model as discussed does not reveal it, Burnham's concept provides for technological variability of three types. These are identified as long-linked technology, mediating technology, and intensive technology. Briefly these three kinds of technology differ according to routineness, interdependence, and variability, respectively.

Burnham's thesis is that educational programs of different kinds of educational institutions may be characterized as one of these kinds of technology. He provides some support for his position based on an intensive case study method applied to a public school district, community college, and a continuing education division of a university.

Long's Heuristic Program Planning Model

Huey Long's (1983a) model was explicitly designed for macro purposes. As is true for the models proposed by Boone and Burnham, the program planning activity is associated with organizational conditions. Long's Heuristic Program Planning Model is designed to plug into any selected micro program planning processes such as needs assessment, objectives, and so forth as determined by the program planner. In other words this model focuses on the broader environmental context. See Figure 3.1.

Long's model contains six steps that should be taken before engaging in the micro planning activities. They are labeled as philosophical purposes, historical character, structural factors in the environment, organizational mission and readiness, environmental interpretation and local/target groups.

The first step, philosophical purposes, involves examining the purposes of education as implied by the organization. For example, some organizations may value educational activities that are designed to reproduce knowledge whereas others may be con-

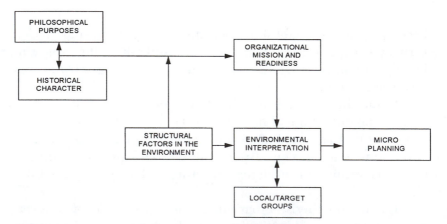

Figure 3.1 Long's Heuristic Educational Program Planning Model incorporating historical and macro elements (Long, 1983a). Reproduced by permission of author.

cerned more with transformative knowledge. See Schroeder (1980) for a slightly different approach where it is suggested that the orientation of the agent system is a major consideration.

The historical character of educational activities, philosophy, and so forth should be reviewed and clearly articulated. Inquiry into the organizational mission and readiness addresses the relationship between the organization's mission and its educational philosophy and history. The readiness factor concerns the organization's ability to provide certain kinds of service, consistent with its mission, in a timely fashion. In other words, can the agency provide an efficient and effective response in a timely fashion? and should it? It is obvious that these three initial analytical steps do not have to be repeated for every program. But they should be completed with sufficient frequency to note any changes that may occur in the philosophy and short-term historical trends, mission, and readiness.

The initial actions are informed by studies and analyses of the larger environment. Organizations interact with the broader society as well as with more local communities. The first is referred to here. The latter is discussed later. Structural factors in the environment include such things as social events and developments, changes in economic structure and activity, shifts in values and customs, politics—some of the kinds of things addressed by Naisbitt (1990), Toffler (1990), and others.

The local/target group element includes two possible subelements. One is the local area as determined by the organization. For some it may be a multistate region, for another it could be a state, finally for another it may be a community within a city or rural area. The second element is the target group. The target group may manifest propinquity or it may be a group of specialists scattered around the world.

Environmental interpretation is the heart of the model. It is the central information processing step where information from the broader society, the local/target group, and the organization is examined collectively and interpreted. The interpretation leads to the creation of program ideas that are then processed through micro planning steps as suggested by Burnham's technology model.

The model has not been subjected to direct empirical testing. Evidence to support the model can be inferred, however. For example, Long (1983a) suggested that broad social developments in the 1960s and 1970s were related to the development of certain kinds of adult and continuing education programs such as adult literacy programs, continuing education for women, and educational program for older adults. It is argued that these educational programs were directly related to structural factors in the environment such as a heightened social consciousness, demographics, and governmental support. In the 1980s and early 1990s things have changed and programs that might be related more directly to the structural factors include continuing professional education (especially in the health-related fields), worker training, and management development.

Morrison's ED QUEST

James Morrison's ED QUEST (1987) program planning model has received recognition for its flexibility and adaptability to different organizations. As with each of the previously discussed models, it also has the advantage of addressing questions of organizational development as well as educational program development. As in Long's model, environmental analysis and interpretation are central to Morrison's scheme; the term *environmental scanning* is used by Morrison for this activity. He defines environmental scanning as the systematic collection of external information to reduce the randomness of information flowing into an organization and to provide advance warnings of changing external conditions. The process, however, is not a simple one. It requires systematic attention to key sources of demographic, economic, political, social, and/or technological intelligence. These sources may include financial data, census reports and similar documents, or news magazines and newspapers such as the *Wall Street Journal*. A key to the process is the selection of the information sources and the commitment and skill of individuals who scan them. Ptaszynski (1989) indicates the use of ED QUEST is beneficial to organizations. Specifically, it seems as if the process has a positive effect on the total organization's communication, shared vision, strategic planning, strategic management, and future organization.

Environmental scanning has been employed by diverse organizations, some for use in educational planning and some for other organizational planning efforts. The United Way Strategic Institute (1990) illustrates the latter. Simpson, McGinty, and Morrison (1987) report its use by educational institutions including the University of Georgia Center for Continuing Education and the Catonsville (Maryland) Community College. Martin (1987) suggests the following process for continuing education organizations: (1) establish a committee of scanners, (2) develop a scanning taxonomy, (3) identify literature sources and data bases, (4) train the scanners, and (5) review the information. As with any condensed list of steps, the above sequence proposed by Martin fails to reveal the detail required in the process, but adequately illustrates it.

Schroeder's Typology of Adult Learning Systems

Wayne Schroeder's (1980) model describes the purpose of his system as a search for order as a means to analyze agent systems, client systems, and program planning processes. Schroeder's model appears to be more concerned with explicitly specifying decision points than other models discussed in this chapter. Accordingly, he identifies three decision points at each of two planning levels: the macro and the micro. At the macro planning level the three decision points concern the educative need, program objectives, and program procedures. The micro decision points are related to learning needs, learning objectives, and learning experiences.

Schroeder provides the practitioner and researcher with an analytic structure for identifying and determining the nature of control in educational decision making. Furthermore, he divides his concept into two major distinct, but interacting systems: the agent system and the client system. Analysis may be limited to either of these systems or may include both at the macro or micro levels.

Basically, it appears that the agent system tends to include the more institutionalized and traditional educational and social organizations that are usually task directed. It is possible that a long-linked technology as proposed by Burnham (1988) is suggested here. The client system, in contrast, seems to be composed of the more flexible, transitory, and person-centered groups as implied in mediated or intensive technology identified by Burnham. The degree of control exerted by the respective systems will be reflected by the judgments concerning decisions about educative needs, program objectives, and program procedures (agent system elements and macro decisions) and learning needs, learning objectives, and learning experiences (client system elements and micro decisions).

The following illustrates the relationship between the macro level decisions and micro level decisions identified by Schroeder. The decision points are described as follows:

Macro decisions
- Educative needs—a gap in capability that obstructs successful attainment of agent or client goals.
- Program objectives—general directional statements that note the educational need to be addressed and the client group.
- Program procedures—the program structure design and how its operation will be supported or facilitated.

Micro decisions
- Learning needs—specific cognitive and other gaps that are believed to be important obstacles to developing identified capabilities.
- Learning objectives—specific directional statements concerning learner performance and the criteria for measurement.
- Learning experiences—the learning structure and how it will be established and maintained.

According to Schroeder agent and client inputs constitute identical categories. Macro inputs and micro inputs are identified as follows:

Macro inputs
- Values
- Goals
- Resource capabilities and dispositions

Micro inputs
- Performance standards
- Agent (learner) capabilities and dispositions.

Schroeder discusses seven propositions concerning potential relationships among three hypothetical program types. These propositions are too lengthy to be reported in detail here, but will be summarized. First, it is suggested that adult education agent systems are more often concerned with external clients; however, some business, corporate, and voluntary membership organizations may have external and internal clients. Compliance is believed to be more easily obtained with internal clients. Institutional agencies that serve external nonmember clients usually serve broad geographic, demographic, and interest groups.

Education programs are typed by Schroeder as being of three kinds based on control patterns and orientation (who controls the program decisions, whose values and goals are most important, etc.) as indicated by macro/micro directions and procedures. They are agent centered, client centered, and eclectic. He provides 14 propositions concerning these relationships. In summary, he suggests that client-oriented systems, e.g., those dependent upon external support are more sensitive to client input. In contrast, agencies that depend upon legal or social mandates for their programs are less client oriented. Stated another way, the degree of client centeredness is associated with the degree of control or freedom the client has to accept or reject the agent's programs. It is important to note that decision control and orientation patterns at the micro level appear to mirror the macro level patterns. In other words, agent- or client-centered control will likely exist at both levels rather than a mixed relationship.

Simerly's Model

Robert Simerly's model is unlike the other models in the absence of theoretical consideration. It is a detailed practical discussion of how to proceed through the planning process based on his experience in continuing higher education. It is not exactly a cookbook approach, but it is a nuts and bolts treatise. The illustrative figure provided by Simerly (1990) demonstrates the relationships among 14 identified steps. The steps, moving from the first to last, according to Simerly's model are as follows:

1. Idea for program
2. Test ideas and seek advice
3. Small group
4. Advisory committee
5. Decision to proceed—or reject
6. Planning committee
7. Establish clear goals
8. Assign planning responsibilities
9. Program planning

10. Logistics
11. Financial management
12. Develop and execute plans
13. Evaluation
14. Wrap-up
15. Follow-up
16. Future agenda identification

The terseness of the items in the model is moderated by an accompanying narrative provided by Simerly. The detail, even in the narrative description, is limited however. For example, step 2— test ideas and seek advice—is described as follows:

> ... It is essential to find out whether or not the basic idea for a program is marketable. An effective way to do this is through discussion and feedback from small groups and advisory committees, as described in the next two steps. (p. 3)

Despite the suggestion that the process of how to test ideas may be clarified in the narration concerning steps 3 and 4, the comment may be too general to provide the guidance needed by novice program planners.

As steps 1–8 are further described by Simerly in Chapter 1 of his book, Simerly refers the reader to that chapter for guidance. Chapter 1 does provide help; for example, 18 tips for program design and development are shared. These tips include conceptual issues such as distinguishing between advisory and planning committees as well as an interview schedule that might be used to obtain information from selected individuals concerning a program idea. Other chapters in his book provide exhibits and suggestions on how to carry out steps 9–14.

DISCUSSION

Similarities and differences exist among the models selected for description in this chapter. At least four similarities, identified below, exist. First, all with the exception of Simerly's model have implied connections with the larger organizational purpose. Educational programming in this sense is perceived to be an extension of the organization that impacts upon it in important ways. Development of educational programs becomes a process that is organically related to the philosophy, mission and history of organiza-

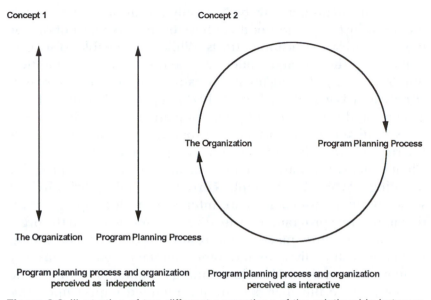

Figure 3.2 Illustration of two different perceptions of the relationship between the organization and the program planning process.

tion. Figure 3.2 illustrates two significantly different perceptions of the relationship between program planning and the organization.

A second similarity found among the models proposed by Boone, Long, Morrison, and Schroeder is a kind of systems analysis. Provisions for the recognition and consideration of two interacting systems, referred to by Schroeder as the agent system and client system, are explicitly included in Boone, Long, Morrison, and Schroeder and implicitly in Burnham.

The emphasis placed on the larger environment is a third common element among the models. Interpretation of the environment contributes to the identification and development of educational program ideas. The process is more of an intelligent one than procedural, however. Procedural provision is necessary, but is not sufficient to contribute meaningful results. Staff members have to develop the ability to interpret the environment.

Fourth, all of the models except Simerly's are based on theoretical concepts derived from social science and/or systems analysis. The larger social system of which educational and other organizations are subunits is represented as being an important factor in program planning activity. Not only are most of the models theoretically based, most of them have been the subject of one or more empirical verification efforts. While it is possible to suggest that each of the selected models may be used with little modification by a variety of agencies and organizations, previous research (Brady and Long, 1972; Everitt, 1974) suggests that prior backgrounds and experiences of program planners affect the perceptions of the relative importance of program planning outcomes. It is also likely that the differences among both agent systems and client systems will have a significant impact upon the program planning process. For example, corporate training divisions and some voluntary associations are interested in developing educational/training programs that are directly associated with the organization's structure, mission, and results. In contrast, continuing higher education divisions and some voluntary organizations may be more frequently involved in planning programs for others. The outputs, to use Burnham's term, have limited impact upon the provider in such instances. Preplanning is expected to reflect important differences among agent systems and client systems. Agent systems that serve their internal client systems may have a greater interest in strategic planning, predicting the organization's future and designing programs directly associated with these scenarios. Another aspect of this element is reflected in Burnham's discussion of his model where he identifies three different kinds of educational institutions with three different kinds of technology that he labels long-linked, mediated, and intensive. It does not seem to be an accident that the kinds of institutions he studied reflect different kinds of technology. It may not be necessary for those institutions to be identified with the kinds of technology he described. However, Schroeder explicitly notes that certain types of organizations may have specific kinds of relationships with the client system that affect the details of the process.

Even though the models discussed in this chapter differ in some ways from the models reported in the previous chapter they also directly or indirectly include some of the same elements. Some of these are (a) originating ideas, (b) developing ideas, (c) setting objectives, (d) designing the educational activities, (e) recruiting participants, (f) identifying and securing resources, and (g) evaluating the program. See Table 3.2 for a comparative listing of the major elements identified in six models.

Entire chapters of books have been written on many of the

Table 3.2 Major Planning Elements in Each of Six Selected Program Planning Models

Boone	Burnham	Long	Morrison	Schroeder	Simerly
• Organization renewal • Design planned program • Implement • Evaluation and accountability	• Originate program ideas • Develop program ideas • Establish objectives • Design program • Ensure participation • Secure resources	• Determine philosophical purposes • Identify historical character • Identify organization mission/readiness • Identify structural environmental factors • Interpret environment • Local/target groups • Micro planning	• Scan environment • Analysis	• Note values • Set goals • Identify and secure resources • Set performance standards • Determine agent (learner) capabilities and dispositions	• Identify ideas • Form advisory group • Form planning committee • Set goals • Program planning • Logistics • Financial management • Develop and execute plans • Evaluate • Wrap-up • Follow-up • Future agenda

above procedures, therefore, it is unwise to attempt to describe them in detail here. For example Long et al. (1992) report on the range of potential needs assessment procedures used by selected professionals. The study identified four major concepts of ways of arriving at decisions concerning educational activities for professionals. They are as follows:

1. Decision by edict or authority, e.g., an approach that provides unilateral decisions through a variety of rational-logical procedures employed by individuals in positions of authority;
2. Decision by market forces, e.g., an approach whereby providers of education service respond to enrollment demands;
3. Decisions by needs determination, e.g., providers of educational services respond to educational practice needs as established through a variety of mechanisms; or
4. Some combination of the above.

Long et al. (1992) sought to determine (a) how different professional continuing education groups approach education needs assessment, (b) how individuals represented by those groups believe that needs assessment should be conducted, and (c) the role of needs assessment procedures in planning educational services. A literature review identified 13 sources for inferring needs: (1) authorities or expert practitioners, (2) advisory groups of a general nature, (3) specialized advisory groups, (4) self-perceived needs and interests of individuals, (5) self-perceived needs of society, (6) self-perceived needs of the local community, (7) self-perceived needs of the sponsoring organization, (8) needs based on a body of knowledge and wisdom, (9) advisory committees, (10) clinical assessments, (11) knowledge of social developments, (12) professional experts, and (13) theoretical constructs supplemented by demographic and other data. Ultimately, six sources were used in the survey to determine which sources were used and which sources the respondents believed should be used in their organizations. In addition, data were collected concerning the usefulness versus practicality of 17 needs assessment procedures.

Long et al. (1992) arrived at five conclusions. First, data based on perceptions are more often used for education assessment than performance data. Second, expert and staff opinions are important in identifying educational needs in the organizations represented. Third, the procedures perceived to be the most useful are not always the most practical. Fourth, the respondents have signifi-cantly different perceptions on a number of items on the survey form. Fifth, the instrument appears to be a useful tool for identify-ing the perceptions of professionals concerning educational needs assessment.

The above illustrates the complexity of only one of the activ-ities associated with program planning. Furthermore, Long et al. (1992) report that a number of differences existed among the five professional groups studied. Thus, we are reminded of the point made at the beginning of this chapter that program planning is more art than science. The program planner, as the artist, begins with a set of elements and procedures rather than colors and canvas, and attempts to skillfully select from an array of procedures and then to apply them according to various considerations such as the nature of the agent system and the characteristics of the client system. Thus, it is extremely difficult to become prescriptive in describing the sequence and the detail of selected program plan-ning techniques (technology according to Burnham). It is note-worthy to observe, however, that some common agreement on some of the techniques or procedures involved in program plan-ning seems to exist. Most models include the following elements: some kind of needs identification, objective/purpose, identifica-tion of resources needed, design of the relationship among the resources, evaluation, and management (financial and human).

The six alternative program planning models described above contain sufficient generality of procedures to accommodate most agencies and clients. For example, Boone's procedure of "trans-lating expressed needs into macro needs" (1985, p. 61) may be done by one program planner using a deductive reasoning process while another may be more comfortable with an inductive process. Only by controlled experimentation could we definitively deter-mine which procedure is most effective under a given set of circum-stances. And even then we might be disappointed in the results. Similarly, Long's and Morrison's model can be used by a variety of agencies and organizations. Schroeder describes his model as one that may be used by training units and voluntary and social agen-cies as well as educational institutions. Of the six, Simerly's model seems to be the most focused on higher education programming. However, even though the action categories may be similar when applied to training or to liberal education, or to cooperative extension service activity, or to voluntary agency programming, some major differences may affect the specific planning steps. As suggested by most of the models discussed here, provider agencies differ in many respects including clientele, history, mission, philosophy, and readiness. These differences will impact on the general categorical action steps in diverse ways. As a result, most effective program planning results from tailoring one or more planning models to specific organizations.

QUESTIONS FOR STUDY AND DISCUSSION

While the models discussed in this chapter provide some useful ideas for program planners in a variety of agencies and organizations, some provocative questions remain to be addressed. Some of these are as follows:

1. Needs analysis is common to most program planning models. How would you conduct a needs analysis for your organization?

2. Client or audience identification is explicit in most of the models. However, the process or procedures by which clients may be identified is not discussed in detail. If you were to identify a target group for an educational or training program in your organization, how would you do it?

3. Development of program ideas is common to most of the planning models. But this activity is not fully described. How would you develop program ideas in your organization, and how would you select from among them?

4. How would you design an investigation to test the application of Boone's model?

5. What structural factors in the environment would you examine to help in program planning decisions in your organization?

6. Burnham identified long-linked technology (a concern with routine, repetitive tasks) with the public school district he studied and the intensive technology (based on use of expert consultants) with university continuing education. Will all public school districts and university continuing education divisions reflect the same kind of technology? If so, why? If not, why not?

7. What are some sources to include in an inventory of techniques that may be applied to program planning?
8. Program planning procedures may vary in effectiveness and efficiency when applied under certain circumstances. Should an attempt be made to identify the variables that affect the outcomes when one technique is used rather than another? If so, how can this be done?
9. Following Schroeder's concepts of agent direction and orientation and client direction and orientation, determine whether an organization with which you are familiar primarily provides educational program service to an internal or external client group. Then determine the degree to which the macro and micro decision points enumerated above reflect agent (institutional) orientation and client (learner) orientation.
10. Select one of the models in this chapter and discuss why you believe it would work better with one agency (of your choosing) than with another agency.

Answers to pretest: 1d, 2c, 3b, 4a, 5c, 6c.

REFERENCES

Apps, J. W. (1979). *Problems in continuing education.* New York: McGraw-Hill.

Boone, E. J. (1985). *Developing programs in adult education.* Englewood Cliffs, NJ: Prentice-Hall.

Brady, H. G., & Long, H. B. (1972). Differences in perceptions of program planning procedures. *Adult Education, 22,* 122–135.

Burnham, B. R. (1988). Program planning as technology in three adult education organizations. *Adult Education Quarterly, 38,* 211–223.

Buskey, J. H., & Sork, T. J. (1982). From chaos to order in program planning: A system for selecting models and ordering research. *Proceedings of the Adult Education Research Conference,* 54–59.

Carpenter, R. G. (1980). The programming process in non-formal adult education, 1959-1979. (Doctoral dissertation, North Carolina State University, 1980). *Dissertation Abstracts International,* 42-02A, 500.

DeVries J. (1978). Agricultural extension and the development of Ujamma villages in Tanzania: Toward a dialogical agricultural extension model. (Doctoral dissertation, University of Wisconsin-Madison, 1978). *Dissertation Abstracts International,* 39-04A, 1991.

Everitt, J. M. (1974). Perceptions of the importance of adult education program planning procedures. (Doctoral dissertation, University of Georgia, 1974). *Dissertation Abstracts International,* 35-10A, 6425.

Long, H. B. (1983a). *Adult and continuing education: Responding to change.* New York: Teachers College Press.

Long, H. B. (1983b). *Adult learning: Research and practice.* New York: Cambridge Books.

Long, H. B. (1996). *Adult learning: Research and practice.* (rev. ed.). Englewood Cliffs, NJ: Prentice-Hall.

Long, H. B., Cervero, R. M., Cheroff, R., Pollack, L. E., Wolkin, P. A., & Wood, F. H. (1992). The range of potential needs assessment methods. *The CLE Journal and Register,* 36, (1), 5–13.

Martin, L. G. (1987).Conceptualizing an environmental scanning process for continuing education organizations. [Summary] *Proceedings of the Midwest Research to Practice Conference in Adult and Continuing Education.* East Lansing, MI, October.

Mazmanian, P. E. (1980). A decision-making approach to needs assessment and objectives setting in continuing medical education program development. *Adult Education,* 31, 3–17.

Morrison, J. L. (1987). Institutionalizing environmental scanning in the ED Quest Process. Paper presented at the American Education Research Association meeting, Washington, DC, April.

Naisbitt, H. J. (1990). *Megatrends 2000.* New York: William Morrow and Co.

Pennington, F., & Green J. (1976). Comparative analysis of program development processes in six professions. *Adult Education,* 7, 13–23.

Perrow, C. (1967). A framework for the comparative analysis of organizations. *American Sociological Review,* 32, 197–208.

Ptaszynski, J. G. (1989). ED QUEST as an organizational development activity: Evaluating the benefits of environmental scanning. (Doctoral dissertation, University of North Carolina at Chapel Hill, 1989). *Dissertation Abstracts International,* 50-11A, 3660.

Schroeder, W. L. (1980). Typology of adult learning systems. In J. M. Peters & Associates. *Building an effective adult education enterprise* (pp. 41–77). San Francisco: Jossey-Bass.

Simerly, R. G. (1990). *Planning and marketing conferences and workshops.* San Francisco: Jossey-Bass.

Simpson, E. G., McGinty, D., & Morrison, J. L. (1987). Environmental scanning at the Georgia Center for Continuing Education: A progress report. *Continuing Higher Education Review,* 3, 1–19.

Sork, T. J., & Buskey, J. H. (1986). A descriptive and evaluative analysis of program planning literature, 1950–1983. *Adult Education Quarterly,* 36, 86–96.

Spencer, B. B. (1980). Non-directive group interviews: A needs assessment approach for older adults. *Proceedings: Lifelong Learning Research Conference.* College Park, NY: April.

Toffler, A. (1990). *Powershifts.* New York: Bantam Books.

United Way Strategic Institute. (1990). Nine forces reshaping America. *Futurist,* XXIV, 4, 9–16.

## 4

The Role
of the Programmer

Travis Shipp

ABSTRACT

With specific organizational contexts, the role of the program planner is both multidimensional and subject to continuous change. Going beyond traditional textbook or job descriptions, this chapter reviews several ways program planning roles are changing in the number, variety and scope of activities. Additionally, time-use studies suggest that program planning roles encompass more than professional skills in techniques and methods of education and training.

ASSESSMENT

1. Identify the different roles you play in your position as an education or training planner. Which roles have been fairly stable over time? Which roles appear to be in flux? Which roles will be yours in the future?
2. In which of the roles do you feel particularly strong?
3. Are there any roles for which you do not feel particularly prepared?
4. How do others in your organization regard your performance in your program planning roles? Are there specific actions you can take to enhance the perspective they have toward your overall performance?

KEY TERMS

Factors of production   The land, labor, capital, and information required to achieve the organizational goals. Land includes all the physical facilities and real estate. Labor includes the skills, competencies, and knowledge required. Capital includes the machinery and tools of production as well as the financial assets. Information includes the data banks, files, and communications systems.

Management   The process of designing and maintaining an environment in which people working together achieve individual, group, and organizational goals.

Organization (also **Community**)   A group of individuals formed to achieve specific, mutually agreed upon economic or social goals.

Organizational development   The long-range effort to improve an organization's problem solving, decision making, and renewal through the management of change in structure, skills, knowledge, and culture so as to meet the organizational goals.

Programmer of adult education and training   The individual to whom is delegated the functional authority to identify, assess and, through planned learning opportunities, help develop skills, competencies, and knowledge which enable people to perform current or future jobs. The process is called adult education, corporate education, training, staff development, human resource development, etc.

Staff (also **Line**)   Those in line positions having *direct* authority over certain assigned processes, practices, and policies relating to the activities of those who produce the goods and services of the organization. Those in staff positions have *functional* or *advisory* responsibilities for the assigned processes, practices, and policies which support the activities of those who produce the goods and services of the organization.

Strategic plan   The process of setting major organizational objectives and developing policies which will guide organizational activities to the achievement of those objectives over the next 5 years or more.

INTRODUCTION

Bob, the chief trainer for XYZ Products & Services, Inc., has just received a memo directing him to present the training budget for the next fiscal year. The memo also mentions that the new responsibility-centered, zero-based budget will be fully implemented at the beginning of the fiscal year and urges him to justify each budget item in dollar terms. None of this worries Bob, because he's been with XYZ for over 20 years, first in manufacturing, then in college recruiting, and now in training. He's seen lots of changes and feels that none of them really makes much difference. He has good presentation skills and thinks well on his feet. Besides, everyone knows the training staff does a good job so he knows he has nothing to worry about.

The next day in the conference room he begins, "Here's a summary of the training programs we did last year. It shows the number of trainees, the content of each program, and the costs of training materials and purchased programs. The last page is a summary of our trainee evaluations. You'll notice all were really pleased and said they would recommend the training to their coworkers." Bob is starting to sweat. This isn't going well; the panel is fidgeting and doesn't look too happy. This is the first time the cost accountant, the operations vice president, and the marketing vice president have attended his budget presentation. He finishes, "We'll need about 10% more than we did last year. Are there any questions?"

"I have some," Mary, the cost accountant says. "What are your direct labor costs, your direct materials costs, and overhead requirements for next year? And how do you justify each one?"

Obviously agitated, Stan, the operations vice president, asks, "Wait a minute. Before we get into that, I want to know how much it will cost to train for the new production line we're planning for year after next."

Mike, the marketing vice president interjects, "Yes, we're adding some new lines and dropping some of the old ones. That'll change everything and if we have to pay for training under this new budget, I want to make sure we get our money's worth. What kind of return can we expect on our training investment?"

Becoming defensive, Bob responds, "Training is always a

good investment and everybody knows we've always done a good job. Just look at these requests for more programs."

Recognizing his subordinate's difficulty, Sam, the vice president for human resource management, declares, "Let's adjourn for now and continue this at our next meeting." He then turns to Bob, and says, "Thanks, Bob, I'll let you know when we'll get together again. In the meantime, you may want to concentrate more on the quantitative aspects and less on the qualitative as you get ready to present again. Pay particular attention to return on investment of the training dollar."

When Bob leaves, the others look at each other and Sam says, "Well, this a tough situation. Bob simply can't grasp the budget process and doesn't have any real understanding of how training relates to overall company goals or management objectives. I've been thinking about moving him to a straight instruction role and hiring a manager of training."

Stan comments, "I agree. Everybody likes Bob and people really enjoy his programs but I've been concerned that we can't get a handle on what we get back for our training dollar."

As Mike begins to toss his papers into his briefcase, he remarks, "We've used a lot of resources for strategic planning, but Bob doesn't seem to be focused on the long-range requirements. I'm worried that we're going to get caught short in our skills inventory with this ad hoc approach to training."

Picking up his folder, Sam walks back with Mike to his office. "OK," he tells Mike, "I've worked up a job description so I'll start looking. I should have someone for you to meet in a few weeks. I'd like to have your input before we hire anybody. After all, you've got to have confidence that the new person can meet your needs. I'll talk to Bob. I have a feeling he'll be relieved."

A month later Sam calls the group together to introduce the finalist for the position of manager of training and strategic planning. When he passes out copies of Elaine's resume Stan whistles and says, "This is more like it. Look, a masters degree in adult education with courses in budgeting, management, and organization theory. I'm impressed."

"I like this, too," Mike adds. "Her experience in skills inventory forecasting looks really good and I particularly like the stuff she's written about organizational change. Let's get her in and see how she does with her presentation."

An hour later the candidate has finished her presentation and left the room. Sam tells those present, "I really like the way she integrated the training plan with the company strategic plan. It's the first time I've thought of training as being the driving force for meeting future conditions. What do you think? I'm all for making her an offer."

"Me, too," Stan enthusiastically responds. "She sold me when she pointed out the relationship of training costs to higher quality and productivity."

"When can she start?" Mary asks. "I'm all for anyone who makes customer satisfaction the number one priority."

What happened here?

What did Bob do or not do that caused dissatisfaction with his report and budgeting process?

What did the other managers want that Elaine provided?

How has the field of adult education programming changed from Bob's approach to Elaine's?

I have been involved in many deliberations about the requirements for the training manager of the future in both the public and the private sectors. This case, although fictional, accurately represents the wishes and needs of organizational management. A discussion of the new role of adult education programming follows.

THE CHANGING ROLE OF THE PROGRAMMER

The programmer of adult education and training is rapidly becoming the chief organizational resource for orchestrating changes in the skills and knowledge of the workforce to meet the long-range needs of the enterprise.

Working within the management structure, the programmer is the individual primarily responsible for ensuring that skills and knowledge are available when needed in the quantities required to meet organizational goals. This process of changing current skill inventories to meet organizational goals through training is also the process of managing change. Change does not occur only because skills change, rather change occurs because employees understand the benefits of the change to themselves. Managing change through training requires the programmer to be a change agent who uses education and training techniques as the instrument of change. The programmer's effectiveness will have a major impact on how human resources are prepared to meet the challenges of the future.

Neither the importance of effectively meeting change nor the difficulties is new. In 1514 Machiavelli (1985) observed:

> It should be borne in mind that there is nothing more difficult to arrange, more doubtful of success, and more dangerous to carry through than initiating changes.... The innovator makes enemies of all those who prospered under the old order and lukewarm support ... from those who would prosper under the new.... Support is lukewarm partly from fear of their adversaries who have the existing laws on their sides and partly because they ... never really trust new things until they have tested them by experience.

Being a change agent is highly challenging and the rewards are often not consistent with the magnitude of that challenge.

Responsibility for developing training programs is not a staff function. It is actually a management responsibility, but, to ensure that it is done competently, the responsibility is assigned to an individual, often in the human resources management department. It is possible to profile the activities considered relevant to the education and training function. The model presented in this chapter is based on a study of the work of professionals in human resource development, adult education, and training. Developing adult education programs is essentially the implementation of change and response to change, both planned and unplanned, in an organization. In the long-range component, the programmer must be able to analyze the strategic plan of the organization to understand the skills, knowledge, and competencies that will be required and then develop plans for training and retraining in order to ensure that the inventory is available when needed.

In any organization, the board and top management provide broad policies relating to the overall enterprise which include human resource matters. The operating level of management (intermediate level) has primary responsibility for implementing that policy. Managers and administrators at this level spend increasing amounts of time on programs and on various reporting requirements and it is often difficult to convince them that human resource matters are integral to the overall objectives of the organization. Not only is effective, efficient training of the workforce crucial to the success of any education or training effort in an organization, but also is educating of all levels of management about potential changes and the necessity for an adequately trained workforce to meet those changes. Many progressive organizations have increased the authority, staff, and budgets of the programmer to deal with human resource development and training activities.

The education/training staff function has expanded in the number, variety, and scope of its activities. It has also changed in the nature of roles performed and which roles are emphasized. Naturally, programming is a direct reflection of the overall emphasis on the one factor of production that is still responsive enough to meet the rapidly demanding changes of the workplace, i.e., the factor of labor.

The primary change in the programming function is the emergence of new activities. At one time a programmer well versed in survey techniques, with a good repertoire of presentation skills and some knowledge of the commercial programs available in the field, could be successful. Today's programmer needs to have a much broader understanding of the overall objectives of the organization, more managerial skills, more budgeting skills, and the ability to interact on a peer level with higher levels of management. A composite advertisement for a programmer might look like this:

> **Manager of Employee Development and Training.** Responsible for identifying, developing, implementing and evaluating policies, practices, and programs which assist in optimizing return on investment in employees; selecting and developing highly effective members of the organization; assisting employees in developing the knowledge, skills, and competencies for increased productivity, higher performance, and improved quality of work life.
>
> Reports to the Vice President for Human Resources; interacts with managers of compensation, benefits and employment, employee services, health and safety, communications and information systems. Staff positions in the unit include employee development, employee planning, executive development, management/supervisor development, and program design and development (including training programs, appraisal programs, and program evaluation).

This new position description is a radical departure from the old concept of the adult education training programmer.

Traditionally, those involved in the education and training of adults have seen themselves set apart from the more mundane aspects of the business world and the hurly-burly of economic life. The value of educating adults was considered to be so well understood that it was neither necessary to make adult education consistent with the overall goals of the sponsoring organization nor to try to evaluate the contribution of the training and education effort in view of the overall organizational objectives. For several years the trend has been to move away from that philosophy and move toward integrating the education and training into the overall economic and organizational scheme and providing sound evaluation (in dollars and cents terms as far as possible).

Much of the impetus for this change comes from economic changes since World War II that are just now becoming apparent worldwide. In a world economy, training a workforce to compete for jobs that require only minimal educational or technical skills is no longer useful. These jobs have been exported to Third World countries and simply will not return to the industrialized nations. The programmer must have some overall knowledge of the economic and social trends facing industrialized countries in the foreseeable future. These trends are readily apparent. Heavy industry and assembly line manufacturing, for example, are jobs that require relatively little education or technical skills and can be performed by citizens of Third World countries for much lower wages than are necessary to provide a decent quality of life in an industrial nation. The programmer, therefore, must understand and be prepared to meet the trends for training employees and other adults for rapid changes in skills, knowledge, and competencies to meet the demands of changing work requirements. The programmer can best do this by instilling the belief that learning is a major part of the everyday work life of employees and management alike. As the industrialized nations move to meet the new demands of a world economy, keeping abreast of economic trends reported in print media is an absolute necessity for the programmer of the future.

THE PROGRAMMER OF THE FUTURE

The adult education and training programmer of the future will be first and foremost a business manager committed to the goals of the business. The programmer understands how (in quantitative terms) training, human resource development, and education contribute to the organizational goals. More and more, the position of programmer includes the following requirements.

Develop and Manage Budgets. The programmer will be requested to establish and justify the education and training budget showing the contribution of expenditures to organization success. The view that "training is good so let's give them some money since business is good this year" is now a part of the past. The programmer must understand and use new budgeting procedures. Relatively few companies continue to operate on the basis of across the board increases in budgets. Rather, budgeting in most organizations, private as well as public, now operates from a zero base in which the programmer will be required in each budget period to justify every expenditure and show how the organization will recover the training or educational investment. One indication that this new budgeting skill among adult education and training programmers is successful is that, rather than cutting the budgets as had been done in the past, in the recent recession many companies actually increased their investment in training and education, thereby taking advantage of the slack time to help employees become more efficient by helping them acquire new skills.

Understand the Organizational Structure. The programmer is required more and more to understand the strategies and elements of growth and development in different organizational cultures. The programmer must be prepared to interact with managers in other parts of the organization or the community in the restructuring and redefining of the organization as it and the community strive to meet new demands, new responsibilities, and new missions. Knowledge of organizational change processes and strategies is critical.

Manage Team Building. The work team concept is being increasingly used in both the public and private sectors to achieve organization goals. The increased pace of life in the industrialized world has encouraged the tendency for personnel to be brought together to do a task rather than trying to find a way to achieve a task within an already existing organizational structure. Therefore, "form follows function." The form of the organization will be dictated by the function to be achieved. When the function has been achieved, the form shifts to perform the next function. This phenomenon is also being manifested in the public and quasi-public sectors of the economy. Even in the more rigid bureaucracies of government, the increased responsibilities of governmental agencies with either reduced or static budgets require that work teams be formed to produce more effectively rather than trying to meet the new requirements by hiring additional people.

Hiring patterns in both the public and private sectors are also changing. The traditional method of hiring has been to hire a person whenever a skill was needed. The emerging trend is to analyze the new demand in the organization, ascertain what skills are necessary, and then build that inventory of skills in the existing workforce. This trend puts greater responsibility on the programmer to understand the overall business concepts as well as the training function.

Manage Strategic Planning. There is a trend to change the title of the adult education and training programmer from manager of training to manager of training and strategic planning. Most organizations, both public and private, are in a situation in which there will be relatively little increase in two of the factors of production: land and capital. The major increases will be in other factors of production: labor and information. The development of labor's skills and the enhancement of the employees' abilities to communicate and use information effectively are the responsibility of the adult education and training programmer. Thus, the success of the organization is largely dependent on the programmer. Effective strategic planning is based on group involvement in setting suitable goals and devising the steps necessary to achieve those goals. The programmer will rely on team building and group facilitation processes to help management in developing plans and making decisions by consensus. The programmer's group process skills and knowledge of workforce training needs and characteristics will make the strategic plan a working document rather than just another paper to be filed and forgotten.

Act as an Internal Organizational Development Consultant. Organizational development is the restructuring of the organization to meet the demands of the future. Restructuring means change. Change implies learning. Again, the adult education programmer has to have an intimate knowledge of all aspects of the organization in order to assist in the restructuring and training.

Adult education and training programmers will need to first review their own qualifications based on the new requirements of the job and design a personal professional development plan to ensure that they have or acquire the needed skills. Writers on ethics in human resource development suggest that for the adult education and training programmer to be unprepared to meet the future demands of the organization is tantamount to unethical behavior. Facing the future with the skills of the past cheats the organization and its members by preparing them for the world of the past rather than the world of the future. Failure to update qualifications jeopardizes security and violates the concept of being a good steward of other people's assets.

HOW IS THE PROGRAMMER'S TIME SPENT?

Research over the past 10 years indicates that most adult education and training programmers spend about *20% of their time in organizational management activities* rather than in training activities.

The programmer is a member of the organization's management team with the responsibility of helping meet organizational objectives. As a manager, the programmer understands the relationship of training to the profits of the organization and can advise other managers on appropriate training solutions to problems. Because managers have a responsibility to ensure that resources under their control are used effectively to meet the goals and objectives of the strategic plan, training resources must be directed toward those ends.

Education and training programmers spend over *15% of their time in needs assessment and research.* There is relatively little reliance on surveys to determine training needs (sending questionnaires to prospective trainees and their supervisors) and more on analysis of organizational problems that may be solved by training. Thus the programmer must be able to communicate well with other managers and understand their perspectives.

A part of this needs assessment and research process involves analysis of articles, books, and other sources of information about training solutions to problems. The programmer must be able to review each report critically to ascertain if the research design is appropriate, if the research is valid, if the conclusions accurately follow the findings, and so on. Good research can save the organization much time and money but using bad research can cost a great deal. Research involves investigation into management, technical aspects, and teaching methods. Research can help the programmer to run the training enterprise as an efficiently operating unit.

Another *10% of the adult education and training programmer's time is spent in dealing with financial and budget matters.* As time goes on this percentage undoubtedly will grow. As money becomes tighter, the need to keep accurate cost records for training and associated job performance changes will require more time in developing and managing systems to accumulate, store, and analyze changes in job performance attributable to training (in financial terms in order to justify expenditures). Organizations, both public and private, are requiring returns on investments in education and training. The programmer will have to establish the relationship between the program costs and its economic benefits.

Approximately *10% of the adult education programmer's time is spent in the area of communications in written and oral presentations* to internal and external audiences outside of the training activity. A large part of the communications required of the programmer involves promoting the value of education and training in general to the organization as well as promoting the benefits of specific programs to potential trainees and their supervisors. The emphasis on this aspect of communication is on understanding the needs, wants and expectations of others. What *benefits* do they expect to receive from the training efforts? How can they use training to solve their problems? This communication requires a high degree of proficiency in listening and negotiation as well as skill in written and oral communication.

Another 10% of the programmer's time is spent in evaluation. This refers to the time spent in planning evaluation, conducting evaluation, communicating evaluation results and modifying training programs in accordance with those results. There is an increasing emphasis on evaluation in economic terms, i.e., money saved, profits increased, productivity increased, turnover decreased.

The remaining 50% of the adult education programmer's time is fairly evenly divided among records management, supervising employees, and two other areas that probably will become even more important as time goes on: planning organizational change and human resource forecasting. There is little in the literature of 20 years ago or in the memories of old-time programmers concerning planning organizational change or human resource forecasting as part of the programming role. Planning organizational change was a function of "legitimate" personnel managers other than training staff. Now, as part of the role of the programmer, it requires understanding planning models, differentiating between single use project plans and standard operating plans, and coordinating short-range and long-range plans among different parts of the organization. In the past 20 years, human resource forecasting and functions have increased to a point where they consume about 15% of the programmer's time. Here, the programmer must anticipate the skills as well as the number of personnel needed to meet each stage of the long-range plan. The programmer must know the training requirements for new people and existing personnel, and must know how to deal with attrition in meeting the skill requirements of the long-range plan. Developing a strategy for moving from the existing workforce skills inventory to the needed inventory as indicated by the long-range plan is an increasingly important technical aspect of the job as new computer-assisted techniques for forecasting are developed.

The adult education training programmer will spend relatively less time as a direct provider or standup instructor and more time as a manager or administrator of the adult education or training program for the business. However, increased emphasis on the training programmer as a business manager has not diminished the importance of professional knowledge and skill in the techniques and methods of instruction. Rather, it has placed even more responsibility on ensuring that every training activity is focused on the goals and objectives of the organization and is delivered in the most effective and efficient manner possible. This emphasis on achievement of quantitative goals does not imply that adult education or training geared to morale and personal development will become less important. If anything, it will be seen as materially contributing to a motivated, stable workforce and informed citizenry and a major factor in improving organizational and national productivity. What will disappear is reliance on the "grab and groom" canned programs that only marginally reflect the needs of the employee, the work team, or the organization. Such packaged programs will be replaced by education and training efforts tailored to specific needs in accordance with the mission and philosophy of the organization. The emphasis in training has shifted from presentation skills to content expertise.

SUMMARY

In summary, being a professional skilled in the techniques and methods of education and training is not enough anymore. The successful adult education and training programmer of today and tomorrow must be able to help individuals go beyond the definition of their work and be able to help the organization use and reward that contribution. The programmer of the future will understand that societal, economic, and organizational changes are not only training opportunities but training necessities. As an organization manager as well as a training professional, the programmer will assist other managers in using training to help the organization meet the challenges of an ever-changing future. The future programmer of adult education and training is: first, an employee of the organization committed to customer satisfaction; second, a manager committed to helping group of individuals achieve organizational goals; and third, a training professional committed to helping identify and produce the skills, competencies, and knowledge needed for attaining future objectives.

QUESTIONS FOR STUDY AND DISCUSSION

1. Adult educators have long maintained that trying to use a good manager, salesperson, engineer, etc., as a trainer without giving them the benefit of retraining in adult education principles and methods is ineffective. If this is so, it follows that an adult educator without training in the management of the organization is similarly disadvantaged. What do you suggest as a plan to ensure that the adult education programmer be a contributor to the organizational goals?
2. How can your plan best be followed?
3. How would you evaluate the effectiveness of your plan?
4. What course of action would you suggest for adult educators already in the field who are beginning to find themselves in Bob's situation?
5. How would you present a proposal to management to retrain the training staff?
6. How would you present a proposal to the training staff to help them understand the need for their own retraining in management skills?

REFERENCES FOR FURTHER STUDY

American Society for Training and Development. (1983). *Models for excellence.* Washington, DC: ASTD.

Byers, K. T. (1974). *Employee training and development in the public sector.* Chicago: International Personnel Management Association.

Clement, R. W., Pinto, P. R., & Walker, J. W. (1978, December). Unethical and improper behavior by training and development professionals. *Training and Development Journal,* 10–12.

Cosner-Lotto, J. (1988). *Successful training strategies.* San Francisco: Jossey-Bass.

Drucker, P. F. (1992). *Managing the non-profit organization.* San Francisco: Harper.

Houle, C. O. (1972). *The design of education.* San Francisco: Jossey-Bass.

Hussey, D. E. (1988). *Management training and corporate strategy.* London: Pergamon Press.

Koonty, H., & Weinhoich, H. (1988). *Management.* New York: McGraw-Hill.

Laird, D. (1985). What do training and development officers do? In *Approaches to training and development.* Reading, MA: Addison Wesley, 17–32.

Machiavelli, N. (1985). The prince. (A new translation, with an introduction by H. C. Mansfield). Chicago: University of Chicago Press.

Mitchell, G. (1989). *The trainer's handbook.* Washington, DC: American Management Association.

Nadler, L. (1985). *Handbook of human resource development.* New York: John Wiley.

Powell, G. N., & Posner, B. Y. (1980, September). Managing change: Attitudes, problems and strategies. *Group and Organizational Studies,* 310–323.

Shipp, T. (1985). The HRO professional: A macromotion study of the practice, *Proceedings of the Lifelong Learning Conference.* College Park, MD: University of Maryland.

Taylor, B., & Lappett, G. (Eds.) (1983). *Management development and training handbook.* New York: McGraw-Hill.

5

Philosophical and Ethical Considerations

Ralph G. Brockett and Roger Hiemstra

ABSTRACT

Program planning is not a "neutral" activity. In fact, it can be argued that the development of adult education programs involves the implementation of values. Therefore, decisions about the content and process of adult education programming are clearly rooted in underlying philosophical assumptions. Similarly, ethics serves as one of the most practical applications of philosophy. The purpose of this chapter is twofold. First, the importance of philosophy in the program planning process will be explored. Second, the importance of ethics in program planning will be addressed by identifying some of the major dilemmas facing program planners and by describing a process for promoting ethical practice.

ASSESSMENT

1. Several basic philosophical frameworks (e.g., humanism, idealism, realism, progressivism) are available to guide our thinking. Can you identify the framework or frameworks that guide your practice?

2. What features of your unique cultural heritage impact on your personal values in some way?

3. How does what you think about values or ethics guide the educational content you build into your programs?

4. How have your professional experiences impacted on your philosophical view of ethical practice?

5. It is important to be consistent in your values and the way they affect your professional practice. What types of educational methods do you favor that reflects such consistency?

6. Much current adult education literature talks about the dignity and worth of each learner. What can you say about your respect for each program participant's desire for autonomy and independence?

7. Are your individual values, philosophical views, and ethical behavior in line with those of your employer or employing agency? If they are not, what are the implications for program planning?

INTRODUCTION

Program planning does not take place in a vacuum. It is driven by values: values of the organization, values of the adult education practitioner, values of the clientele, and values of society. In fact, it can be argued that the purpose of any adult education activity is either to promote change or to maintain the status quo. This simple observation clearly illustrates that virtually any decision relative to adult education program planning will be rooted in values.

The purpose of this chapter is to examine the centrality of values in the planning process. This will be accomplished in two ways. First, the importance of philosophy as an element of the program planning process will be explored. This will include a discussion about how program planners can examine and articulate their own philosophies of practice. Second, the chapter will focus on ethical issues that can arise in the planning process. Ethics is one of the most important, yet most frequently overlooked, applications of philosophy. By introducing a process that can be used in ethical decision making, we hope to encourage readers to consider the importance of ethics in decisions surrounding the development of programs for adult learners.

Philosophy has held an important place throughout the history of the adult education movement. From classic works such as *The Meaning of Adult Education* (Lindeman, 1926) and *The Meaning of a Liberal Education* (Martin, 1926) through more contemporary writings such as Elias and Merriam's (1995) *Philosophical Founda-*

tions of Adult Education and Apps's (1985) *Improving Practice in Continuing Education,* there is ample evidence that many adult educators have struggled with questions of values and philosophy relative to effective practice. Indeed, a central premise of this chapter is that program planning, at its most basic level, is a process involving the implementation of values.

To illustrate this point, consider two very different approaches to adult literacy. One approach stresses the development of clearly identifiable basic competencies that will allow a person to function effectively in contemporary society. A different approach stresses that literacy can be a tool for helping those who have traditionally been disenfranchised to have a clear voice in decisions that affect their lives. While both approaches stress the importance of developing literacy skills, the ends of the two approaches are very different; thus, the process by which these programs are implemented are built on very different sets of assumptions. Philosophy serves as a tool for effective practice. In the view of de Chambeau (1977), philosophy must be a priority for educators of adults because "the question of *why* must precede questions of *what* or *how*" in the development of educational programs (p. 308). This means that before making decisions about the content and format of a workshop or training program, it makes sense to question why the activity is being planned, whose needs are being served, and what consequences (positive and negative) may result from the activity. By asking such questions at the outset of the planning process, the questions serve as a framework against which subsequent decisions can be measured.

According to Apps (1985), there are several benefits of philosophical analysis to the practitioner:

> It can help us become critically aware of what we do as practitioners; show us alternative approaches to program planning, teaching, budgeting, and so on; help us become aware of how values, ethics, and esthetics can be applied to continuing education practice; illustrate to us the importance of our personal histories and how they influence what we do as educators; and free us from dependence on someone else's doctrine. (p. 16)

Similarly, the role of philosophy in program planning is further described in the following observation from Boyle (1981):

> Our beliefs, values, and attributes provide the basis for many of our actions in developing continuing education programs. Thus, con-

tinuing education programmers need to identify and utilize a set of beliefs about such things as education, continuing education, continuing education agencies, the learner, the programmer, and the program development process.... Efforts to construct a philosophy will help us to better understand the gaps between the reality of problems, clientele and programs and the way we want things to be. A well developed program in continuing education, then, is one in which there is consistency between the beliefs of those involved and the actual program. (pp. 18–19)

Developing such consistency does not automatically happen. It usually requires experience and a clear understanding of one's own philosophy. Thus, there are at least four reasons why a program planner should develop a personal statement of philosophy:

1. A philosophy promotes an understanding of human relationships.
2. A philosophy sensitizes ... [one] to the various needs associated with positive human interactions.
3. A philosophy provides a framework for distinguishing, separating, and understanding personal values.
4. A philosophy promotes flexibility and consistency in working with adult learners. (Hiemstra, 1988, p. 179)

We believe it is important to talk openly with colleagues about personal values, philosophical views, and ethical standards. These can be topics for consideration during staff meetings, for example, to elicit recognition of the importance of developing programs that match the values of both the organization and individual program planners. One may even want to include discussion of values or ethical expectations during the hiring of new employees, in orientation training, and in organizational policy manuals. In other words, we recommend that such concerns about values and ethical standards be raised early in any program planning process.

VALUES ARE AT THE HEART OF EFFECTIVE PROGRAM PLANNING

It has been our observation that a person's values impact on professional practice in various ways. Unfortunately, some people either have difficulty expressing their values and philosophical underpinnings or have never attempted to do so. Others may be at odds with their employing organization or influential decision-makers within the organization. As Knox (1991) notes, "Value judgements and assumptions tend to be implicit and unexamined unless one deliberately and critically reflects on the desirability of goals" (p. 231). One of our intents in writing this chapter is to encourage others to develop a good self-understanding of personal values and reflect critically on their professional decision-making activities.

Other authors also believe values lie at the heart of effective program planning. For example, Schroeder (1980) calls values, those of the sponsoring agency and of the client, one of the three most important input variables in any adult program development process: "Thus values are of primary significance, for they affect the other two macro variables, goals and resource capabilities and dispositions" (p. 59). Cunningham (1982) describes some of her concerns related to the development of programs in isolation from stated or recognized values: "What is worrisome is that continuing educators develop and operate programs without a clearly visualized set of values in which the adult learner and societal well-being are central concerns" (p. 85).

Lawson (1991) believes that people's philosophical perspectives may be implicit in their educational activities, "but are not recognized as such ..." (p. 282). Tyler (1974) recognized the value of understanding a personal philosophy in developing educational programs. Caffarella (1988) believes a system of personal beliefs guides planning activities. Wislock and Flannery (1991) believe that a working philosophy is important to informing subsequent practice.

Some program planning models contain components or steps that overtly address issues of values, beliefs, and ethics. For example, Caffarella (1988) believes that integrating basic principles and practices related to adult learning into a basic philosophy of planning is crucial. She identifies a "philosophy of program development for adults" as part of her program planning model's first component (p. 32). Sork and Caffarella (1989) believe that an organization's philosophical orientation usually affects how planning proceeds right from the first step. Within what is labeled "analyzing the planning context," they believe such concerns as organizational missions and any philosophical constraints must be addressed.

Many adult educators today approach practice from a value

system rooted in humanist beliefs. They understand the value of an adult learner's previous experience and believe such learners often can undertake considerable responsibility for aspects of planning or implementation. However, this has not always been the case. Much of adult education research and what we know about the planning process in the 1960s and 70s was based on positivist paradigms and quantitative or scientific research methods (Merriam, 1991). Scholars such as Skinner (1954) and Tyler (1974) stressed behavior modification or fairly structured components as part of any planning process. Only during the past couple of decades have interpretive paradigms evolved where humanism and phenomenology served as foundations for our thinking and development work (Marsick, 1988).

Some planners accept many humanistic beliefs as foundational to their own values and ways of working with others. However, they can work in an organization where primarily behavioristic approaches to working with people are required. Thus, the planning process can create conflicting situations that are not easily resolved.

There are several shared elements between humanist and behaviorist orientations:

1. Learning tends to focus on practical problem solving.
2. Learners enter an educational setting with a wide range of skills, abilities, and attitudes, and these need to be considered in the instructional planning process.
3. Any learning environment should allow each learner to proceed at a pace best suited to individual abilities.
4. It is important to help learners continuously assess their progress and make feedback a part of the ongoing planning process.
5. A learner's previous experience is an invaluable resource for future learning and thus should be considered in the planning process.

Therefore, we urge individual program planners to address any conflicts by examining the values of both humanist and behaviorist views and, in essence, extracting the best of both in building a planning approach. As an example, we suggest that educators examine written policies and mission statements pertaining to work with adult learners. Are these written statements consistent with actual practice and with the values held by members of the organization? As we will address later in this chapter, inconsistencies between organizational mission and personal philosophy often give rise to ethical dilemmas.

We recommend that each professional identify a personal philosophy of adult education (Hiemstra, 1988). By better understanding personal values and philosophical views, we believe program planners will be better prepared to reconcile institutional beliefs or expectations that differ from their own. In addition, a recognition of personal values and beliefs combined with a personal statement of philosophy often results in a foundation for subsequent professional activities and ethical decision making.

A tool we have found particularly useful in providing insight into personal philosophy is the Philosophy of Adult Education Inventory (PAEI) (Zinn, 1990). The PAEI contains 75 statements designed to assess the degree to which one ascribes to five of the philosophical positions discussed by Elias and Merriam (1995) (i.e., liberalism, progressivism, behaviorism, humanism, and radicalism). For the past several years, we have regularly used this instrument in some of our graduate-level courses and off-campus workshops in conjunction with asking participants to write a statement of personal philosophy. For many learners, the PAEI can help to confirm individual views, provide new insights, and raise possible contradictions between ascribed values and actual practice.

The process that we typically use to help educators develop their personal philosophy statements includes the following steps:

1. We make a general presentation that describes various philosophical systems, using such sources as Elias and Merriam (1995) and Zinn (1990).
2. We involve participants in understanding some of the ways such systems impact or drive educational aims, methods, and content. For instance, a behaviorist's reliance on prior conditioning might result in implementing multiple practice sessions while a humanist's expectations about autonomous action might mean emphasizing self-directed study on a topic.
3. We administer the PAEI, a self-scoring instrument, and then facilitate some general discussion about findings, reactions, and insights into personal values and beliefs.

4. Next, we ask participants to begin developing a written statement of personal philosophy. We suggest some questions on
philosophical beliefs, philosophical models, and educational
methods they might use to guide their initial work on a statement. In order to guide this process, we typically provide a
worksheet with space for participants to address the following
areas (Hiemstra, 1988, p. 187):
   • Philosophical beliefs
     —Philosophical system
     —Meaning
     —What is reality?
     —Nature of being human
   • Professional practice
     —Educational aims
     —Educational methods
     —Educational content
5. We facilitate discussion in both small groups and among the
total group for those who wish to share aspects of their statement and who desire feedback from colleagues in the developmental process.
6. Finally, we provide written feedback on the statement participants submit to us. Generally, this includes observations on the
completeness of the statement, identification of possible inconsistencies, and suggestions for future consideration.

Typically, we suggest that educators who develop a statement
of personal philosophy use it as a guide or framework for subsequent practice as adult education professionals. Some will benefit
by using it as a basis for redesigning programs they plan or courses
they teach. Others will be able to use it to determine sources of
conflict they have had in the past with individuals or policies within
the organization. We also encourage educators to periodically
reexamine their statement to see if changes are appropriate based
on their own growth and development.

To summarize, the value of philosophy in program planning
resides in two main ideas: that planning is the implementation of
values and that the need to ask "why" must precede asking "what"
or "how." There are many benefits to be derived from analyzing
one's values. Taking the time to develop a personal philosophy

statement and to reflect upon it periodically (and make revisions when appropriate) is well worth the initial investment.

ETHICS IN PROGRAM PLANNING

One of the most practical applications of philosophy to program planning can be found in an examination of ethical principles relative to planning. Program planners regularly make decisions that impact the lives of those served by such programs. Thus, planners are often in a position where they wield a great deal of power. And while the decisions that adult education program planners make rarely have the "life and death" circumstances faced by, say, health professionals, these decisions nonetheless do have an impact on the lives of others. For example, planners are often called upon to make decisions about whose needs are to be served, who will have access to information about programs and to the programs themselves, how programs will be delivered, and how information about program outcomes will be gathered and utilized.

While we work from the assumption that most adult educators are committed to acting in an ethical manner, we also recognize that decisions such as those listed above provide an opportunity for misuse of power, whether such misuse is intentional or not. Ethical dilemmas arise when one is faced with a conflict of values or, as stated by Purtilo and Cassel (1981), "when acting on one moral 'conviction' … means breaking another" (p. 5). Or, as Mirvits and Seashore have stated, ethical dilemmas often arise "not because roles are unclear but because they are clearly in conflict" (1979, p. 771). Thus, a program planner who has been approached about developing a workshop on a topic that has the potential of bringing negative publicity to the institution may be faced with a dilemma in that serving the stated needs of potential learners could have negative consequences for one's employer. Similarly, role conflict is often a reality for the individual, such as a trainer in a business setting, charged with doing an evaluation of the effectiveness of an "in-house" training program.

Sork (1988) has identified nine ethical issues relevant to program planning and addresses several key questions relative to each issue. The issues are as follows:

1. Responding to "felt" or "expressed" needs of adult learners.
2. Basing a program on a need not acknowledged by the learner.
3. Basing the planning process on the learning "deficiencies" of adult learners.
4. Claiming that specific capabilities will be developed by learners who participate in a program.
5. Designing programs in which participation is compulsory.
6. Maintaining confidentiality of information.
7. Selecting instructional and other resources.
8. Deciding who will be involved in the planning process.
9. Determining fees for programs. (pp. 39–46)

Sork's intent in developing this list was to stimulate discussion about relevant ethical issues and questions. While a thorough discussion of all nine issues is beyond the scope of this chapter, an illustration of one issue might be helpful. Consider, for a moment, the issue of who should be involved in the planning process. Historically, a hallmark of "good" adult education practice has been the idea that participants play a role in planning and implementing adult education programs (e.g., Lindeman, 1926; Knowles, 1980). However, findings have been mixed in several studies on the impact of involvement on achievement and satisfaction. Ewert (1982) has suggested four potential problems with involving learners in the planning process, each of which has implications for ethical practice:

> (1) adult participation in the teaching and learning process may result in equating an audience's verbalization of a perceived need with an external promise for a programmatic solution to that need; (2) adult participation in program planning may lead to conflict within the existing political system; (3) adult participation in program planning violates the traditional roles of teacher and learner and may cause frustration until the new process in internalized; and (4) adult participation in program planning may threaten the established order (particularly where it reduces the level of dependence upon that order) and cause administrative resistance to effective implementation of that program. (p. 31)

The point to be stressed here is that Ewert is not suggesting that involving learners in planning is inherently unethical; rather, he makes the point that it is important to avoid uncritical acceptance of ideas that are often taken for granted as universally appropriate principles of practice.

A FRAMEWORK FOR ETHICAL PRACTICE

How might a program planner resolve ethical dilemmas that can arise in practice? Several years ago, the first author developed a model designed to help guide adult educators through the process of ethical decision making (Brockett, 1988). Essentially, this model suggests that one way to arrive at ethical decisions is to engage in a three-step process that begins with an examination of one's personal values, moves to a consideration of one's "multiple responsibilities" as an adult educator, and finally leads to acting in accordance with one's values.

In reexamining this model in the years since its original publication, it seems that a clearer way to look at the process is to point out that the process of ethical decision making is made up of at least three key elements—values, obligations, and consequences—and that the process is not linear, but rather, a mix of these elements. Each of these elements can be understood by asking key questions. These are addressed below.

Values

As we have stated, values are at the heart of effective program planning. So, too, are values at the heart of ethical practice. A vital element of ethical practice is the need to understand one's basic beliefs and the extent to which one is committed to them. Thus, this element of ethical decision making centers on two key questions:

1. What do I believe?
2. How committed am I to my beliefs?

The first question is actually comprised of several subquestions. First, it is important to ask, "What do I believe about human nature?" The adult educator who believes that human nature is basically good will have a much different outlook on practice from one who holds that human nature is basically evil, or is entirely shaped by one's environment. Second is the question of "What do I believe about adult education and adult learners?" The program planner in an industrial training setting who, for instance, views adult learners as lazy or manipulative will likely take a very different approach to planning than a person who typically views adult learners as having virtually unlimited potential for growth. A third subquestion involves asking, "What do I believe about moral obligation?" While an extensive discussion of ethical theories is beyond the scope of this chapter, it is important to note that one set of ethical theories defines right and wrong behavior in terms of fulfilling duty (deontological), while another view stresses that what is ethical is defined by the consequences of one's actions (teleological) (Thiroux, 1986). Here, the intent is to create a result that produces the greatest good and the least harm.

A second key question relative to values involves the degree to which an individual is committed to personal beliefs. Values can be internalized at different levels. As an example, consider the context of literacy education. An educator who is deeply committed to the belief that the sole purpose of literacy programs should be to promote empowerment and social change is probably not likely to be fulfilled or successful working in a literacy program that uses a competency-based approach to teaching functional life skills. A second literacy educator, on the other hand, who believes that social change should be one of several purposes served by a literacy education program, may be able to find ways to work effectively in a setting where a degree of personal dissonance is often experienced. As another illustration of how values can be internalized in different ways, one professor in the continuing education division of the local university might provide service to the community by serving on advisory councils, working with a local professional association, and volunteering in a senior center. Another colleague, however, thinks of service as involving consultancies with the training divisions of various organizations. Each professor values an outreach opportunity, but they have placed different values on the nature of such involvement. The first professor might even resent the second professor's requirement that remuneration always be involved in a service effort, while the second person may think the colleague to be naive in terms of valuing the worth of any service provided. As has been noted elsewhere, "The more deeply committed one is to a particular point of view, the greater the likelihood of polarization when the issue at hand is discussed" (Brockett, 1988, p. 11).

It is in this realm of personal values where the importance of having a personal philosophy of adult education becomes important. The suggestions offered earlier in this chapter and elsewhere (e.g., Hiemstra, 1988; Apps, 1985) can be useful in addressing these questions of personal values. Another tool that can be useful is a three-question "ethics check" offered by Blanchard and Peale (1988). In assessing whether an act may be unethical, it is suggested that one ask the following questions:

1. Is it legal?
2. Is it balanced?
3. How will it make me feel about myself?

The first question addresses possible violations of civil law or organizational policy. Here, it should be pointed out that, in our view, law is actually a subset of ethics. There may be laws, such as Jim Crow laws that until fairly recently mandated racial separation in many states, which are clearly unethical. There are times, then, when we believe that ethics must supersede law. Yet, the question, "Is it legal?" remains a viable ethics check for most situations in daily practice. The second question is essentially the question of justice. It emphasizes the belief that what is ethical is what is "fair" and, thus, will produce "win-win" situations. Finally, the third question is quite powerful, indeed, for it reflects the popular phrase of "being able to look at oneself in the mirror each morning." It is important to be able to be proud of the decisions one makes, and the third question addresses this concern directly.

Obligations

A second dimension of ethical decision making centers on the notion of obligations. As educators, our obligations extend in many directions. Two key questions that address the questions of obligations are:

1. To whom am I responsible?
2. To what extent is the dilemma a result of conflicting obligations?

In considering the first question, it is not difficult to come up with a list of "stakeholders" to whom one's obligations extend in a given situation. Typically, an educator will have obligations to oneself, the learners, the institution, the community, society in general, and the profession.

In most instances, the first question is fairly easy to answer. It is the second question that directly targets issues of ethical practice. As was stated previously, most ethical dilemmas arise when there is conflict in one's roles (i.e., when fulfilling one role can lead to conflict in another role). What happens, for instance, when a group of individuals approach an educator or institution with a request to offer a workshop on a topic that may be highly controversial, with the potential for negative publicity for the institution? If the institution has a clear mission statement, and the proposed topic clearly lies outside of that mission, it would seem appropriate to deny the request (and, possibly, assist the group in finding a provider whose mission is more in line with the request). But what if the mission of the institution is broadly defined, such as that of a land grant university, which purports to be dedicated to ideals of academic freedom and public service? Here, there is likely to be ample room for interpretation and, thus, the possibility for an ethical dilemma exists.

An illustration of this issue can be found in one of the major controversies currently facing cooperative extension programs in many states. Some extension professionals subscribe to the traditional view that the role of the extension professional is to disseminate research-based knowledge to the public. Others, however, believe that extension must take more of an "advocacy" role by taking public positions on certain social issues. This may not be an easy dilemma for many to resolve, as both positions emphasize serving the learners' needs by providing relevant information and both views seem to stress what is believed to produce the "greatest good." Perhaps the question is most easily resolved by either (1) finding a way to serve the needs of both the client and the institution or (2) determining which obligation is most central to one's values. Of course, most situations are not "either/or" dilemmas, and the optimal response may be some combination of possibilities.

Consequences

A third dimension of ethical practice focuses upon the consequences of the actions that one may take in an ethical dilemma. Here, three key questions are:

1. What are my options?
2. What are possible consequences of my options?
3. Which option is most consistent with my values?

In most ethical dilemmas, the program planner is going to have a range of options from which to choose. At the same time, each option presents a different set of possible consequences. While it is clearly not always possible to predict the outcome of one's decisions beforehand, it behooves the program planner to try and think through possible outcomes in order to make as informed a choice as possible. Ethical decision making means that educators have choices in how they will respond to a given dilemma, but it also stresses that educators must be responsible for their decisions.

In order to illustrate the issue of choice and consequences, take the case of a public affairs specialist for a state extension service who has been approached by a group of citizens interested in organizing to oppose dumping of waste in the local river by a major industry in the community. The specialist clearly has several choices, among which are the following:

1. Inform the group that such involvement is outside of the scope of the specialist's position;
2. Help the group identify other community agencies that can assist them with their efforts;
3. Agree to present a workshop providing information about the disposal of hazardous waste;
4. Work with the group to assist them in developing and implementing a plan of action.

Each of these choices involves an increasing degree of involvement by the specialist. In the first option, the specialist chooses not to get involved in the situation. The second option allows the specialist to acknowledge the clients' need, but to do so without getting directly involved. The third option focuses on providing fact-based information that the clients can use in taking action. Finally, the fourth option involves direct intervention on the part of the specialist.

The process that has been discussed throughout this section is not designed to provide prescriptive solutions to specific ethical dilemmas. Rather, it is intended to raise questions and identify principles that bring ethics to the forefront of one's practice. As such, the process is a way for planners to engage in reflective practice relative to ethics.

CREATING AN ETHICAL ENVIRONMENT

What can educators do to promote ethical practice? Because ethics is so often an emotional, controversial, or even taboo topic, it is sometimes difficult for educators to confront this question. Our view of ethics is based on the assumption that the vast majority of adult education program planners are basically "good" people who truly want to "do the right thing." The difficulty, as was mentioned earlier, comes in the form of competing obligations, where fulfilling one responsibility means not fulfilling another. So, what can be done to create an environment where ethical decision making, such as the process described above, is valued and actively promoted?

We believe that three strategies can be particularly useful in working toward the creation of an ethical environment. First, it is important to begin by looking at ourselves. As is stated elsewhere, "Being ethical is a personal choice. But until we can understand and articulate our own values, it is difficult to exercise this choice in an informed way" (Brockett, 1990, p. 10). One of the best ways to promote ethical practice in one's own work is to *model* ethical practice. Developing a personal philosophy statement and using instruments such as the Philosophy of Adult Education Inventory, which were discussed earlier, can help to facilitate this process. Other tools can include the development of critical thinking skills (Brookfield, 1987) and the use of reflective practice techniques (e.g., Peters, 1991), which encourage individuals to engage in a continuous process of reflecting and analyzing their own practice.

Second, we believe that it is necessary to "demystify" and "destigmatize" ethics. As long as ethics is considered a controversial or taboo topic, it will be difficult to get practitioners to talk openly about ethical issues, particularly within their own organizations. One way to address this problem is to strive toward the development of trust and caring within the organization, where staff members can feel free to openly share ethical questions or concerns in a nonthreatening or nonaccusatory way. If educators can set aside the stigma of being labeled "unethical," it may be possible to begin a true dialogue that can lead to constructive practice and ethical decision making rather than blame placing and finger pointing.

One developing trend in the corporate world is "ethics training" (e.g., Harrington, 1991). Some organizations are hiring ethics "specialists" to address ethical issues in practice. While this can be helpful in bringing ethics to the forefront of the organization, few adult education programs can afford such resources. The point is that whether such activities are formally instituted or take place in less formal, open discussions, it is possible to create an ethical environment if staff members are willing to engage openly in dialogue about ethical concerns.

Third, it may be helpful to gain insights from ethical issues in other fields. While adult education program planners face ethical dilemmas that, in substance, differ from those faced by other professionals, a general understanding of professional ethics can help to uncover some general issues and themes that are central to ethical practice.

CONCLUSION

Program planning is the implementation of values. Basic decisions about who should be served by programs and the way in which clients are served reflect a set of philosophical assumptions. All models of program development are rooted in one or more philosophical orientations. For this reason, it is important for educators and trainers of adults to have an awareness of their personal philosophy and an ability to clearly articulate this philosophy.

A practical application of philosophy can be seen in the link between ethics and practice. Ethics is often an emotionally charged topic and, as such, is often avoided. However, choosing not to address ethical issues can be very costly in terms of personal and institutional reputation, program effectiveness, and long-term success. By asking key questions about ethical practice and by striving to create an environment where ethics can be discussed in an open and nonthreatening manner, it is possible to successfully resolve many of the ethical dilemmas that arise in the planning of programs for adult learners.

QUESTIONS FOR STUDY AND DISCUSSION

1. Develop a statement of your personal philosophy of adult education. In this statement, be sure to describe your basic assumptions about human nature, adult learners, and ethics. Which philosophical approaches most directly guide your practice?
2. Reflect on a time when you were faced with an ethical dilemma in planning a program for adults. Write down a brief description of the incident. Use the questions in the section on the

ethical decision-making process to "work through" the dilemma. How similar is your response to the way in which you actually resolved the dilemma?

3. Describe examples of the nine ethical issues described by Sork. What ethical "principles" are reflected in each of these issues?
4. Should there be a code of ethics for adult education program planners? What are the arguments for and against such a code? Who would develop and enforce an ethical code?
5. To date, there has been very little research on ethics in adult education. What do you believe might be some appropriate questions for research in this area? How would you design such a study?

REFERENCES

Apps, J. W. (1985). *Improving practice in continuing education.* San Francisco: Jossey-Bass.

Blanchard, K., & Peale, N. V. (1988). *The power of ethical management.* New York: Ballantine Books.

Boyle, P. G. (1981). *Planning better programs.* New York: McGraw-Hill.

Brockett, R. G. (1988). Ethics and the adult educator. In R. G. Brockett (Ed.), *Ethical issues in adult education* (pp. 1–16). New York: Teachers College Press.

Brockett, R. G. (1990). Adult education: Are we doing it ethically? *MPAEA Journal of Adult Education, 19*(1), 5–12.

Brookfield, S. D. (1987). *Developing critical thinkers.* San Francisco: Jossey-Bass.

Caffarella, R. S. (1988). *Program development and evaluation resource book for trainers.* New York: John Wiley.

Cunningham, P. M. (1982). Contradictions in the practice of nontraditional continuing education. In S. B. Merriam (Ed.), *Linking philosophy and practice (New Directions for Continuing Education,* No. 15, pp. 73–86). San Francisco: Jossey-Bass.

de Chambeau, F. A. (1977). How? what? or why? Philosophy as a priority for educators of adults. *Adult Leadership, 25* (June), 308.

Elias, J. L., & Merriam, S. (1995). *Philosophical foundations of adult education* (2nd ed.). Malabar, FL: Krieger.

Ewert, D. M. (1982). Involving learners in the planning process. In S. B. Merriam (Ed.), *Linking philosophy and practice (New Directions for Continuing Education,* No. 15, pp. 29–38). San Francisco: Jossey-Bass.

Harrington, S. J. (1991). Ethics training: What corporate America is teaching about ethics. In R. B. I. Frantzreb (Ed.), *Training and development yearbook 1992/1993* (pp. 7.144–7.150). Englewood Cliffs, NJ: Prentice Hall.

Hiemstra, R. (1988). Translating personal values and philosophy into practical action. In R. G. Brockett (Ed.), *Ethical issues in adult education* (pp. 178–194). New York: Teachers College Press.

Knowles, M. S. (1980). *The modern practice of adult education* (Revised and updated). New York: Cambridge.

Knox, A. B. (1991). Educational leadership and program administration. In J. M. Peters, P. Jarvis, & Associates, *Adult education: Evolution and achievements in a developing study* (pp. 217–258). San Francisco: Jossey-Bass.

Lawson, K. H. (1991). Philosophical foundations. In J. M. Peters, P. Jarvis, & Associates, *Adult education: Evolution and achievements in a developing field of study* (pp. 282–300). San Francisco: Jossey-Bass.

Lindeman, E. C. (1926). *The meaning of adult education.* New York: New Republic. Reprinted in 1988. Norman, OK: Oklahoma Research Center for Continuing Professional and Higher Education.

Marsick, V. J. (1988). Learning in the workplace: The case for reflectivity and critical reflectivity. *Adult Education Quarterly, 38,* 187–198.

Martin, E. D. (1926). *The meaning of a liberal education.* New York: Norton.

Merriam, S. B. (1991). How research produces knowledge. In J. M. Peters, P. Jarvis, & Associates, *Adult education: Evolution and achievements in a developing field of study* (pp. 42–65). San Francisco: Jossey-Bass.

Mirvits, P. H., & Seashore, S. E. (1979). Being ethical in organizational research. *American Psychologist, 34*(9), 766–780.

Peters, J. M. (1991). Strategies for reflective practice. In R. G. Brockett (Ed.), *Professional development for educators of adults* (*New Directions for Adult and Continuing Education,* No. 51, pp. 89–96). San Francisco: Jossey-Bass.

Purtilo, R. B., & Cassel, C. K. (1981). *Ethical dimensions in the health professions.* Philadelphia: Saunders.

Rosenblum, S. H. (1985). The adult's role in educational planning. In S. H. Rosenblum (Ed.), *Involving adults in the educational process* (*New Directions for Continuing Education,* No. 26, pp. 13–25). San Francisco: Jossey-Bass.

Schroeder, W. L. (1980). Typology of adult learning systems. In J. M. Peters and Associates, *Building an effective adult education enterprise* (pp. 44–77). San Francisco: Jossey-Bass.

Skinner, B. F. (1954). The science of learning and the art of teaching. *Harvard Educational Review, 24*(2), 86–97.

Sork, T. J. (1988). Ethical issues in program planning. In R. G. Brockett (Ed.), *Ethical issues in adult education* (pp. 34–50). New York: Teachers College Press.

Sork, T. J., & Caffarella, R. S. (1989). Planning programs for adults. In S. B. Merriam & P. M. Cunningham (Eds.), *Handbook of adult and continuing education* (pp. 233–245). San Francisco: Jossey-Bass.

Thiroux, J. P. (1986). *Ethics: Theory and practice* (3rd Ed.). New York: Macmillan.

Tyler, R. (1974). *Basic principles of curriculum and instruction.* Chicago: University of Chicago Press.

Wislock, R. P., & Flannery, D. D. (1991). A working philosophy of adult education: Implications for the practitioner. *MPAEA Journal of Adult Education, 20*(2), 3–10.

Zinn, L. M. (1990). Identifying your personal orientation. In M. W. Galbraith (Ed.), *Adult learning methods* (pp. 39–77). Malabar, FL: Krieger.

## 6

Reflecting on What Program Planners Really Do

Ronald M. Cervero and Arthur L. Wilson

ABSTRACT

To reflect on program planning practice, program planners need a different starting point than offered by traditional planning models because such models do not account for what real planners actually do (Cervero & Wilson, 1994a, 1994b). In this chapter, Cervero and Wilson offer an image of planning as the negotiation of interests. They invite readers to use this new language to reflect on their own practice, thereby drawing attention to what practitioners now do and may do better. The first part of the chapter describes the image of negotiating interests as what program planners should reflect on. The second part of the chapter illustrates this image using an actual case, thereby showing how planners can reflect on their practice. The concluding section explains why this new image can help improve planning practice.

ASSESSMENT

The following questions are intended to help orient you to the perspective on program planning taken in this chapter. Select the answer that most closely corresponds to your view of your own program planning practice.

1. When planning educational programs for adults:
   a. I try to keep politics out of the planning process.
   b. I hope that politics won't intrude; but it always does and I have to try to deal with it on an ad hoc basis.
   c. I assume that politics always affects planning practice and I try to anticipate this so that I can deal with it systematically.
2. When planning educational programs for adults:
   a. I always try to follow the adult education program planning models.
   b. I just do what works; the standard program planning models don't help me out much.
   c. I have had to develop my own approach that combines the techniques of the standard planning models with an understanding of the politics of my own setting.

If you selected (c) as your response to the above questions, then this chapter is consistent with your understanding of program planning practice in adult education. If you answered (a) or (b) to the questions, this chapter may challenge some of your conceptions about how to improve your planning practice.

KEY TERMS AND CONCEPTS

Program planning practice   This is a social activity in which people negotiate personal and organizational interests to construct educational programs for adults.

Negotiate   We use this term to encompass the variety of techniques planners use and forms of interpersonal interactions and relationships they engage in to construct programs. Its dictionary definition is: "to communicate or confer with another so as to arrive at the settlement of some matter; meet with another so as to arrive through discussion at some kind of agreement or compromise about something." This definition highlights the social character of program planning. It acknowledges that planning is carried out both in situations where there is widespread consensus and in situations that are characterized by conflict. The point is that a course of action is chosen through the social interaction among the planners.

Interests   This is a term we borrow from critical theory, and Habermas (1971) in particular. Interests are the human social purposes that give direction for getting along in and transforming the lived-in world. They are a complex set of predispositions, goals, values, desires, and expectations that lead people to act in certain ways and to position themselves in a particular manner when confronted with situations in which they must act (Morgan, 1986).

WHAT IS IMPORTANT TO REFLECT UPON?

Program planning practice in adult education is a social activity in which planners negotiate personal and organizational interests. The educational programs constructed through these practices do not just appear, showing up fully formed on a brochure or in a classroom. Rather, they are planned by real people in complex organizations replete with particular sets of historical traditions, relations of power, and human wants and interests. These planners construct educational programs out of the judgments they make in this messy, though normal, everyday world. Any account of educational program planning must face these realities.

Few, if any, educational planners would deny these realities. This should not be surprising for as Forester (1989) points out, planning while "ignoring the opportunities and dangers of an organizational setting is like walking across a busy intersection with one's eyes closed" (p. 7). However, these realities have rarely been taken as a source of insight for theories of program planning. In our view, everyday practice is the terrain on which the struggles occur to provide educational opportunities for adults. This chapter explores the practice of planning programs for adults and assesses the challenges and opportunities that are encountered in this pursuit.

Program planners have had at their disposal many theories for use in their practice about adult learning, program design, and organizational behavior. Important as these are, they are theories *for* the practice of planning rather than *of* it (Griffin, 1983). This chapter attempts to provide an alternative to those views by offering an account of planning practice in adult education. Our central thesis is that planning practice must be seen as a social activity in which planners negotiate personal and organizational interests. In this view planners would be able to significantly improve the quality of education by learning how to anticipate and deal with the interests they must routinely negotiate in their daily work.

Although the literature on educational program planning offers numerous principles of good practice, such as always assess the needs of your audience, these principles do not seem to account for the important things educators do when planning programs. In many ways, these principles sell practice short. For example, decisions about whether or how to assess the needs of the audience depend on a number of factors, such as the values and interests of others involved, organizational and interpersonal power relationships, available resources, and a knowledge of the history of planning efforts. Thus, reflecting on our own experiences and those of others, it is important to try to account for the political richness, the practical judgments, and the complexities of planning practices.

Others involved in adult education have recently voiced similar concerns (Millar, 1989; Usher & Bryant, 1989). Those who plan programs on a daily basis are quite direct about this. In an editorial, Pittman (1990) argued that: "Graduate programs could improve their image and utility to practitioners by giving serious, considered, scholarly attention to some of the problems and challenges their students will encounter when they enter continuing education" (p. 30). Brookfield (1986) noted that the conventional program planning models are generally treated with a great deal of skepticism, especially by those with "years of experience dealing with organizations in which personality conflicts, political factors, and budgetary constraints alter neatly conceived plans of action" (p. 202). These practitioners indicate that "they are unable to recognize themselves in the pages of most program development manuals" (Brookfield, 1986, p. 206). In their comprehensive review of the literature on planning programs for adults, Sork and Caffarella (1989) conclude that there are "shortcomings in the planning literature that need to be addressed. Building a theory that takes into account the exigencies of day-to-day responsibilities of practitioners" (p. 243) must be done if planning theories are to be taken seriously.

This recent questioning of the foundational principles of program planning in adult education is similar to a movement that has been underway for over 20 years in the field of curriculum planning for schools. The clarion call was issued by Schwab (1969): "The field of curriculum is moribund, unable by its present methods and principles to continue its work and desperately in search of new and more effective principles and methods.... There will be a renewed capacity to contribute to the quality of American education only if the bulk of curriculum energies are diverted from the theoretic to the practical.... It is the discipline concerned with choice and action" (p. 1). Since that time the field of school-based curriculum planning has been deeply involved in teasing out the implications of this turn away from the conventional planning theories (Atkins, 1986; Beyer & Apple, 1988; Cornbleth, 1988).

This chapter is our effort to move away from conventional planning theories, but not from theory about program planning. Of course, it is important to recognize that models don't plan programs, people do. Nevertheless, we agree with Forester's view of the importance of planning theories, which "can help alert us to problems, point us to strategies of response, remind us of what we care about, or prompt our practical insights into the particular cases we confront" (1989, p. 12). All models, however, leave something out because each is a simplified version of a complex reality. The important question of what does any particular model indicate is really important in planning practice. We believe that to be truly useful, any model must come to terms with the situationally specific nature of planning practice. Several chapters in this book (for example, Donaldson, Sork, and Cookson) have taken the first step in this direction by addressing the need for the program planner to take into account the various contexts which influence program planning judgments.

A New Image of Practice: Negotiating Interests

We believe the essential issue confronting program planning theory in adult education is that it does not adequately account for the important things that real educators must do in everyday practice. The crucial first step in redirecting theory is to move planning out of the minds of individual planners and into the social relations among people working in institutional settings. Thus, planning is essentially a social activity in which educators negotiate with each other in answering questions about a program's form, including its purposes, content, audience, and format. An educational program is never produced by a single planner acting outside of an institutional and social context. Rather, these programs are produced by people with multiple interests working in specific institutional contexts that profoundly affect their content and form.

By locating practice in its social context, it becomes inextricably linked to the complex world of human and institutional interests. *Interests* is a concept we borrow from critical theory (Habermas, 1971), but expand its meaning to include a complex set of predispositions, goals, values, desires, and expectations that lead people to act in certain ways and to position themselves in a particular manner when confronted with situations in which they must act (Morgan, 1986). Interests make the real world as they are manifested through human action. Thus, interests are the human social purposes that give direction for getting along in and transforming the lived-in world (Carr & Kemmis, 1986; Habermas, 1971). Each planner is working with a complex array of interpersonal and institutional interests that ultimately become expressed in the final program. Program planners must work with situation-specific institutional and human interests, which are often in conflict, are constantly changing, may be invisible, and may be at variance with the planner's own values and intentions. Yet these interests define for planners what is possible, desirable, and at times, imaginable.

How does a program come to be? Every program will be constructed out of the negotiation of these interests in the social context. Its ultimate form, both in the abstract nature of a brochure or syllabus and as experienced by participants, emerges from the everyday activities of those who planned it. Programs are fashioned through the planning practices of many people in the concrete settings of common institutional life. In our view questions about a prospective program's purposes, content, audience, and format are important, but they are not givens to work with or toward. Rather they are practical and political problems to be formulated and continually reconstructed through daily practice (Forester, 1989). How program planners negotiate interests to answer these questions is the central problem of their practice.

REFLECTING ON PLANNING PRACTICE: A CASE OF NEGOTIATING INTERESTS

The purpose of this section is to illustrate how our image of program planning can be used to reflect upon program planning practice in the real world. Specifically, we will show how two planners, Pete and Joan, constructed a program by negotiating interests. We encourage the reader to reflect on this case by asking how they would have acted in the same situation. Having tried out this image of planning practice to reflect on Pete and Joan's case, we suggest that readers use this new lens to reflect on their own planning practice, both retroactively as well as in an anticipatory way in planning future programs. After briefly describing how we collected the data for the case, we provide an overview, the historical background, a description of the three interests affecting the planning, and an analysis of how the planners negotiated the interests to construct the purposes and format for the program. A more complete analysis would also show how the planners negotiated the interests in constructing the audience and content for the program. However, due to space limitations of this chapter, we are presenting only a partial analysis of the case.

In collecting data for the case, we sought out people responsible for planning programs and asked to observe their planning activities for an upcoming educational program. Our data collection methods used observations, interviews, and document analysis. We asked to observe any planning meetings that were held. We audio-taped these meetings and at least one of us was present. We then interviewed the principal planners usually for 30 to 45 minutes as soon as we could after the meeting, asking them to comment on judgments that were made about the program. In addition to the interviews keyed to the planning meetings, we conducted several other interviews with the planners to capture other judgments that were being made outside of the public meetings. Finally, we interviewed the primary planners within a week after the program had actually been offered. We also examined available planning documents such as meeting agendas, program objectives, institutional mission statements, and marketing materials.

The Introduction to the Case

The Phoenix Company is a service-oriented business with 1280 employees in the southeastern United States. The company had conducted an annual management retreat for 10 years, which was planned by the president, to inform department directors of the company's plans for the upcoming year. By virtue of his position as vice president for human resource development, Pete was one of the primary planners for the 1997 annual retreat. The other primary planner for this retreat was Joan, whom Pete had recently hired as the company's director of customer service. As we shall see, Pete and Joan had an interest in changing the purpose and format of the retreat. They changed the retreat from an activity where vice presidents provided information about their plans for the upcoming year into a management education program designed to remedy an organizational problem.

The Institutional Setting

The company has a president, six vice presidents, and 31 department heads. Figure 6.1 shows the company's formal organizational chart. Pete reports to the president through the executive vice president, although all the vice presidents sit on the company's policy management team and comprise the top management team. Joan is one of six department heads who report directly to Pete. The company's middle management has two levels: the 31 department heads and the 65 line supervisors. However, 20 supervisors who report to the department heads in the professional services part of the company are technically trained for and have responsibility for the company's core product. As a result, these 20 people have authority and span of control similar to the depart-

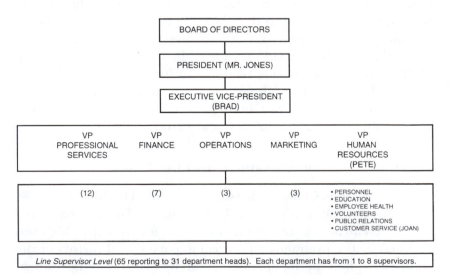

Figure 6.1 Phoenix Company organizational chart.

ment heads although their positions are not at that level in the formal organizational chart. All previous management retreats had included the president, the six vice presidents, and the 31 department heads. In comparison, the 1997 program had a significantly larger and different audience because it included for the first time the 20 technically oriented supervisors as well as all the new department heads who were appointed in the normal employee turnover.

The Program Planners

Pete, a cheerful and gregarious individual who considers himself a "humanist," has worked in this company for 10 years. In his position as a vice president, which he has held for 6 years, he is responsible for a number of functions in the company, including customer service, public relations, personnel, employee health, education, and volunteers. Joan had worked at the company for several years as the director of customer service. She left the company in March 1995 for a position at another firm. She remained at the new firm until September 1996 when she was rehired for her previous position at the Phoenix Company. Pete is pleased to have Joan back working at the company because the woman he hired to replace her left after 12 months, having been rebuffed by the president and executive vice president in her attempt to change the organizational culture.

Pete and Joan have a great deal of respect for one another and, having worked together for several years, have a relationship with which both feel comfortable and in which they believe they complement each other. For example, in describing how they planned for a recent meeting with the company president, Joan said, "We'll sit and we'll talk" about what to do because "Pete and I are real idea people and we bounce things off each other." Then she went off and prepared the meeting agenda because "he likes it done but I'm the one who does it. That's just my personality. We've worked together long enough. He knows that's the way I am and that's okay." Pete echoed this interpretation of their relationship in describing how they prepared an agenda for another meeting with the president: "I asked Joan to write it up for us but we agreed about what to put on the agenda and Joan put it down on paper for us."

Both planners had an interest in using the retreat to remedy a problem in the organization. Their interest was to change the retreat so that it served an educational rather than an informational function. Joan considers herself to be a "driver personality" who becomes impatient at the amount of time it takes to change the way her organization operates. Although Pete also is deeply committed to changing problems within the organization, he expects it will take time: "If adults become aware of some deficiencies and problems, then many times they're willing to try to change them. And if we give them the right tools and the right encouragement, many times they're successful in doing so. I don't think we can dictate or manipulate behavior too much. But if people see the need and know that's what we're expecting, sometimes a light comes on."

Pete has a fair amount of latitude in planning the company's overall management education program. His department offers many programs for all levels of company management during the year, many of which are planned based on input from the target audience. For example, his department conducts surveys and phone polls in order to get "input from people and be responsive and at the same time move our needs along." Moving the company's needs (as defined by top management) along takes top priority. As Pete explains: "if we [top management] think it's important, then they [participants] think it's important. We are pretty directive in our approach to planning things. I guess I'm pretty directive because I see myself as kind of the internal organizational development person who has my finger on what's happening ... and I feel pretty strongly that my ideas are valid and felt by the managers."

The History

Pete and Joan were the primary planners of the management education program being discussed in this chapter. Now that you have met them, we turn to the historical background leading up to the development of the 1997 management retreat. The annual spring retreats at the company had been a "real sacred cow," according to Pete. The company president, Mr. Jones, planned them as an opportunity for each vice president to outline plans and policies for the coming year. "It was very directive and everybody rotated to each VP and were told this is what we're doing and here's our budget plans and then you went home," said Pete. One year the retreat would be held in town and the next year out of town. There had not been a history of using the annual retreat for educational purposes until the most recent one in 1995. That planning process was extremely contentious and provides the necessary background for understanding the planning efforts for the 1997 retreat.

Pete had wanted to develop a retreat program in the spring of 1995 (just after Joan had left the company) that was more of a "communication, interaction kind of thing but Mr. Jones was not ready to do it at all ... he said that he might want to do it in the fall but I never heard from him again until I was confronted by Brad, the executive vice president." As Pete described it: "We got into a couple of real shouting matches in the budget preparation. I didn't understand why but apparently the executive VP believed I was trying to undermine his authority and that I was questioning his judgment in an inappropriate way. He really got upset about it. So then in the summer of 1995 we continued to have disagreements and that's when he shook his finger in my face one day in July and said: 'Where is our retreat, Pete? The boss said he wants to have a retreat; I just talked to him last night and he wonders why you haven't planned it and his understanding was that you were going to do one in August and why haven't you got this together.' That's exactly what he said in front of a whole group of people when I had not even heard the word *retreat* in the last 60 days. Much less had been given the mandate to do it."

So Pete pulled together a retreat using Harvard Business School cases as directed by Brad, secured the site, and hired an outside consultant from a nearby university to facilitate the session. However, just 2 weeks before the program he had not been able to get final approval for the retreat agenda, so he suggested to Brad that they "go in to talk with the boss." When they met with the president, Pete was "very surprised because I expected him to support me and instead of supporting me he was very critical of the fact that I hadn't planned it earlier, hadn't gotten final approval ahead of time. So apparently the executive VP had done a real good job of letting him hear his side of it before I ever got there and I felt like a lamb taken to slaughter." During the meeting, Brad pointed his finger in Pete's face again, saying: "This consultant woman, you are responsible and accountable for every word she says and if she does anything inappropriate, it's your head."

It is not surprising that Pete had been quite concerned going into the program. However, the program "ended up being a real success, very positive. I felt like my values were confirmed ... that's the kind of retreat we needed to have, and as a real surprise, at the end of the retreat the president presented me with a sweater with the logo of the retreat center and said just what an outstanding retreat it was. But I was still in this struggle because I threw it together at the last minute, I planned it under pressure, I didn't go to the right person for direction, so I really did a lot of reflecting on why I screwed up and why I had gotten blamed for not doing a good job. But I felt I knew the group and I kept coming back to my values of what I thought was appropriate." The outcome of this retreat was a fulcrum point in changing Pete's role in the organization. By the fall of 1996, Pete saw himself as the point person in moving along the organizational change: "... I feel like I've been given permission and authority to be the organizational culture person and to push things. So I feel like they depend on me. I feel like I've got the leadership role there." He was also feeling much more confident about his place in the organization than during the planning for the previous retreat: "I'm in a much different position in the organization as far as the politics of this management team, because you see the last time I was a sinking ship going into this thing and this time I'm on top of things."

The annual retreat had not been held since that time because, according to Pete, the timing was not right. So the group of vice presidents had not gotten together in a retreat (or any other educational program) for over a year at the time that Joan was rehired in September 1996. At that time, then, Pete and Joan began to identify organizational problems that needed to be addressed through management education. This was the situation at the Phoenix Company as Pete and Joan embarked on planning the management retreat.

As shown in Figure 6.2, the program planning took approximately 4 months. This included three initial meetings with the company president, Mr. Jones, during January and February 1997. During the third meeting, Pete and Joan received approval to hire George (the director of a leadership center at a nearby university) as a consultant to facilitate the program. Pete, Joan, and George

2 January 1997	Pete and Joan have first meeting about the upcoming retreat with Mr. Jones, the company president
17 January 1997	Second meeting with the president
13 February 1997	Third meeting with the president
21 February 1997	Pete and Joan send memorandum to audience announcing retreat purpose and dates
6 March 1997	Pete and Joan have first meeting to plan the retreat with George, an outside consultant hired to facilitate the retreat
20 March 1997	Second meeting with George
7 April 1997	Pete and Joan send memorandum to audience with final retreat schedule
28 April 1997	Third meeting with George
8–9 May 1997	"Phoenix Company Management Retreat"

Figure 6.2 Program planning calendar.

had three planning meetings during March and April. The retreat was held in May.

In the next section we describe the primary outcome of their efforts which culminated in the 1997 Phoenix Company Management Retreat.

The Program: "Phoenix Company Management Retreat"

The retreat was held on a Thursday and Friday in early May at a resort inn 50 miles from the company. Of the 65 people invited to attend, 62 were present. They arrived late Thursday morning for the lunch which opened the retreat. That evening everyone except the president shared a sleeping room with another participant. The program ended at 1:30 Friday afternoon. Figure 6.3 shows the retreat schedule as it was distributed at the opening session on Thursday.

Thursday was primarily devoted to team-building exercises facilitated by an outside consulting firm, Executive Adventure. The planners contracted for this packaged program; they had no role as facilitators, but rather were participants along with all the company employees. These exercises were conducted in five groups of 12 or 13 participants, which had been selected by Pete and Joan ahead of time. The dinner Thursday evening was held at the inn with the social activities organized by Pete and Joan.

Each of the three activities Friday morning was designed to

Phoenix Company Management Retreat
May 8–9, 1997
Agenda

Retreat Objectives:
1. To increase the awareness of the importance to the Phoenix Company of communicating as a team member. This includes, but is not limited to, supporting others, leading in a positive manner, working cooperatively with other departments, projecting a positive image about the department and Phoenix Company, and resolving problems in a quiet, positive manner for the good of the company.
2. To provide skill-building opportunities on how to conduct a meeting.
3. To provide opportunities to develop skills in handling difficult questions, conflict, and confrontation when conducting a meeting.

Thursday, 8 May

12:00–1:00 p.m.	Lunch
1:00–1:15 p.m.	Welcome, Overview & Purpose of Retreat: Pete
1:15–5:15 p.m.	Executive Adventure Exercises
5:00–7:00 p.m.	Free Time
7:00 until ?	Outdoor Bar-B-Que and Social Time

Friday, 9 May

7:00–8:00 a.m.	Breakfast Buffet
8:30–8:40 a.m.	Overview and Purpose of Morning Activities: Pete
8:45–10:00 a.m.	Department Meetings—Disaster or Success: George
10:00–10:15 p.m.	Break
10:15–11:15 a.m.	Desert Survival Exercise: George
11:15–12:15	Departmental Meetings Exercise: Pete & George
12:15 p.m.–1:15 p.m.	Lunch with Table Topics
1:15–1:30 p.m.	Summary and Wrap-up: Joan
	Closing Comments: Mr. Jones

Figure 6.3 The retreat schedule.

facilitate the achievement of the stated retreat objectives. All three activities used both small and large groups. In the "Departmental Meetings—Disaster or Success" activity, George asked the small groups to identify characteristics of successful and unsuccessful meetings. This was intended to give the participants ideas about how to conduct effective meetings. In the "Desert Survival Exercise" small groups simulated being lost in the wilderness and trying to save themselves. In the large group discussion after this, George led people to see different ways that they "saved themselves," which would show the importance of communicating as a team member. For the "Departmental Meetings Exercise" Pete wrote three role play scenarios based on actual problems that the company was facing, such as the implementation of a new smoking policy for employees. These role plays, which were intended to help participants learn to deal with difficult questions when conducting a meeting, were enacted in small groups. George facilitated the large group discussion that sought to draw out lessons from the role plays.

At the lunch to close the retreat, participants were to discuss at their tables certain aspects of the material covered at the retreat and how these ideas might apply back at the company. Closing comments were made by Joan and Mr. Jones. Evaluation forms, which asked participants to rate different aspects of the program, were distributed and collected before participants left the retreat site.

In the following sections, we return to September 1996 and show how Pete and Joan's negotiation of interests constructed the Phoenix Company Management Retreat. We first explain the three primary interests that Pete and Joan were negotiating as they planned the retreat. After that, we show how their negotiation of these three interests in their everyday world shaped the purpose, audience, content, and format for the retreat. The chapter concludes with a discussion of Pete and Joan's evaluation of the retreat in terms of the interests which guided their practices.

Interests and the Phoenix Company Management Retreat

Pete and Joan continually negotiated three critically important interests in planning this specific educational program. The primary interest was to improve the way that the company's management (100 people) communicated to the rest of the company's employees (approximately 1200 people). This interest was shared by all of the significant planners, in contrast to the other two interests that were shared primarily by Pete and Joan. In addition to the primary interest in fixing an organizational problem, they also had interests in (1) changing the approach of management education in the company to a more problem-based and experiential mode and (2) strengthening the support for the company's human resource development function.

Improving organizational communication. There was widespread agreement among top management that the processes of communicating information throughout the company were not working well. This problem was causing conflict and was so disruptive that the work of the company was not as effective and efficient as it needed to be. Therefore, top management had an interest in improving the organizational communication practices so that (1) their decisions were clearly communicated by middle management to all company employees and (2) middle management was capable of effectively dealing with potential or actual problems at a local level and preventing them from blowing up and disrupting the entire company.

The president's interest was clearly in preventing the disruptions that had been occurring because his management team did not communicate effectively with company employees. Pete explained that Mr. Jones "has this monthly meeting with hourly employees and they keep telling him over and over again that they don't know what's going on, their supervisor doesn't answer their questions. They criticize other departments in a department meeting and they never get any follow-up." The president believed that lack of effective communication had been an ongoing problem at the company. As Joan noted, at the time she was interviewing for her position the president "talked with me about the need to have better communication from department level up and down." The president's interest, then, was not in changing the organizational relations of power between management and staff but rather fixing the current system so that it would run more smoothly.

Based on the problems they had observed and experienced over the past several years, both Pete and Joan shared the interest of other members of top management in wanting to minimize staff disputes and more effectively communicate the directives of the company's formal leaders. Pete was very direct, for example, in articulating this interest to George in the March 6 planning meeting. In explaining a recent event in the company, he said: "Yesterday in a first line supervisory training program, they claimed they had never even been told about a major new component of our wage and salary program. Well, we published it in the employee newsletter. It's a policy." Pete followed with the key statement of interest: "But for their manager never to sit down and communicate— that to me means we're missing something." From this view, if the company were to function smoothly, department heads would need to be able to communicate the decisions of top management.

Not only must department managers communicate these decisions to company employees, but they must do so in a way that employees feel they are members of the company "team" and have the opportunity to ask questions and voice complaints. This view of communication did not mean that employees were being given a role in making the decisions. Rather, they needed to be better informed and motivated so they could further the company's agenda as defined by top management. Pete was very clear about this interest in a particular form of communication and teamwork. During the March 6 planning meeting he explained this view to George: "How do you conduct a meeting with thirty hourly employees so that you give clear information? You allow for questions and challenges and complaints. But you then keep a teamwork spirit; you keep a positive representation of the company as you respond without criticizing top management."

In addition to representing the interests of top management in his role as vice president, Pete had a vested interest in improving the communication skills of the managers. He said, "I'm the person that hears all the grievances and I'm the person who goes to federal court when we get a lawsuit for terminating someone. So I have a real applicable and valuable reason for managers being good communicators ... and I find also that by the time I'm called in to resolve a problem in a department, it's usually some confrontation, some resistance to communication and facilitation that's been building for months. And I was just eaten up and spit out for lunch recently in a two-and-a-half hour meeting with a group of twenty employees who were just so angry that they weren't being heard in their department meetings." Because of his role as human resources vice president, Pete personally dealt with problems that occurred when middle managers did not effectively communicate to the employees. He was left with cleaning up the messes "that should have been taken care of a little bit at a time over the last three or four months." Thus, we see that Pete's personal and organizational interests converge in wanting to improve communication practices at the company.

Reorienting management education at the company. For several years prior to the 1997 program, Pete had had a clear interest in changing management education from an information-oriented, didactic format to a more problem-based, experiential approach. He believed the way that management education was being done was not effectively improving the Phoenix Company. Although Pete attempted to convey this interest, it was generally not shared by other members of top management or by the president. As explained in the earlier section, at prior management retreats planned by the president, vice presidents gave information to middle mangers in a didactic format. Pete tried to change this orientation for the 1995 retreat by introducing the "concept of executive adventure and focus on team building and communication with employees, but that was not an option. They would not approve that." There had been simply no support for reorienting management education among the company's top management team.

Since the previous retreat, however, Pete had been actively promoting this new orientation to management education in his other planning efforts by, for instance, having department directors "facilitate management training programs ... when we have not done much of that before." Pete's department was moving toward focusing more on the company's problems as a basis for education and thus needed to use internal "facilitators" because "they're usually more in tune with what our needs are than someone from the university. But they know where we are and are usually real familiar with the terms." In the interview Joan conducted to hire George, she explained their orientation for the upcoming retreat in these same terms. The focus of the retreat this time was to change the managers' awareness or behavior "by doing group activities versus lecturing about how do you be a good manager. Let's look at practicing it." Pete and Joan's interest in reorienting management education was historically evolving and exhibited in many of their current program planning efforts.

Strengthening the human resource development function. Historically, the human resource development department in the Phoenix Company had relatively less power than the other units represented by the vice president team: finance, marketing, professional services, and operations. One of Pete's major interests was to secure the power necessary to operate effectively within the top management team so that he could influence the direction of the company. Pete's near powerlessness was demonstrated in the problems he encountered in planning the 1995 retreat. Since then, however, Pete had begun to solidify support for the human resource development function.

Yet, he was not fully secure as he began planning for the 1997 retreat. In going into the January 2 meeting with Mr. Jones, he was less concerned about obtaining approval for the retreat than he was about protecting himself from the president "coming up at the last minute and saying 'where's the retreat?'" as happened in planning the 1995 retreat.

Pete was in a continual battle to secure support and power for his role from the president and other members of the top management team. His planning strategy for this retreat was a direct expression of his interest in strengthening his role within the company. Based on his experience from the last retreat, Pete decided that he would not include the executive vice president at all in planning the 1997 program. "I was going to make sure that Mr. Jones was part of every step. And so I intentionally excluded Brad because I did not want his input. But I had the power and support to get around him." However, Pete knew that he needed approval for this new approach for the retreat from other key vice presidents. He learned from the last retreat that "there are some political players in the vice president team, so it is good to go and run ideas by them and warm them up to what's going on. So I went by and talked to three vice presidents about this whole idea." Pete hoped this would build support for his function in the company among the other members of the top management team.

This section described the three primary interests that were negotiated in giving form to the retreat. The following two sections show how the planners negotiated these interests in making judgments about the purposes and format of the program. A complete analysis would show how the planners negotiated these interests also regarding the audience and content for the program. However, due to space limitations in this chapter, only the purpose and format judgments are discussed.

Negotiating Purposes

The purpose of the retreat was negotiated primarily by Mr. Jones, Pete, and Joan who shared the interest of improving the way that top and middle managers communicated to the rest of the company employees. The overall purpose that they negotiated was to improve the managers' communication practices. Although many employees in the company desired better communication practices from the managers, the important point is that top management's interest defined those communication needs. No other interests, such as those of the middle managers or the other 1200 company employees, were negotiated. Thus, top management's definition of the company's communication needs determined the fundamental purpose of the program. During the activities in which the program's purpose was negotiated, Pete and Joan experienced little conflict because no potentially competing interests were involved. The negotiation of program purposes are illustrated in two areas of their planning practices described below.

The first, and most important, part of Pete and Joan's negotiation strategy was to clearly define who was going to be a player in the negotiation of the purposes. Besides themselves, there was no doubt that the president would be the only other significant actor in these negotiations. As Joan said, after she and Pete considered the possibility of using the company's annual retreat to focus on internal communication, "The first thing we have to do is to talk to Mr. Jones and see what he would like us to do." At their first meeting with the president on January 2, the overall purpose of the program was easily negotiated because the same interest was shared by all three people. Joan felt that based on this first meeting, "we had a good feeling for what he wanted accomplished. I think we were all thinking along the same lines." The president thought that it had been long enough since the last retreat and, according to Joan, "gave us the go-ahead" for a spring retreat. At the first meeting, then, the planners successfully negotiated approval to have the retreat because Mr. Jones felt that "communication and having good department meetings were very valid things for us to emphasize."

After the completion of the program, Pete explained that the strategy of representing the president's interests was a crucial aspect of their planning practices. As the final speaker at the Friday lunch, Mr. Jones spoke passionately about the importance of the retreat's purpose and "really tied in the whole communication focus and how employees want to be communicated to." It was unusual that the president was able to do such a good job because "he is not a real good speaker and he tends to ramble, but he was just wonderful, he was articulate, he was on the point, he was motivational." Pete reasoned that Mr. Jones was able to do this because of his role in negotiating the retreat's purpose: "He helped identify the issues in January, and we built the whole retreat around issues that were near and dear to him.... We were able to brainstorm and get him to identify issues that were also our issues." Thus, we see the institutional interests of top management directly expressed in the program itself.

Pete and Joan were equally clear about who would *not* be involved in negotiating the program's purpose. In their first planning meeting on March 6, George wanted to know if any other interests were being represented when he asked, "Have the people who are coming bought into the fact that we need some guidance and updating in how to conduct good meetings?" Joan's response was "I don't know." Pete gave his rationale for this response in the interview after the meeting. It wasn't that he did not want to seek input from the managers, but that he didn't need to because "I feel pretty strongly that my ideas are valid and are felt by managers." In other words, Pete believed that the middle managers shared his ideas about the retreat's purpose. George pushed this issue of who would negotiate the purpose by suggesting that a survey be sent to the audience. This would be acceptable to Pete if the survey would "help warm them up and get some buying in. Allow them to participate but not allow them to dictate what we're going to be doing." It was important that top management define the purpose because as Pete said, "We are running a business."

George's attempts to negotiate the program's purpose with Pete and Joan offer a second illustration of how they managed to exclude other interests through their planning practices. The fundamental issue was the way in which George interpreted Pete and Joan's interest in improving the communication practices of managers as an attempt to move the organization to more participatory forms of management. George believed this was a better form of management and assumed that Pete and Joan shared this interest and were trying to reshape the relations of power at the company. Through the negotiation around this issue in the March 6 planning meeting, the retreat's fundamental purpose became clearer. The point was made during the discussion about sending out a questionnaire to the audience to determine their views about positive and negative aspects of meetings in the company. George interpreted this effort to involve the managers to mean that the

purpose of the retreat was to move the company to a more participatory form of management. However, Pete responded to a question from George about whether this was the purpose by clearly
restating the purpose as defined by top management: "I think the
heart of a good meeting, whether you are participatory or not, is
in being approachable so that people feel comfortable in raising
their hands.... And I don't think a lot of times our managers set the
climate for people to raise their hands." Pete stopped George's
effort to negotiate the program's fundamental purpose by reiterat-
ing top management's view of effective meetings, namely that
employees feel that their managers are "approachable." This is
quite in contrast to George's view of effective meetings as those
in which employees are involved in making decisions for the company.

In the debriefing after the March 6 meeting, Pete explained
that he wouldn't allow George's view to shape the program's purposes because the managers "would be real threatened by opening
the thing up and really talking a lot about participation and participatory decision making.... So I kind of sidestepped him but I think
I made it clear to him that we're more directive than we are
participatory." This explains why it was so important for Pete to
successfully silence George's view in negotiating the program's
purpose. Although Pete himself was not necessarily opposed to
participatory management, he indicated that "I see us phasing
into that and I think we really have to lay a foundation with Mr.
Jones to get something like that pulled off." Even though George's
interest was in moving organizations toward more participatory
forms of management, he recognized that Pete was protecting a
very important organizational interest and did not try to further
negotiate the purpose.

Negotiating Format

All three primary interests discussed earlier came into play as
Pete and Joan negotiated the many aspects of the retreat's format.
Of the many judgments the planners made about the format, four
were critically important in furthering the interests being negotiated. The first was the *location* at which the retreat was to be held,
with the specific issue being whether it would be held in the same
town as the Phoenix Company or at a remote site. The second

concerned the overall *schedule* for the retreat, with the specific issue being whether the retreat would be held on Thursday/Friday or Friday/Saturday. The third related to the selection of *instructors* for the retreat and centered on the selection of the Executive Adventure consulting firm and on why George was hired to be the primary facilitator in addition to Pete. The final area of judgment focused on the design of *learning activities* for the retreat, which were highly interactive in contrast to the didactic methods used in previous retreats.

Location

The primary interest of improving organizational communication was given form in the selection of the location for the retreat. In Pete and Joan's January 17 planning document, which was used that day for their second meeting with the president, the issue was stated as: "Do we plan an overnight retreat out of town or do we try to meet locally and have half a day plus a day on site?" As they went into the meeting Pete and Joan had felt that "we wanted it out of town" even though there was the downside of "cost and taking that many key roles out of the company at the same time." Pete explained the out-of-town location was necessary for the program to accomplish its objectives "because it was a communication type workshop. We would really benefit from the informal time together and the socialization would be a big part of it." In order to improve organization communication and build teamwork, Pete and Joan felt strongly that the participants need to be removed from their work setting where the problems existed. This was especially important because they envisioned the retreat as an environment where the participants could temporarily have more equal roles in contrast to the hierarchical relations of power that existed at the company. The location was such an important issue that they broached it with Mr. Jones as early as the January 2 meeting when they asked "Should we look at an overnight retreat or should we do something in town?" And Joan remembered that Mr. Jones said "Overnight would be great." So when they formally brought up the options of in-town or out-of-town during the January 17 meeting with the president, it was not surprising that he "just said 'out-of-town'" with no discussion. The president had been involved in negotiating all of the important issues for the retreat, and the location was no exception.

Schedule

Unlike the location issue, the actual days on which the retreat would be held was not centrally related to the primary interest of improving organizational communication. The major question here, as stated in the Pete and Joan's January 17 planning document, was "Do we schedule the retreat for a Thursday afternoon/ Friday or for a Friday afternoon/Saturday morning?" Neither planner believed that the actual days would have made a major difference in furthering the primary interest; Joan personally preferred Thursday/Friday because she wanted to be home with her family on the weekend, whereas Pete preferred Friday/Saturday "because it won't be as difficult to staff the management of the company." Because this judgment did not involve negotiating the primary interest, Pete engaged in planning practices that furthered his interest of strengthening the human resource development function. Specifically, he met with three of the other vice presidents to find out what they thought about the issue and the finance VP recommended Friday/Saturday because the participants "won't miss as much work time and it will be easier operationally." Two other VPs recommended Thursday/Friday because "we work hard enough, people want to take their Saturdays." He was able to present these two viewpoints to the president at the January 17 meeting who, according to Joan, "just said 'Thursday/ Friday.' I mean he didn't bat an eye, he just said it." Where Pete and Joan did not need to negotiate the primary interest, which was done only with Mr. Jones, they could afford to involve other members of the top management team in the planning. This involvement would not only help the other vice presidents buy into the retreat itself, but also would give them more exposure to Pete's ideas about management education.

It was not until after the January 17 meeting that Pete and Joan "started playing with the schedule and started talking about time frames and agendas and what would work." By this time they had negotiated the major areas of content with Mr. Jones and now the two of them alone negotiated the overall schedule, with the major question being the relationship of Executive Adventure and the remainder of the program. As Pete explained: "If we do Executive Adventure, would we do that the first afternoon and then come back the next day and try to reinforce it with small group interaction? Or should we do Executive Adventure on the second day?"

They made this decision before the March 6 meeting with George so they could say that Executive Adventure was going to be held on Thursday afternoon and that he wasn't responsible for this. They asked him to help them come up with other exercises so that Friday morning "would be more interactive than it was lecture." By circumscribing the areas of the program that George was allowed to negotiate, Pete was able to maintain control over the primary interests out of which the retreat was being negotiated.

Selecting Instructors

In order to further the interest of strengthening his function within the company, Pete decided to be one of the facilitators for the retreat. However, he knew that because of his ongoing relationships with the members of the audience, he would need to hire facilitators from outside the company to further the primary interest of improving organization communication. He did this by selecting the consultants from Executive Adventure for the Thursday afternoon session and George as the facilitator for Friday morning. Pete and Joan selected Executive Adventure because they needed people from outside the company to help "break down the barriers and relax the group so that the group would really give honest feedback." As they explained, many of the department directors and supervisors work together every day but "they don't really know each other." Pete also needed an outsider for the Friday sessions to "bring some credibility as opposed to the administration saying" how the participants needed to improve their communication practices. Another reason that Pete selected an outsider to facilitate the Friday sessions was that "I've got some critics and that's one reason I thought to have a neutral person who has a good reputation."

Although Pete's judgment to use an outside facilitator was a result of negotiating the primary interest, his selection of George from the three people interviewed was a result of negotiating the other two interests. They interviewed George prior to the February 13 meeting with the president partly to ensure that he was "free and willing" to work on the retreat. As part of their negotiation to reorient management education, they needed to make sure he "understood our values and objectives" related to the interactive nature of the retreat and that "he would be comfortable with them." In the interview, Pete and Joan indicated that "we were not looking for the expert, we were looking for the facilitator to help the group learn themselves." By selecting someone who shared these values, they tried to ensure that the negotiation about the structure of Friday morning activities would proceed without conflict. Importantly, Pete's selection of George also furthered his third interest of building support for his function in the company. As Pete explained about the interview, "One green light was that he had just met with the president and executive vice president about something different. And it had been a fairly positive experience with them." Thus, George would add some credibility to the retreat, "because he has some recognition in the community that the president and vice president would buy into." All of this made for a smooth negotiation at the February 13 meeting when Pete recommended and Mr. Jones approved hiring George. Pete could further both interests in negotiating the form of the retreat, then, by selecting George to facilitate the Friday morning part of the retreat.

Design of Learning Activities

Pete and Joan strongly believed in the importance of using interactive learning methods at the retreat, which would be in contrast to the highly didactic approach used in previous retreats. Giving this kind of form to the retreat was a result of negotiating the primary interest of improving organizational communication as well as Pete's interest in reorienting management education. The learning activities constructed for the retreat clearly and directly represent Pete's attempts to change all management education programs to a more problem-focused and interactive approach. This was not simply a blind trust in this type of format; rather, Pete believed that the interactive format was the most effective way to meet all three retreat objectives and thus further the overall purpose.

This type of design for the learning activities conflicted with the way the president had organized previous retreats and thus presented Pete with one of the most difficult areas of negotiation. At the February 13 meeting Pete and Joan negotiated with Mr. Jones about using the Executive Adventure segment, which they were concerned he might not agree to "because two years ago he would not buy into it at all." Although they did their best sales pitch, they were actually vague about exactly what would be going on as part of the activity: "We sort of told him what the goal of that part of the program was all about which is team building" but didn't go into detail because "he didn't ask us." The president agreed to the activity, Pete explained, because "I think he knows what we can do and part of his going along with us is he can tell we feel strongly about what we want to accomplish." Likewise, at the same meeting, Pete and Joan explained to Mr. Jones more about the interactive nature of the Friday morning sessions, "of using a group process to try to promote the skills of a manager's communication." They "got him to buy off on that kind of exercise," which was important if they were going to be able to hire and work with George to plan the specific activities for Friday morning. Having successfully concluded these negotiations with the president over the type of learning activities, Pete and Joan could proceed with the design of the specific activities at their March 6 planning meeting with George.

REFLECTING ON THE EVERYDAY WORLD OF PLANNING PRACTICE

This image of planning as a social activity in which planners negotiate interests can improve practice in three ways. First, we can make sense of much of the apparent noise of daily work once we recognize that program planning is a social activity of negotiating interests. The daily informal conversations, public planning meetings, countless telephone calls, memoranda, letters, and faxes now endemic in the modern organization are the media through which these negotiations are conducted. By using an image that moves planning out of the minds of planners into the social relations among people, we can now account for the everyday activities of planning practice.

Second, this image identifies planning inescapably as a political activity. One simply cannot plan an educational program without attending either to interests of the institution or its relations of power. The negotiation of these interests along with those of the planner, the potential learners, those providing funding for the program, as well as the larger public is fundamentally a political act. Some interests will become central to the planning of a program while others will be downplayed. In those instances where there is a great deal of consensus among all of the interests regarding the purposes, content, audience, and format of a program, the negotiation will appear to proceed easily. However, this should not mask the fact that negotiation is occurring. Much more often, there will be uncertainties, ambiguities, and conflict that must be resolved in planning a program.

Third, the ethical responsibilities of planners are more clearly defined. Because planners are no longer neutral actors, the central ethical question is, "Which interests will be selected to organize the planning?" This is made more difficult because it is not a judgment to be made once and for all at the beginning of the planning; rather, interests are continuously being negotiated throughout all of the activities that give form to a specific program. In the messy world of organizational politics, it is often easiest to do "what works." However, program planners frequently feel at odds with the dominant organizational interest. This can happen, for example, when the organizational interest to make a profit from a program by enrolling large numbers of participants creates an educational format that effectively silences participants. This image does not offer ethical standards that must be applied in every situation. However, by drawing attention to the centrality of interests in planning it can identify the important types of judgments planners routinely make in shaping every educational program.

So what is new here? By developing a pragmatic account of planning practice, we hope to draw attention to what practitioners now do and may do better. We want to argue that although theories of learning, program design, and organizational behavior may be distinguished from each other in the abstract, they must be integrated in any activity of educational program planning. If we go even part way toward capturing the essential aspects of planning practice, and at the same time stimulate others to carry out similar work, we believe these arguments can enrich both our understanding and our practice of planning programs for adults.

QUESTIONS FOR STUDY AND DISCUSSION

1. At the beginning of the chapter, we asked two questions regarding the politics of planning practice and the nature of planning models. Reconsider your responses to those questions. Would you change your initial responses? Why or why not?

2. Put yourself in Pete and Joan's position. What planning judgments would you have made given those circumstances? Which interests would you have represented? What might have been the consequences of having made those judgments? How might the final program have changed?
3. Reflect on your own institutional context. What are the major interests, who represents them, and how do they affect the educational programs that you plan?
4. Consider your own planning practice. How effective are you at anticipating, representing, and negotiating interests? In which ways?
5. We have attempted to make visible the political reality and ethical nature of planning programs in institutional contexts. How can an understanding of the central place of interests contribute to more effective planning practice? In what ways?
6. Planning models, which are meant to be idealized guides to planning action, "can alert us to problems, point us to strategies of response, remind us of what we care about, or prompt our practical insights into the particular cases we confront" (Forester, 1989, p. 12). In what ways does a model of planning as the social negotiation of interests alert you to problems, point out strategies of response, and remind you of what you care about?

REFERENCES

Atkins, E. (1986). The deliberative process: An analysis from three perspectives. *Journal of Curriculum and Supervision, 3*(4), 265–293.

Beyer, L. E., & Apple, M. W. (Eds.). (1988). *The curriculum: Problems, prospects, and possibilities.* Albany: State University of New York Press.

Brookfield, S. D. (1986). *Understanding and facilitating adult learning.* San Francisco: Jossey-Bass.

Carr, W., & Kemmis, S. (1986). *Becoming critical.* London: Falmer Press.

Cervero, R. M., & Wilson, A. L. (1994a). *Planning responsibly for adult education: A guide to negotiating power and interests.* San Francisco: Jossey-Bass.

Cervero, R. M., & Wilson, A. L. (1994b). The politics of responsibility: A theory of program planning practice for adult education. *Adult Education Quarterly, 45,* 249–268.

Cornbleth, C. (1988). Curriculum in and out of context. *Journal of Curriculum and Supervision, 3*(2), 85–96.

Forester, J. (1989). *Planning in the face of power.* Berkeley: University of California Press.

Griffin, C. (1983). *Curriculum theory in adult and lifelong education.* London: Croom Helm.

Habermas, J. (1971). *Knowledge and human interests* (J. J. Shapiro, Trans.). London: Heinemann.

Millar, C. (1989). Educating the educators of adults: Two cheers for curriculum negotiation. *Journal of Curriculum Studies,* 21(2), 161–168.

Morgan, G. (1986). *Images of organization.* Beverly Hills, CA: Sage.

Pittman, V. (1990). Some things practitioners wish adult education professors would teach. *Adult Learning,* 1(3), 30.

Schwab, J. J. (1969). The practical: A language for curriculum. *School Review,* 78(1), 1–24.

Sork, T. J., & Caffarella, R. S. (1989). Planning programs for adults. In S. B. Merriam & P. M. Cunningham (Eds.), *Handbook of adult and continuing education* (pp. 233–245). San Francisco: Jossey-Bass.

Usher, R., & Bryant, I. (1989). *Adult education as theory practice. and research: The captive triangle.* London: Routledge.

7

Examining the External Context

Peter S. Cookson

ABSTRACT

Education and training programs are planned within specific contexts. The focus of this chapter is on the context external to the organizational sponsor of the education or training programs. The chapter is divided into two parts. The first describes some aspects of the external context which affect the design, implementation, evaluation, and follow-up of programs. The second suggests how the planner can attain an understanding of the different factors and use them to increase successful learning for program participants.

ASSESSMENT

For each one of the four scenarios described below, decide which external conditions are affecting the implementation of the planning of education or training programs. For each condition, identify the specific conditions of the external context that seem to be impacting the program planning process. Think about how the program planner in each scenario might respond to those conditions.

Scenario 1

In the firm Delila's Delicious Cookies, Robert, as director of personnel, has among his many functions responsibilities for the orientation of new workers. One main objective of this training is to enable the new workers to accomplish their tasks safely and with sufficient speed to not slow down the work of the more experienced workers. Because the firm is in the process of expanding, each month more and more employees are hired. With all his other duties, the director finds it increasingly more difficult to conduct the orientation training for the new workers while simultaneously coordinating all the other programs for the sales personnel, supervisors, and operatives.

Recently, Robert submitted to the upper management a proposal to employ, for the coming year, an assistant director with major responsibility for the coordination and implementation of training. Although the proposal was adopted, a drop in the international market prices for sugar and chocolate, significant increases in the costs of the raw materials needed for the company, and disruptive labor and social unrest experienced among the primarily ethnic minority workers have impacted on the organizational climate of the company. Under such conditions, the upper management has declared a moratorium in the hiring of new employees, thus suspending Robert's plans to name an assistant training director. Without any reduction in the other tasks, the programs that he plans will be shorter and offered with less frequency than he would like.

Scenario 2

Juanita is an engineer and recently was elected as one of the vice presidents of the National Engineers Society. One of her responsibilities is the organization of the educational program of the biannual conference of the society. She has been thinking about the program and a series of lectures to be conducted following the congress. She believes that one of the reasons she won the election was her strong support for continuing professional education of the society.

In planning the national conference, she would like to address two areas of concern. Because she regularly reads several professional engineering journals, she realizes several basic technologies are likely to transform the ways in which many engineers perform their work. At the upcoming congress, she would like to highlight several new technologies that have been widely adopted in several countries. She believes that it is only a matter of time until these same technologies will be adopted in her own country. Another of her concerns is that due to several accidents caused by structural weaknesses in bridges on the national highways, as well as in several high rise buildings, the national government legislators have mandated that all civil engineers in the country must renew their licenses every 5 years by an examination on the new technologies.

Scenario 3

Josephine is the associate dean of the College of Humanities and Social Sciences in a state university. After her children graduated from secondary school, she returned to higher education and completed two academic degrees. Perhaps that is why she has become very interested in expanding the study opportunities in higher education for other adults who cannot pursue a full-time university career. In the college academic council meetings she has argued eloquently in support of building outreach and nontraditional programs of study that correspond to the life style, free time, and energy level of men and women who work full time while carrying the weight of numerous family responsibilities.

Unfortunately, her voice is lost in the discussions. Other administrative officers are more concerned with the education of youth who, upon their graduation from the secondary schools, find an insufficient number of spaces available in higher education. For that reason, Josephine has arrived at the conclusion that her institution—due not only to the endemic lack of resources but also to an entrenched institutional inertia and lack of vision—will probably not change direction this side of her retirement. Recently she has been meeting with a group of administrators from other universities and other interested people to discuss the possibility of establishing a new university that will have as its central mission the provision of higher education services to adults who want to study for degrees part time.

Scenario 4

Oscar works with a nongovernmental, grass-roots organization that establishes *people's banks* for low income and primarily ethnic minority, inner city residents. He has organized *study circles* of inner city residents to learn how to set up credit unions and prepare to manage small community banks. He has discovered that instead of recruiting people as individuals to form such *circles*, his greatest success has come in organizing study circles within existing groups. He has also discovered he has greater success in organizing the groups during the spring and fall seasons when the weather conditions are less extreme than during the winter and summer months.

WHAT IS THE EXTERNAL CONTEXT?

No training or education program for men and women occurs in a vacuum. As one of Houle's (1972) underlying assumptions states, every program takes place within the framework of a specific situation and is profoundly influenced by that fact. In this chapter we examine some of the elements of the extra-organizational situation which affect both how the program is carried out and how the sponsoring organizations carry out their program-related functions.

The external context impacts on several programming elements. Of course, many factors internal to the organization also influence the selection of programs, their contents, methods, goals and objectives. The internal or organization context of planning is treated in the chapter that follows. Although an endless litany of factors external to the organization could be mentioned, the program planner may benefit from paying particular attention to the following:

- Characteristics of the society
- Demographic attributes of the population: size, density, fecundity, ethnicity, age profile, level of schooling
- Attributes of the economy: level of production, average income per capita, rate of employment/unemployment/underemployment
- Culture: level of literacy and schooling of the population, availability of books and libraries, educational programs via communications technologies
- Ideology and political culture of the country, dominant tendencies of the country, degree of official hegemony of the government and armed forces, values assigned to the functions of education and training, degree of class consciousness and consciousness of class conflicts

- History of the geographical areas in which the organization operates and with which it relates
- Climate
- Abundance and availability of natural resources

PATTERNS OF INFLUENCE OF EXTERNAL FACTORS

In the four scenarios above we see how the work of planners may be either or both circumscribed and enhanced by conditions over which they do not have control. In each scenario the alternatives are clear: either the planners will adjust their own actions in accordance with the conditions or they will be restricted by them. To perform with knowledge and confidence, planners need to become aware of the conditions of the external context that affect their work. Thus an inventory of such conditions can serve as a first step toward improvement in the practice and art of planning. Depending on the administrative and organizational arrangements of the education or training unit, this inventory can be prepared by the planner alone, by a group of planners, or with an advisory committee. It may be a simple and informal process or a systematic and formal process. Some organizations hold fast to a philosophy of always involving prospective program participants in the design of their own learning activities.

This process of becoming aware of the conditions of the external context is not the same as the separate program planning step of assessing learning needs. The effects of these external conditions are not limited to a single program. On the contrary, they affect the process and procedures of planning in general. Hence this program planning step of surveying the external context provides data and insights that transcend the informational requirements of any specific education or training program.

The conditions of the external context which impact on the program planning can be varied, extensive, and ever subject to change. To keep up to date with these conditions, it is essential that planners stay alert and continually and critically process the information from a number of sources about different aspects of the external context. The methods of knowing may be as simple as reading the daily newspaper, listening to the informative radio and television programs, or consulting with well-informed professional colleagues, representatives of the target learners, or consultants.

Methods may also include detailed inquiries, search of relevant literature, or formal research. In the following sections, particular attention is paid to two methods: participation in professional associations and interaction with advisory committees.

PROFESSIONAL ASSOCIATIONS

Membership and active involvement in an association of professional colleagues—whether of the same profession that the planner serves or of other planners from a variety of fields—can increase awareness of events that impact significantly on planning practice. In periodical meetings, it is possible to discover the external conditions that affect not only one's own organization but also many others. Speaking with counterparts, the planner can learn about solutions that have been tested and the corresponding outcomes. Without the necessity of firsthand experience, the planner can learn the most effective solutions. By meeting together, planners can deepen their understanding of themes of common interest, including those related to changing external conditions which affect their organizations.

Instead of only accommodating such conditions as individuals, they also think about uniting their efforts to face shared conditions. When there is a need to shape new policies that fortify education or training efforts, such united projects can result from association among planners in a professional organization. Without such an association, it is easier for training and education decisions to be made by people who overlook the criteria of excellence in lifelong education.

ADVISORY COMMITTEES

The famous anthropologist Margaret Mead (1955, p. 289, cited in Boyle, 1981, p. 91) once wrote, "Every change should be introduced with the full awareness and participation of those whose daily lives will be affected by the change." Before designing relevant and practical programs, it behooves us to inform ourselves about the realities of those who participate in our programs. Advisory committees permit us to act in accordance with those realities. The members of such committees gain valuable experience in serving others, practice in democratic activities, opportunities that raise confidence in self-expression, informal learning experiences, and skills in accepting and carrying out responsibilities.

In the planning of specific programs, committees that assume duties in relation to numerous aspects of program development can play a very significant role. However, in this chapter we limit our discussion to functions of committees that offer advice *prior* to planning a specific program. As such, these advisory committees comprise persons who collectively represent a given area of practice. For example, an advisory committee for a school of computation could be made up of representatives from a university program of computational science and from data processing or computation departments in government ministries, banks, businesses or other organizations—all of which presumably have a vested interest in an adequate supply and demand of trained personnel in computing. By the same token, an organization that offers training in leadership for directors of cooperatives could benefit from the support and advice of a committee made up of past and present cooperative officers. The main function of these committees would be to bring the planner up to date about trends, events, and changing conditions to consider in organizing learning activities for their corresponding areas of interest.

Upon inviting the representatives of the area to serve, it is important to explain the nature of their duties and responsibilities. They deserve to know how much time will be required of them, the length of expected service in the position, and whether the appointment will be voluntary or remunerated. If the members see how their work on the advisory committee results in programming which benefits their profession or area of occupational commitment, the lack of remuneration will not be an obstacle to their participation. When they meet together it would be appropriate to provide some refreshments; if the meeting lasts all day, it would be appropriate to provide meals.

Below is a list of recommendations offered by Knowles (1980) with respect to advisory committees. Although these recommendations are directed to lifelong education programs offered to the public, they may be adapted in accordance with the reality unique to many types of training or education programs. Some of the functions that can be assigned to an advisory committee include:

- Assist in designing and conducting needs assessment strategies (surveys, focus groups, key informants, etc.).
- Inform the program planner about community issues that could be addressed by specific programs.
- Suggest criteria for the setting of priorities among program purposes and objectives.
- Recommend policies and procedures for program planning and implementation.
- Act as an advocate for the programs before policy-making groups, administrators, and other stakeholders whose influence and decisions affect education or training operations.
- Generate ideas for new programs.
- Recommend resource people for specific program activities.
- Liaise with different segments of the population served by the program.
- Provide voluntary assistance with various program activities such as registration, evaluation, receptions, and other social gatherings.
- Assist in program evaluation.
- Support program promotion and marketing activities. (pp. 74–75)

In selecting advisory group members, Knowles (1980, p. 75) recommends three types of representation:

1. Representatives of the sponsoring organization
2. Representatives from the external context of the sponsoring organization—these might include members from target groups to be served, representatives of organizations and/or agencies with which the sponsoring organization cooperates, and other stakeholders outside the organization whose interests are served by education and training programs
3. Specialists in selected areas of practice or who represent specific fields of expertise relevant to specific education and training programs

Upon forming an advisory committee, it is important that the planner takes seriously the assistance that it can provide. Some years ago the author was involved with an evaluation of a training program for Spanish-speaking labor union leaders in Chicago. The program had a *Latino* director and an advisory committee made up of *Latino* community leaders and trade unionists. When the committee realized that none of their recommendations or suggestions had been accepted by the project planners, there was a dramatic decrease in activity further advisory committee meetings and an almost total desertion from the project. In subsequent meetings, instead of the 12 people present during the earlier meetings, only 3 or 4 would attend.

Advisory committees can help planners to become aware of significant changes in the external environment which, in turn, precipitate significant changes in such things as the need for constant changes within the organizational unit responsible for training and education. The importance of organizational correspondence to the changes in the external environment (in systems theory referred to as the *supra-system*) was reported to me some years ago by the director of a technical continuing education program for adults. When informed by the advisory committee for a technical education program in office equipment repair that soon mechanical typewriters and calculators would be replaced with electronic machines, the director of the extramural studies program of a large urban community college alerted the technical and structural subsystems of his organization. As a result those responsible for courses and certification programs relating to office machine maintenance and repair coordinated a modernization process, with instructors undergoing advanced training from the manufacturers of the new electronic equipment. Because his organization was the first in the area to effect the updating process, the continuing education program captured all the recruitment and retention activities for a particular group of adult students in the community; as a result, several proprietary schools, less attuned to the imminent changes in the external environment, suddenly found themselves unable to compete and subsequently phased out a whole line of formerly prosperous programs.

SUMMARY

One of the main purposes of an advisory committee is to provide information and recommendations to the planner. Such a committee can function as an invaluable instrument and source of information with respect to the external conditions that will affect subsequent program planning. The identification of such conditions enables us to be sure that our programs address the reality of those whom they serve. If we make an analytical and critical inventory, we will not be satisfied to know only the superficial reality but will seek to find positive alternative answers. In elaborating subsequent plans of many programs, we will consider the findings and conclusions that are formed in this first step.

QUESTIONS FOR STUDY AND DISCUSSION

1. Evaluate the merits of participating in a professional association in which other lifelong educators participate. What would be your expectations in belonging to and participating in such an association? What could you offer to help such an association reach its objectives? How could such an association enable you to keep up to date and to respond responsibly to the external conditions which affect your duties as a program planner?
2. Analyze the merits of forming an advisory committee with membership from outside (possibly as well as from within) your organization to provide information and counsel concerning external conditions which impact on your education or training programs. Describe the composition and functions of such a committee. What would you do to help the members of the committee feel useful?
3. Describe the exact steps that you could take to learn about the conditions of the external context that affect programming within your own organization.

REFERENCES

Boyle, P. G. (1981). *Planning better programs.* New York: McGraw-Hill.

Houle, C. O. (1972). *Design of education.* San Francisco: Jossey-Bass.

Knowles, M. S. (1980). *The modern practice of adult education: From pedagogy to andragogy.* New York: Cambridge.

Mead, M. (Ed.). (1955). *Cultural patterns and technical change.* New York: The New American Library.

8

The Nature and Role of the Organizational Sponsor

Joe F. Donaldson

ABSTRACT

Organizations and organizational situations are complex, ambiguous, paradoxical, and difficult to understand. Yet, because the organization is a significant component of each programming situation, it is essential that program planners understand the organizational context of planning. This chapter is dedicated to broadening and improving program planners' understanding of their organizations. To achieve this understanding requires program planners to "complicate their thinking" about organizations by developing the ability to analyze organizations and situations using multiple perspectives. Four different ways of viewing organizations are considered: organizations as machines, as organisms, as political arenas, and as cultures. The theories supporting each viewpoint are briefly described, as are the major analytical concepts associated with each. A case vignette is used to illustrate how these multiple perspectives can be used to analyze the organizational context of program planning.

ASSESSMENT

The following questions are intended to assist you in gaining insight about the ways you think about and act in your organization. There are no correct answers. But it is important that you answer honestly so you can obtain an accurate understanding of how you approach the organizational context when you plan programs.

1. When making programming decisions, for me the most important organizational factor is:
   a. the chain of command in my organization.
   b. the needs of my organization.
   c. understanding who has power.
   d. the unwritten values and norms of my organization.

2. When developing a program, (select only one):
   a. I take the organizational context for granted, since I understand it from having worked here for some time.
   b. I sometimes take time to analyze how my organization influences my program planning.
   c. I always take time to analyze how my organization influences my program planning.

3. When thinking about your work, with which one of the following statements are you most comfortable?
   a. My job is to fulfill the duties outlined in my position description.
   b. My job is to bring in resources for the organization.
   c. My job is to negotiate and resolve conflicts.
   d. My job is to participate with others in making our work meaningful and in establishing unwritten rules for working together.

If you are like most people, this brief self-assessment has shown that you have a preferred way of thinking about the organizational context of program planning. It most likely has also shown that, in the day-to-day pressures of program planning, we take little heed of the organizational context of each program planning situation. This chapter, however, takes a different approach. It argues that (a) we need to broaden our thinking about organizations beyond our preferred ways of thinking, and (b) we need to take stock of the nature and role of our organization for each program planning situation we face.

KEY TERMS AND CONCEPTS

Milieu or setting   "Broadly speaking, the total social and physical environment surrounding a [program planning] situation at a given time and place" (Houle, 1972, p. 233). This chapter focuses upon one aspect of the milieu surrounding program planning situations—the institutional or organizational context of planning.

Organizational analysis   A systematic means of examining organizations and organizational situations for the purposes of gaining increased understanding of the organization and of discerning the character of organizational situations. Organizational analysis also has the purpose of providing insights to guide our actions.

Metaphor   A figure of speech in which a word or phrase ordinarily used for one thing is used in place of another to suggest a likeness between them. The comparison is figurative rather than literal. For example, "the man is a lamb."

Metaphorical analysis   A form of organizational analysis in which different metaphors of organization are employed to obtain particular insights about organizations and organizational situations, as well as a more comprehensive understanding of organizational situations.

Analogy   In this chapter, a particular use of metaphors in which organizations and organizational situations are compared with metaphors to determine whether features of the situation and the metaphor are shared or not.

Nature of the organization   The character of the organization as we understand it. The nature of the organization also implies an understanding of what we mean by organization and our role (as program planners) in them.

Role of the organization   The function the sponsoring organization plays with respect to program planning. As will be seen, the organization's role varies with its nature.

INTRODUCTION

The purposes of this chapter are twofold: (1) to underscore the importance of the organizational sponsor in program planning and (2) to provide a way for program planners to gain deeper and broader understandings of their organizations and the organizational situations they face on a day-to-day basis. The approach taken in the chapter is based upon five assumptions about program planning and the organizational context in which it occurs.

The first is that program planning is set within a specific milieu of which the planner's organization is a significant component (Houle, 1972). Further, the planner's organization profoundly influences the planning of each program. Examples of ways the organization influences programming are plentiful. Boyle (1981) and Knowles (1980) provide guidance, for instance, about the organizational structures, policies, and climate that they believe are ideally needed to support program planning. Pennington & Green (1976) identify several organizational factors, including resource availability, that constrain planning. Burnham (1988) points to the way organizations do their work (their technology) as having consequences for programming. Mills, Cervero, Langone, and Wilson (1995) delineate how organizational structure and culture, available resources, and power relationships constrain or enable program planning practices. Cookson (1989) and Donaldson (1989) illustrate the relation between organizational factors and the recruitment and retention of adult learners. Schroeder (1980) uses a typology of sponsor organizations (e.g., institutional and voluntary agencies) to inform our understanding of the different types of organizations for which we work and the implications these different types have for planning. However, while the organizational context is recognized as important, we are sometimes so overwhelmed by other aspects of programming that it does not receive the attention it deserves.

Second, understanding the organization is an essential ingredient in effective program planning practice. Forester (1989) notes, for example, that "ignoring the opportunities and dangers of an organizational setting is like walking across a busy intersection with one's eyes closed" (p. 7). Constraints to the planning process remain unidentified; opportunities within the planning situation are missed; and organizational expectations are misunderstood. Knox (1981) points out that the adult educator's challenge lies between the constraints and demands of the organizations for which we work. Constraints come in such forms as organizational mission, policy, and resources, that limit what we can do. Demands, on the other hand, are expectations of the organization that we cannot fail to ignore (for example, the organization's requirement that programs be fully self-supporting). The latitude between constraints and demands determines the quantity and the types of choices that we can make in programming. Understanding our organizations is therefore essential. It is also essential to identify those constraints and demands that limit our work. Only when identified can we take action to have them reduced, so the quantity and types of choices available to us are increased (Donaldson, 1990).

The third assumption is that organizations are by their very nature complex, ambiguous, and filled with paradox (Morgan, 1986). They are not only difficult to understand, but even when we think we understand them, unexpected developments arise that confound our way of thinking and interfere with our actions. Therefore, we need analytical tools that help us better comprehend and deal with the complexity of organizational situations.

Fourth, how we describe the nature and role of the organizational sponsor of adult education programs (a) will differ according to the perspective we use in understanding the organization and (b) will vary over time. The perspectives we use influence the way we understand our organizations and how they function in relation to the programs we plan. In addition, the organization's nature and role must be considered in dynamic, not static, terms. The infusion of new personnel, changes in the organization's external environment, propagation of new policies, for instance, all change the nature of the organization, even if in subtle ways. As we approach the planning of each program, the role that the organization plays may also differ. For example, in one situation a business may expect that a program be fully supported by the divisions from which participants are drawn. In another situation, however, general company financial support may be available for program development and implementation. The nature and role of the organizational sponsor must therefore be considered for each programming situation.

Finally, and related to previous assumptions, program planners, to be effective, need to develop the analytical skills that contribute to a broad and in-depth understanding of their organizations. For program planners to achieve this form of understanding, they must complicate their thinking about organizations. This assumption is based on two premises. The first is that we each have preferred ways of thinking about organizations and organizational situations. These ways of thinking, or what Argyris and Schön (1974) call "theories-in-use," determine our understanding of organizational situations, help us define the problems embedded in them, and guide our actions. To the extent that we rely upon one preferred way of thinking, our understanding of situations is narrow, our definition of problems constricted, and our choice of actions limited. Second, the need to complicate thinking has a rich tradition in many fields. For example, physicists have for some time known that to understand physical phenomena as fully as possible, theoretical perspectives from Newtonian physics, quantum mechanics, and the new generation of theories (e.g., string theory), are required. No theory or model is considered complete. Instead, a multiplicity of perspectives is required, each of which complements and enriches the others.

The need to employ multiple perspectives is also supported in the organizational literature. Three major, but related tools have been recommended for obtaining multiple perspectives in the analysis of organizations. Scott (1987) and Harmon and Mayer (1986) recommend, for example, the use of concepts from theories of organization. Bolman and Deal (1984, 1991), in contrast, recommend using four frames (structural, human resource, political, symbolic) that they have developed from major schools of organizational theory. Each frame functions like a stencil: Each highlights, as well as hides, different aspects of the situation, but when used together the frames provide a more complete picture than one frame alone. Finally, Morgan (1986) suggests the use of nine metaphors of organization, each again developed from major schools of organizational theory.

Although the tools differ somewhat from each other, their function is similar. They provide a means for increasing our understanding of organizations and how they work. They serve as diagnostic tools, illuminating possibilities for action, stimulating greater understanding of what we and others have done, evoking new and unexpected insights about organizational dynamics, and serving as aids to thinking (Harmon & Mayer, 1986). Each also provides a distinctive but partial view of the organizational situation. Metaphors, for example, provide one-sided insight (Morgan, 1986). To say that a director of training is a spark plug tells us one thing about the director, but does not tell all. To also say that the training director is a lightning rod for controversy deepens and broadens our description and understanding. Taken together, therefore, the different theories, frames, and metaphors, like the theories of physics, complement and enrich each other, providing more complete and deeper understanding than any one could achieve alone.

Although one can approach the analysis of organizations using theories, frames, or metaphors, I prefer metaphors for several reasons. Metaphors have a rich tradition in language and therefore are more easily understood than are theories or frames. Metaphors have been increasingly and successfully employed to understand different facets of adult education theory and practice (see, for example, Candy, 1986; Deshler, 1990; Donaldson, 1991; Proctor, 1991). Metaphors have much power for making the unfamiliar (organizations and organizational theories) familiar (Candy, 1986), for making the ambiguous unequivocal, and for simplifying our understanding with rich images, sufficient in accuracy and novelty to provide us with good and perhaps novel insights (Morgan, 1986). They contribute directly to expanding the repertoire of images that are parts of professionals' practical knowledge (Schön, 1987; Cervero, 1988). Lastly, there are guidelines for using metaphors to gain the one-sided insight they provide, as well as for combining these one-sided views into a more comprehensive understanding of organizational contexts.

I have selected four metaphors of organization provided by Morgan (1986) for our consideration. These are the metaphors of organizations as (1) machines, (2) organisms, (3) political arenas, and (4) cultures. These metaphors have been selected because they correspond to some of the most commonly used theories of organization and because the latter two metaphors can be extended to provide insight about the role organizations play in issues of social justice, an area of particular concern to many adult educators.

In the next section, each of the four metaphors is considered in turn. The theory or theories supporting each viewpoint is briefly described, as are some of the major assumptions and analytical concepts associated with each. Then, we will turn our attention to an examination of how these metaphors can be employed, using a case vignette to illustrate their use.

FOUR METAPHORS OF ORGANIZATION

The Organization as Machine

The fundamental issue in the machine metaphor is, "how do we organize?" Drawn from the literature dealing with theories of bureaucracy and scientific management, this metaphor focuses on how to build an organization with interdependent and highly specialized parts that can be controlled for producing results in a highly efficient manner (a machine). Consequently, the primary focus in this metaphor is on how the organization is structured to do its work, and the organizational chart is often a primary source for analysis. In considering the organizational chart, one focuses on a several concepts:

1. Division of work—How well is each position (represented by each box of the chart and position description) designed in terms of specialization for efficiently achieving organizational goals?
2. Line of command—Who reports to whom? Does each subordinate report to only one superior (unity of command) or to two or more subordinates (matrix form of organization)?
3. Authority—Is it centralized or decentralized and what individuals are in positions of authority?
4. Control—What mechanisms are in place to control the work of specialists so their work is efficient? Is control centralized or decentralized? If decentralized, on what basis is it decentralized—functionally (e.g., a course office and a conference office), geographically (dispersing the adult education operation into different geographic regions), or on the basis of clients served (e.g., one training division works with professional staff; another works with those on the assembly line)?
5. Span of control—Is the number of people reporting to one superior of adequate size to produce efficiency in operation but not so large as to create problems of communication, coordination, and control?

Although aware of the human side of organizations, those who proposed this view were primarily concerned with ways to make humans beings fit the requirements of mechanical organization, so that work could be controlled and made efficient (Morgan, 1986). In addition, because machines are relatively impervious to external influences, this particular view considers organizations to be closed, rather than open, to external environmental influences.

The most common application of this metaphor within adult and continuing education is illustrated by the debate, primarily within continuing higher education (see, for example, Knox, 1982 and Strother & Klus, 1982), about whether continuing education should be centralized or decentralized within institutions of higher education. This debate has historically centered around the issue of control over the continuing education enterprise, with comments about the "fatal embrace" of the university president (Gordon, 1980) or about "keeping others out of my business" (Hentschel, 1991) illustrating how the issue of control is manifested in this context. It also focuses our attention on the organization of the continuing education enterprise within the total organization, raising questions about lines of command, division of labor, and efficiency in doing work. From the perspective of this metaphor, therefore, the nature of the organizational sponsor is that of the structured machine. Its role with respect to programming is providing the structure, control, and specialized roles needed to generate programs in an efficient manner.

The Organization as Organism

Viewing organizations as living organisms has its roots in systems theory, particularly that branch which considers the organization to be open to its environment (natural open systems theory) (Scott, 1987). From the systems perspective comes an understanding of organizations as unitary wholes, made up of interdependent parts or subsystems. But because this metaphor focuses upon the lifelike nature of organizations, concerns about environmental transactions, growth, development, and survival are also central. The fundamental issue within this metaphor is, "what are we doing?" (Chaffee, 1985, p. 222). Because openness to the environment is a central assumption, answers to the fundamental issue are judged against the organization's relation to and transactions with its external environment (its suprasystem) and the extent of organizational congruence with that environment. Key analytical concepts in the metaphor include (Katz & Kahn, 1978):

1.   Homeostasis—This refers to the organization's ability to maintain a steady state through negative feedback about deviations

from preestablished standards and norms. Negative feedback from participants about a program, for example, allows program planners to take corrective action, keeping their organizational unit and its programs in a steady state.

2. Negative Entropy—Newton's second law of thermodynamics states that there is a natural tendency for systems to run down or deteriorate. But, as an open system the organization is able to take in more energy than it expends, thereby reversing entropic processes to create negative entropy. Consequently, importation of energy is another key concept in this metaphor.

3. Inputs—Inputs are resources that supply energy to the system. These resources take a variety of forms, including, for an adult education program, money, participants, and information needed to make programming decisions.

4. Throughputs—Throughputs are the activities of the organization associated with transforming inputs into products. The teaching/learning transaction is, for example, an organizational throughput for changing participants' knowledge, attitudes, or skills. Another term for throughput is organizational technology, or the way in which the organization does its work. In the case of programming, it can be the particular pattern employed in developing a program.

5. Outputs—These are the products of an organization. In the case of a program, it can be program alumni with changed knowledge, attitudes, or skills.

6. Functional Differentiation and Integration—As changes occur in the environment, the organization has the capacity to differentiate its functions to respond to these environmental changes. For example, in light of the rapid development and growing use of telecommunications technologies, a human resource development unit might choose to differentiate its functions by developing one unit that specializes in face-to-face instruction and another that specializes in distance education. The corollary of differentiation is integration. The more differentiation that an organization has, the more integration is required to keep different specialized functions (and perhaps units or part of the system) coordinated and working toward organizational goals. The need for integration is also based upon the view of an organization (system) as a group of interrelated and interdependent subsystems.

7. Equifinality—In an open system many different means are available for achieving the same end result. Face-to-face classroom instruction, face-to-face tutorials, and a variety of distance education methods can be used, for example, to produce the same changes in program participants' knowledge, attitudes, and skills.

This metaphor has been used more extensively than the others by adult and continuing educators to analyze and understand the administration of adult and continuing education, as well as the development of programs for adults. Some examples will illustrate. At the organizational level, Peters and associates (1980) employ an open systems perspective to examine a "whole range of adult education enterprises, regardless of their organizational base" (p. xi). Knox (1981) uses open systems theory to explore the continuing education agency's relationship with its parent organization. Votruba (1987) focuses our attention on the organizational survival of continuing education units by detailing ways to build internal support for continuing education. Beder (1978) uses open systems theory to analyze the adult education agency's interactions with its external environment, and more particularly the potential of interorganizational linkages for overcoming the organizational constraints of resource dependency and insecurity. Donaldson (1992) also focuses on the external environment by highlighting the importance of continuing higher educators' boundary-spanning role in helping institutions of higher education adapt to their environments and affect these environments in advantageous ways.

At the program planning level, Cookson (1989) uses many of the central concepts listed above to consider recruiting and retaining adult students. He concludes from his analysis, for example, that student retention is enhanced by the inputs of social reinforcement and program linkages, the satisfying, nurturing, and supportive qualities of the throughput, and congruence between student expectations and actual outcomes (outputs). When Knowles (1980) draws our attention to the importance of understanding the needs of the organization in program planning, he is employing the organism metaphor, since "an organization or institution is a living organism that has needs, too" (p. 97).

Burnham (1988) focuses exclusively on the throughput dimension of this metaphor in his study of program planning as organizational technology, or the way the organization does its work (in this case, how it plans programs). Three types of organizational technologies identified by Thompson (1967) are used by Burnham. The first, long-linked technology, is assembly line in nature. Planning occurs in lockstep manner, and the adult education agency offers a stable number of programs from one year to the next. The second, a mediating technology, focuses upon adult educators' brokering role between instructors and participants, in which responses to needs are mediated on the basis of available instructional resources. In the intensive technology, each planning event differs, and is characterized by thorough diagnosis (as in medicine) of educational needs and the planning situation (Burnham, 1988).

Lauffer (1978), on the other hand, focuses almost exclusively on the importance of adult educators assessing the programming task environment, or that segment of the environment that most affects programming. He identifies four groups of people and organizations in the task environment that are important for adult educators to know about and understand—the program's regulatory publics or internal and external groups that establish policies, rules, and laws that affect programming; the input publics or resource providers; potential competitors and collaborators in programming; and actual and potential consumers (outcome publics) of the outcomes of programs—for example, employers of program participants.

From the perspective of this metaphor, the nature of the organizational sponsor is similar to a living organism interacting with its environment, importing and processing resources to produce a product so that its survival is ensured. The role of the sponsor in this case includes (a) the provision of resources (money, instructors, philosophical support, perhaps program participants in the case of human resource development programming), (b) the use of a dominant program planning technology, (c) the existence of other organizational subsystems upon which the adult education unit depends for doing its work, and (d) relations with various segments of its external environment that influence the adult education unit and its programs. This metaphor moves us away from a focus on structure and control to an organic view of the nature and role of the organization.

The Organization as Political Arena

Although many adult educators are uncomfortable with politics, a reality of organizational life is that it is indeed political. This metaphor draws our attention to this reality, asking us to view organizations as political arenas. The fundamental issue in this metaphor is, "how are scarce resources allocated and by whom?" The metaphor focuses our attention on the following factors:

1. The roles, uses, and sources of power and influence;
2. Individual interests, as well as special group interests;
3. Organizational stakeholders, or those individuals and groups that have a stake in the organization and its programs;
4. The natural tendency for there to be conflict within organizations;
5. The importance of networking and the building of political coalitions;
6. The processes of bargaining, negotiating, coercion, compromise, and cooptation; and
7. Viewing the program planner primarily as a political actor.

Systematic analysis of organizations as political arenas requires a focus on the relations between interests, conflict, and power (Morgan, 1986). Interests are a complex set of predispositions, goals, values, desires and expectations that lead people to act in certain ways and to position themselves in a particular manner when confronted with issues and questions (Morgan, 1986). Power, on the other hand, can be considered from the perspective of whether it is associated with positions of formal authority (position power), is derived from an individual's expertise in a particular domain (expert power), or is associated with a person's interpersonal skills and ability to form relationships with a wide variety of individuals and groups (personal power) (Donaldson, 1990).

According to this metaphor, "power is the medium through which conflicts of interests are ultimately resolved. Power influences who gets what, when, and how" (Morgan, 1986, p. 158). This metaphor also incorporates the assumption that few solutions to problems are optimal. Rather, they are only satisfactory because they have been arrived at after considering and mediating all relevant interests. Finally, the goals of the organization are not seen as existing apart from the political process. Instead, organizations are coalitions of multiple goals and interests which express themselves in different ways depending upon who or what group is in power.

Analysis of organizations using this metaphor requires us to address several different questions: What interests exist within the organization and what individuals and groups are associated with those interests? Who are the organization's internal and external stakeholders? Who are the informal opinion leaders (people who, although not in positions of power, have much influence due to their expert and personal power)? Are group interests the same or are they in conflict? If in conflict, how is the conflict resolved—through negotiation, coercion, compromise, or cooptation? Who is involved in resolving these conflicts, i.e., who is exercising the power to resolve them?

This metaphor can be further employed by considering unitary, pluralistic, and radical perspectives of interests, conflict and power. In the unitary view, interests are seen as common, conflict as rare, and power associated almost exclusively with positions of authority. In the pluralistic view, interests are diverse; conflict is inherent and ineradicable; and power is a central variable in mediating the diverse interests and resolving the inevitable conflicts that will arise from them. In the radical view, interests are contradictory "class" interests; conflict is inevitable and is derived from class conflicts in the broader society; and power, being associated with broader issues of social control, is unequally distributed among groups both within and outside the organization (Morgan, 1986).

Morgan (1986) expands upon the radical view of interests, conflict, and power to develop yet another metaphor—the metaphor of organizations as instruments of domination. This latter perspective is closely akin to the social reform philosophy within adult education (Darkenwald & Merriam, 1982). It raises questions about whether organizations of adult and continuing education support dominant group interests (Jarvis, 1985) and draws our attention to the underrepresented among adult education participants, a subject of much concern among many adult and continuing educators.

In addition, Cervero and Wilson (1994) have used pluralistic and radical perspectives on power, conflicts, and interests, and the work of Forester (1989), to develop an analytical template to aid program planners in identifying the political constraints (or forms of political boundedness) they face in planning situations. The template considers both the sources of power relationships and whether individual and group interests are generally the same (consensual) or different (conflictual). "In terms of the source of power relationships, some may be *socially systematic*—they are tied to existing organizational designs or political structures—and others may be relatively *ad hoc*—they derive from temporary organizational conditions or interpersonal relationships" (Cervero & Wilson, 1994, p. 129). This template and its theoretical underpinnings provide program planners with not only a means to assess the form of political boundedness they face in a programming situation, but also guides for action in each form of political boundedness. The template illustrates how the concept of the political metaphor can be used to develop an insightful and powerful analytical tool for assessing the political nature of organizational planning situations.

From the perspective of this metaphor, the sponsoring organization is a stage upon which a political drama is continuously played. Its role for program planning is to provide us a part in this drama, a part in which we work to secure the scarce resources needed for programs, to mediate and negotiate the various interests of people and groups that have a stake in them, and to participate in the resolution of conflicts which are sure to arise during the program development process. The radical perspective of interests, conflict, and power also draws our attention to the role our organizations and programs play in society. The drama in this instance broadens to one in which issues of social justice, equity, involvement, and access become central themes. Our part becomes one of critically analyzing our organizations and programs in light of these themes in an effort to gain the understanding necessary for action that works to correct the imbalance of power and the forces of domination.

The Organization as Culture

One of the more recent developments in organizational theory is the increased focus given to cultures of organizations. Holt (1987) defines organizational culture as "... the unspoken and unwritten norms that fashion and direct organizational life" (p. 169). When viewing organizations as cultures we focus primarily upon the systems of values, norms, beliefs, and cultural expressions or symbols (language, rituals, sagas, myths) that hold the organization together, make it distinctive, and define acceptable ways of doing work. For this reason, the central issue in this metaphor is, "why are we together?" (Chaffee, 1984, p. 222) Because norms, values, and beliefs are unspoken and unwritten, analysis of an organization using this metaphor requires us to delve beneath the surface of standard operating procedures, explicit policies, and organizational charts to determine what is implicit and tacit in the character and work of the organization.

Although many concepts undergird the consideration of organizations as cultures, two are especially relevant. These are the concepts of social contract and a socially constructed reality (Chaffee, 1985). The concept of social contract holds that organizations are composed of individuals who have freely entered into a cooperative enterprise to work together. As a result, this concept requires us to view personnel as participants in creating the culture of the organization rather than just as "organizational members" who have little control over the organization's work, culture, and direction. The concept of socially constructed reality holds that reality and meaning are constantly being created as organizational participants work together and interact with one another. Consequently, organizational culture is continually taking form and shape as meaning is made through interaction among an organization's participants.

Taken together these two concepts also ask us to reconsider our views about organizational goals. In the previous three metaphors, especially in the machine and organism metaphors, goals are considered to be *of* the organization, developed by upper management and held up as ends to which each organizational member is to work. In the culture metaphor, however, goals are most often viewed as goals *for* the organization, arrived at through forms of interaction and negotiation (to arrive at the social contract) by all participants in the life of the organization. From this perspective, the written mission statement and goals of an organization have less relevancy in a programming situation than the unwritten and unspoken norms and goals that have been arrived at over time through social interchange.

The culture metaphor draws our attention to the need to

establish, through development of organizational culture, an image which is positive and well accepted by a program's publics (Deal, 1987). This is particularly important in the recruitment of program participants. It also asks us to focus on the language we use and the ways in which programming activities communicate symbolic meanings. It calls, for example, for the careful use of language in promotional material, language that communicates the identity and character of the sponsoring organization and unit. And it helps us realize that many of our activities (for example, use of advisory committees, holding graduation exercises) carry symbolic meaning as well as serve functional ends (Donaldson, 1989).

Morgan (1986) has also used the culture metaphor as a platform from which to develop yet another metaphor—the organization as a psychic prison. In this metaphor, meaning is again socially created, but organizational members become trapped by the very meaning and reality they create and sustain (Morgan, 1980). This leads to dominant ways of thinking and to creation of a dominant ideology from which a large segment of the population may be alienated. Morgan (1980) links this metaphor to a radical humanist paradigm which calls for examining how human thought and action can be linked to transcend alienation. As such, this metaphor has themes with the same roots as those which undergird several approaches to administration, teaching, and learning in adult education—e.g., praxis (Freire, 1970), critical theory (Cervero, 1988), and transformative learning (Mezirow, 1991).

If the metaphor of the political arena provides us with a stage upon which a political play is enacted, the culture metaphor provides us with the drama itself. However, the script of this drama remains unwritten and can only be discerned by looking beneath the obvious. In this metaphor the nature of the organization can be represented by what Holt (1987) calls the unwritten manual of standard operating norms (SONs) that guide our and others' participation in the organization. The role it plays is providing us with the SONs that guide our actions and judgments in programming, with meanings associated with our work and programs, and a variety of symbols which express those meanings. However, the organization might also act like a psychic prison, constraining our ways of thinking and limiting the perspectives we have on the role our programs play in society.

USING METAPHORS FOR DIAGNOSIS, UNDERSTANDING, AND ACTION

The examples used to illustrate these metaphors provide a glimpse of how metaphors can be used to more fully understand organizations and the particular organizational situations we face in program planning. Yet, to use metaphors most effectively requires us to employ them in systematic fashion. The goal of such analyses is to arrive at as complete an understanding of the organizational situation as possible. This necessitates the use of several different metaphors, as well as a means to blend the one-sided insight obtained from each into a more comprehensive view of the situation.

The first step in analysis is to perform a diagnostic reading of the situation using each metaphor separately and in turn. The purpose of this diagnostic reading is to "… discern the character of the situation" from the perspective of each metaphor (Morgan, 1986, p. 328). In this step of the process, metaphors are treated as "… idealized points of reference against which the situation … can be compared" (Morgan, 1986, p. 328). These comparisons will result in three types of analogy: a positive analogy in which the metaphor and the situation share elements in common; a negative analogy in which the metaphor and the situation have elements which they do not share; and a neutral analogy in which we are uncertain whether features belong to the positive or negative type of analogy (Keeley, 1980). According to Keeley (1980), each type of analogy provides us with guidance about how the metaphor can be used:

> The positive aspect suggests *descriptive* considerations: How well does a … [metaphor] reflect what's going on? The neutral aspect suggests *heuristic* considerations: Is a … [metaphor] likely to be a constructive tool for [further] inquiry [into the situation]? The negative aspect suggests *normative* considerations: Does a … [metaphor] have reasonable implications for … [organizational] change? (p. 340)

From this we can see that metaphors provide not only a basis for description and understanding, but for further inquiry and action as well. For example, if a particular feature of a metaphor is found lacking in a situation (e.g., lack of programming unit identity), then action can be taken using concepts from various metaphors as guides to correct the situation. By linking inquiry, understanding, and action, this form of organizational analysis provides us with a means for linking theory and practice (Morgan, 1986).

The second step is to conduct a critical evaluation of each interpretation produced by the different metaphors (Morgan, 1986). This requires considering the different types of analogies obtained from application of each metaphor, as well as determining which interpretation(s) provide the most significant and useful insights. We also have to consider how the different interpretations might be reconciled to generate a more comprehensive view of the situation. To accomplish this reconciliation, Morgan (1986) recommends integrating those interpretations that are most useful into what he calls "the most effective story line" (p. 329). Developing the "story line" is the point at which we move from description and interpretation to evaluation in order to arrive at an opinion about the situation. At this point, the story or explanation we develop is based on metaphorical analysis, but it is no longer confined to it. The metaphors fade into the background as we bring the story forward to describe more completely what is going on in a particular situation. Consequently, the critical evaluation of our interpretations results in our playing one interpretation against another and has the potential of our choosing among them (Morgan, 1986).

A case vignette has been developed to illustrate this type of analysis. It is to this case that we now turn.

ILLUSTRATING METAPHORICAL ANALYSIS— AN EXAMPLE

Jean sits at her desk trying to figure things out. Earlier in the week she had received a call from the vice president of a major manufacturing firm, requesting that her university offer a major noncredit program on strategic planning for personnel in the division he leads. As head of the noncredit programs office in the university's office of continuing education, Jean informed her boss, the director of continuing education, of the contact. She also called Tim, the outreach program coordinator in the College of Business to tell him of the call and to ask that he pursue the program request with appropriate persons within his college.

Tim has been on the job less than a year, having been appointed by the college's dean. His position, which reports to the college's associate dean of instruction, was created using incentive funds provided by central administration to stimulate college involvement in continuing education programming for business and industry. Tim has been successful in increasing the size of the college's outreach program, but is frustrated by his lack of budget and policy control, which still resides in Jean's office and the university's office of continuing education, a unit of the university's provost for academic affairs. Tim and Jean have developed a very good working relationship, though, sharing similar philosophies about the importance of continuing education for the college and the university. But having to work constantly through Jean's office to offer programs has at times seemed inefficient and awkward to Tim.

After two days, Jean received a call from Tim who informed her that everything had been worked out, although he did have some concerns. Apparently the head of the college's management department had already had contact with the company's vice president, an influential alumnus of the department—even before Jean had received her call from the vice president. In this contact, the department head and vice-president had discussed program topics, and compensation for each faculty member who participated in the program had been established. The department head had also discussed these arrangements with the college's associate dean of instruction.

As Jean learned, the compensation package was twice the amount normally paid college faculty for teaching noncredit programs and three times the amount normally paid other faculty in the institution for like work. Earlier, it had been agreed that College of Business faculty would be paid more than other faculty for teaching noncredit programs. This position was supported by the provost, since market pressures demanded that a similar differential be used in establishing the salaries of College of Business faculty members. However, the agreement had not become formal policy and remained a tacit agreement between Tim and Jean, as well as between the director of continuing education and the college's dean.

Tim and Jean agreed that offering this program would be a good thing for the college and university. It would respond to central administration's agenda to expand the college's outreach offerings, and it would be a programmatic response to one of the most important businesses in the state. The program, if offered on a contractual basis, would cover the compensation package that had been negotiated, as well as bring a good deal of money into the continuing education office; and it would allow Jean and Tim to develop relationships with an academic unit that until now had not participated in continuing education programming. Tim also explained that the faculty of this department had grown accustomed to receiving large honoraria for their consulting activities, and because of departmental size and prestige, had routinely been able to garner support of college and university leadership for its various initiatives. Tim noted that the department chair had informed him that no program would be offered unless faculty received the amount of pay that he had negotiated. Tim and Jean also admitted, however, that agreeing to pay the larger amount for teaching went against their instructor compensation policy and might very well set a bad precedent for future programming.

The decision is really up to Jean, since her boss has delegated responsibility in this area to her. Offering the program would have positive and negative consequences. So too would not offering the program. What is she to do?

Diagnostic Reading

This case illustrates the complexity, ambiguity, and paradoxical nature of organizational situations faced by program planners. As Jean sits at her desk, she might be tempted to respond emotionally, pointing to personality attributes of any of the actors in the case. A more systematic analysis would, however, give her more information and point to some action she could take.

The Machine Metaphor. Let's start with the machine metaphor. Using this metaphor, we notice that something is amiss with the organizational structure. Tim has responsibility but little authority and control, especially in allocating resources; Jean has control, but her responsibility is not tied as directly as Tim's to the college's programs. Because Jean's and Tim's roles and positions overlap somewhat, there is some lack of clarity about who does what. The structural arrangement has given rise to inefficiencies because many different people, reporting in different chains of command, must confer before any decision is made. In addition, tracing the chain of command through the organizational chart shows that the situation would actually have to go all the way to the provost for resolution, since both the college's dean and director of continuing education report to the provost. Another reporting line for Tim, either to Jean or her boss, would help centralize responsibility and authority, creating a more efficient organizational arrangement. So too would be a transfer of both programmatic and budget control and responsibility to the college and in turn to Tim. From this viewpoint, the nature of the organization is confusing and the role of the organization for providing a structure for programming is less than ideal.

The Organism Metaphor. From the perspective of the organism metaphor, we notice that the institution is indeed open to environmental influences, the request of the company's vice president creating a potentially precedent-setting situation for the university, the college, and the office of continuing education. The company can be viewed as both a resource and consumer public. Offering the program to the company would generate some important inputs to the institution in the form of program participants and money, contributing to negative entropy and, in turn, to organizational growth and survival. In addition, the program's alumni (outputs), with improved knowledge and skills, would return to their jobs better able to assist the company in its strategic planning. Responding would also increase noncredit programming in business, assisting the university in adapting to its environment.

We also observe that the establishment of Tim's position is a form of differentiation, since an office specializing in business programming for a particular segment of the adult learner population responds to this principle. Interdependencies are also very much in evidence, with Tim's and Jean's offices being dependent on each other to offer the program. However, we also note that integrating mechanisms are weak: Tim and Jean are left primarily to their own devices to deal with the situation. The nature of the organization is therefore an open one, affected by the external environment, but also able to adapt to it. The organization has also provided Jean and Tim with resources for programming in the form of faculty expertise and funding for Tim's position. Although the case is not specific about this, we can safely assume that other resources are also available. But the level of integration necessary to coordinate activities, even with these resources, is not what it could be.

The Political Arena Metaphor. Use of the political arena metaphor results in the identification of another whole set of factors. As you recall, the central focus of analysis using this metaphor is the relation among interests, conflict, and power. Several interests are evident in the case. The vice president of the company is interested in obtaining some programs for his division's employees. The university's central administration is interested in improving the college's responsiveness in outreach, having demonstrated that interest by funding Tim's position. Although not clear in the case, we might expect that the provision of this money was tied to some expectations for increased programming.

Both Tim and Jean are also interested in expanding the college's offerings and, except for the problem with instructor compensation, this situation affords them an opportunity to pursue their interests in this area. Tim has an interest in dealing with the inefficiency which he has experienced in programming. One interest of the department head and his faculty is abundantly clear— they wish to be compensated well for the time and effort they put into offering the program. But both Tim and Jean are interested in maintaining, to the extent they can, an equitable compensation policy in the college. In addition, Jean is concerned about how such a deviation from the compensation policy might be received by other parts of the campus.

There are many areas where interests coincide in the case, but there is also a significant area of conflict. We can also ask whether there is a coalition of interests at work as well. For example, how do the interests of other faculty in the College of Business relate to those of the faculty in question?; is the dean supportive of the department head's approach?; what interest does the provost have in this matter?; and will faculty in other colleges feel exploited if the department head is successful in obtaining the amount of pay he is requesting? The case does not provide us with this information, but it is information that Jean may wish to obtain to the extent she can before proceeding.

The next step is for us to ask who has the power to reconcile this conflict and how. The college dean, Jean, and her boss appear to have position power in this instance (as does the provost, if the problem were to be referred up the chain of command), but position power appears to be matched and perhaps exceeded by the expert and personal power of the department head and his faculty. Apparently, the dean and provost have regularly conceded to departmental wishes on a host of other issues. Coercion certainly does not seem to be a fruitful course of action in this case. Even if used successfully, the long-term impact might be to interfere with most actors' interest in expanding the college's continuing education offerings. It appears that negotiation and some form of compromise might work. Perhaps establishing a funding pool for the department (for professional travel, graduate assistants, etc.), using the difference between what Jean and Tim want to pay and the amount the department head demands, would resolve the conflict. But would the department be interested in this? If not, will Jean have to bow to the source of power inherent in this situation and just live with the long-term consequences?

The Culture Metaphor. The culture metaphor focuses our attention on the implicit values, norms, and beliefs that are at work in the situation. It also asks us to look for symbols of meaning that may give us additional insight. According to this metaphor, standard operating norms develop over time through human interaction. It appears that some of these norms have developed to guide Tim's and Jean's working relationship. But it also may be that they have confronted too few conflict situations to develop a shared belief system and way of dealing with such occurrences. Conflict in values is readily apparent in the value that different actors place on money. The department head and his faculty value it highly, evidently viewing it as the dominant instrumental motivation for their participating in the program. Jean and Tim appear to place more value on the intrinsic worth of continuing education itself and the importance of institutional responsiveness to adult learner needs. They are not only frustrated but puzzled about how a faculty could take such a "mercenary" approach in this situation.

This conflict in values also suggests that two subcultures exist in the case. Perhaps this can be attributed in part to (a) the college's association with business and industry and the profit motive which serves as a primary value in this segment of society, (b) the value departmental faculty place on consulting and the extra compensation they derive from it, and (c) Jean's and Tim's beliefs about continuing education in which the value of service dominates. Viewing the situation from the perspective of subcultures also brings into question how well Tim has been socialized into his new culture and whether over time he might increasingly buy into the subculture of the college or become increasingly alienated from it.

When we look for symbols, none is obvious. Perhaps the most we could say is that, other than extra compensation, there is an absence of symbols associated with different types of faculty rewards for participation in the college's and institution's continuing education programs. As a result, the faculty of the department have been drawn to the only symbol available, one with which they have worked in the past and with which they feel comfortable.

Critical Evaluation

Having generated these four interpretations of the case, the next step is to critically evaluate the usefulness of each interpretation in order to arrive at a synthesis of relevant points. This synthesis, or "story line," would minimally have to integrate the following observations:

1. The apparent deficiency in organizational structure
2. The lack of integration needed to deal with differentiation in function
3. Contributions the program would make to additional environmental adaptation
4. The conflict in interests that exists over the issue of extra compensation
5. The power that is at work in the situation
6. Differences in values that may be associated with different organizational subcultures

If one decides that lack of control and coordination are central to understanding the situation, then factors 1 and 2 become the focal elements of the story line, and the remaining factors become supporting themes. In this case a negative analogy is obtained in which a gap is apparent between what is observed and what the metaphors recommend. As a result, guides to action are provided. If actions were taken to introduce more control and coordination, then one would have to consider what effect these actions would have on factors 3 through 6. The nature of the organizational sponsor in this instance is one characterized by loose structure and poor coordination. The role of the organization to provide the coordination and structure for programming is lacking, and information about how its role can be strengthened is provided.

We might choose to focus on the cultural dimensions of the situation. However, we notice that only sketchy information about this aspect of the case is available. An analysis using the cultural metaphor results, therefore, in a neutral analogy in which we are unclear about whether the cultural features of the case belong to the negative or positive type of analogy. Choosing this particular focus would consequently require us to inquire more into this aspect of the situation so that we could determine whether a positive or negative analogy was more applicable.

If, however, we decide that the character of this situation is primarily political, then factors 4 and 5 come to the fore, and the remaining factors are viewed as elements which serve only to complicate the conflict and power play which characterize the situation. One can argue that use of the political arena metaphor results in a positive analogy because it best reflects what is going on in this situation. As a result, it provides us with the best understanding and explanation of the most relevant organizational dynamics. It also provides us with guides for action. But in this instance, the guides are not corrective, as for a negative analogy, but reflective and suggestive of how we might proceed in the situation as it currently exists. For example, if one chose to negotiate in this situation, factors 1, 2, 3, and 6 serve not as guides to action, but rather as additional knowledge to inform the approach one might take in attempting to resolve the conflict.

The development of different story lines is a critical element in an organizational analysis of this type. It has the strength of providing program planners with different pictures of organizational situations, as well as with guides for different actions to take in dealing with them. As Morgan (1986) notes,

> The process of *critical evaluation* thus requires that we explore competing explanations and arrive at judgments regarding the way that they fit together. Rather than attempt to make the facts of a situation fit a given theoretical scheme (as happens in much conventional organizational analysis), the method developed here takes account of the complexity of a situation by playing one interpretation against another and, when necessary, choosing between them. Again, in contrast with many conventional approaches, the process does not hinge on spotting isolated problems and finding piecemeal solutions. Rather it is an open-ended mode of inquiry that allows problem

definitions and possible solutions to emerge from the readings on which the analysis is based. (p. 331)

But understanding organizational situations does not alone provide all the information needed to make a judgment about how to proceed. Other information, including detail about the broader situation, as well as about one's own philosophical approach to adult education and program planning, must be factored into decision making. How Jean will proceed will depend upon her own philosophical orientation, as well as upon other data she may have about the situation. This case not only illustrates the importance of understanding our organizations, but it also underscores the philosophical, ethical, and other dimensions which comprise the complex situations that program planners face.

CONCLUDING REMARKS

This chapter has been dedicated to describing a means by which program planners' understanding of their organizations can be broadened and deepened. Several metaphors of organization have been presented, and a way has been described to use metaphorical analysis to obtain a more complete understanding of our organizations and the particular situations we face in them. This chapter has provided only an introduction to several metaphors that can be employed in such analyses. Other metaphors are also recommended for consideration, and readers are referred especially to Morgan's (1986) *Images of Organization* and Bolman and Deal's (1984, 1991) books on organizational frames for further information and inquiry about the metaphors reviewed, as well as about others.

Initially, use of this form of organizational analysis takes time and effort, especially for those unfamiliar with the metaphors and the mode of analysis they require. Through practice, however, metaphorical analysis can become second nature, affording us an approach to organizational analysis that occurs naturally and is built into other patterns of thought we commonly employ in planning programs.

But metaphorical analysis is also predicated upon a continual process of adding to one's store of images. To use it most effectively, we must be open to learning about metaphors developed from new concepts about organizations. You are also encouraged to develop your own metaphors of the organizations in which you work, metaphors which also have the potential for increasing understanding and guiding action (Morgan, 1993). For instance, metaphors have been recently employed to describe different dimensions of organizations of continuing higher education. Edelson (1989), suggests, for example, that continuing education is like a sailboat, dependent upon the changing winds of enrollment patterns for its direction and locomotion. Drawing on continuing education's place at the boundary of the institution (the organism metaphor), King and Lerner (1992) see continuing education as the institution's front parlor, where those internal and external to the institution gather for dialogue. Donaldson (1992) has built upon this front parlor metaphor to describe continuing education as the front porch of the institution, a location less hampered by institutional boundaries and a place where those outside the institution feel more comfortable and welcome—a metaphor that deals in part with the issue of access.

These are just some examples of the way metaphors can be used to help us understand the nature and role of the organizational sponsors of adult and continuing education programs. But they are also examples that help guide our actions and provide meaning for the activities to which we are dedicated. Metaphors serve as powerful analytical tools and capture much of the meaning we associate with our work. The key, however, is not to become so comfortable with preferred metaphors that they limit our thinking. Metaphors empower us only to the extent that we employ a variety of them, including ones we create, to add richness to the repertoire of images that make up our professional knowledge.

QUESTIONS FOR STUDY AND DISCUSSION

1. What other "story lines" might you develop for the case presented in this chapter? What do these tell you about the organizational situation, and what suggestions do they have for your action?
2. The case vignette is set within the context of university continuing education. If this is not your practice context, think about how the case might be modified to fit your situation (some elaboration of details would also be acceptable). Having revised the case, what interpretations would you make, and to

what "story lines" could these lead? How do these inform your understanding of the situation and how might they guide your actions?

3. Most people have a preferred way of viewing organizations. Which of the several metaphors presented do you prefer? Why? How might you further complicate your thinking to strengthen your ability to analyze the organizational situations you face?

4. The metaphors of organizations as instruments of domination and as psychic traps were introduced in the chapter but were not used in the metaphorical analysis. What additional insights about the case do these two metaphors provide? What additional actions do these insights suggest?

5. Put yourself in Jean's position. Using the different metaphors as guides, what additional information about the situation would you seek? What action would you take in this situation? Why?

6. Think about a program planning situation that you have recently faced or that you have recently observed. Then apply the metaphors to analyze the organizational context of this situation. What positive, neutral, or negative analogies can you derive from this analysis? What insights have you gained about the situation? What further information gathering does the analysis suggest? What guides to action result from your analysis?

7. What metaphors can you develop that help you better understand the nature and role of your organization in program planning? How do these guide your actions?

REFERENCES

Argyris, C., & Schön, D. A. (1974). *Theory in practice: Increasing professional effectiveness.* San Francisco: Jossey-Bass.

Beder, H. W. (1978). An environmental interaction model for agency development in adult education. *Adult Education, 28,* 176–190.

Bolman, L. G., & Deal, T. E. (1984). *Modern approaches to understanding and managing organizations.* San Francisco: Jossey-Bass.

Bolman, L. G., & Deal, T. E. (1991). *Reframing organizations: Artistry, choice, and leadership.* San Francisco: Jossey-Bass.

Boyle, P. G. (1981). *Planning better programs.* New York: McGraw-Hill.

Burnham, B. R. (1988). Program planning as technology in three adult education organizations. *Adult Education Quarterly, 38,* 211–223.

Candy, P. C. (1986). The eye of the beholder: Metaphor in adult education research. *International Journal of Lifelong Education, 5,* 87–111.

Cervero, R. M. (1988). *Effective continuing education for professionals.* San Francisco: Jossey-Bass.

Cervero, R. M., & Wilson, A. L. (1994). *Planning responsibly for adult education: A guide to negotiating power and interests.* San Francisco: Jossey-Bass.

Chaffee, E. E. (1984). Successful strategic management in small private colleges. *Journal of Higher Education, 55,* 212–241.

Chaffee, E. E. (1985). Three models of strategy. *Academy of Management Review, 10,* 89–98.

Cookson, P. S. (1989). Recruiting and retaining adult students: An organizational theory perspective. In P. S. Cookson (Ed.). *Recruiting and retaining adult students (New Directions for Continuing Education,* No. 41, pp. 13–22). San Francisco: Jossey-Bass.

Darkenwald, G. G., & Merriam S. B. (1982). *Adult education: Foundations of Practice.* New York: Harper & Row.

Deal, T. E. (1987). Building an effective organizational culture: How to be community oriented in a traditional institution. In R. G. Simerly & Associates. *Strategic planning and leadership in continuing education* (pp. 87–102). San Francisco: Jossey-Bass.

Deshler, D. (1990). Metaphor analysis: Exorcizing social ghosts. In J. Mezirow & Associates. *Fostering critical reflection in adulthood: A guide to transformative and emancipatory learning* (pp. 296–313). San Francisco: Jossey-Bass.

Donaldson, J. F. (1989). Recruiting and retaining adult students in continuing higher education. In P. S. Cookson (Ed.). *Recruiting and retaining adult students (New Directions for Continuing Education,* No. 41, pp. 63–78). San Francisco: Jossey-Bass.

Donaldson, J. F. (1990). *Managing credit programs in continuing higher education.* Urbana, IL: University of Illinois.

Donaldson, J. F. (1991) New opportunities or a new marginality: Strategic issues in continuing higher education. *Continuing Higher Education Review, 55,* 120–128.

Donaldson, J. F. (1992). The organization of continuing higher education: Responding to the 90's. *Metropolitan Universities, 3*(2), 26–35.

Edelson, P. (1989, October). *Some observations on model building in continuing education.* Paper presented at the Region II National University Continuing Education Association Conference, Baltimore, MD.

Forester, J. (1989). *Planning in the face of power.* Berkeley, CA: University of California Press.

Freire, P. (1970). *Pedagogy of the oppressed.* New York: Seabury Press.

Gordon, M. (1980). Organization. In H. J. Alford (Ed.). *Power and conflict in continuing education: Survival and prosperity for all?* (pp. 168–198). Belmont, CA: Wadsworth.

Harmon, M. M., & Mayer, R. T. (1986). *Organization theory for public administration.* Boston: Little, Brown and Company.

Hentschel, D. (1991). The case for the hybrid model for implementing the continuing education mission. *Continuing Higher Education Review, 55,* 155–167.

Holt, M. E. (1987). Using evaluation to monitor plans and assess results. In R. G.

Simerly & Associates. *Strategic planning and leadership in continuing education* (pp. 168–184). San Francisco: Jossey-Bass.

Houle, C. O. (1972). *The design of education.* San Francisco: Jossey-Bass.

Jarvis, P. (1985). *The sociology of adult and continuing education.* London: Croom Helm.

Katz, D., & Kahn, R. L. (1978). *The social psychology of organizations* (2nd ed.). New York: John Wiley.

Keeley, M. (1980). Organizational analogy: A comparison of organismic and social contract models. *Administrative Science Quarterly, 25,* 337–362.

King, B. K., & Lerner, A. W. (1992). Organization structure and performance dynamics in continuing education administration. In A. W. Lerner and B. K. King (Eds.). *Continuing higher education: The coming wave* (pp. 83–99). New York: Teachers College Press.

Knowles, M. S. (1980). *The modern practice of adult education: From pedagogy to andragogy* (revised and updated). New York: Cambridge.

Knox, A. B. (1981). The continuing education agency and its parent organization. In J. C. Votruba (Ed.), *Strengthening internal support for continuing education* (*New Directions for Continuing Education,* No. 9, pp. 1–11). San Francisco: Jossey-Bass.

Knox, A. B. (1982). *Leadership strategies for meeting new challenges* (*New Directions for Continuing Education,* No. 13). San Francisco: Jossey-Bass.

Lauffer, A. (1978). *Doing continuing education and staff development.* New York: McGraw-Hill.

Mezirow, J. (1991). *Transformative dimensions of adult learning.* San Francisco: Jossey-Bass.

Mills, D. P., Jr., Cervero, R. M., Langone, C. A., & Wilson, A. L. (1995). The impact of interests, power relationships, and organizational structure on program planning practice: A case study. *Adult Education Quarterly, 46*(1), 1–16.

Morgan, G. (1980). Paradigms, metaphors, and puzzle solving in organization theory. *Administrative Science Quarterly, 25,* 605–622.

Morgan, G. (1986). *Images of organization.* Beverly Hills, CA: Sage.

Morgan, G. (1993). *Imaginization: The art of creative management.* Newbury Park, CA: Sage.

Pennington, F., & Green, J. (1976). Comparative analysis of program development processes in six professions. *Adult Education, 27,* 13–23.

Peters, J. M., & Associates. (1980). *Building an effective adult education enterprise.* San Francisco: Jossey-Bass.

Proctor, R. F. II. (1991). Metaphors of adult education: Beyond penance toward family. *Adult Education Quarterly, 41,* 63–74.

Schön, D. A. (1987). *Educating the reflective practitioner.* San Francisco: Jossey-Bass.

Schroeder, W. L. (1980). Typology of adult learning systems. In J. M. Peters & associates. *Building an effective adult education enterprise* (pp. 41–77). San Francisco: Jossey-Bass.

Scott, W. R. (1987). *Organizations: Rational, natural, and open systems* (2nd ed.). Englewood Cliffs, NJ: Prentice-Hall.

Strother, G. B., & Klus, J. P. (1982). *Administration of continuing education.* Belmont, CA: Wadsworth.

Thompson, J. D. (1967). *Organizations in action: Social science bases of administrative theory.* New York: McGraw-Hill.

Votruba, J. C. (1987). From marginality to mainstream: Strategies for increasing internal support for continuing education. In R. G. Simerly & Associates. *Strategic planning and leadership in continuing education* (pp. 185–201). San Francisco: Jossey-Bass.

9

What We Need to Know about Adult Learners

Jovita M. Ross-Gordon

ABSTRACT

This chapter reviews what we know about adult learners who participate in education and training programs. The vast literature on physiological changes that accompany movement through the life cycle, together with their implications for program planning, are described. Adults are subject to a variety of motivations to participate in educational programs. The process whereby they learn has been described in terms of behaviorist, cognitivist, humanistic, social learning, andragogical, transformative, and adult development theories of learning. Theoretical explanations of the changes that accompany aging are discussed in terms of life cycle theories, developmental stages, and life events. The literature on learning and cognitive styles is reviewed and the topic of underrepresented groups is highlighted. All of this information is then analyzed and summarized. The chapter concludes with a detailed description of three situations that illustrate the characteristics of adults as learners reviewed: learning disabled adults in an adult basic education setting, women and minority employees in a corporate training program, and a group of older adults enrolled in a community college program on voluntarism.

ASSESSMENT

1. What are the most typical motivations for adult learning? Do these represent primarily intrinsic or extrinsic influences?

2. Describe several learning theories, including at least one geared specifically toward adult learning.
3. What are the basic assumptions associated with andragogy?
4. Explain the key concepts associated with two life cycle or phase theories of adult development as well as two stage theories. Also identify two or more life events which may serve as triggers for adult learning experiences and explain how these events are likely to influence the learners' motivation and choice of learning content.
5. What do you see as the meaning and significance of the term *learning style* with reference to planning educational programs for adults?
6. Identify three instruments or methods of assessing learning style that you are familiar with. What dimensions of learning style do they measure? Is there one best instrument?

KEY TERMS AND CONCEPTS

Andragogy A term popularized by Malcolm Knowles. It is used to describe a set of assumptions about adult learners, linked with correlated principles for the instruction of adults. Andragogy has been traditionally distinguished from pedagogy—the art and science of instruction, commonly associated with the "schooling" of children and young adults. More recently dichotomies between pedagogy and andragogy based on age have been less rigidly drawn (Knowles, 1980, 1984).

Cohort A group of individuals bound by a common set of life experiences, often discussed relative to having lived during a major historical epoch or social event while in a given developmental period (e.g., the "Baby Boom Generation," or "Children of the Depression" or "Flower Children of the 60s") but can be used in a more restricted sense (e.g., class of 1995; incoming freshmen; those entering the work force in 1998).

Developmental task A task "which arises at or about a certain period in the life of the individual, successful achievement of which leads to his happiness and to success with later tasks, while failure leads to unhappiness in the individual, disapproval by the society, and difficulty with later tasks" (Havighurst, 1953, p. 2).

Cognitive style; learning style An individual's preferred style of learning. The terms will be used interchangeably here because clear distinctions in their use have not been maintained in the literature (Bonham, 1988). Learning style has been used to refer to a number of types of preferences including modality preferences (e.g., visual, auditory, haptic), environmental preferences (e.g., quiet, with background music), interactive preferences (learning alone versus learning in groups), and preferences for taking in and processing information (assimilator, diverger, converger, or accommodator). Cognitive style has more often been discussed as relatively stable characteristics or traits which affect everything the individual does in organizing experience (Brundage & MacKeracher, 1980).

Participatory planning Assumes the greatest involvement of participants, potential participants, or their representatives in the vital stages of program planning, from goal setting to evaluation.

Transition An event or non-event resulting in change (Schlossberg, 1984, p. 43). A non-event in this case can be conceptualized as a desired or anticipated occurrence, which by its failure to occur prompts change in the individual. For instance, the lack of a job promotion can act as a non-event, leading to dissatisfaction with the job situation and providing an impetus for learning.

INTRODUCTION

Curriculum design typically incorporates assessment of learners' skills and abilities as well as subject matter expertise. Generally going beyond traditional curriculum design models by emphasizing involvement of participants and potential participants, or their representatives in the planning process, program planning models drawn from adult education rely to a greater extent on general knowledge of adult learner characteristics. To effectively incorporate such dimensions, the program planner will need to draw on a large body of information about both common patterns and individual variability among adult learners.

This chapter will focus on the commonalties, with the caveat that knowledge of these common characteristics provides only a basis from which to come to know the individual learners in a particular program. As such, the chapter will aim to familiarize or reacquaint the reader with current theories and research findings regarding the impact of aging on the learning processes, motivations of adult learners, adult development, learning styles and preferences, and particular considerations for learners often underrepresented in certain kinds of programs.

SUMMARY OF THE LITERATURE

Physiological and Intellectual Changes with Aging

Sensory Changes

Aging in the visual system appears to take place at two levels (Fozard et al., 1977). First, changes between the ages of 35 and 45 affect the transmission of light to the retina and the ability of the eye to accommodate. These are reflected in presbyopia (far-sightedness), and changes in sensitivity to glare, sensitivity to color, and depth perception (Perlmutter & Hall, 1985). The second level of changes affect the retina and nervous system, contributing to slowing in visual processing. Illumination needs can be compensated for with increased lighting in the learning environment. Yet, Perlmutter and Hall (1985) note that "No matter how much the light level is raised, 60-year olds cannot see as clearly as 20-year olds" (p. 186).

Gradual but consistent decline in hearing capacity begins around age 25, with noticeable changes starting during the mid-30s (Perlmutter & Hall, 1985, p. 189). The progressive age-related loss of the ability to hear high-pitch sounds is called presbycusis. Tinnitus (ringing in the ear) is another common hearing problem associated with age. Hearing losses result from sensory, neural, metabolic, and mechanical changes, leaving 16 percent of the population deaf by age 75. Most of us are aware of reduction in sound volume in our older relatives, colleagues, and friends, and we may assume that speaking louder or using a hearing aid to magnify sounds will compensate for this problem. Changes in ability to discriminate speech sounds, above and beyond actual changes in sound perception, make this assumption invalid. Many

hearing aids do not differentially amplify sounds, leaving low frequency sounds too loud as they amplify everything equally. It is also
likely that because of a low level of social acceptance of hearing
aids, older adults may be less likely to get corrective aids for hearing
loss than for visual loss. Yet, hearing loss can have a significant
impact on their ability to communicate effectively in group learning situations. This calls for teachers to be sensitive to signs of
difficulty in hearing. Perlmutter and Hall (1985) suggest that
"Hearing difficulties of older people can be eased if their conversa-
tional partners lower their voices, speak slowly and distinctly, and
look directly at them while talking" (p. 191). Their suggestion
implies the benefit of preferential seating near the front of a room
for individuals of any age with a hearing loss, and the disadvantage
of scheduling large groups of older individuals in an environment
that does not allow this type of adaptation.

Intellectual Changes

Early studies of adult intellectual functioning done by Thorndike and others, cited in Merriam and Caffarella (1991), concluded
that intelligence peaked in late adolescence to early adulthood,
then began to decline. These conclusions have been challenged
over the years, and we now know that it is possible "to teach an old
dog new tricks." Lorge (1944) was among the first to question the
extent to which timed tests led to an impression of reduced functioning as an artifact of slowed processing speed with aging. The
work of Cattell (1963) and others built on this discovery, suggesting
that adults exhibited diminished performance with age only on
certain abilities, particularly such abilities as memory span and
spatial perception—associated with what is called *fluid intelligence.*
With respect to other abilities, associated with what is referred to as
crystallized intelligence (abilities depending on judgment and experience, vocabulary, general information, and arithmetical reasoning), adults were found to remain stable in abilities or even show
improvement. Schaie and Parr (1981) hypothesized that different
stages of life may well call for different learning abilities.

Clearly one's definition of intelligence and means of measurement of intelligence have an impact on the conclusions one draws
regarding adult intellectual abilities. Definitions of intelligence
and means of measurement to date have tended to focus on a
limited range of abilities closely associated with academic perfor-

mance (Merriam & Caffarella, 1991). Differences in research methods have also influenced conclusions regarding intellectual change with aging. Cross-sectional studies comparing different age groups tend to exaggerate age differences, but also measure differences related to poor health and cohort effects (Cross, 1981; Merriam & Caffarella, 1991). Longitudinal designs, however, may minimize age-related changes due to selective dropout, with the healthiest and best educated remaining in follow-up samples longer (Merriam & Caffarella, 1991). Based on alternative designs which combine cross-sectional and longitudinal components (following several age-cohorts over a period of time), Schaie (1979) concluded that reliable age decrement in intellectual abilities does not occur for all abilities and all individuals until as late as the 80s. Significantly for adult educators, it has been found older adults are amenable to training of certain abilities, with limited periods of training and learning strategies leading to full restoration of earlier levels of ability (Willis & Schaie, 1985).

The bottom line for adult educators is that research on age-related change in intellectual abilities of adults suggests that their capacities remain stable well into their later years. Future research, focusing on a broader range of intellectual abilities, such as Gardner's (1983, 1995) seven factors of intelligence and Sternberg's (1985, 1994) triarchic theory of intelligence, may tell us more about adults' practical as well as academic intelligence and the effects of experience and culture on learning abilities.

Why Adults Participate and Why Not

The well-informed program planner is likely to have some understanding regarding the various reasons adults have been found to participate in educational programs, as well as some understanding of a variety of factors which may serve as barriers to their decisions to participate. Houle's (1961) qualitative case studies of 22 men and women who were exceptional adult learners is often cited as the seminal work in the area of adult motivations for learning. Based on focused interviews, he developed a three-way typology, the elements of which continue to appear today in typologies generated by factor analytic procedures. Houle described three types of adult learners. *Goal-oriented* learners use learning to meet specific objectives, such as learning to supervise employees or learning to effectively parent teenage children. Authors writing subsequently to Houle repeatedly suggest this is the most common group of adult learners (Boshier & Collins, 1985; Tough, 1979; Aslanian & Brickell, 1980). The second group of learners, those who are *activity-oriented*, participate primarily for the sake of activity itself. They may learn in order to collect credits or to escape boredom, but exhibit minimal interest in the content of the learning, either for its own sake or its practical value. The third type of adult learner was referred to by Houle as *learning oriented*; they pursue learning for its own sake and seek continual opportunities for learning in their choices of work and leisure activities.

The fundamental nature of Houle's work can be found in the similarities of his findings and those of subsequent researchers using a variety of methods. Tough (1979) used interviews with adults engaged in self-directed learning projects as the source of his conclusions regarding adult motivations to learn. Although his findings suggest that adults frequently have multiple reasons for learning, the three patterns he identified as origins for learning projects bear remarkable similarity to Houle's typology: (1) some learners start with an awareness that they want to do something and seek out learning activities that provide needed knowledge and skills; (2) some learners start with a basic curiosity and seek learning to broaden their awareness or understanding related to the topic or issue in question; and (3) some learners start with a decision to spend some extra time on learning, deciding subsequently what they will learn during that time.

Subsequent research on motivational typologies comprised such techniques as factor analysis (Burgess, 1971; Morstain & Smart, 1974) and cluster analysis (Boshier & Collins, 1985) to develop typologies of adult learners. Yet, parallels can be drawn between typologies developed through these methods and the earlier work of Houle (Merriam & Caffarella, 1991).

Survey questionnaires have provided an alternative method of identifying adults' motivations for participation (Carp, Peterson, & Roelfs, 1974), adding information on what adults study to the more abstract typologies of why they study. Results from such surveys, including the most recent triennial survey by National Center for Education Statistics (NCES), indicate that most adults are involved in adult education for practical reasons. The 1984 NCES triennial survey revealed that 64 percent of adult education participants were involved in adult education to get a job or advance in their present job (Snyder, 1988), supporting the findings reported by Tough (1979) and Aslanian and Brickell (1980) that transitions related to career life are a major impetus for adult learning. Cross (1981) concluded from her analysis of studies of adult participation that most adults give practical, pragmatic reasons for learning. Yet, she also pointed out that "Motives differ for different groups of learners, different stages of life, and most individuals have not one but multiple reasons for learning." In explicating some observed patterns relative to learning differences, she noted:

> Learning that will improve one's position in life is a major motivation. Just what will "improve life" varies with age, sex, occupation and life stage in rather predictable ways. Young people are primarily interested in education for upward career mobility; adults with a good job want a better one and those reaching career levels where additional education promises few extrinsic rewards are often interested in learning that will enhance quality of life and leisure. (1981, p. 97).

Learning Theories

One's conceptualization of adult learning and program planner roles depends, at least in part, on one's perspectives with regard to learning theory. While some may argue that they consider each learner and situation on an individual basis, the "adult educationalists" are likely to be aware of multiple theoretical frameworks, to have considered the match between their own educational philosophy and each of the prevailing learning theories, and to have come to appreciate one or more learning theories as providing a better fit with the typical learner clientele and situation with which they are most frequently in contact.

To aid the program planner in achieving the role of thoughtful educationist, a review will be presented here of the major learning theories applied across the life span, as well as two theories framed more particularly with regard to adult learning.

Behaviorist

One of the major pervasive theoretical models of learning is that of behaviorism. It is associated with the work of theorists like Thorndike, Tolman, Hull, and perhaps best known is the work of B. F. Skinner (Dubin & Okun, 1973; Merriam & Caffarella, 1991). Merriam and Caffarella (1991), citing Grippin and Peters (1984), reviewed three basic assumptions common to behaviorist learning theories. First, observable behavior rather than internal thought processes is the focus of study; in particular, learning is manifested by a change in behavior. Second, the environment shapes one's behavior; what one learns is determined by the elements in the environment, not by the individual learner. And third, the principles of contiguity (how close in time two events must be for a bond to be formed) and reinforcement (any means of increasing the likelihood that an event will be repeated) are central to explaining the learning process (Merriam & Caffarella, 1991, p. 126). According to this view of the learning process, the teacher's role is one of designing an environment that will elicit desired behavior and extinguish undesirable behavior. The influence of behaviorist theory is more easily observed in adult education contexts which utilize programmed instruction, competency-based education, and computer-assisted instruction as well as more generally in adult job training and vocational education. Yet, the influence of a behaviorist model is pervasive in program planning models applied to a diversity of settings, insofar as such models build on the curriculum development models of Ralph Tyler (Pennington & Green, 1976; Tyler, 1959).

Cognitivist

An early challenge to behaviorist learning theories came from Gestalt learning theorists, who placed emphasis on perception, insight, and meanings (Hergenhahn, 1988). To a Gestaltist, learning often flows from a flash of insight—placing the locus of control with the individual rather than the environment. This shift to the individual learner's mental processes is a feature of cognitivist learning theories. Classical cognitive theorists like Piaget, Ausubel, and Bruner have focused on the internal processes whereby individuals acquire and make meaning of information. Despite this commonality, distinctions among these theories and their implications for instruction are discernible. For instance, Ausubel's emphasis on reception learning through linking new knowledge to existing cognitive structures suggests an active role for instructors in investigating the learner's prior knowledge and presenting new information so as to clarify its connections to prior learning. Bruner, on the other hand, emphasizes learning through discovery, with the process of transforming evidence to gain new insights;

the instructor's role is limited to arranging the environment to facilitate the learner's independent discovery. A cognitive theorist sometimes referred to as a neobehaviorist (Dubin & Okun, 1973; Merriam & Caffarella, 1991). Gagne, Briggs, and Wager (1988) have detailed the precise types of learning and associated instructional processes. Contemporary research and theory formation in the cognitivist tradition include schema theory, artificial intelligence, information processing models, and "learning to learn" models (Smith, 1982).

Humanistic

Humanistic learning theorists focus on learning from the perspective of human growth. Maslow's theory of human motivation as a hierarchy of needs earns him consideration as the founder of humanistic psychology. Indeed the highest need in his hierarchy, self-actualization, often serves as the slogan of supporters of humanistic learning theories. Carl Roger's (1983) principles of significant learning describe the kind of learning he perceives as leading to personal growth and development. Such learning is characterized by personal involvement, self-initiative, its pervasiveness, and provision for evaluation by the learner. Clearly the work of these humanistic theorists has had a significant influence on Malcolm Knowles and his concept of andragogy, as he himself admits (Knowles, 1980) (see also Chapter 2 in this volume).

Social Learning

Merriam and Caffarella (1991) add to their list of conventionally discussed general learning theories, the more socially oriented and often overlooked theories of Bandura and Rotter. Consistent with cognitive theories, Bandura focused on cognitive processes involved in attending to a model and learning vicariously through observation. Unlike the cognitive theorists, he emphasized the reciprocal relationships between individuals and their environment, and unlike behaviorists, he emphasized their self-regulatory ability to influence their environment. Similarly, Rotter's theory incorporates features of behaviorism, cognitivism, and personality theory in his concept of expectancy; behaviors are said to be more likely to occur if the individual perceives a particular (valued) reinforcement as a consequence of the behavior. Such expectations grow out of the social context of prior experience.

Linked to this theory is Rotter's more widely known concept of locus of control, with some individuals exhibiting a personality that is more externally controlled, while others exhibit a greater degree of internal control. Strategies consistent with social learning theories such as those of Bandura and Rotter include mentoring, apprenticeship, on the job training, and internships. Each involves learning contextually in a social situation whereby novice learners are influenced by the modeling of more experienced teachers or coworkers.

Constructivism

Receiving increasing attention over the last several years has been a viewpoint on learning and knowledge development referred to as *constructivism*. A paradigm shift can be recognized in the literature of a number of subdisciplines of education, ranging from early childhood education through teacher professional development. A central tenet of the constructivist viewpoint is a focus on reality as determined by the experiences of the knower; external phenomena take on meaning as they are interpreted by the mind (Cooper, 1993). Hence, learning is seen as an active process of interpretation, integration, and transformation of one's experiential world (Pratt, 1993). Phillips (1995) points out that there are multiple strands of constructivism, and discusses the conceptual origins of these various strands in the work of such varied theorists as Dewey (1960), James (1920), Piaget (1980), and Vygotsky (1978). The contemporary re-analysis of these theories and their implications for educational practice has led to changes in classrooms which diminish at least some of the distinctions in education practice typically drawn between adult education practice and schooling. For instance, Feden (1994), in a discussion of "powerful new instructional strategies," emphasizes active learning through such strategies as teaching students strategies for learning, using cooperative learning strategies, and adapting to differing learning styles.

Andragogy

Each of the learning theories discussed so far have been proposed without regard to age of the learner and may thus be regarded as theories of human learning, though not specifically adult learning. A chapter on program planning for adult learners would not be complete without some mention of prominent theories regarding adult learning. Most notable of these is Knowles's conception of andragogy, summarized by Knowles himself in Chapter 2 of this volume. Indeed, considerable debate has emerged in recent years regarding whether it is more a theory about adult learning or a philosophical stance (Pratt, 1993), whether this is a theory of learning or teaching (Hartree, 1984), whether it provides a complete and unified theory of learning (Hartree, 1984; Tennant, 1986), whether it describes adult learning as it is or prescribes some ideal standard of adult learning (Brookfield, 1986; Tennant, 1986), and whether it is a theory which actually distinguishes child learning from that of adults (Day & Baskett, 1982; Geber, 1988; Hartree, 1984; Pratt, 1988; Tennant, 1986). The depth of this debate does not diminish the importance that those who plan programs for adults should be aware of this prominent theory; such awareness is essential if the reader is to critically assess both the theory and its critique (Pratt, 1993). Whether a theory of learning or instruction, five basic assumptions about adult learners lie at the core of andragogy as discussed by Knowles (1980, 1984).

First, it is presumed that adult learners generally have a psychological disposition towards self-direction. Knowles claims that adults exert self-direction in most aspects of their lives, and resist educational environments which restrict their ability to exercise self-direction in their learning. While he admits in later writings (Knowles, 1984) that adults may not always be prepared for self-directed learning and that children are capable of self-direction in specific situations, he nonetheless sees adults as generally preferring and capable of a significant degree of self-direction. This is the assumption which appears to be most widely debated (Brookfield, 1986; Day & Baskett, 1982; Geber, 1988; Grow, 1991; Pratt, 1988) with some recent authors discussing situational and personal variables which influence interest and preparedness of adults for self-direction (Grow, 1991; Pratt, 1988). This assumption has critical implications for program planning, since it is at the heart of Knowles's insistence that adults have significant involvement in the program planning process. Relatively little research has actually been undertaken to determine the extent to which participation in the planning process makes a difference in program outcomes (Rosenblum, 1985).

A second assumption of andragogy is that adults bring a vast reservoir of experience to the learning situation which can and should be utilized. This assumption suggests that planners should encourage instructional design which builds on and expands adults' experiential base through techniques such as case study, role play, discussion, and simulation. Some authors have debated whether adults hold unique advantages in experience, particularly with regard to depth versus breadth (Day & Baskett, 1982; Hartree, 1986; Tennant, 1986). Anyone who has made the mistake of competing with a child expert in playing computer video games should be keenly aware of the experience advantage children can hold in selected areas. But generally, there has been a greater acceptance of this assumption as describing a difference between child and adult learners.

The third assumption of andragogy is that adults' readiness to learn is influenced by developmental tasks associated with adult roles in family and work life. This suggests a problem-centered basis for identifying content of adult education programs. Knowles indicates that readiness to learn is determined in most cases for school children by expert-determined subject matter curriculum. It seems obvious that there are numerous instances of subject-matter driven programs of adult education and Boyle (1981) describes these as institutional programs. It may be helpful to recall that aside from mandated and degree-centered education, adults are likely to select the general areas of their learning based on current problems at work or home. Thus, even subject matter curriculum can be designed to allow some flexibility as to learners' problem-centered needs.

The fourth assumption regarding adult learners has to do with immediacy of application. Related to their problem-centered pursuits, adults often bring an urgency for learning needed in the present or very near future. Knowles maintains that children, on the other hand, are preparing for the long-range needs of future adulthood. If immediacy of application is a concern, particularized needs assessment, once learners enroll in a program, seems essential to identify their most urgent concerns and to allow for some tailoring of objectives and activities to meet their goals.

A final assumption of andragogy, added by Knowles in more recent years (1984), is related to motivation. Adults are said to be primarily intrinsically motivated, although they may have access to and respond to extrinsic rewards. Indeed, to the extent that adults engage in learning for purposes of curiosity and self-fulfillment, it would seem true that they are intrinsically motivated. In listing multiple reasons for adult learning, adults do identify these motivations as important (Cross, 1981). It also seems obvious, however, that a significant number of adult learners come to programs as involuntary learners—required or expected to learn to get or keep a job, to earn or renew a license. The very goal-centered nature of adult learning suggests a mix of intrinsic and extrinsic motivations as a minimum for many learners, with others who may participate for almost purely extrinsic reasons. In planning education and training programs for adults the key is to design instruction so as to foster rewards for intrinsic learning and provide mechanisms to enhance the motivation of those who have not arrived out of self-motivation.

Transformative Learning

Another theory of learning developed specifically with adults in mind is Mezirow's transformative theory of adult learning (Merriam & Caffarella, 1991). Building on Habermas's categorization of learning into three categories (instrumental, dialogic, and self-reflective), Mezirow focuses specifically on self-reflective learning, which is concerned with "gaining a clearer understanding of oneself by identifying dependency-producing psychological assumptions acquired earlier in life that have become dysfunctional in adulthood" (Mezirow, 1985). In the uniquely adult learning process referred to as perspective transformation, Mezirow sees individuals as "becoming critically aware of how and why psychocultural assumptions constrain the ways in which we perceive our world," and developing more inclusive and discriminating ways of integrating and acting on experience (Mezirow, 1985, p. 22). This is accomplished through learning processes which include: learning to further differentiate within existing meaning schemes; developing new meaning schemes following the realization of the inadequacy of current assumptions. This transformative theory of adult learning emerged out of Mezirow's study of reentry women in the mid-70s (Mezirow & Marsick, 1978) and has been developed over the years since (Mezirow, 1981, 1985, 1990). Applications of perspective transformation may be critical to the program planner. Clearly one who believes in perspective transformation as an essential element of adult learning will aim to structure learning activities which encourage self-examination and critical reflection. Brookfield (1989) referred to this mode of facilitation as the "critical paradigm," distinguishing it from more traditional modes of facilitation associated with adult education, the humanist and behaviorist paradigms. In characterizing this mode he says:

> The educational activity is often described in terms of a dialogue between facilitators and learners who bring to the conversation markedly diverging experiences, expectations, perspectives and values. Within this learning conversation, the particular function of the facilitators (where this is not being performed by other members of the learning group) is to challenge learners with alternative ways of interpreting their experiences. Prompting people to scrutinize their previously unexamined values, actions, and ideas is difficult and intimidating for even the most experienced facilitators. Yet in doing this, facilitators can help adults to become critical thinkers engaged in a continual process of inventing and reinventing their personal, occupational, and political worlds. (p. 205)

Adult Development

Although a topic of relatively little interest until recent years, there is now considerable discussion of continuing development during the adult years and its implications for education. Several conceptual frameworks have emerged in the literature on adult development. Each will be discussed briefly here, along with a few cross-cutting concepts.

Life-cycle Phases

Perhaps best known to the general audience are life-cycle theories which are also called phase theories (Cross, 1981). Theorists taking this perspective emphasize changes that occur as adults move through different phases of the life cycle, often linked with age. Among the best known theorists in this category include Levinson (1978), author of *The Seasons of a Man's Life* and Sheehy (1976), author of *Passages: Predictable Crises of Adult Life*. Levinson discusses the building and rebuilding of the life structure as adults move in and out of periods of stability and transition. His work was based on interviews with 40 mid-life men in various walks of life. He and his associates proposed six sequential periods of development:

1. Early adult transition or leaving the family
2. Entering the adult world

3. Age 30 transition
4. Settling down
5. Midlife transition
6. Restabilization or middle adulthood

This work was later criticized for its focus on men, and the model has since been investigated with reference to women (Roberts & Newton, 1987). Studies of women's lives indicate qualitative differences in the nature and timing of these phases which Levinson and others originally postulated to be universal.

After interviewing 115 men and women Sheehy focused on the predictable turning points in the lives of adults. She can be credited with popularizing the term *mid-life crises*. Like Gould (1972) and others, Levinson (1978) and Sheehy (1976) attached ages to the time periods associated with the various life changes, and Levinson in particular stressed the supposed universal nature of these age frameworks.

Less tied to age and more deeply rooted in social context are the propositions about life phases postulated by others (Havighurst, 1953; Lowenthal et al., 1975; Neugarten, Moore, & Lowe, 1968). It is Havighurst from whom the familiar terms *developmental task* and *teachable moment* arose. He listed developmental tasks associated with young, middle, and older adulthood, but assigned only broad age ranges to his list of tasks, with tasks arising from social expectations and personal values. For instance, tasks associated with middle age included:

- Achieving adult civic and social responsibility
- Establishing and maintaining an economic standard of living
- Assisting teenage children in becoming responsible and happy adults
- Developing adult leisure-time activities
- Relating to one's spouse as a person
- Accepting and adjusting to the physiological changes of middle age
- Adjusting to aging parents (adapted from Havighurst, 1953)

Obviously, Havighurst's list of tasks does not provide a perfect fit with the great variations in lifestyle common in today's society. Yet, the notion of performing certain developmental tasks either on time or off-time in the eyes of society (Neugarten, Moore, &

Lowe, 1968) still seems to affect the way we perceive ourselves or others perceive us, even in an increasingly fluid environment with regard to age norms (Neugarten, 1979). Some researchers have attempted to avoid age-based normative assumptions by focusing solely on social roles. Lowenthal et al. (1975) followed this approach by studying men and women at four different junctures in the life cycle: high school seniors, newlyweds, middle-age parents, and retired couples. They found both role-related and gender differences in concerns. More recently Juhasz (1989) has developed what she terms the triple-helix model of adult development, symbolized by spiraling and intertwining elements representing the varying importance placed on work or career, family life, and personal development at differing times in our lives.

Developmental Stages

Like Cross (1981) I have made a distinction here between phases of the life cycle and developmental stages of growth and maturity. Stage theories can be distinguished by an assumption of some hierarchical progression along an identified dimension, with the implicit assumption that it is "better" to be at a higher level or position. Cross (1981) maintains that stage researchers generally provide a stronger theoretical basis, devoting as much attention to explanations of the stage and its origins as to description. Examples of stage theory with implications for planning education programs for adults include the work of Loevinger (1976) on ego development, Perry (1970) on intellectual development, and Kohlberg (1969) and Gilligan (1981) on moral development. All share the description of movement from simple to more complex forms of reasoning.

Life Events

Another strand of discussion in adult development literature focuses on life events and associated transitions. With regard to the concepts of transition, this discussion in fact overlaps with the work of some authors already mentioned in the context of life cycle/ phase development. For instance, Levinson speaks of the marker event, one which often triggers the reassessment process association with transition periods. Lowenthal et al. (1975) studied the anticipation and responses to impending events among men and women at four transitional periods of life, finding that women in all stages experience more stressful life experiences than men. Focusing more specifically on life events, developmental scholars have categorized them in a number of ways. Hultsch and Plemons (1979) contrast individual events (e.g., birth, death, marriage, divorce) that define one's personal life with cultural events which arise out of societal and historical occurrences (e.g., wars, the civil rights movement, political assassinations) that have an influence on individual lives. The salience of events has also been postulated as related to timing (congruence of the event with personal or social expectations regarding when it should happen); cohort specificity (whether the event selectively influences a particular generation); and probability (normative events being those with a high probability of occurrence, nonnormative being those that are unlikely to occur) (Brim & Ryff, 1980; Merriam & Caffarella, 1991; Reese & Smyer, 1983).

Closely related to the discussion of life events are the concepts of triggers and transitions. Aslanian and Brickell (1980) might be credited with introducing the concept of *triggers* for learning—events that provide an impetus for participation in some form of adult learning. In their nationally representative study 83 percent of adult learners interviewed identified some past, present, or future transition in their lives as the reason for their participation. Most (56 percent) reported changes in jobs or careers as precipitating learning; transitions in family lives ranked second. Schlossberg reminds us that transitions include "not only obvious life changes (such as high school graduation, job entry, marriage, birth of first child, bereavement) but also subtle changes (such as the loss of career aspirations and the nonoccurrence of anticipated events, such as an expected job promotion that never comes through)" (1984, p. 43). She suggests that in helping adults negotiate a transition it is important to assess the type of transition (anticipated or not), the context, and the impact on the person's existing relationships and roles.

Much of the developmental literature has been criticized for its focus on white, middle class males. Early adjustments came in the form of testing existing theories' applicability to women (Roberts & Newton, 1987; Stewart, 1977). More recently, a new path of research has begun to investigate women's development (Belenky, et al., 1986; Caffarella & Olson, 1993). While avoiding the tendency to use the terms *levels* or *positions*, Belenky et al. have described five characteristic "ways of knowing" as postures through which women greet new knowledge. As developmental theory has become more widely known, more and more researchers are now aware of the benefits of studies focused on women and of the need to include significant numbers of women in their samples. The status of research is still quite limited with regard to cross-cultural differences (Gutmann, 1982), particularly as applied to cultural differences *within* the North American context where much of theory has been generated (Ross-Gordon, 1991). Meanwhile, program planners need to exercise caution in assuming that adult development theories apply to females, racial/ethnic minority adults, individuals with disabilities, or others typically discussed in our emerging awareness of cultural diversity.

Learning and Cognitive Style

Differences in adult learning style, cognitive style, or learning preference should be considered as a significant dimension of program planning, particularly in the instructional design phase.

The reader who makes a foray into the literature on learning styles and cognitive styles will find a bewildering plethora of terms, theories, and instruments. Bonham (1988) aptly captures the confusion in the literature by first discussing underlying differences in two streams of work on cognitive styles and learning styles, then describing the difficulty in clearly differentiating these streams as researchers and instrument developers have come to use the terms interchangeably. A discussion by Claxton and Murrell (1987) sheds some light in the effort to sort and categorize the vast literature. Their discussion is embedded in the context of college instruction, leaving it with greater utility for understanding adult learning style than literature reviews on learning styles in children but limited by its focus on the collegiate setting and studies that have primarily focused on college "young adults." At the same time, their framework seems to offer a heuristic for organizing available research findings and learning styles instruments as well as suggesting future research focused on adult populations.

Claxton and Murrell (1987) follow Curry (1983) in applying the metaphor of an onion to the analysis of learning styles. At the center of the onion they place style differences related to basic characteristics of personality, as measured by instruments like

Witkin's Embedded Figures test of field dependence and field independence and the Myers-Briggs Type Indicators. In the next layer they place learning styles related to information-processing models, describing how persons take in and process information. Kolb's (1976) model of experiential learning and his Learning Styles Inventory fit here. At the next layer of the learning styles onion, Claxton and Murrell place social-interaction models dealing with how students tend to interact and behave in the classroom. Grasha and Reichmann's Student Learning Style Scales measure this type of learning style. Finally, at the outermost layer are found learning styles models focusing on learning environments and instructional preferences, with Hill's Cognitive Style Inventory as an exemplary instrument. Consistent with Bonham's (1988) contrast between cognitive style and learning style, Claxton and Murrell (1987) suggest traits at the center are most stable and least subject to change in response to intervention by the researcher or instructor. They maintain that as layers proceed outward, traits and preferences are less stable and more susceptible to change (and thus of greater interest to instructors), making them increasingly difficult to measure reliably.

Having heard much about the need to attend to adult differences in learning style, cognitive style, and learning preferences, the program planning practitioner may be surprised to hear that controversy exists over terminology, concepts, theories, and instrumentation. After choosing an instrument or strategy to identify learning style, the central question may be how to use this information in instructional planning. The limited amount of research linking learning style based instruction with satisfaction or effective learning among adults makes this a difficult question to answer. Yet, several strategies are worth sharing, along with examples of their applications. Cross (1976) wonders if simply "matching" learners to their preferences is necessarily the best strategy, noting for example, that it may be preferable to encourage field independent learners to learn to work cooperatively with others rather than to arrange all their learning to accommodate their more independent learning preferences. This kind of matching is referred to as a "challenge match"—one that places learners in an uncongenial or conflict setting in order to expand their repertoire of skills. She would also suggest this kind of match to expand the repertoire of field dependent learners who often are at some risk in formal educational environments, which frequently place a high premium on the skills associated with field independent learning. Another kind of matching, "compensatory matching," allows students to compensate for deficiencies in one skill area by using skills that are more adequately developed in other areas.

Some conclude that the best advice is that offered by Sternberg (1994). He states: "Teachers must accommodate an array of thinking and learning styles, systematically varying teaching and assessment methods to reach every student.... You probably know all these methods and have used them in the past, yet most teachers regularly use only a few" (1994, p. 38).

For the adult educator who wonders how either instructors or planners can reasonably make adaptations to individual learning styles, Sviniciki and Dixon's (1987) discussion of applications of the Kolb model may offer some guidance. Building on the experiential learning model which underlies Kolb's Learning Style Inventory (Kolb, 1981), they delineate instructional activities that support different aspects of the learning cycle, beginning with concrete experience, then moving on to reflective observation, abstract conceptualization, and finally active experimentation.

Each of four learner types (*divergers, assimilators, convergers,* and *accommodators*) are determined in Kolb's model by determining intersections of learner preferences along two dimensions: (1) preferences for information input by either concrete experience or abstract conceptualization, and (2) preferences for information processing by either internal reflection or external action. Convergers' dominant learning abilities are abstract conceptualization and active experimentation (Kolb, 1981). They are especially good at the practical applications of ideas, using hypothetical-deductive reasoning to focus knowledge on the solution of specific problems. Divergers are best at concrete experience and reflective observation. Their strength lies in their imaginative ability, as they see things from many perspectives. Assimilators' dominant learning abilities are abstract conceptualization and reflective observation. They are apt at creating theoretical models and excel in inductive reasoning. Accommodators are best at concrete experience and active experimentation. They are risk-takers, preferring active involvement to a greater extent than the other three learning styles. Thus, an instructional sequence that moves through each of the four modes of learning provides an opportunity for each learner to operate within a preferred learning mode. Sviniciki and Dixon (1987) suggest activities associated with each of the four poles of the learning cycle:

1. Concrete experience—laboratories, field work, readings, problems, examples
2. Reflective observation—journals, discussion, brainstorming
3. Abstract conceptualization—lecture, papers, projects
4. Active experimentation—case study, laboratory, simulations

Another use of learning style information is to empower students to understand their own learning styles as well as the learning and teaching styles of their instructors. Claxton and Murrell (1987) describe efforts at Mountain View Community College where both students and teachers were mapped according to Hill's Cognitive Style Inventory and "students were helped to understand their own cognitive style, select courses consistent with their own style, and develop strategies for succeeding in courses where a mismatch occurred" (p. 50). Claxton and Murrell suggest dialogue between teachers and learners about learning and teaching styles and how to make accommodations on each side is in itself beneficial to the teaching-learning process.

Underrepresented Groups

Adult education programs today generally aim to serve a broad-based population. Yet, participation statistics repeatedly reveal that certain populations of adult learners are less likely to participate in adult education programs. These groups include racial and ethnic minorities, and older adults. Data from the National Center for Education Statistics indicate that 8.1 percent of blacks, 8.2 percent of Hispanics, and 14.5 percent of whites participated in adult education in 1984 (Snyder, 1988). Among adults age 55 and over, 5.7 percent participated in adult education in 1984, while 16.9 percent of those age 35 to 54 participated. Adults with disabilities also constitute an underserved population ("Building Effective Program Linkages," 1991; Gloeckler, 1991), one whose needs are being addressed through the recently organized National Association for Adults with Special Learning Needs and its *Journal.* It is more difficult to describe the extent of their underrepresentation since they have not been counted as a category in major studies and statistics compiled by the National Center for Education Statistics. Some discussion of these groups seems warranted if program planners hope to increase their level of participation in the future. Demographic changes associated with the growth in minority and aging populations and legislative mandates through the Americans with Disabilities Act (West, 1990) suggest the importance of program planners' knowing more about the barriers leading to diminished participation among these groups and ways to overcome these barriers.

Minority Adults

Barriers to minority participation are numerous. These include dispositional barriers such as negative perceptions of education and educators based on schooling experiences which include tracking into lower-ability groups and accompanying reduced teacher expectations (Darling-Hammond, 1985; Rosenbaum, 1976); resistance to educational enterprises seen as "unfriendly" to their communities (O'Brien, 1990); and lack of identification with teachers and curriculum not linked to their own experiences (Darkenwald, 1975). This category of barriers may seem difficult to overcome, but program planning that shows sensitivity to the cultural backgrounds of individuals in the target audience and instructors who show respect for minority adults as capable individuals can make a difference (Ross-Gordon, Martin, & Briscoe, 1990). One way to enhance this outreach effort is by involving members of the underrepresented groups as planners and instructors (Podeschi, 1990). In addition to dispositional barriers, institutional and situational barriers often prevent the participation of minority adults in educational programs. To the extent that minorities are disproportionately represented among those with low incomes, the cost of participation becomes a barrier for many. Funded projects, scholarship programs, and collaboration with employers can be strategies to reduce the impact of this barrier (Moe, 1990). Institutional barriers include selection of ineffective marketing strategies which leave minority adults with inadequate information regarding educational programs for adults. In addition to traditional promotional vehicles like radio, television, and direct mail, recruitment through face-to-face channels such as churches and community-based organizations should be considered as important supplements when recruiting those segments of the minority population which are traditionally underserved by formal adult education programs. Staff development efforts may be an effective tool in helping adult educators identify and overcome racism in their own practices which may translate into barriers for students (Amstutz, 1994; Hayes & Colin, 1994). One key to improved service to underserved minority adults is learning from such organizations which have traditionally provided informal educational opportunities within minority communities (Briscoe & Ross, 1989).

Older Adults

While underrepresented relative to younger adults, the presence of older adults in educational programs has been rising due to at least two factors: a demographic shift toward an older population and the rising educational level of older adults compared to earlier generations (U.S. Bureau of the Census, 1989). Although older adults frequently choose to continue their learning through self-directed means or participation in nonformal environments such as churches, clubs, libraries, and senior centers, many choose to participate in formally sponsored adult education programs as well. Courtenay (1989) suggests that intrinsic motivations are the driving force behind most adult learners, and that lack of interest has been identified as the major barrier for older adults. He goes on, however, to describe additional barriers which may prevent participation in programs by older adults, including poor health, feeling too old, lack of transportation, lack of discretionary time and costs. Although program planners may not be able to influence factors such as health, and may have limited influence on older adults' acceptance of cultural stereotypes of older people as unable to learn, they may be able to reduce barriers due to situational factors such as cost or lack of transportation by offering programs in accessible places or arranging transportation services. Courtenay (1989) points out that it is older adults at the lowest socioeconomic levels who are least likely to participate, and when they do are more likely to participate in programs related to pressing needs. He notes that most funding for older adult education comes from fees or voluntary support rather than public support, but adds that simply increasing funding for older adult education may not directly lead to increased participation due to the disproportionate numbers with low educational levels. He effectively raises the issue whether education for older adults will continue to go primarily to the most able, who are already best educated, or whether more efforts might be directed toward the underserved and isolated. Finally, Courtenay discusses the purposes of education for older adults, suggesting that diverse purposes and providers suggest a wide variety or programming including that which is intergenerational. Program planners directing programs toward the elderly will need to consider the above issues. They should also work with instructors to make changes in the learning environment and instructional methodology to accommodate changes in sensory processes with aging (Beatty & Wolf, 1996). For instance, meeting rooms should be in barrier-free locations, and have good lighting and acoustics and limited background noise. Instructors should be encouraged to speak slowly and clearly facing the group; present material in short, manageable units; and compensate for reduced hearing with large-print visual aids.

Adults with Disabilities

A population of learners with special instructional needs about which we as a field know very little is those adults with disabilities. I include here physical disabilities, specific learning disabilities, the developmentally disabled, the mentally disabled, and those with sensory impairments (deaf or hearing impaired; blind or visually impaired). Clearly all these disabilities cannot be understood as one homogeneous grouping since each brings different challenges and program adjustment requirements (Fettgather, 1989; Malone, 1986; Ross, 1987). Travis (1985) also makes the point that age of the individual at the onset of the disability is a factor to consider, with the implications that disability occurring in adulthood represents a major intrusion into the life process and requires significant learning simply to readjust and cope with these changes. The concerns of Travis that we not leave andragogy at the door when dealing with disabled adults are echoed in Fettgather's discussion of the dissonance between theory and practice when retarded adults are simultaneously trained to act like adults and treated like children.

The programming needs of adults with disabilities are not unlike those of other adults. They include education for occupational, vocational, or professional competence; education for social and civic competence; education for personal or family competence; and education for self-realization (Boyer-Stephens, 1987). Critical needs in the occupational/vocational area are demonstrated by estimates that 50 percent to 80 percent of disabled adults are unemployed or underemployed (Sarkees & Scott, 1985). Programs to train the disabled for work as well as programs to train employers to understand and make accommodations for workers with disabilities will become a growing area of opportunity as the Americans with Disabilities Act (ADA) is implemented (West, 1990). Yet, without appropriate accommodations for such learners within adult education programs dismal failure rates can be predicted. Boyer-Stephen's (1985) provides a useful literature overview, discusses initiatives originating in the U.S. Office of Special Education and Rehabilitation Services (OSERS), and describes programs aimed at adults with varying disabilities. Program planners should also become familiar with ADA since their programs will generally come under its auspices (West, 1990; "Americans with Disabilities Act," 1990). Although physical barriers may be the obvious ones, countless other barriers exist within adult education programs, ranging from stereotypical attitudes of instructors or learners to inappropriate means of preliminary assessment and final learner evaluation. Appropriate accommodations may be as simple as changing the arrangement of chairs in a room to facilitate lip reading, allowing an alternative form of evaluation, or using large print overheads; or as complex as hiring a sign language interpreter or making a classroom wheelchair accessible. Adult educators can have a vital role to play in enabling adults with disabilities to acquire full access to society, but this will require some new ways of thinking as we develop and implement programs (Gadbow & Du Bois, in press; Jordan, 1996).

ANALYSIS OF THE LITERATURE

I have frequently heard the remark "We have so little research on adult learning." Yet, the literature presented above supports both the idea that we seem to know a great deal about adult learners and the concern that we need to know a great deal more. Indeed, a number of suppositions have guided our practice which have yet to stand the scrutiny of empirical testing. The results are not yet in, for instance, on whether adults really are inclined to act as self-directed learners in formal learning situations. "Knowing" if this is true would provide a clearer guide to practice. Or would it? One of the challenging aspects about putting some of our theories about adult learning to the test is the great diversity of adult learners and learning situations. What holds for one group may not hold for the other, although often our research findings have been reported as if generalizing to a much broader population than the samples with which the studies were conducted. Contemporary researchers seem more likely to remind us that results may not generalize beyond the young to the middle-aged, white, middle-class, male (and increasingly female), able-bodied sample used. But that leaves those of us who are developing programs for older, minority, working class, or disabled students uncertain about what we can assume about these groups of learners. Then there is that troubling reality of individual differences. In addition to learner diversity, we must be curious about the relationship between setting or context of adult learning programs and learner expectations or preferences. Learners in a workplace training program may hold different conceptions of their roles than those in a college classroom or those in a community organization.

Having suggested suitable caution in interpreting the existing body of research as universally generalizable, I will review several of the conclusions which seem apparent on the basis of literature reviewed here.

1. Although decline in sensory abilities, as with those facets of intelligence highly dependent on perceptual accuracy and speed, is seen an inevitable concomitant with aging, it now seems quite evident that healthy adults retain their ability to learn well into old age. Program planners should make accommodations for sensory changes in hearing and vision as learners age, but should not lower their expectations of older adults' learning abilities due to their age.

2. Adults learn for a multitude of reasons; even a single individual may have multiple reasons. Prominent among adults' reasons for learning, however, are pragmatic reasons rooted in the desire to improve their occupational, family, and community lives. The wise program planner or instructional designer will determine the problems or situations which motivate adult participants and build learning experiences around these needs.

3. The theory of learning one embraces is likely to influence the nature of program planning. Program planners with differing

world views on the purpose of adult education, intended clientele, relationships between learners and teachers, and appropriate methods may plan radically different programs involving radically different processes. It is possible nonetheless for certain learning theories to be more compatible with certain contexts than with others, e.g., self-development programs with humanistic or transformative learning theories; job training programs with behaviorist, cognitivist, or social learning theories.

4. Andragogy and transformative theory are two theories of learning specific to adults, although andragogy has been challenged as uniquely describing or benefiting adults. Both theories assume the value of adult experience; transformative learning theory places more emphasis on the change which occurs in the individual as a reaction to unsettling life experiences or a series of gradual awakenings. Those who accept either of these theories will seek to use methods which capitalize on adults' presumed readiness for self-direction and critical thinking. Both theories call for avoidance of instructional approaches which call for adults merely to learn from experts.

5. Adults encounter challenges and tasks as they seek to respond to life events or prepare for anticipated events. Such triggers often give rise to what has been referred to as the teachable moment. It is debatable whether in contemporary Western society these events can still be easily associated with given ages. Transitions can be overwhelming, or they can inspire growth. It is those which inspire growth which often brings adults to our programs, although the challenges may seem greater than the opportunities at first. Programs will be more effective to the extent that they assist adults in responding to these changes, whether a promotion with new responsibilities or unexpected job displacement, whether the need to cope with teenage children or the need to participate in community action programs to stop hazardous dumping in a local neighborhood.

6. According to most developmental stage theories, adults move from simple interpretations of reality to more complex ways of viewing the world. In a given learning group, however, adults may be as diverse in developmental stages as they are in age or height. Part of the challenge in planning activities aimed at

developing or enhancing critical thinking is allowing for the varying stages of cognitive, ego, or moral development which may exist in one learning situation.

7. While there is little agreement on the most effective tools to determine cognitive or learning style, there is agreement that some efforts should be made to accommodate varied learning styles in most adult groups. Instructors may work to match or challenge the learning styles of individuals or the group, but it is unrealistic to expect perfect matches of instructional style and learning style. Still, Kolb's theory on the learning cycle underscores the value of the deliberate variation of methods aimed to suit diverse learning styles.

8. Certain groups, including minority adults, older adults, and adults with disabilities, are among those underserved in educational programs. We must know more about their interests, motivations, and barriers if we are to solve problems of access. We must broaden our own knowledge, attitudes, and competence in working with learners whose experiences differ from our own if they are to be better served in our programs.

APPLICATIONS OF THEORY TO PRACTICE CONTEXTS

To illustrate possible applications of the information presented here on adult learning for planning educational programs, three cases will be presented, each in a different setting. The first setting is a program for learning disabled adults in adult basic education classes. The second is a corporate training program aimed at enhancing the preparedness of women and minorities for managerial positions. The third is a community college sponsored program for older adults interested in becoming more effective volunteers in local youth programs. Each example will discuss the possible influence on the program planning and evaluation process related to:

- Accommodations needed due to aging of participants (if applicable)
- Predominant motivations for participation
- The guiding learning theory
- Developmental phases and stages of learners

- Learning and cognitive style patterns in the group
- Access barriers and program strategies related to underrepresented status of the learners

Example 1—An Adult Basic Education Class

For a variety of reasons, 12 participants have come to participate in a program for adults with learning disabilities. Several came to improve their basic skills as a precursor to gaining employment. Three have reasonably good basic skills but in the past gave up on high school completion due to frustration. Now they are ready to study for the GED (General Education Development) examination. One woman is mainly interested in being able to help her child with homework that is becoming more difficult since her daughter entered fourth grade. Another woman enrolled after successive failures in three adult basic education (ABE) classes because she had heard this group might provide an experience more akin to a learning disabilities (LD) resource room experience in school. Two men have been referred by the local Office of Vocational Rehabilitation. They wish to study mechanical trades but did not score well on the portions of the aptitude test which depend greatly on measurements skills, so they cannot yet enroll in the training program. All of these learners are "ready to learn" although their long histories of educational difficulty may challenge the instructors to use their full array of motivational strategies. The diversity of their motivations as well as their varying skill levels suggests the value of a fairly individualized program. Yet, their common needs to enhance self-esteem suggest the benefits to be gained from group activities.

The coordinator for the ABE program has been highly trained in cognitive learning theories. She believes that it is important to develop cognitive strategies that enable adults with learning disabilities to become aware of their own learning patterns, replacing ineffective strategies with new ones. She also believes that Ausubel had much to offer when he talked about building on the learners' existing experience and prior knowledge as new material is introduced. For this reason, she will encourage teachers to have clear, sequentially organized lesson plans that foster the development of independent learning strategies. Hearing more and more about andragogy, she also wants for teachers to use students' interests as a source of ideas for selection of relevant instructional materials. She is concerned that some teachers have fostered too much dependence in their students through infantilizing behaviors sometimes observed in those working with retarded adults.

Developmental stages of the adults enrolled in the program have not yet been considered as an aspect of the program planning. It is likely that as the teachers follow up on the coordinator's suggestions to investigate the adult learners' motivations and interests, they will realize that those interests stem from developmental tasks associated with family and work life.

The coordinator has had fairly extensive training in perceptual learning styles, and is working with teachers to get them to use more varied forms of sensory input as they develop teaching strategies. They are becoming accustomed to thinking of the needs of auditory learners who benefit from taping class lectures or recording their compositions before they write them, as well as the visual learners who like the use of overheads, flip charts, prints, and videos. They have not yet been introduced to the concept of the experiential learning cycle (Kobl, 1981). The coordinator became intrigued by Kolb's Learning Style Inventory when she used it in a workshop and read the description of her type—an accommodation like many educators. She has invited teachers to a staff development session where an expert on the inventory will administer it and talk about its potential applications in small group and individualized instruction.

Finally, consideration is given to the status of this group of learners as disabled, but this is kept in perspective with their abilities. One aim of the program is to help them identify and describe their own learning strengths and weaknesses as a step toward greater independence in developing compensatory strategies without the assistance of an instructor.

Example 2—A Corporate Training Program

The human resources manager at a mid-sized corporation has been asked to develop a managerial preparation program for women and minorities at the company. Critics have recently commented that their strong affirmative action recruitment efforts have diversified the general workforce in a way seen as valuable to the long-term growth of the company, but despite more than a decade of such efforts there is only one woman manager and none who represent racial or ethnic minorities. Potential participants have been identified in two ways. Supervisors have been contracted to provide a list of women and minority workers perceived as having management potential. Individuals have also been invited to submit an application to the program explaining the basis for their interest in the program and the strengths they would bring to a managerial position. The participants finally selected include 10 white women, 3 African American women, 4 African American men, 3 Hispanic men, and 1 Hispanic woman. This group of 21 seems highly motivated, although several long-term employees have expressed some doubts about the real impact the program will have on their promotability. Each has been with the firm for a minimum of 5 years and has had no more than one job promotion in that time. Although all state in their applications their interest in remaining with the firm, three of the white women and one African American man actually see the program as another way to enhance their job mobility outside the company, having already become frustrated with the ultimate prospects of rising to the top in this particular company. Thus, a group that appears highly motivated for purposes of job advancement also has some doubts about the program.

Bill Brown has been chosen to conduct the training program. He is aware that as a white male his experiences in the company may be different from those of the participants, but he is interested in listening to determine what they perceive as their greatest learning needs and most significant barriers to advancement. His humanistic orientation makes him especially interested in developing and delivering this program; many programs he has developed have been more technical in focus. He sees it as an opportunity to maximize the personal growth of those individuals who participate, while also significantly benefiting the company in terms of public relations and improved work climate. Such a program seems critically needed as the workforce becomes more diversified. Reflecting his program planning philosophy, on two occasions before the program started he invited several members of the group to lunch to plan the training sessions.

The developmental stage of the participants is considered in terms of life cycle theory—most are in their mid-30s, an age associated in Levinson's model with rising aspirations for achievement in the work domain among men; career-oriented women have been shown in some research to show similar developmental progression to the men in Levinson's model (Roberts & Newton, 1987). Bill also sees these employees as mid-career professionals who are looking for new work responsibilities to stimulate their continued high rate of performance. In each case, the developmental phase suggest a high level of motivation. Bill has no information about the levels of cognitive, ego, or moral development of these workers. As the program progresses, he has wondered about one man who always seems to be uncomfortable when the group gets into a lively discussion of issues they have faced in the workplace. The man reminds them that they should be grateful to be employed with Newstyle Company and should stay in line with company expectations. He does not like the discussions of case studies when the group is asked to map out alternative strategies for response. He would much prefer that the instructor, as expert, recommend the most effective strategy without all the discussion. His conventional thinking leads him to take issue with the techniques which place so much emphasis on the opinions of his trainee colleagues.

The group was most interested in using the Myers-Briggs Personality Type Indicator to determine their personal work and learning style preferences. Several members of the group became so excited about the results that they persuaded others in their work group to complete the instrument as well. In the classes, Bill has organized participants into work groups so as to maximize the diversity of Myers-Briggs Types in each group. This challenges them to become aware of what happens in their interactions with supervisors or employees who are quite unlike themselves, whether in type or culture.

The nature of this training program permits the group to openly discuss what the group members have perceived to be barriers to their own advancement in the past. Lack of mentors within the organization is one problem they identified. As members of underrepresented groups, they have found it harder to find colleagues higher up in the organization with whom they can naturally cultivate the close ties associated with mentoring relationships. The group has suggested that they and others in the organization who are interested be matched with new workers who sign up for a structured mentoring program.

This program illustrates how a workplace learning program can be built on humanistic assumptions and utilize andragogical instructional strategies. The humanistic influence has been consistent throughout the program, including the frequent informal feedback given by learners as a way of redirecting program elements that are not working successfully.

Example 3—A Community College Sponsored Program

Metropolitan Community College is sponsoring a program for older adults. Because the median age of students attending the community college is 36, the current director of continuing education and public service is interested in expanding programming for older adults. Although this age group comprises 12% of the adult residents in the local community, it comprises only 3% of the participants in noncredit programs offered by the community college.

A course called "Retirement on a Shoestring Budget" is being offered as a pilot course aimed specifically at the over-60 market. Since demographic data suggest many of the residents in this age group must make ends meet on Social Security checks supplemented by small pension checks, the topic should provide some degree of motivation to participate. The content area is clearly designed to appeal to the life cycle developmental stage of older adulthood. Additional motivation will be likely since the instructor used the first morning of the five sessions to identify the particular needs of the group that signed up. He found out that all of the participants in this predominantly female class are especially interested in identifying ways to obtain adequate housing and health care coverage in a town where the costs of both have been rising faster than their fixed incomes. Several of the women are finding it especially difficult to live on their deceased husbands' Social Security benefits alone, having limited work histories of their own and thus no significant amount of supplementary funds.

The instructor hired for the class is firmly rooted in cognitive learning theory and seems to know a fair amount about structuring learning experiences to provide for the greatest possible receptive learning. The continuing education director sees the benefit of having an instructor who knows a great deal about financial resources in the local community and how to maximize cognitive strategies used by older learners. She is interested, additionally, in encouraging the instructor to apply a bit of social learning theory by both using active demonstrations of budgeting techniques and inviting as models older adults from the community who have already been learning to live more comfortably using some of the information and techniques discussed.

The continuing education director has reduced some access barriers for the older adults by offering the program for a nominal fee of $20 for five sessions. Also, the class is offered late in the morning, avoiding hours in the late afternoon or evening when the older adults might feel less safe to attend due to rush hour traffic in darkness. The college is located on a public transportation bus line, making it possible for several participants without cars to attend; a car-pool list was also generated at the first meeting for the convenience of several participants who drive.

Keeping in mind physiological changes with aging, the director and the instructor generated a list of accommodations. A room has been scheduled that has good natural lighting and minimal background noise from the heating and cooling system. The instructor, who has a tendency to talk rapidly, has practiced slowing down so these students can hear him more clearly. He introduces content with clear overview statements and briefly reviews each topic before moving on the next. He is using more than the usual number of visual aids so as to provide an additional visual cue for those who may have difficulty hearing. In addition, he asked on the first morning if anyone needed preferential seating due to hearing difficulty. He remembers to watch the group for signs that members are straining to hear. His handouts are printed with large print on yellow paper. To reduce the effects of fatigue, the group meets for only 80 minutes with a short break in the middle of each session, unlike many of the adult classes at the community college which meet for two to three hours a time. These accommodations make a more pleasant learning experience for the older adult participants.

Summary

Each of the program planners presented in the preceding cases is taking an active role, along with the instructional facilitators, in using knowledge about adult learners to plan the most

effective program possible. Each will utilize formative and summative evaluation strategies aimed at identifying ways to improve the
programs while in progress and for future audiences.

QUESTIONS FOR STUDY AND DISCUSSION

1. What myths about aging and learning have been dispelled
    through research, although they are sometimes still believed
    by the general public? What changes associated with the aging
    process are important to consider in planning educational
    programs for adults? What actual changes might you make in
    the learning environment or instructional design to accommo-
    date these changes among older learners?
2. How may knowledge of anticipated participant motivational
    patterns aid the program planner?
3. Explain how your director's or your own theory of adult learn-
    ing might affect your program planning practices.
4. How would you describe your own learning style? Of what
    value is awareness of an individual's learning style? How might
    knowledge of learning styles permit a match of teaching and
    learning styles?

REFERENCES

Americans with Disabilities Act. (1990). [Special Issue]. *Work life: A publication on
    employment and people with disabilities, 3*(3).
Amstutz, D. (1994). Staff development: Addressing issues of race and gender. In
    E. Hayes & S. Colin (Eds.), *Confronting racism and sexism* (*New Directions for
    Adult and Continuing Education,* No. 61, 39–51). San Francisco: Jossey-Bass.
Aslanian, C. B., & Brickell, H. M. (1980). *Americans in transition: Life changes as
    reasons for adult learning.* New York: College Entrance Examination Board.
Beatty, P. T., & Wolf, M. A. (1996). *Connecting with older adults: Educational responses
    and approaches.* Malabar, FL: Krieger.
Belenky, M. F., Clinchy, B. M., Goldberger, N. R., & Tarule, J. M. (1986). *Women's
    way of knowing: The development of self, voice, and mind.* New York: Basic Books.
Bonham, L. A. (1988). Learning style use: In need of perspective. *Lifelong Learn-
    ing, 11*(5), 14–17.
Boshier, R., & Collins, J. B. (1985). The Houle typology after twenty-two years: A
    large-scale empirical test. *Adult Education Quarterly, 35,* 113–130.
Boyer-Stephens, A. (1987). Disabled adult learners: Meeting the needs in commu-
    nity education programs. *Lifelong Learning: An Omnibus of Practice and Re-
    search, 11*(2), 12–14.

Boyle, P. G. (1981). *Planning better programs.* New York: McGraw-Hill.

Brim, O. G., & Ryff, C. D. (1980). On the properties of life events. In R. Baltes & O. Brim (Eds.), *Life-span development and behavior* (Vol. I.3). New York: Academic Press.

Briscoe, D. B., & Ross, J. M. (1989). Racial and ethnic minorities and adult education. In Sharan Merriam & Phyllis Cunningham (Eds.), *Handbook of adult and continuing education* (pp. 583–598). San Francisco: Jossey-Bass.

Brookfield, S. (1986). *Understanding and facilitating adult learning.* San Francisco: Jossey-Bass.

Brookfield, S. (1989). *Developing critical thinkers: Challenging adults to explore alternative ways of thinking and acting.* San Francisco: Jossey-Bass.

Brundage, D. H., & MacKeracher, D. (1980). *Adult learning principles and their application to program planning.* Toronto, Ontario: Ministry of Education.

Building effective program linkages. (1991). Proceedings of a conference held by the Offices of Vocational and Adult Education and Special Education and Rehabilitative Services. Washington, DC.

Burgess, P. (1971). Reasons for adult participation in group educational activities. *Adult Education, 22,* 3–29.

Caffarella, R. S., & Olson, S. K. (1993). Psychosocial development of women: A critical review of the literature. *Adult Education Quarterly, 43,* 125–151.

Canfield, A. A. (1983). *Canfield learning styles inventory. Form 5-A manual.* Birmingham, MI: Humanics Media.

Carp, A., Peterson, R., & Roelfs, P. (1974). Adult learning interests and experiences. In K. P. Cross, J. R. Valley, & Associates (Eds.), *Planning nontraditional programs: An analysis of the issues for postsecondary education.* San Francisco: Jossey-Bass.

Cattell, R. B. (1963). Theory of fluid and crystallized intelligence: A critical approach. *Journal of Educational Psychology, 54*(1), 1–22.

Claxton, C. S., & Murrell, P. H. (1987). *Learning styles: Implications for improving educational practices.* ASHE-ERIC Higher Education Report. (ERIC Document Reproduction Service No. 293478).

Cooper, P. A. (1993). Paradigm shifts in designed instruction: From behaviorism to cognitivism to constructivism. *Educational Technology, 33*(5), 12–19.

Courtenay, B. C. (1989). Education for older adults. In Sharan Merriam & Phyllis Cunningham (Eds.), *Handbook of adult and continuing education* (pp. 525–537). San Francisco: Jossey-Bass.

Cross, K. P. (1976). *Accent on learning.* San Francisco: Jossey-Bass.

Cross, K. P. (1981). *Adults as learners: Increasing participation and facilitating learning.* San Francisco: Jossey-Bass.

Cross, K. P., Valley, J. R., & Associates (1974). *Planning nontraditional programs: An analysis of the issues for postsecondary education.* San Francisco: Jossey-Bass.

Curry, L. (1983). *An organization of learning styles theory and constructs.* Paper presented at American Educational Research Association, Montreal, Canada.

Darkenwald, G. G. (1975). Some effects of the obvious variable: Teacher's race and holding power with black adult students. *Sociology of Education, 48,* 420–431.

Darling-Hammond, L. (1985). *Equality and excellence: The educational status of black Americans.* New York: College Board Publications.

Day, C., & Baskett, H. K. (1982). Discrepancies between intentions and practice: Reexamining some basic assumptions about adult and continuing professional education. *International Journal of Lifelong Education, 1*(2), 143–155.

Dewey, J. (1960). *The quest for certainty.* New York: Capricorn.

Dubin, S. S., & Okun, M. (1973). Implications of learning theories for adult instruction. *Adult Education, 24,* 3–19.

Feden, P. D. (1994). About instruction: Powerful new strategies worth knowing. *Educational Horizons, 73*(1), 18–24.

Fettgather, R. (1989). "Be an adult!": A hidden curriculum in life skills instruction for retarded students? *Lifelong Learning: An omnibus of practice and research, 12*(5), 4–5, 10.

Fozard, J. L., et al. (1977). Visual perception and communication. In J. E. Birren & K. W. Schaie (Eds.), *Handbook of the psychology of aging* (pp. 497–534). New York: Van Nostrand Reinhold.

Gadbow, N. F., & Du Bois, D. A. (in press). *Adult learners with special needs.* Malabar, FL: Krieger.

Gagne, R. M., Briggs, L. J., & Wager, W. (1988). *Principles of instructional design.* (2nd ed.). New York: Holt, Rinehart & Winston.

Gardner, H. (1983). *Frames of mind.* New York: Basic Books.

Gardner, H. (1995). Reflections on multiple intelligences: Myths and messages. *Phi Delta Kappan, 17,* 200–209.

Geber, B. (1988, December). The problem with andragogy. *Training,* 31–39.

Gilligan, C. (1981). Moral development. In A. W. Chickering & Associates (Eds.), *The modern American college: Responding to the new realities of diverse students and a changing society.* San Francisco: Jossey-Bass.

Gloekler, L. C. (1991). Lifelong learning for individuals with disabilities: Beginning to coordinate services in the state of New York. *Journal of the National Association for Adults with Special Learning Needs, 1*(1), 35–45.

Gould, R. (1972). The phases of adult life: A study in developmental psychology. *American Journal of Psychiatry, 129,* 521–531.

Grippin, P., & Peters, S. (1984). *Learning theory and learning outcomes.* New York: University Press of America.

Grow, G. O. (1991). Teaching learners to be self-directed. *Adult Education Quarterly, 41,* 125–149.

Gutmann, D. (1982). The crosscultural perspective: Notes toward a comparative. In K. W. Schaie & J. Geiwitz (Eds.), *Readings in adult development and aging.* Boston: Little, Brown.

Habermas, J. (1971). *Knowledge and human interests.* Boston: Beacon Press.

Hartree, A. (1984). Malcolm Knowles's theory of andragogy: A critique. *International Journal of Lifelong Education, 3,* 203–210.

Havighurst, R. J. (1953). *Human development and education.* New York: Longmans & Green.

Havighurst, R. J. (1972). *Developmental tasks and education* (3rd ed.). New York: McKay.

Hayes, E., & Colin, S. A. J. (1994). Racism and sexism in the U.S.: Fundamental issues. In E. Hayes and S. A. J. Colin (Eds.), *Confronting racism and sexism (New*

Directions for Continuing and Adult Education, No. 61, pp. 53–62). San Francisco: Jossey-Bass.

Hergenhahn, B. R. (1988). *An introduction to theories of learning* (3rd ed.). Englewood Cliffs, NJ: Prentice-Hall.

Hill, J. E. (1972). *How schools can apply systems analysis.* Bloomington, IN: Phi Delta Kappa Educational Foundation.

Hill, J. E. (1976). *The educational sciences.* Bloomfield Hills, IL: Oakland Community College.

Houle, C. O. (1961). *The inquiring mind.* Madison: University of Wisconsin Press.

Hultsch, D. F., & Plemons, J. K. (1979). Life events and life span development. In P. B. Baltes & O. G. Brim (Eds.), *Life-span development and behavior* (Vol. 2). New York: Academic Press.

James, W. (1920). Remarks on Spencer's definition of mind as correspondence. In W. James, *Collected essays and reviews.* London: Longman.

Jordan, D. R. (1996). *Teaching adults with learning disabilities.* Malabar, FL: Krieger.

Juhasz, A. M. (1989). A role-based approach to adult development: The triple helix model. *International Journal of Aging and Human Development, 29*(4), 302–315.

Knowles, M. S. (1980). *The modern practice of adult education: From pedagogy to andragogy* (2nd ed.). New York: Cambridge.

Knowles, M. S. (1984). *The adult learner: A neglected species* (3rd ed.). Houston, TX: Gulf.

Kohlberg, L. (1969). Stage and sequence: The cognitive-developmental approach to socialization. In D. A. Goslin (Ed.), *Handbook of socialization theory and research.* Chicago: Rand McNally.

Kolb, D. A. (1976). *Learning style inventory: Technical manual.* Boston: McBer.

Kolb, D. A. (1981). Learning styles and disciplinary differences. In A. W. Chickering & Associates (Eds.), *The modern American college: Responding to the new realities of diverse students and a changing society* (pp. 232–255). San Francisco: Jossey-Bass.

Levinson, D. J. (1978). *The seasons of a man's life.* New York: Knopf.

Loevinger, J. (1976). *Ego development: Conceptions and theories.* San Francisco: Jossey-Bass.

Lorge, I. (1944). Intellectual changes during maturity and old age. *Review of Educational Research, 14*(4), 438–443.

Lowenthal, M. F., Thurnher, M., Chiriboga, D., & Associates. (1975). *Four stages of life: A comparative study of women and men aging transitions.* San Francisco: Jossey-Bass.

Malone, O. (1986). The adult deaf learner: A very neglected species. *Lifelong Learning: An Omnibus of Practice and Research, 10*(3), 8–11, 23, 30.

Merriam, S. (1988). Finding your way through the maze: A guide to the literature on adult learning. *Lifelong Learning, 11*(6), 4–7.

Merriam, S. B., & Caffarella, R. S. (1991). *Learning in adulthood.* San Francisco: Jossey-Bass.

Mezirow, J. (1981). A critical theory of adult learning and education. *Adult Education, 32*(1), 3–27.

Mezirow, J. (1985). Concept and action in adult education. *Adult Education Quarterly, 35*(3), 22.

Mezirow, J. (1990). *Fostering critical reflection in adulthood: A guide to transformative and emancipatory learning.* San Francisco: Jossey-Bass.

Mezirow, J., & Marsick, V. (1978). *Education for perspective transformation: Women's reentry programs in community colleges.* New York: Teachers College, Columbia University Center for Adult Education.

Moe, J. (1990). Education, democracy, and cultural pluralism: Continuing higher education in an age of diversity. In J. M. Ross-Gordon, L. G. Martin, & D. B. Briscoe. *Serving culturally diverse populations* (*New Directions for Adult and Continuing Education,* No. 48, pp. 31–44). San Francisco: Jossey-Bass.

Morstain, B. R., & Smart, J. C. (1974). Reasons for participation in adult education courses: A multivariate analysis of group differences. *Adult Education, 24*(2), 83–98.

Neugarten, B. L. (1979). Time, age, and the life cycle. *American Journal of Psychiatry, 136,* 887–893.

Neugarten, B. L., Moore, J. W., & Lowe, J. C. (1968). Age norms, age constraints and adult socialization. In B. L. Neugarten (Ed.), *Middle age and aging.* Chicago: University of Chicago Press.

O'Brien, E. M. (1990, Mar. 1). Continuing ed programs not reaching minority populations, officials admit. *Black Issues in Higher Education,* 6–8.

Pennington, F., & Green, J. (1976). Comparative analysis of program development processes in six professions. *Adult Education, 27*(1), 12–23.

Perlmutter, M., & Hall, H. (1985). *Adult development and aging.* New York: John Wiley.

Perry, W. (1970). *Forms of intellectual and ethical development in the college years.* New York: Holt, Rinehart & Winston.

Phillips, D. C. (1995). The good, the bad, and the ugly: The many faces of constructivism. *Educational Researcher, 24*(7), 5–12.

Piaget, J. (1980). The psychogenesis of knowledge and its epistemological significance. In M. Piatelli-Palmarine (Ed.), *Language and learning.* Cambridge, MA: Harvard University Press.

Podeschi, R. (1990). Teaching their own: Minority challenges to mainstream institutions. In J. M. Ross-Gordon, L. G. Martin, & D. B. Briscoe, *Serving culturally diverse populations* (*New Directions for Adult and Continuing Education,* No. 48, pp. 55–66). San Francisco: Jossey-Bass.

Pratt, D. D. (1988). Andragogy as relational construct. *Adult Education Quarterly, 38,* 160–181.

Pratt, D. D. (1993). Andragogy after twenty-five years. In S. Merriam (Ed.), *An update on adult learning theory* (*New Directions for Adult and Continuing Education,* No. 57, pp. 18–14). San Francisco: Jossey-Bass.

Reese, H. W., & Smyer, M. A. (1983). The dimensionalization of life events. In E. J. Callahan & K. A. McCluskey (Eds.), *Life-span developmental psychology: Nonnormative events.* New York: Academic Press.

Reichmann, S. W., & Grasha, A. F. (1974). A rational approach to developing and assessing the construct validity of a student learning style scales instrument. *The Journal of Psychology, 87,* 213–223.

Roberts, P., & Newton, P. M. (1987). Levinsonian studies of women's adult development. *Psychology and Aging, 2*(2), 154–163.

Rogers, C. R. (1983). *Freedom to learn for the 80's.* Columbus, OH: Merrill.

Rosenbaum, J. E. (1976). *Making inequality: The hidden curriculum of high school training.* New York: John Wiley.

Rosenblum, S. H. (1985). *Involving adults in the educational process* (*New Directions for Continuing Education,* No. 26). San Francisco: Jossey-Bass.

Ross, J. M. (1987). Learning disabled adults: Who are they and what do we do with them? *Lifelong Learning: An Omnibus of Practice and Research, 11*(3), 4–7, 11.

Ross-Gordon, J. M. (1990). *Serving culturally diverse populations: A social imperative for adult and continuing education* (*New Directions for Adult and Continuing Education,* No. 48, pp. 5–15). San Francisco: Jossey-Bass.

Ross-Gordon, J. M. (1991). Needed: A multicultural perspective for adult education research. *Adult Education Quarterly, 42*(1), 1–16.

Ross-Gordon, J. M., Martin, L. G., & Briscoe, D. B. (1990). Serving culturally diverse populations. In J. M. Ross-Gordon, L. G. Martin, & D. B. Briscoe (Eds.), *Serving culturally diverse populations* (*New Directions for Adult and Continuing Education,* No. 48, pp. 31–44). San Francisco: Jossey-Bass.

Sarkees, M., & Scott, J. (1985). *Vocational special needs.* Alsip, IL: American Technical Publishers.

Schaie, K. W. (1979). The primary mental abilities in adulthood: An exploration in the development of psychometric intelligence. In P. B. Baltes & O. G. Brim (Eds.), *Life-span development and behavior,* Vol. 2. New York: Academic Press.

Schaie, K. W., & Parr, J. (1981). Intelligence. In A. W. Chickering & Associates (Eds.), *The modern American college: Responding to the new realities of diverse students, and a changing society* (pp. 117–138). San Francisco: Jossey-Bass.

Schlossberg, N. K. (1984). *Counseling adults in transition.* New York: Springer.

Sheehy, G. (1976). *Passages: Predictable crises of adult life.* New York: Dutton.

Smith, R. M. (1982). *Learning how to learn: Applied learning theory for adults.* Chicago: Follett.

Snyder, T. (1988). *Digest of education statistics.* Office of Educational Research and Improvement and the National Center for Education Statistics. Washington, DC: Government Printing Office.

Sternberg, R. J. (1985). *Beyond I.Q.: A triarchic theory of human intelligence.* Cambridge, MA: Cambridge University Press.

Sternberg, R. J. (1994). Allowing for thinking styles. *Educational Leadership, 52*(3), 360–40.

Stewart, W. A. (1977). A psychosocial study of the formation of the early adult life structure in women. *Dissertation Abstracts International, 38,* 381 B. (University Microfilms No. 7714849).

Sviniciki, M. D., & Dixon, N. M. (1987). The Kolb model modified for classroom activities. *College Teaching, 35*(A4), 141–146.

Tennant, M. (1986). An evaluation of Knowles' theory of adult learning. *International Journal of Lifelong Education, 5*(2), 113–122.

Tough, A. (1979). *The adult's learning projects: A fresh approach to theory and practice in adult learning* (2nd ed.). Toronto: Ontario Institute for Studies in Education.

Travis, G. Y. (1985). Andragogy and the disabled adult learner. *Lifelong Learning: An Omnibus of Practice and Research,* 8(8), 16–20.

Tyler, R. (1959). *Basic principles of curriculum and instruction.* Chicago: University of Chicago Press.

U.S. Bureau of the Census, Department of Commerce. (1989). *Statistical abstracts of the United States.* Washington, DC: Government Printing Office.

Vygotsky, L. (1978). *Mind in society. The development of higher psychological processes.* Edited by M. Cole, et al. Cambridge: Harvard University Press.

West, J. (Ed.). (1990). *The Americans with disabilities act: From policy to practice.* New York: Milbank Memorial Fund.

Willis, S. L., & Schaie, K. W. (1985). Practical intelligence in later adulthood. In R. J. Sternberg & R. K. Wagner (Eds.), *Intelligence in the everyday world.* New York: Cambridge University Press.

## 10

Determining Program Needs

Sandra Pearce

ABSTRACT

Programmers have a central role in determining needs. By describing the tacit decision process used by experienced programmers, the intent of this chapter is to allow programmers to reflect on their approaches to needs assessment and to become more aware of how they exercise professional judgment. The literature on needs assessment is reviewed with emphasis on both the practical considerations of programmers and the conceptual approaches which underlie programmers' decisions. It offers two conceptual approaches—the functional (positivist) perspective and the empowerment (subjectivist) perspective. While recognizing the pivotal role that programmers have in the process of determining program needs, current practice and pertinent literature are discussed from both perspectives.

ASSESSMENT

- I always do a needs assessment before I go ahead with a program. No Yes
- I find needs assessments are useful in some circumstances. No Yes

An earlier version of this chapter appeared in Sandra Pearce (1975), Needs assessment: Constructing tacit knowledge from practice, *International Journal of Lifelong Education*, *14*(5), 405–419.

- I think needs assessments are a waste of time.   No   Yes
- I believe that needs assessments are antithetical   No   Yes
  to the whole process of learning.

How many yes answers did you circle? How many nos? As you no doubt have surmised, there are no correct answers. These statements are representative of the range of beliefs about determining program needs that are held by various program planners. Without knowing the contextual situation of programmers, we cannot make judgments about the "rightness" or "wrongness" of these statements. If you are a training director for municipal fire-fighters, you will likely answer "yes" to the first question and I would agree with you since I would certainly prefer to be rescued by a firefighter who knew, and could apply, the skills of that trade. On the other hand, if you are a community development worker helping the people who live in fishing villages to confront government regulations and controls on their livelihood, you may be engaged in an activity in which needs assessment is not relevant.

The field of adult education and training is so broad that there are many different, yet equally valid, conceptions regarding how one goes about determining program needs, or even if one should be involved in that process. These differing approaches are the result of at least two factors—the type of work the program planner is involved in, as in the examples just mentioned, and the programmer's beliefs and values.

The purpose of this chapter is to help experienced program planners reflect on how they determine program needs by posing a series of questions. These questions emphasize the programmer's pivotal role in determining needs. They also form the basis for a programmer's decision making within that process.

What conceptual model underlies my thinking about needs assessment?
What are needs?
Whose needs do we assess?
How do we determine program needs?

Following a discussion of these questions, a new approach to needs assessment is introduced. This approach is drawn from practice and recognizes the skill and expertise of experienced programmers.

KEY CONCEPTS

Needs assessment The process of discovering program needs. It is variously called task analysis/job analysis in training, field work or social animation in community development, a self-diagnosis by an individual learner, or pre-program evaluation. As well as a process, it can also refer to a product—usually an instrument such as a survey or a questionnaire.

Programmer Used in this chapter as a shortened form of *program planner*. It is treated as a generic term to cover those adult educationists who are engaged in determining program needs.

WHAT CONCEPTUAL MODEL UNDERLIES MY THINKING ABOUT NEEDS ASSESSMENT?

There are several conceptual approaches that can underlie our work as programmers, and therefore influence the ways in which we choose to discover program needs. While a needs assessment instrument may be an end product, determining needs is a process as well. The beliefs and values we hold form the basis for our professional decision making, and influence the ways we understand and implement the process of determining needs. A good deal of the program planning literature recognizes the influence that programmers' values have on their work (Knox, 1986; Apps, 1985; Boone, 1985), underscoring the fact that needs assessment, as part of the educational process is never neutral or value free. Although a number of philosophical beliefs can underlie our work as programmers, this chapter uses two broad categorizations—one has a positivist orientation and the other a subjectivist orientation. The positivist approach is apparent in the functional perspective and the subjectivist orientation in the empowerment perspective.

The Functionalist Perspective

The functionalist approach has been the most prevalent in North American adult education and training. Variously labeled rational, technical, or positivist, the functional view assumes that needs can be identified objectively and that they are measurable. The functionalist perspective underlies most program planning models in adult education and training (Boone, 1985; Boyle, 1981; Houle, 1972; Knowles, 1980; London, 1960). Program design comprises stating needs as objectives, attempting to meet those objectives, and evaluating the outcome to see if the needs were indeed met.

The functionalist approach is based on scientific empiricism—the idea that knowledge and the need for it are objectives that can be empirically discovered. In adult education practice, this view draws to a great extent on the work of John Dewey who applied the logic of science to education. Education is helping people learn to solve problems through the scientific method. It assumes that the source of knowledge lies outside the learner, and that educators must help people access that knowledge. This is the kind of knowledge that is often labeled "how-to." If you use this approach in your programming, your determination of program needs will focus on what people need to know in order to do something better than they are doing it now. Many programs are even titled with "how-to" (e.g., "How to Write and Give a Speech"), while with other programs the "how-to" is implied (e.g., "Motivating Staff for Improved Performance").

The Empowerment Perspective

The empowerment perspective has as its goal empowering individuals, communities, or societies. It suggests that the purpose of any educational undertaking is to reduce the power and influence that various systems have on our lives—the ultimate goal is to change the system itself and the oppressive conditions it creates for individuals who are part of it. If you adopt the empowerment perspective, you are working toward change at the system level—the educational system, the system of government, the economic system, or the political system.

The subjectivist paradigm, on which the empowerment perspective rests, suggests that social reality is constructed and constantly changing. Your perceptions of reality may not be mine, but to each of us they are real. Reality is constructed by the individual and social reality reflects our shared perceptions (see discussions by Berger & Luckman, 1966; Cunningham, 1988). Apps (1985) notes that many scientists take this definition of reality one step further—they include objective as well as social reality.

Within the empowerment approach, determining needs is a process but the end product of the process is seldom a "program" in the traditional (functional) sense, although a "program" may be part of the overall process. The empowerment approach underlies such diverse areas as feminist pedagogy, some environmental education, feminist jurisprudence, and liberation theology and is reflected in the work of Freire (1970), Alinsky (1972), Illich (1971), and Ohliger (1988), among others. Although the philosophical bases represented in this approach, as well as the methods that are used, are all very different, in all cases, the intent is to change a given system and free the people within it from oppression. In the empowerment view, needs assessment is part of the whole educational process, a learning and needs-meeting tool of its own.

Choosing a Perspective

These two perspectives are not always as sharply defined in practice as they have been here. Distinguishing them in this manner though, allows programmers to reflect on the underlying question, "What is my reason for doing this program?" By coming to grips with your underlying beliefs regarding the program you are working on, you will become more aware of how you will go about assessing the need for it. A program, a needs assessment, or any educational activity, is only the beginning. It is usually impossible to discern the underlying reasons for doing the program by its title or description. Let's look at an example of this in practice.

One of my own programs is titled, "Working with People in Chronic Pain." It is designed for professionals in the health and human service fields. From a functionalist perspective it offers these professionals new knowledge and skills—which is clearly indicated from its "how-to" title. However, it was designed from an empowerment perspective not a functional one. The underlying belief is that you and I as individuals should be in control of our own health, and that the role of health professionals is to provide their expertise to us, as it is needed. At this point in time, though, health professionals are more likely to be in charge than the person they are caring for. From the empowerment perspective then, the professional community's power over the health system must be

transferred to the people who use their services. This is the conceptual approach underlying this program and it is seen as one of
many small steps in changing the health system. The participants in
the program do indeed learn new skills and knowledge, but the
entire focus of the program is aimed at helping these professionals
move the locus of control away from the professional health community.

The conceptual approach that underlies our work as programmers will influence how we go about determining program needs,
and indeed our beliefs about needs themselves.

WHAT ARE NEEDS?

Need, according to Leagans (1964) is "an innocent appearing, four letter word, but probably the most deceptively complex,
basically significant, and far reaching in its implications of all the
major terms in the vocabulary of the adult educator" (p. 89). Most
program planning models in adult education are based on Tyler's
(1949) belief that a need is the difference between an individual's
current state of knowledge or skill and a specified norm. As
Knowles (1980) explains it, this gap or deficiency on the part of the
learner creates the motivation to learn. This conception of need as
a deficiency to be remedied has formed the basis not only for the
majority of program planning models (see for example, Boone,
1985; Houle, 1972; Knowles, 1980; London, 1960) but has also
created a lengthy discussion in the literature about the nature of
educational needs.

Needs have been described as being of two types—felt needs
which are needs expressed by the individual and normative or
ascribed needs which are those set by an outside authority. While
many other descriptive labels have been used (see for example,
Boshier, 1986; Bradshaw, 1972; Sork, 1987) the overall intent is clear
as far as individual learners are concerned. They either feel a need
to learn something, or they are told to learn something.

While applying different terminology, Boshier (1986), Bradshaw (1972), and Sork (1987) are among those who have noted that
felt needs themselves can be of two types—deficiency needs or
growth needs. While deficiency needs are clearly gaps in our learning, growth needs reflect the developmental tasks generated by
various life stages (Havighurst, 1976).

The concept of need, as discussed to this point, reflects the conceptual approach of the functionalist perspective so prevalent in the literature today. Working within this view, a need is a gap or discrepancy that the learner is trying to change. In his review of the literature on the concept of need, Long (1983) reiterates the conclusions reached by Monette (1979) by noting, "The term *need* ... always implies ... some standard or valued state of affairs or certain social norms against which need is measured" (p. 187).

This functionalist concept of need has resulted in a great deal of literature that attempts to discover what constitutes "real" educational need and tries to distinguish between "real" needs and mere wants or desires (Bryson, 1936; Clark, 1990; Sheasha, 1961). The discussion, while interesting from a conceptual approach, has little to do with the reality of program planning. For a programmer working within the rationalist perspective, the salient point is that people believe they have something to learn-whether theoreticians would consider their need to be "real" or not. For those working from an empowerment perspective, the discussion is simply not relevant.

While debate on the technicalities of needs may not be critical for programmers who are making needs assessment decisions, it does offer us another opportunity to engage in critical reflection and so learn more about our conceptual approach to needs assessment. The discussion on what constitutes a real need reflects the technical/rational approach that dominates the literature, i. e. the belief that a real need exists, and that people need to measure up to it. The alternative paradigm of the empowerment perspective suggests that needs, like social reality, are constructed. This paradigm underlies the empowerment approach to determining needs. By casting our thoughts about program planning within this paradigm, we can see that all needs are real—whether they are classified as needs, interests, wants, or desires.

These diverse conceptualizations of needs leads us to the next question—whose needs are we concerned with as program planners?

WHOSE NEEDS DO WE ASSESS?

The discussion of needs in the literature focuses almost exclusively on the needs of the individual learner. This reflects the dominance of the ethos of the individual in North American, particularly U.S., adult education. Moving only slightly beyond the emphasis on individuals in the adult education literature brings us a broader perspective and a wealth of knowledge about needs. Training and development shows the dominance of organizational needs, continuing professional education reflects the dominance of professional norms, and community development emphasizes the needs of community and society. The needs that we are assessing then can belong to an individual, a private or public sector organization, a professional or voluntary association, a community, or a society. Many discussions of needs refer to some or all of these differing kinds of needs (see Apps, 1985; Boone, 1985; Boshier, 1986; Clark, 1990; Houle, 1972). Despite this diversity, the assessment of individual needs tends to dominate the literature.

Private and public sector organizations have needs for skilled employees. Professions also exert a normative standard on their members, as do various trades. Training needs analysis in organizations has reached a degree of sophistication unrivaled in public continuing education. The focus is often competency based, and draws heavily on the functionalist perspective. While the earlier discussion indicated that the discussion of needs variables vs. wants in the literature had little relation to program practice, in the broader context of organizational needs, the difference becomes more important. "Employees often want training in specific areas that are irrelevant to their jobs or inconsistent with organizational objectives" (Nowack, 1991, p. 69) and so it is important for organizations to distinguish between "training wants and true training needs" (p. 69). Indeed, as Parry (1990) states, "Good training doesn't cost; it pays. But only if it is linked to the organization's business plan, goals, and objectives" (p. 32).

To this point we have considered needs as belonging to either an individual, an organization, or a society. However, considering needs from a different angle shows us that there are two general groups that programmers are concerned with—those that constitute a captive audience, and those that constitute a public audience. The needs, and the assessment processes, will be very different for each.

Public Audiences. This group represent those people who can choose to participate in programs. While quite diverse, they represent a major portion of the audience for noncredit adult education programs offered by universities, colleges, YM-YWCAs, community associations, and many other private and public agencies. Public audiences also represent communities and special interest groups for community development specialists. While the label "general public" is too broad, these are the people who take part in programs or processes by choice.

Captive Audiences. This group is composed of people who have only limited choice about participating in a program, as opposed to public audiences who have a great deal of choice. This distinction is seldom made in the adult education literature—there is a general assumption that participation is voluntary (Knowles, 1980). However, it may be more correctly said that learning is voluntary, even though program participation may not be. Captive audiences have quite limited choice about participating in a program.

Programs developed for captive audiences include:

- in-house training and development programs whether for a private company, a public agency, or the military;
- programs leading to initial licensure or certification, e.g., university degrees, licenses for skilled tradespeople, or professional accreditation;
- curative or punishment programs required by a court of law, e.g., unsafe drivers must take driver education, or wife batterers must take programs to change their behavior;
- programs offered exclusively for the members of a particular profession or trade, which would include most continuing professional education as well as continuing trades training.

Since captive audiences are much more homogeneous than public audiences, needs assessments can be much more precise. At the same time, the cost of more elaborate needs assessment techniques can be justified based on that homogeneity and the fact that the program planner has fewer concerns about participation.

HOW DO WE DETERMINE PROGRAM NEEDS?

The dominant perspective in North American adult education and training is the functionalist approach. Most of the literature on determining needs takes a prescriptive approach (Long, 1983; Sork and Buskey, 1986) and most conventional program planning models state that needs must be identified. Boone's (1985) exhortation typifies these models: "Adult educators must identify, assess and analyze learners' expressed/felt needs.... It is imperative that adult educators thoroughly understand the needs concept if they are to function effectively" (p. 12). Clearly, this statement fits the functional perspective well, the empowerment approach less so.

The assumption underlying the standard writings on needs assessments is that it is both possible and desirable to determine needs. This reductionist belief is valid only within the rational-functional framework—and even programmers working within that perspective often do not carry out needs assessments. Many highly successful programs have had no needs assessment component (Pennington & Green, 1976). It is generally agreed that although there is a plethora of prescriptive needs assessment models, few are ever applied in practice (Apps, 1985; Cervero, 1988; Pennington & Green, 1976; Sork & Buskey, 1986; Sork & Caffarella, 1989).

Although the functionalist perspective is dominant in the literature, some scholars such as Cervero (1988) and Brookfield (1986), among others, have suggested that it does not adequately describe the process of assessing needs. After reviewing many program planning models, Sork and Buskey (1986) point out that none take into account the contextual situation of the programmer, while Monette (1979) emphasizes their lack of recognition of the programmer's values.

Monette (1979) draws on Freirian concepts to suggest that programmers should focus on values rather than a deterministic approach to needs. He suggests that programmers need to reflect on their own views of the human person and human learning and what values they want to encourage. By drawing on these two sources, they can then find appropriate learning activities.

Following Monette (1977 and 1979), then, the initial question the programmer must deal with is not, "What are the needs to be met with this program?," but the much broader question, "What is my reason for doing this program?" Answering that question will allow programmers to reflect on their beliefs and experience and will clarify which conceptual approach the programmer will adopt to guide the whole process of determining needs.

Since the literature in the field appears to be at odds with practice, it may be useful to reflect on what constitutes effective practice. Experienced programmers develop a sense of professional judgment that can almost be described as an intuitive feeling for the ins and outs of the process of determining program needs. Schön (1987) describes it as professional artistry, and labels it knowing-in-action. He notes that knowing-in-action is similar to tacit knowledge, "... the knowing is in the action. We reveal it by our spontaneous, skillful execution of the performance; and we are characteristically unable to make it verbally explicit" (p. 25). In everyday life, we know how to ride a bicycle—the knowledge we have is in the action of riding the bicycle—it is not something we are able to describe. In our professional lives as effective programmers, we know when, why, and how to engage in needs assessments— yet like riding a bicycle, it is not readily described.

It is clear that the functionalist prescriptive treatments of needs assessments are not congruent with practice since they fail to take into account the professional artistry, the knowing-in-action, of program planners. Schön notes that descriptions of tacit knowledge, or knowing-in-action, cannot be prescriptive since knowing-in-action is dynamic, while prescriptions are static. Schön goes on to observe that, "... it is sometimes possible by observing and reflecting on our actions, to make a description of the tacit knowing implicit in them" (p. 25). These descriptions are, by their very nature, constructed. Following Schön, and reflecting on the practice of effective programmers, the next section attempts to construct a description of determining program needs that reflects the knowing-in-action of effective program planners.

AN APPROACH TO NEEDS ASSESSMENT

As noted earlier in this chapter, determining needs can be both a process and an end result in the functionalist framework, while in the empowerment perspective, the discovery of needs is usually an intrinsic part of the process of learning and cannot be set apart. The approach to needs assessment suggested here is derived from practice and is described from the programmer's viewpoint. It can be employed by programmers working within the functionalist or empowerment frameworks. It rests on the programmer answering the core question introduced at the beginning of this chapter: "What is my reason for doing this program?"

The process begins with a program idea which is followed by an initial assessment. If the initial assessment is favorable an in-depth assessment is the next step. With favorable answers, the program planner reaches the stage of needs assessment, and determines whether one is necessary and if so, its purpose. Prior to this stage, some programmers working from the empowerment perspective may move directly to program implementation. The process, summarized in Figure 10.1, is described in more detail below.

Program Idea

The program idea can come from a number of sources including content experts, the parent organization, learners, an external agency, or from the programmer.

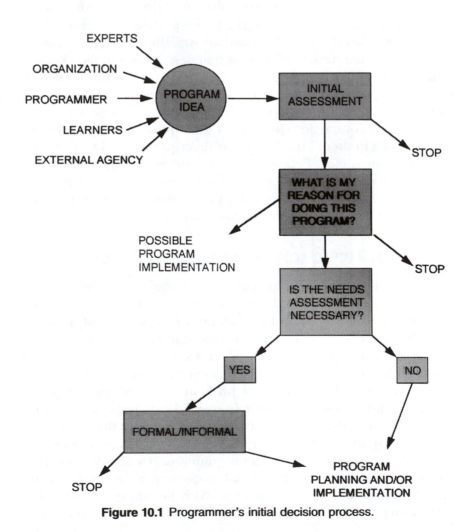

Figure 10.1 Programmer's initial decision process.

Content Expert. The first of these sources, the content expert, is one used reasonably often in continuing higher education. In fact Boone (1985) states that this is the major source of programs. My own experience, and that of others would not support that assumption, but it is a reasonably common source. The scenario goes something like this: Dr. Knowit, an internationally respected expert in her area, calls and says she would be interested in giving a workshop on the topic to professionals in the field.

Parent Organization. Another source of program ideas is the programmer's parent organization. Given that most continuing education agencies are part of larger parent organizations whose major focus is not adult education (Knowles, 1977), demands from the parent organization become program ideas. A YWCA for example may direct its training officer to develop an orientation program for new board members, a university president may direct the continuing education unit to hold a certain conference, or an airline may require its human resource department to develop training that will enhance the customer service capabilities of its ticketing agents.

Learners. A third input for program ideas are the learners. It is with this group that the majority of adult education writing on needs assessment is concerned, since most models demand that learners' needs be evaluated before a program begins. Discovering the needs of learner's has preoccupied the field and numerous methods of doing this have been documented. Strother and Klus (1982) list surveys, direct observation, trial balloons, advisory groups, inquiries and user feedback, interest inventories, and results of performance reviews. Boshier (1986) includes many of the same methods while Knowles (1980) emphasizes self-diagnosis.

Programmer. Program ideas are also generated by the programmer. Although some needs assessment models (Knox, 1986; Cervero, 1988; Nowlen, 1982; Apps, 1985) recognize this source of ideas—Nowlen (1982) refers to it as the programmer's *informed intuition*, while Apps (1985) calls it *creativity*—few models discuss it in detail. In practice however, this is perhaps the most widely used source of program ideas. While there are relatively few studies that have attempted to discover how programmers actually work, the few that do exist note that none of the formal planning steps, including needs assessments are used (see Cervero, 1988; Pennington & Green, 1976). This is one instance where we can see Schön's (1987) concept of knowing-in-action.

External Agencies. Program ideas also come to the programmer
from external agencies that request a specific program or learning
experience and often contract with the programmer, or the programmer's institution, to deliver it. Independent consultants and
training organizations rely on this type of work from clients, as do
programmers in many universities and trade schools. The local
steel plant contracts with the community college to develop a safety
program for their plant workers; a governmental agency asks for
proposals from universities and private consultants for a management development workshop; a neighborhood association approaches an extension outreach programmer to learn how to deal
with city hall.

To summarize then, the first step in determining program
needs is a program idea. Programmers get these ideas from five
sources: (1) content experts, (2) their own organization, (3) potential learners, (4) their own professional experience and (5) external agencies. With a program idea in mind, the programmer does
an initial assessment.

Initial Assessment

The initial assessment is a series of questions the programmer
runs through. Sometimes the initial assessment is as short as a
thirty second review, in other instances it is considerably longer.
During the initial assessment phase, the programmer considers
some, or all, of the following questions.

1. Do I think this is a worthwhile program? This question carries
the most weight because it filters the program idea through the
personal philosophical beliefs and values of the programmer. Although some needs assessment models agree that the programmer's values have some influence on the process, in practice that
influence is much greater than has been acknowledged. Because
the programmer's pre-program decision process reflects knowing-
in-action and is largely tacit in its nature, programmers are generally unaware that they initially ask themselves if they think the
program is worthwhile. This is especially true if the programmer
feels comfortable with the program idea—the question is tacitly
answered "yes"—and the programmer just continues on with the
process of reviewing the other questions in the initial assessment.
Most health educators would feel comfortable with programs

aimed at helping new mothers nurse their babies; most extension specialists would see helping farmers increase their crop yields as worthwhile. If the answer to the first question is "yes," then the question has been tacitly posed and answered with such rapidity as to be unnoticed.

On the other hand, if the programmer does not consider the program to be worthwhile—if it violates a personal sense of values and creates a sense of unease—the programmer is more likely to be aware of these negative feelings, and respond, "No, I don't believe this is a worthwhile program." If this is the response, in most cases the process stops and the program idea is abandoned. Some health educators would have great difficulty with programs aimed at enhancing sexual responsiveness for homosexual couples; some extension specialists would feel unable to advocate increased use of pesticides or herbicides to increase farmers' productivity.

There are instances though, when despite responding negatively to the question, the programmer is unable to voluntarily abandon a program idea. For example, if the program idea is a demand from the parent organization, the programmer is put in a difficult position. It may be possible to think of ways to negotiate with the parent organization to change the demand. If that is not feasible, then the programmer has to reflect on whether it is possible, in good conscience, to do what has been asked (Kaufman, 1991). While it is true that the final decision to offer a program is a process of construction and negotiation, the central, if tacit, role played by the programmer's values and belief systems is critical.

Posing the question "Do I think this is a worthwhile program?" is not only the first step in the initial assessment, it is also the most important. It recognizes and affirms the centrality of the programmer and emphasizes the critical influence of the programmer's beliefs and values. The conceptual approaches to needs assessment presented earlier in this chapter can help programmers clarify and reflect on their thinking. The order of the remaining questions, and whether they are asked or not, depends on the programmer's particular situation.

2. Does this program fit the goals and mission of the sponsoring organization? This question addresses the issue of program congruence with the stated beliefs of the sponsoring organization. University programmers have particular concerns that their programs reflect "university quality," while a trainer in a government department needs to ensure that the program reflects the current government's priorities and directions.

3. *Will people be interested in it?* Will they participate? This question is of particular importance to those planning programs for public audiences—audiences who have a great deal of choice about whether or not they will participate.

4. *Can we afford to do it?* This question focuses on the balance between financial realities and the perceived importance of the program. For many program planners revenue production is important, while for others (such as in-house trainers) cost-benefit ratios are the focus. The subquestions that can be used to examine this issue for public programs are:

- Will it produce revenue?
- If it won't produce revenue, can I get outside funding to support it?
- Is it so important that I should do it anyway and subsidize it from another area?

In-house trainers need to ask if the cost of participants' time away from work is worth the anticipated benefit.

5. *Can I get the resources to do it?* This question refers to instructors, facilitators, cosponsors, advisory groups, specialized facilities and materials.

6. *How much time will it take me to do this program?* This question refers to the personal program mix of the programmer and how this program fits in to the time constraints already in place. Some of the considerations here will be whether the developmental time frame is short term or long range; the type of program (a conference, a seminar, a community action project); and whether the program is one that will be repeated or represents a one-shot effort. In addition, programmers factor into this mix the other requirements of their jobs (e. g. , committee work, research, teaching, management functions) and the demands on their time and creativity from areas of their life outside work.

Armed with the answers to these questions in the initial assessment, the programmer either proceeds to the next phase, or stops consideration of the program idea. The next phase brings the programmer to the core question, "What is my reason for doing this program?"

What Is My Reason for Doing This Program?

If the initial assessment has been favorable, the programmer proceeds to the heart of the process—coming to terms with the reason for deciding to put time, experience, energy, and expertise into the program. The process continues to focus on the programmer's perceptions and beliefs—bringing to the fore the knowing-in-action of effective programmers. There are a number of reasons that programmers may reflect on as they answer the question.

1. *The programmer needs the program.* The program is important either in terms of providing job satisfaction or fulfillment, or because it is seen as necessary for a promotion, job change, or long-term career goal. This response recognizes the missionary zeal that many educators working in the area of social change bring to their life's work. At the same time, it also recognizes the pragmatic needs of educators working in institutions who desire to be promoted or get a better job. While there is a wide range of meanings that can be attached to this response, it recognizes, and emphasizes, the centrality of the programmer and the programmer's needs.

2. *The programmer's work unit wants the program.* Many programmers work within programming agencies that are part of larger organizations—such as HRD training departments in companies, continuing higher education divisions in universities, education and extension units in museums and libraries. All these structured work groups must produce a range of programs at any given time. In order to meet the requirements, the program being considered will often be a repeat of an earlier program, either a successful one with modifications or a program that may have been canceled due to low enrollment. In the case of the latter, there may be changes made in time, location, title, or advertising methods.

3. *The programmer's parent organization requires the program.* This is the case with many in-house training programs, such as keeping the work force up to date with new technology. On the other hand, the program may be required because it reflects the organizational mission—YWCAs, for example, will offer lifestyle and fitness programs for women.

4. *The expertise for the program is available.* This is true for many off-campus credit classes, as well as for specialty degree classes. For example, the doctoral program in Adult Education at Pennsylvania State University offers electives in highly specialized areas in the

spring and summer terms. The content of these electives depends on the expertise of visiting faculty members.

5. *The program has been requested by an external group that will form the potential audience.* This reflects training requested by professional associations, community groups, or other organizations.

6. *The professional judgment of the programmer indicates that this program is a winner.* If not a winner, it at least has a reasonable chance of success.

These are just some of the possible answers to the question, "What is my reason for doing this program?" By concentrating on the heart of the matter, the programmer focuses on what for her or him is the real reason, the underlying purpose, for choosing to be involved with that particular program.

After receiving a program idea, the first two steps in the pre-program decision process (the initial assessment followed by the core question, "What is my reason for doing this program?") focus on the centrality of the programmer's individual values and beliefs. It must be stressed that these first two steps take very little time—in fact this tacit process in its entirety generally takes less than two minutes. However, as anyone who has ever tried to describe how to ride a bike or hammer a nail can attest, constructing a description of knowledge-in-action is considerably lengthier than the action itself—knowing is in the act of doing. For the most part, the literature on needs assessment has tended to ignore these tacit processes.

If the programmer decides that the reason for proceeding with the program is sufficient, it is at this point that other actors may become involved and that the question of needs assessment arises.

Is a Needs Assessment Necessary?

This question may or may not appear as part of the process depending on the type of program and the conceptual approach the programmer has developed. Programmers working in a functionalist framework will proceed to ask the question; those working in the empowerment framework may or may not. In many programs based on the empowerment approach, the program itself begins as the educator and community engage in a dialectic process.

Programmers who proceed to ask whether a needs assessment

is necessary, find that the answer, depending on the program, can be either yes or no. According to the few studies that have been done, the answer is usually no (Pennington & Green, 1976). Here again we see professional judgment at work. As discussed earlier, the norm specified in the literature is that needs assessments must be done. The adult education literature that bemoans the lack of needs assessment used in practice is written from a functionalist perspective. Much to the dismay of authors extolling the many virtues of needs assessments, programmers are not exhibiting poor professional judgment if they choose not to use them. Many highly successful programs have no needs assessment component. As Schön (1987) points out, professional judgment, or artistry, is the quality that moves professional practice beyond the textbook. It is the exercise of this professional judgment that is lost, or over-looked in the current prescriptive approach to needs assessment.

If the programmer decides a needs assessment is necessary, the next step is to decide whether it should be formal or informal.

Formal Needs Assessment

The formal approaches are the ones we are familiar with from the literature—various forms of surveys or questionnaires, usually referred to as needs assessment instruments. The most successful—and indeed the most sophisticated of these instruments—have been developed in organizational training. These assessment instruments have been developed not only to reflect various competencies, but also attitudes and beliefs. One such assessment instrument (Vest, O'Brien, & Vest, 1991) focuses on AIDS: the fear it generates in the workplace and the resulting negative business consequences such as loss of customers and wrongful dismissal suits. The authors describe it as a diagnostic process that determines what managers know and believe about AIDS and it is used to evaluate the causes of managerial fears before training. "The causes for managerial fears then become the focus for training program development. After training, needs assessment data are used to evaluate training program effectiveness" (p. 59). The instrument consists of three separate scales. All the scales were developed and validated on a sample of 248 managers from a government and a range of private sector organizations.

It is clear that the process of developing a needs assessment such as this one is extremely time consuming, and also very costly.

Administering the instrument and analyzing the data are also expensive in terms of both time, expertise, and money. These are the reasons formal needs assessments are normally the bailiwick of programmers working with captive audiences. Those working with public audiences seldom have such resources available. Program planners working with public audiences normally use these methods only in special circumstances. One such circumstance is to meet the requirements imposed by a funding agency. These groups often require a formal needs assessment in order to approve funds for a given project. Formal needs assessments are also used when a potential prod is of such significance (in terms of cost, impact, or risk) to the programmer's parent organization, that the investment in a formal needs assessment is felt to be justified. Universities and governments are notable for striking task forces and commissions as formal methods of needs assessment.

If a formal needs assessment is required, the programmer must decide at what point in the program development process it should be done. This decision point reflects the symbolic use of needs assessment. Although those working in a functionalist mode will find this use of needs assessment irrelevant (and perhaps underhanded), the symbolic role of needs assessments cannot be ignored. Programmers working from an empowerment perspective will be all too familiar with the symbolic power of, for example, the educational system. The symbolic aspect of needs assessment has less to do with needs being evaluated than with validating or enhancing the value of the program or its sponsoring institution. The value of symbolic power is of particular importance to those organizations (like universities, colleges, some public agencies, and hospitals) that produce no tangible product, but rely on public perceptions and beliefs about their value to society (Meyer & Rowan, 1978). Needs assessments can serve these symbolic ends. If this is their purpose, then they may not be done during the pre-program decision process, but at some other point.

Informal Needs Assessment

Informal assessments could be more aptly described as Q & D ("quick and dirty") assessments. Strother and Klus (1982) and Boshier (1986), among others have noted such methods as reviewing trade and professional journals, talking with colleagues in the field, checking out ideas with a network of key contacts, looking over past trends, informal environmental scanning, and offering a program to see what happens. Q & D assessments are used by programmers working with both public and captive audiences; however, those programming for public audiences (programmers in continuing higher education, museum education, or health promotion, for example) use them most extensively.

Informal needs assessments of a different sort are used by programmers in community education and community development, working from an empowerment perspective. Lovett (1975) describes it as "... [going] out into the field to meet the people on their own ground, without any preconceived notions about what is 'good for them'" (p. 25).

Decisions about when, or if, to use a needs assessment, whether formal or informal, is the last point in the process of determining needs. Whether you work from a functionalist or empowerment perspective, determining needs is a process—a holistic process. Needs assessment, whether formal or informal, is just one possible part of that process.

DETERMINING NEEDS

The framework that has been presented has been constructed from practice, and it recognizes the knowing-in-action of experienced program planners. It acknowledges the centrality of the programmer's beliefs and values as well as the professional artistry involved in assessing needs. It attempts to help programmers bring to the surface some of the tacit decision-making processes they engage in while determining program needs and it encourages programmers to reflect on their conceptual approaches to needs assessment. The core question that programmers concern themselves with is, "What is my reason for doing this program?" The framework provides a series of questions and decision points that describe the tacit processes involved in preprogram decisions.

QUESTIONS FOR STUDY AND DISCUSSION

1. What conceptual perspective (functionalist or empowerment) underlies your work as programmer? How is your perspective demonstrated in your approach to determining needs?
2. Recalling an actual example of a program with which you have

been involved, discuss the worth of the needs assessment you used (or didn't use).
3. Can a programmer with a strong personal belief in one perspective work with, or for, an organization that holds an opposite view? Discuss your experiences in this area.
4. As a group choose a topic/title for a program. Using the framework, step through the questions in the pre-program process. Do group members have similar or different responses to the various questions? Discuss the reasons for these similarities and differences. In the final analysis, is your reason for doing the program different from others in your group?
5. Assessing needs is an important part of the literature on program planning. As Sork and Caffarella (1989) observe, there is clearly a gap between theory and practice and it appears to be increasing. They offer three explanations: "(1) practitioners take shortcuts in planning in order to get the job done; (2) contextual factors largely determine how planning is done; (3) planning theory is increasingly irrelevant to practice" (p. 243). What is your opinion? Are there other explanations?

REFERENCES

Alinsky, S. (1972). *Rules for radicals: A practical primer for realistic radicals.* New York: Random House.
Apps, J. W. (1985). *Improving practice in continuing education.* San Francisco: Jossey-Bass.
Berger P., & Luckman, T. (1966). *The social construction of reality.* New York: Doubleday.
Boone, E. J. (1985). *Developing programs in adult education.* Englewood Cliffs, NJ: Prentice-Hall.
Boyle, P. (1981). *Planning better programs.* New York: McGraw-Hill.
Boshier, R. (1986). Proaction for a change: some guidelines for the future. *International Journal of Lifelong Education, 5,* 15–31.
Bradshaw, J. (1972). A taxonomy of social needs. In G. McClachen (Ed.). *Problems and progress in medical care: 7th series* (pp. 69–82). London: Nuffield Provincial Hospital Unit.
Brookfield, S. D. (1986). *Understanding and facilitating adult learning: A comprehensive analysis of principles and effective practices.* San Francisco: Jossey-Bass.
Bryson, L. (1936). *Adult education.* New York: American Book Company.
Cervero, R. M. (1988). *Effective continuing education for professionals.* San Francisco: Jossey-Bass.
Clark, J. (1990). Community education and the concept of need. *International Journal of Lifelong Education, 9,* 317–329.

Cunningham, P. M. (1988). The adult educator and social responsibility. In R. G. Brockett (Ed.). *Ethical issues in adult education* (pp. 133–145). New York: Teachers College, Columbia University.

Freire, P. (1970). *Education for critical consciousness.* New York: Seabury Press.

Havighurst, R. J. (1976). Education through the life span. *Educational Gerontology, 1,* 41–51.

Houle, C. O. (1972). *The design of education.* San Francisco: Jossey-Bass.

Illich, I. (1971). *Deschooling society.* New York: Harper and Rowe.

Kaufman, R. (1991). When good bosses ask for bad things. *Training and Development Journal,* May, 29–32.

Knowles, M. S. (1977). *A history of the adult education movement in the United States.* (revised ed.). Malabar, FL: Krieger.

Knowles, M. S. (1980). *The modern practice of adult education: From pedagogy to andragogy.* Englewood Cliffs, NJ: Prentice-Hall.

Knox, A. (1986). *Helping adults learn.* San Francisco: Jossey-Bass.

Leagans, J. P. (1964). A concept of needs. *Journal of Cooperative Extension, 2*(2), 89–96.

London, J. (1960). Program development in adult education. In M. S. Bowles. (Ed.). *Handbook of adult education in the United States* (pp. 13–36). Washington: Adult Education Association of the USA.

Long, H. B. (1983). *Adult learning: Research and practice.* New York: Cambridge.

Lovett, T. (1975). *Adult education, community development, and the working class.* London: Ward Lock.

Meyer, J., & Rowan, B. (1978). The structure of educational organizations. In M. W. Meyer & Associates (Eds.). *Environments and organizations: Theoretical and empirical perspectives* (pp. 78–109). San Francisco: Jossey-Bass.

Monette, M. L. (1977). The concept of educational need: An analysis of selected literature. *Adult Education, 27,* 195–208.

Monette, M. L. (1979). Needs assessment: a critique of philosophical assumptions. *Adult Education, 29,* 116–127.

Nowack, K. M. (1991). A true training needs analysis. *Training and Development Journal,* April, 69–73.

Nowlen, P. M. (1982). Program origins. In A. B. Knox & Associates. *Developing, administering, and evaluating adult education* (pp. 65–81). San Francisco: Jossey-Bass.

Ohliger, J. (1988). *The fictional adult educator.* Madison, WI: Basic Choices.

Parry, S. B. (1990). Linking training to the business plan. *Training and Development Journal,* May, 32–36.

Pearce, S. D. (1995). Needs assessment: Constructing tacit knowledge from practice. *International Journal of Lifelong Education, 14,* 5, 405–419.

Pennington, G., & Green, J. (1976). Comparative analysis of program development processes in six professions. *Adult Education, 27,* 12–23.

Schön, D. A. (1987). *Educating the reflective practitioner.* San Francisco: Jossey-Bass.

Sheasha, T. (1961). A definition of needs and wants. *Adult Education, 12*(1), 52–53.

Sork, T. J. (1987). Needs assessment as part of program planning. In Q. H. Gessner (Ed.). *Handbook of continuing higher education* (pp. 125–142). New York: Macmillan.

Sork, T. J., & Buskey, J. H. (1986). A descriptive and evaluative analysis of program planning literature, 1950–1983. *Adult Education Quarterly, 36*, 86–96, 31.

Sork, T. J., & Caffarella, K. S. (1989). Planning programs for adults. In S. B. Merriam & P. M. Cunningham. (Eds.). *Handbook of adult and continuing education* (pp. 233–245). San Francisco: Jossey-Bass.

Strother, G. B., & Klus, J. P. (1982). *Administration of continuing education.* Belmont, CA: Wadsworth.

Tyler, R. W. (1949). *Basic principles of curriculum and instruction.* Chicago: University of Chicago Press.

Vest, J. M., O'Brien, F. P., & Vest, M. J. (1991, December). AIDS training in the workplace. *Training and Development Journal,* 59–64.

## 11

Program Priorities, Purposes, and Objectives

Thomas J. Sork

ABSTRACT

This chapter addresses the processes involved in determining priorities, purposes and objectives for adult education programs. It discusses the challenge of conflicting values among stakeholders and the issues involved in progressively narrowing the scope of what often begins as a vague program idea to those needs, purposes and objectives considered of greatest value by stakeholders. Alternative techniques useful in carrying out these tasks are described.

ASSESSMENT

If you can answer yes to all of the questions below, then you should skip this chapter because you already know all the ideas it contains and can carry out the tasks it explains.

* Are you aware of the relationships between needs, purposes and objectives in program planning?   No   Yes
* Are you aware of and can you use at least four different approaches to priority setting?   No   Yes
* Can you name and describe at least eight different criteria that might be used to determine priorities?   No   Yes
* Can you explain the influence the "Tyler Rationale" had on how educators have thought about objectives?   No   Yes

- Are you aware of and can you use at least four
  different ways of preparing objectives?   No   Yes
- Can you describe the advantages and disadvan-
  tages of each of the four ways of preparing objectives?   No   Yes
- Can you identify at least four different alterna-
  tives to objectives in program planning?   No   Yes
- Can you explain the advantages and limitations
  of each alternative to objectives?   No   Yes

KEY TERMS AND CONCEPTS

Priority   Often used to refer to what is more important but used
  here more broadly to mean having an earlier or antecedent
  claim to resources, including time, energy, money and so on.
  Determining priorities involves placing all of the ideas/needs
  identified in an order that reflects the sequence in which they
  will be addressed or in which they will receive resources. If
  there are sufficient resources to address all ideas/needs, then
  there is no need to worry about determining priorities. But
  there are few adult educators who have access to enough
  resources to respond to all ideas/needs that come to their
  attention.

Purpose   A general statement indicating intentions. In the case of
  program planning in adult education, purpose usually refers
  to a statement that indicates what a program is designed to
  accomplish. It provides a rationale for the decision to put time
  and effort into planning. Purposes are often related hier-
  archically to goals and objectives with goals usually being more
  specific than purposes but less specific than objectives.

Objective   As used in program planning, an objective is a detailed
  description of what learners should know or be able to do as a
  result of their participation in an educational event. In most
  cases an objective describes an intended learning outcome as
  reflected in something that the learner is asked to do–that is,
  the learner is asked to perform a task that is considered good
  evidence that the desired learning has taken place. Because
  learning cannot be directly observed, objectives provide a
  basis for inferring the degree to which the intended learning

has occurred. There may be multiple levels of objectives which are related to one another in hierarchical fashion.

BACKGROUND

Determining priorities, purposes and objectives in program planning is part of the continuing challenge of using limited resources to achieve the most valued outcomes. Many adult education programs have their origins in vague or ill-defined needs, ideas, requests, or problems. In these situations the task of those involved in planning is to sharpen the focus of the program so that it can be communicated clearly to those who will have a role to play during instruction and to those who control the resources that will be necessary to offer the program. To be successful, program planners must be able to design offerings that are consistent with the mission or mandate of the sponsor and are considered of value by the learners for whom they are designed. Although determining priorities, purposes and objectives in a systematic way requires some technical knowledge and skills, a more fundamental capability required is understanding and, in some cases, reconciling the conflicting values that are reflected in these decisions.

In most systematic approaches to program planning, needs assessment is used as one means to justify the allocation of resources. Needs assessment is often described as a process in which present states of affairs are determined and judgments are made about more desirable states of affairs. The more desirable states of affairs are *value judgments* made by those who are in a position to articulate their own needs (in which case they are felt or motivational needs) or to claim that others have needs (in which case they are ascribed or prescriptive needs) (Houle, 1972; Beatty, 1981). Needs are much more than lists of topics or program ideas that come from various stakeholders in the educational enterprise. Needs represent competing claims on limited educational resources. Planners can use them to demonstrate that such resources as money, personnel, equipment, facilities, and materials are being used on programs that stakeholders consider valuable. Program planning involves maintaining control over the allocation of scarce resources so that the maximum number of high value programs can be offered to the sponsors' clients in a way that both sponsors and other stakeholders (like governments, boards, community groups, business and industry representatives, professional associations and so on) are satisfied. If stakeholders are not satisfied that "correct" resource allocation decisions are being made, they will usually take steps to communicate their displeasure and to influence the process used to make these decisions in the future. For example, in recent years there has been growing pressure on many public sector providers of adult education programs to make money for their parent institutions. This pressure from the parent institution has come in many forms including new, more restricted mission statements and requirements that the adult education unit begin paying a share of, or increase its contribution to, the sponsor's overhead—rent, utilities, support personnel, supplies, equipment, postage and so on. A natural and necessary response to this pressure is to focus limited resources on programs high in demand or on programs for learners who are both willing and able to pay higher fees to attend. A long-term consequence of this pressure is that the needs of adults who are able and willing to pay higher fees will receive greater attention than the needs of those who are unable or unwilling to pay higher fees. This sometimes subtle transition occurs in the needs assessment and priority setting phases of planning where resource allocation decisions are made.

Although needs assessment logically precedes setting program priorities, purposes and objectives, in practice purposes and objectives are often determined without a needs assessment having first been done. This is possible because, as Houle (1972) rightly points out, needs assessment is only one of many ways that program ideas are identified. Indeed, recent research by Sork (1994) indicates that decisions about what programs will be offered are influenced by dozens of factors, only some of which are related to learning needs.

STATE OF THE LITERATURE

There is a vast literature on the program planning process, but only some of it addresses the topics of this chapter. Determining priorities is often neglected in the literature. Although most books that address program planning in adult education give some attention to needs assessment, only a few authors address priority setting as a distinct topic. Those who do include Boyle (1981), Caffarella (1994), Forest and Mulcahy (1976), Kemerer (1984), Kemerer and Schroeder (1983), Knowles (1980), Misanchuk and Brack (1988), and Sork and Fielding (1987). In addition to these, recently published books on needs assessment by Queeney (1995) and Witkin and Altschuld (1995) each give attention to priority setting, although the second does so in much greater detail than the first.

The process of developing program purpose statements is hardly addressed at all. Most authors seem to assume that purposes are only temporary statements of intent that will be supplanted by more detailed objectives, so the development of objectives receives more attention. But some practitioners seem unsure of the merits of developing instructional or performance objectives to communicate intent. This may be due to the unfortunate association in some people's minds between instructional objectives and behaviorism. It is an unfortunate association because objectives are useful planning tools even for those who totally reject behaviorism. Using instructional objectives in no way endorses behaviorism, but neither is using them inconsistent with behaviorism. This may seem like a paradox to some, but a review of the tenets of behaviorism followed by a look at the ways objectives have been used in planning quickly shows that objectives are simply one means of clarifying instructional intent regardless of the philosophical or theoretical position from which one is working. Questions like, "What kind of objectives should be developed?" "Who should be involved in developing objectives?" and "How should objectives be used to guide instructional design and evaluation?" are all quite relevant. However, the question, "Should objectives be developed for this program?" is more appropriately answered based on preferred planning style, time available and expectations of stakeholders than whether using objectives violates a philosophical or theoretical position.

On the issue of objectives, the most useful literature is not found directly in adult education but rather from other sectors of education. The best analyses of objectives as tools for planning—including reviews of research on the use of objectives and discussion of the arguments for and against using objectives—can be found in Kibler et al. (1981), Davies (1976) and Yelon (1991) while the best sources on developing and using objectives for instruction and evaluation are Mager (1984), Gronlund (1995) and Gagne, Briggs and Wager (1992). Most of these sources will be discussed in more detail later in this chapter as different ways of thinking about priorities, purposes and objectives are presented.

PRIORITIES, PURPOSES AND OBJECTIVES

Determining priorities, purposes and objectives may be done more or less systematically, and it *should not* be assumed that approaches at the more systematic end of the continuum are either better or worse than those toward the less systematic end. However elegant and sophisticated systematic approaches may seem, the real challenge in program planning is to pick a strategy that is suited to the task and to the resources available to the planner.

Determining Program Priorities

The process of determining program priorities has received uneven attention in the program planning literature. In failing to address the issue at all, some authors seem to assume that resources will be available to address all needs, program ideas, or problems that are brought to the attention of the planner. Such an assumption seems both naive and dangerous since there are always constraints on how resources are allocated and expectations about what kinds of programs and related outcomes that will be produced. Other authors have considered priority setting to be an essential element of planning and have offered detailed discussions of the issues involved and processes that might be useful. For example, Boyle (1981) devoted an entire chapter to priority setting which he begins by observing that

> Continuing educators usually face the dilemma of too many problems to work on, too much content to teach, and too many clientele groups to reach with the time and resources available. So, we must make decisions about program priorities. Priority setting is a continuous process of decision making that takes place during all phases of programming including delineating needs, specifying goals, identifying target audiences, defining available resources, and determining necessary actions. (p. 172)

Caffarella (1994) also devoted a chapter to priority setting in which she observed that "Rarely can personnel involved with educational programs design programs for *all* the ideas identified as appropriate for educational programs.... Therefore, they must have a system for determining which ideas will take priority in the planning of actual activities and events" (p. 86). She goes on to propose a process for determining priorities based on four steps: (1) identify the people who should be involved in setting priorities; (2) select or develop appropriate criteria; (3) record the ideas, along with the criteria, on a priority rating chart and assign weighting factors to each criterion; and (4) apply each criterion to each idea using the priority rating chart. Individual values calculated at each step may then be combined to yield a total priority value for each idea (pp. 88–90).

Forest and Mulcahy (1976) developed a priority setting process that could be used by planners in agricultural extension who have to decide each year how they will allocate limited resources to what often seems like unlimited needs of their clients. Others have woven the priority setting process into needs assessment so that when the process is completed, a list of needs in priority order is produced. Scissons (1982), for example, proposed a needs assessment approach in which information about competence, relevance and motivation is gathered and can then be used to establish priorities. Gathering data like this during needs assessment saves time and results in a seamless process in which a prioritized list of needs is the final product.

My own view of priority setting has shifted from a concern with specific techniques to a focus on more general ways of thinking about the task and making deliberate, informed decisions about what factors or criteria should be used to make these important decisions. Following are four ways of approaching priority setting that range from familiar metaphors that can be used in almost any circumstances to more technically demanding and time-consuming approaches that might be used in rare situations where every part of the process must be open to scrutiny by various stakeholders.

Filter Approach

Knowles (1980), Forest and Mulcahy (1976) and Boyle (1981) suggest using filters or screens to make decisions about priorities. Figure 11.1 represents a simple filter using three criteria. In this case, all needs that are competing for resources are placed in the top of the filter. Those that make it through the three criteria are considered priority needs. Knowles (1980) uses a similar approach

ALL NEEDS

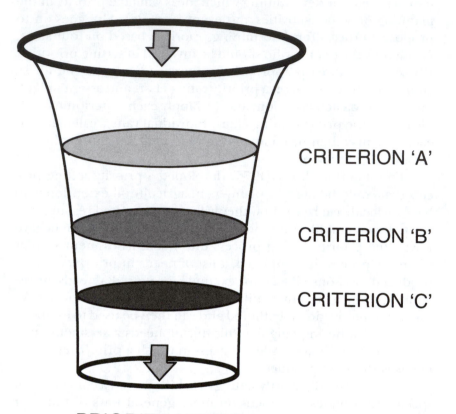

CRITERION 'A'

CRITERION 'B'

CRITERION 'C'

PRIORITY NEEDS

Figure 11.1 A priority-setting filter with three criteria

to determine priorities among program objectives. In his view, all possible objectives are identified and placed into the top of a filter that has three "elements": institutional purposes, feasibility and interests of clientele. Objectives that are not of high priority are screened out by the filters and only high priority objectives come out the bottom. Although the three criteria or elements suggested by Knowles are sensible starting points, there could be dozens of other criteria or factors that might be used to sort out high priority objectives from all those competing for limited resources.

Forest and Mulcahy, writing from the context of agricultural extension, do not specify criteria but indicate instead that they come from four sources: (1) clientele; (2) community and society; (3) the extension organization; and (4) self. Criteria, in their view, can be objective or subjective and should carry different weights in priority decisions because some criteria are simply more important than others. Boyle builds on the earlier work of Forest and Mulcahy by suggesting that needs should be screened through six factors that influence what program priorities should be: (1) personal, (2) organizational, (3) clientele, (4) community, (5) political, and (6) resources. In Boyle's view, "... priorities are what is important or valuable at the present time. Programming situations often have a number of priorities at any given time, so it is necessary to decide which priorities are most important" (p. 178). This comment highlights one of the weaknesses of the filter or screening metaphor as a tool for thinking about setting priorities and that is that filters and screens produce "all or none" outcomes. That is, when objectives, needs or program ideas are filtered or screened, they either make it into the category of "priority" or they don't. This still leaves the planner with the potential problem of determining the relative importance of undifferentiated "priority" needs or objectives. But in most day-to-day priority setting situations, the filter metaphor can be a useful tool for arriving at decisions about which competing objectives, needs or program ideas should be attended to first, second, third and so on.

Recent work by Sork (1994) suggests that it is not difficult for practitioners to identify the relative importance of various criteria used to make priority decisions in their own organizations. Although the set of filter elements (criteria) may change from one priority setting task to another, the idea of figuratively dumping needs or objectives in the top of the filter and allocating resources to those that make it through the various filter elements is easy to apply.

Whether using a filter metaphor or one of the other approaches mentioned below, a key task in priority setting is selecting criteria. No single set of criteria is suitable for all adult education settings. It is likely that most priority decisions are based on a few criteria considered important by the decision makers. Sork and Fielding (1987) identified eight general criteria that they extracted from the literature. Some of these relate to the importance of meeting a need and others to the feasibility of meeting a need. Although most priority setting processes mentioned in the literature focus on priorities among needs, the approaches could as easily be used to set priorities among ideas or objectives. The eight criteria identified by Sork and Fielding are described below with updated descriptions:

Importance Criteria

1. *Number of people affected.* This criterion can be used to establish priority based on the number of people who would potentially benefit if the idea/need was addressed. The greater the number of people benefitting, the higher would be the priority of the need.
2. *Contribution to goals.* This criterion can be used to establish priority based on the degree to which responding to the idea/ need would contribute to the attainment of organizational goals. It is quite possible to identify ideas/needs which are unrelated to the goals of the sponsoring organization. Such needs would be of much lower priority than needs which are directly related to the goals of the organization (or goals of the community).
3. *Immediacy.* This criterion can be used to establish priority based on the degree to which each idea/need requires immediate attention. Immediacy is determined by analyzing how the situation has been changing over time. If waiting to respond to the idea/need would increase hardship or represent an important lost opportunity then that idea/need would be higher priority than one where no increase in hardship or loss of opportunity is expected.
4. *Instrumental value.* This criterion can be used to establish priority based on the degree to which responding to one idea/need will have a positive or negative effect on responding to other ideas/needs. If responding to one idea/need will increase the likelihood that responses to other ideas/needs will be possible, then that idea/need would be high priority. An idea/need that, if responded to, would make it more difficult to respond to other ideas/needs would be a very low priority.
5. *Magnitude of discrepancy.* This criterion can be used to establish priority based on the relative size of the "gap" or discrepancy

between the present and desired capability suggested by the program idea or need. This assumes that the basis for an adult education program is always some explicit or implicit gap between what people know and can do now and what they, or someone else, believe they should know or be able to do. Using this criterion places ideas/needs representing a "big" gap higher in the list of priorities than those with a smaller gap.

Feasibility Criteria

1. *Educational efficacy.* This criterion can be used to establish priority based on the degree to which an educational intervention (program or series of programs) is the best response to the idea/need. Not all ideas/needs are best addressed by providing an educational program. Using this criterion, ideas/needs judged to have high educational efficacy are considered higher priority since the "tool" used by programmers is education. Ideas/needs judged to have low educational efficacy are lower priority and might well be referred to other agencies better able to address the idea/need, or cooperative arrangements might be made to employ education and other means concurrently to eliminate a need requiring more than one approach.
2. *Availability of resources.* This criterion can be used to establish priority based on the degree to which the resources necessary to develop a program would be available if it is decided that the idea/need should be addressed. Use of this criterion involves making a judgment about the potential availability of human, financial, physical, hardware and software resources necessary to organize a program. Ideas/needs for which all or most of the required resources are potentially available (or for which few or no resources are required) would be given higher priority than those for which the necessary resources would not be available.
3. *Commitment to change.* This criterion can be used to establish priority based on the degree to which stakeholders are committed to eliminating the idea/need. Stakeholders are people who have a vested interest in the success or failure of efforts to address the ideas/need; they are often in a position to help or hinder the programmer's efforts to develop and implement programs. Using this criterion involves identifying stakeholders,

deciding the relative importance of each stakeholder's commitment, and assessing the commitment to change of each individual or group.

But these criteria are from the literature and may or may not reflect the criteria commonly used in practice. During the past five years I have surveyed 368 practitioners from Canada and Asia who work in a wide range of adult education settings in an effort to understand the relative importance of 48 different criteria that have been identified as influencing resource allocation decisions. Following is a listing of the 10 "most important" criteria as identified by these practitioners:

1. Potential benefit to participants
2. Availability of funding
3. Contribution to organization's objectives
4. Consistency with organization's philosophy
5. Urgency of the need
6. Potential demand for the program
7. Contribution to organization's productivity
8. Previous success with the program
9. Number of potential participants
10. Contribution to individual performance

This list confirms that many different factors are taken into account before a decision is made to allocate scarce organizational resources to design and offer a program. Although this study reveals something about the criteria that are used to establish priorities, it reveals nothing about how providers approach the task of resource allocation.

In the practical world of day-to-day program planning, decisions about resource allocation are most likely made continuously rather than only after a needs assessment or some other systematic process is completed. So it is more likely that the constant barrage of program ideas, needs, and objectives that planners encounter are figuratively passed through a filter of minimum criteria before they are even given a second look. For example, it's doubtful that any resources would be allocated unless the idea, need or interest was considered within the mandate or mission of the organization or group in which the planner worked. There may be other similar *minimum* criteria used to make an initial assessment before any additional time or money is spent on planning. The metaphor of a sluice box may be a better fit with the realities of practice. A sluice box is a device used in placer mining to separate the valuable (gold) from the worthless (sand, gravel and dirt). Gold-bearing material is placed in the sluice box through which a stream of water runs. The force of the water flushes the lighter worthless material out the end of the box while the heavier gold is trapped by "baffles" placed in the bottom of the box. In a similar fashion, a constant flow of program ideas and needs competing for attention become known to various adult education providers who then apply criteria to sort out those that will receive attention from those that will not. In effect, providers of adult education become adept at selecting from the flow of ideas and needs those that are consistent with their mission and with the criteria they use to allocate resources. The key to being successful at this task is both to be aware of program ideas and needs and to have a clear understanding of what criteria should be used to decide which ones will receive attention.

Importance-Feasibility Approach

Another relatively straightforward way of thinking about priority setting is to consider only two broad dimensions of each need: importance and feasibility. Importance is not an empirically derived characteristic of ideas/needs but is a judgment made by people after considering such factors as the consequences of not taking any action, the value that various stakeholders attach to responding to the ideas/need and so on. Feasibility is also a judgment that is made after considering such issues as whether the resources required to respond are available, whether the effort to respond will encounter active resistance or support, the degree to which an educational intervention is the most suitable response and so on. A useful device for applying these two judgments in setting priorities is a two-dimensional graph like that represented in Figure 11.2. For each need, judgments are made about importance and feasibility. In the case of Figure 11.2, these judgments are simply represented by the words "low" or "high," but they could just as easily be represented by numbers on a scale with 1 representing very low importance and feasibility and 5 or 10 representing very high importance and feasibility. The judgments for each need are plotted on the graph and fall into one of the quadrants. Those

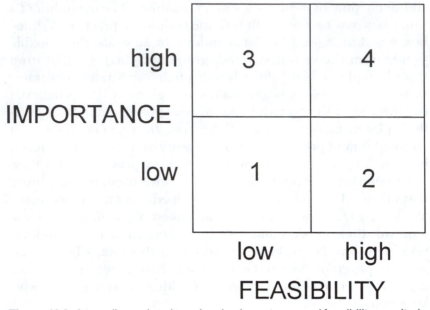

Figure 11.2 A two-dimensional graph using importance and feasibility as criteria

needs falling in Quadrant 1 are low in both importance and feasibility and therefore would not likely be allocated resources. Those falling in Quadrant 4 are high in both importance and feasibility and would call for immediate and thorough attention. Those in Quadrants 2 and 3 fall somewhere in between. Needs that are low in feasibility but high in importance (Quadrant 3) could be addressed using an innovative but experimental approach requiring modest resources and low levels of "political" support. In other words, a relatively risk-free pilot project would be a suitable response because it would be considered an "experiment" and as such would not require a substantial commitment of resources and would be relatively nonthreatening to those who might otherwise be opposed to programming in that area. It may also be desirable to respond to needs that are high in feasibility but low in importance (Quadrant 2) if doing so would make it easier to respond to other needs, now or in the future.

Determining priorities using the two-dimensional graphing approach is straightforward and easy to explain but is limited in that it results in decisions based on only the two broad dimensions of importance and feasibility. For some planners in some settings, decisions using only these two dimensions may not be defensible in which case a ranking or rating approach may be more useful.

Ranking Approach

For planning situations requiring a more systematic approach to priority setting, a ranking chart can be used. Figure 11.3 is a simple ranking chart that can be used to establish priority among competing program ideas or needs. Those making decisions about priorities would select criteria (A, B, C, and so on), would determine "weighting" of each criterion, and then rank each idea or need under each criterion. Weights are whole numbers like 1, 2, 3, and so on that are multiplied by the ranking to give a "weighted ranking" for each need. A weighting of "1" would be given to the criterion that should carry the *least* weight in priority setting while a higher number would give proportionally more weight to a criterion in the final decision. Although it may seem illogical to assign more important criteria higher numbers when the higher priority ideas/needs are assigned lower numbers, the process has the desired effect of increasing the influence of the more heavily weighted criteria on the final priority ranking while maintaining the convention of using #1 as the *highest rank*.

The best way to apply the weighting scheme is to first rank each idea or need under each criterion without considering the weightings and then go back and multiply the rankings by the

Ideas/ Needs	Criteria					Sum of Weighted Ranks	Final Rank
	A Wt.= x3	B Wt.= x1	C Wt.= x4	D Wt.= x2	E Wt.= x2		
# 1	5 x3=15	6 x1= 6	7 x4=28	5 x2=10	6 x2=12	71	6
# 2	3 x3= 9	2 x1= 2	2 x4= 8	1 x2= 2	3 x2= 6	27	2
# 3	1 x3= 3	3 x1= 3	1 x4= 4	2 x2= 4	2 x2= 4	18	1
# 4	7 x3=21	5 x1= 5	3 x4=12	7 x2=14	5 x2=10	62	5
# 5	4 x3=12	4 x1= 4	5 x4=20	4 x2= 8	4 x2= 8	52	4
# 6	2 x3= 6	1 x1= 1	4 x4=16	3 x2= 6	1 x2= 2	31	3
# 7	6 x3=18	7 x1= 7	6 x4=24	6 x2=12	7 x2=14	75	7

Figure 11.3 A simple priority ranking chart with weighted criteria and sample data

weighting factor for each criterion. For example, if criterion 'A' was "number of people affected" then the need affecting the most people would be ranked '1,' the need affecting the next largest number of people would be ranked '2' and so on until all needs had been ranked under each criterion. If Criterion 'A' had a weighting of '3' (as it does in Figure 11.3), then each of the original rankings in column 'A' would be multiplied by 3 to arrive at weighted rankings. The weighted rankings of each need would then be summed across the chart and a final sum of weighted ranks calculated. In this example, the idea/need with the lowest sum of weighted ranks would be *highest priority*, the one with the highest sum of weighted ranks would be *lowest priority*, with all others falling somewhere in between. This technique works best with a limited number of needs since the chart and the task of ranking would get quite unmanageable with more than a dozen or so needs.

Rating Approach

One of the weaknesses of using the ranking approach is that it is very difficult to apply if there are more than ten or so ideas or needs under consideration. It is simply too difficult a task to rank more than this number of ideas or needs. A simple solution to this problem is to switch to a rating approach. The only difference between the two is that instead of ranking all ideas or needs—that is, assigning each idea or need a rank from 1 to n where n is the total number of ideas or needs—each idea or need is rated on a scale from 1–5 or 1–10 in which the lower numbers represent lower priority ideas/needs and the higher numbers represent higher priority needs. Determining and using the weighting factors for the criteria would be the same as described above for the ranking approach. As indicated in Figure 11.4, each idea/need is rated between 1 (lowest priority) and 5 (highest priority). Ratings are then multiplied by weights and a sum of weighted ratings is calculated. Each sum is then divided by the number of criteria to yield a mean rating for each idea/need. The higher the mean rating, the higher the priority of that idea/need, so in Figure 11.4, idea/need #7 is the highest priority. The reason this is the reverse of the ranking approach is that in ranking a lower number is considered "higher in rank" and in rating a higher number is considered "higher rated."

Ideas/ Needs	Criteria					Sum of Weighte d Ranks	Final Rank
	A Wt.= x2	B Wt.= x1	C Wt.= x4	D Wt.= x5	E Wt.= x2		
# 1	4 x2= 8	3 x1= 3	5 x4=20	2 x5=10	3 x2= 6	47	9.4
# 2	3 x2= 6	5 x1= 5	3 x4=12	2 x5=10	2 x2= 4	37	7.4
# 3	5 x2=10	2 x1= 2	1 x4= 4	4 x5=20	3 x2= 6	42	8.4
# 4	1 x2= 2	1 x1= 1	1 x4= 4	2 x5=10	2 x2= 4	21	4.2
# 5	2 x2= 4	1 x1= 1	3 x4=12	3 x5=15	3 x2= 6	38	7.6
# 6	4 x2= 8	3 x1= 3	1 x4= 4	4 x5=20	5 x2=10	45	9
#7	2x2=4	4x1=4	3x4=12	5x5=25	4x2=8	53	10.6

Figure 11.4 A simple priority rating chart with weighted criteria and sample data

These four ways of thinking about setting priorities are certainly not the only ones available to adult educators. Those interested in other ways of approaching the task may wish to read the work by Kemerer (1984) and Kemerer and Schroeder (1983) who focus on setting priorities in community development work and Misanchuk and Brack (1988) who discuss a paired-comparisons approach to setting priorities in university extension work.

Determining Program Purposes and Objectives

The "objectives movement" has had a powerful influence on education during the past 30 years, but it has not been without its critics. Brookfield (1986) captured well the strong feelings held by some about an overemphasis on using specific objectives in adult education. He said that "As both professor and student, nothing has proved more irksome to me than the insistence that for educational encounters to be valuable there must always be clearly specified learning objectives that are being assiduously pursued" (p. 215). Overzealous promoters of behavioral or performance objectives share some of the blame for the backlash that has occurred in reaction to the objectives movement. This backlash has been so strong that some authors have rejected outright the use of objectives in adult education because they are seen as instruments for undemocratic, institutionally based control of educational experiences that serve only the interests of dominant groups (Jones,

1982). Unfortunately, these critics have reached a verdict on objectives largely based on their *misuse*. Objectives are planning tools which, like any tool, can be used properly or improperly. There is nothing inherently undemocratic about objectives but there are certainly undemocratic uses of objectives. There is nothing inherently self-serving about using objectives, although they can certainly be used in a self-serving fashion. And the matter of control in planning is a red herring since every effort to plan is an effort to control. The question is not whether control will be exercised but who will be making the decisions and influencing the direction of the educational experience. If learners develop their own objectives or have substantive involvement in the development of program objectives, then control is democratized. If an institution develops objectives that are rigidly pursued and nonnegotiable, then control is centralized. Since the objectives movement had its origins in schools where learners had little say about expected outcomes, it's not surprising that there is a suspicion about *any* objectives which learners are not directly involved in developing.

Objectives are useful planning tools because they clarify the intentions of those who are involved in planning and can then be used to communicate those intentions to potential participants, sponsors, instructors, and so on. When properly used, they are also the most powerful tool available for clarifying the expected effects a learning experience will have on the capabilities of participants. When misused, they become excuses for inflexible, teacher-oriented, coercive instruction, and overly behavioral, quantitative evaluation approaches.

Over the past 45 years many proposals have been made about what constitutes a useful objective. Following are brief summaries of several of the better-known proposals beginning with Tyler's formulation. Each of these proposals, it should be noted, was designed to overcome weaknesses that were thought to accompany earlier formulations.

Tyler's Approach

Although Tyler (1949) was not the first to argue that clearly stated objectives were important tools in educational planning, his curriculum planning framework, with its emphasis on developing objectives that described expected changes in learners, was very influential. Tyler criticized objectives that described what the teacher expected to do during instruction, or that described in vague or imprecise fashion what students would learn, and proposed that the most useful objectives were those that described significant changes in student behavior. He asserted that "Since the real purpose of education is not to have the instructor perform certain activities but to bring about significant changes in the students' patterns of behavior, it becomes important to recognize that any statement of the objectives of the school should be a statement of changes to take place in students" (p. 44). He proposed the development of objectives that have two components: one component indicates the kind of behavior to be developed and the other describes the area of content or of life in which the behavior is to be applied (p. 47).

Although Tyler's framework was intended to guide curriculum development in the schools, it had a significant and lasting impact on adult education as well. The origins of many contemporary program planning models can be traced quite easily to what became known as the "Tyler Rationale."

Mager's Approach

In the early 1960s when behaviorism was still on the ascendency, Mager (1962) produced a thin volume which was designed to help educators—especially those developing programmed-instruction materials—prepare clear and unambiguous instructional objectives. Mager introduced the idea that useful objectives should contain three elements. If any of these three elements was missing, an objective was less useful than if it contained all three. Mager's text, itself a programmed-instruction manual, used humor, clear writing and dozens of examples to show how "fuzzies"—vague or ambiguous statements of intended outcomes—could be converted into useful objectives. The three elements that Mager proposed should be included in useful objectives are as follows:

- **Performance**—An objective always says what a learner is expected to be able to do.
- **Conditions**—An objective always describes the important conditions under which the performance is to occur.
- **Criterion**—An objective describes the criterion of acceptable performance by describing how well the learner must perform in order to be considered acceptable (Mager, 1984, p. 21).

Mager's approach to writing objectives was attractive to educators because he provided an easy-to-follow formula to arrive at useful objectives that fit well with current thinking about the importance of focusing on student performance. His approach also made it much easier to evaluate student learning because the objectives contained not only a description of what students would be expected to do, but also the conditions under which they would do it and expectations about how well they would do it. Although Tyler also proposed using objectives as the basis for evaluating learning, it was Mager who helped educators develop such specific objectives that made evaluating student learning a much easier task. Developing Mager-style objectives was not in any sense mindless work. He required precise language and careful selection of the verbs used to describe performance. He forced planners to be specific about outcomes much earlier in the curriculum development process than they had previously and this was considered an important advance over other approaches. By putting a great deal of energy into developing unambiguous objectives, the selection of instructional methods and evaluation procedures became much less arduous.

Gronlund's Approach

Gronlund's (1995) style of preparing objectives has the advantage of being somewhat less mechanistic than Mager's (1984) approach. He views objectives as descriptions of intended learning outcomes that emphasize what students will be able to do following instruction. What makes Gronlund's approach different from the others is that he proposes using two types of statements to represent intended learning outcomes. The first statement he calls a general instructional objective. These statements provide an overall view of the intended outcomes and use language that Mager would consider "fuzzy." For example, a Gronlund-style general instructional objective would be, "Understands common terms used in adult education." Such a statement would not be acceptable to Mager because it does not describe a performance, identify conditions, or set criteria for acceptable performance, although it would likely be considered acceptable to Tyler. But Gronlund suggests that all general instructional objectives should be accompanied by statements describing specific learning outcomes which would be more acceptable to Mager. Examples of specific learning outcomes related to the above general instructional objective are:

- *Defines each term as it is commonly used in the literature.*
- *Distinguishes between similar terms.*
- *Uses each term accurately in an original sentence.*

Gronlund emphasizes that specific learning outcomes are only samples of a vast array of statements that could represent evidence that the intended learning had occurred—in the case of the sample objective above the intended outcome is *understanding*. In Gronlund's view verbs like *defining, distinguishing* and *using* represent student actions that provide evidence that understanding has been achieved.

> The fact that specific learning outcomes simply serve as samples of the types of performance we are willing to accept as evidence of the attainment of our general instructional objectives has implications for both teaching and assessment. Our teaching efforts must be directed toward the general objectives of instruction and not toward the specific samples of performance we have selected to represent each objective. (p. 9)

Gronlund also argues that objectives are less likely to limit the activities and choices of the instructor if they do not contain conditions and standards. Although he recognizes that objectives which include conditions and standards are very useful in programmed instruction and in simple training programs, he is concerned that such specific statements, when used in more complex instructional settings, can limit the options open to the instructor and reduce spontaneity and creativity.

Gagne, Briggs and Wager's Approach

Gagne and his colleagues (1992) suggest a five-component objective that they believe communicates instructional intent even more precisely than Mager- or Gronlund-style objectives. In their view, "An *objective* is precisely described when it communicates to another person what would have to be done to observe that a stated lesson purpose has in fact been accomplished. The statement is imprecise if it does not enable the other person to think of how to carry out such an observation" (p. 126). In developing the case for precision in preparing objectives, they make an important point that seems to escape many critics of the objectives movement.

> We cannot directly observe that someone has acquired a new capability. We can only infer that the capability has been attained through the observation of satisfactory performance by the learner on a task that employs that capability. Often, the particular performance (action) exhibited by the learner is confused with the capability. The five-component method of writing objectives seeks to avoid this confusion by specifying two verbs: one to define the capability, and a second to define the observable action. (p. 127)

Gagne et al. are responding to the same concern that Gronlund had when he proposed using both general instructional objectives and specific learning outcomes to communicate intent. In both cases the authors were concerned that those reading objectives would confuse the verbs describing the performance with intended learning.

The five components of objectives suggested by Gagne et al. are as follows:

1. **Situation**—The stimulus situation faced by the learner when asked to perform.
2. **Learned capability verb**—One of nine verbs used to indicate the type of learning expected.
3. **Object**—The content of the learner's performance.
4. **Action verb**—A verb, other than a learned capability verb, that describes how the performance is to be completed.
5. **Tools, constraints, or special conditions**—A description of equipment/devices that will be used, performance standards, and other circumstances under which the learner must perform. (pp. 127–129)

Following is an example of a five component objective with each component labeled:

> [Situation] Given a random listing of assumptions underlying andragogy and pedagogy, the learner [learned capability verb] classifies [object] those related to each model by [action] placing a "p" next to pedagogical assumptions and an "a" next to andragogical assumptions [tools, constraints, conditions] as Knowles discusses them in *The Modern Practice of Adult Education* (1980).

Gagne et al. do not claim that all objectives should have all five components. They state that "If you can communicate unambiguously without all five components, then do so" (p. 136). Many of their examples include all except the tools, constraints, and special conditions component. While their approach to developing objectives may be considered too detailed and mechanistic for some, it does represent a powerful, albeit time consuming, tool for clarifying intended outcomes.

In some program planning situations developing explicit objectives may be neither necessary nor desirable. For example, in cases where the role of the adult educator is to animate a group of adults so that its members take responsibility for identifying what they want to learn, how they want to learn it and for organizing the resources necessary to support their learning, then developing objectives in advance may hinder the group more than help it. Also, in situations where the learning outcomes cannot reasonably be anticipated or where the outcomes are sufficiently complex that they cannot be adequately represented in objectives, forcing the development of objectives may trivialize the nature of the program and mislead learners about the complexity of expected outcomes. In these cases, it may be more useful to prepare a narrative description of the intended outcomes free of the constraints imposed by more systematic approaches to preparing objectives. The price to be paid when doing this, however, is that the planners may be accused of having a hidden agenda that they are not willing to reveal to others (Millar, Morphet, & Saddington, 1986) or that they have not thought carefully enough about intended outcomes since if they had, they surely could prepare a list of objectives.

Alternatives to Objectives in Program Planning

It seems apparent from talking with dozens of practitioners and participating in planning many different kinds of programs that developing explicit objectives is not necessary for success in program planning. But what is necessary for success is a relatively clear understanding of the intentions of those who are involved in planning. Objectives are one means to clarify intentions, but there are other tools available that may be used individually or in combination to provide adequate clarity for many planning situations. Following are brief descriptions of several alternative approaches which are not as powerful as objectives, but that can be effective ways of clarifying intended outcomes if developing program or instructional objectives is not considered the best use of limited planning time.

Purposes Approach

This approach relies on a description of the purpose of a program to communicate intended outcomes. Statements of purpose generally lack the precise language of objectives and cannot be used in the same ways as objectives to guide instructional planning or evaluation. But a clear and concise purpose statement is a very good way to suggest what the program is designed to accomplish and can give potential participants and instructors a reasonably clear idea of why the program is being offered. Example: "The purpose of this program is to encourage participants to adopt innovative approaches to conflict resolution and to show how conflict resolution strategies can be used to improve organizational effectiveness." This example of a purpose statement does not say anything directly about what participants will be capable of doing as a result of the program, but it does allow some inferences to be made about outcomes. From this statement it would be reasonable to conclude that participants will learn about "innovative" approaches to conflict resolution in organizations and that the program will help them develop the skills and knowledge necessary to use these approaches in their own work.

In some cases, the word "purpose" may not be used at all, but if the statement can be prefaced with the phrase, "The purpose of this program is …" and it makes sense, then the purposes approach is being used.

Processes Approach

The processes approach relies on descriptions of what will take place during the educational program to communicate intended outcomes. Most descriptions of process only hint at intended outcomes rather than describe them directly, so it may only be possible to infer outcomes from descriptions of process. Example: "This program will provide participants with an opportunity to assess their current assertiveness skills, to practice new assertiveness skills in simulated work situations, and to develop strategies to help them to apply assertiveness skills appropriately in their work, family, and social lives." The three parts of this statement describe what will be happening during the program, but it is not difficult to read into these statements what at least some of the intended outcomes are. For example, by the end of the program participants will *understand* what assertiveness skills they already possess, will have developed the ability to *apply* new skills at work and will have learned how to *develop* a plan of action to use their current and new skills in their lives. Again, these outcomes must be inferred from the descriptions of instructional processes, but this is not a difficult process.

Content Approach

This approach relies on listing and discussing program topics or content and often leaves it to the reader to infer intended outcomes from the listing. Example: "This program will include: An Introduction to Transformational Learning; Distinguishing Transformational Learning from Other Types of Learning; Recent Research on Transformational Learning; Facilitating Transformational Learning; Evaluating the Outcomes of Transformational Learning." This listing contains no direct statements of intended outcomes, but by analyzing the topics it is possible to infer the outcomes. Potential participants reasonably expect some indication of program content before they decide to participate, and many institutions and agencies seem to rely on the content approach exclusively. This practice is potentially dangerous because the inferences that people make about outcomes can go far beyond the ability of the program to deliver. Listing topics to be covered can lead learners to believe that they will develop more than a superficial understanding of—or will develop advanced skills related to—those topics. When used as a planning tool, the content approach can be useful because it helps to clarify what will be included in the program. But if used exclusively, it leaves a great deal open to interpretation and may lead to misunderstandings between planners and instructors and between program sponsors and participants.

Benefits Approach

This approach involves describing the anticipated benefits to participants of attending the program. Example: "By attending this program you will be able to (1) have greater influence on people, (2) add power and polish to your professional image, and (3) handle difficult people." Statements such as these are similar to goals and objectives but they lack the specificity of well-written objectives. They communicate intended outcomes more directly than some of the other approaches because few inferences have to be made from them. However, they are not as specific as objectives and, since they often describe benefits related to a job or family life, are very difficult to use as a basis for program evaluation. In other words, benefits are useful for communicating the focus of a program and for marketing a program, but they may create expectations that the program cannot fulfill.

Combined Approaches

Combinations of these approaches are also used to clarify intended outcomes of programs. Some planners may prefer to clarify outcomes by beginning with a purposes approach, then move to more specific descriptions using an objectives processes, content or benefits approach. An analysis of program descriptions would likely reveal that combined approaches are the most frequently used means to clarify intended outcomes with clients.

Regardless of the process used, it is always important to keep in mind the relationships between the various elements of program planning. Clarifying outcomes—whether done using purposes, objectives, benefits or any other approach—is one element in program planning that is related to many others. For example, clarifying outcomes is directly related to both instructional planning and evaluation. In conventional program planning, outcomes are defined and then instruction is crafted to promote those outcomes. Evaluation is concerned, in part, with determining the degree to which the program produces the expected outcomes. So the process of clarifying outcomes is never an end in itself but rather is one element in the complex process of program planning.

QUESTIONS FOR STUDY AND DISCUSSION

1. What processes are used in your day-to-day practice to focus the planning of programs?
2. What factors or criteria influence the day-to-day decisions where you work about what needs, purposes or objectives will be addressed and which ones will not?

3. Who benefits and who is not well served by the decisions that are made about priorities, purposes and objectives?
4. What program characteristics influence the decision about which approach to clarify intended outcomes will be used?
5. How can objectives be used more effectively to guide the design of instruction and to construct an evaluation strategy for the program?
6. If developing objectives is not a regular part of program planning, what approach is used to clarify intended outcomes and how well does it work?
7. What kind of research would be useful to deepen our understanding of processes used to determine priorities, purposes and objectives in adult education?

REFERENCES

Beatty, P. T. (1981). The concept of need: Proposal for a working definition. *Journal of the Community Development Society, 12*(2), 39–46.

Brookfield, S. D. (1986). *Understanding and facilitating adult learning.* San Francisco: Jossey-Bass.

Boyle, P. G. (1981). *Planning better programs.* New York: McGraw-Hill.

Caffarella, R. S. (1994). *Program planning for adults: A practical guide for adult educators, trainers, and staff developers.* San Francisco: Jossey-Bass.

Davies, I. K. (1976). *Objectives in curriculum design.* London: McGraw-Hill.

Forest, L., & Mulcahy, S. (1976). *First things first: A handbook of priority setting in extension.* Madison: Division of Program and Staff Development, University of Wisconsin—Extension.

Gagne, R. M., Briggs, L. J., & Wager, W. W. (1992). *Principles of instructional design* (4th ed.). Fort Worth: Harcourt Brace Jovanovich.

Gronlund, N. E. (1995). *How to write and use instructional objectives* (5th ed.). New York: Macmillan.

Houle, C. O. (1972). *The design of education.* San Francisco: Jossey-Bass.

Jones, R. K. (1982). The dilemma of educational objectives in higher and adult education. *Adult Education, 32*(3), 165–169.

Kemerer, R. (1984). Setting priorities: The adult educator's dilemma. *Lifelong Learning, 7*(7), 7–8, 26.

Kemerer, R. W., & Schroeder, W. L. (1983). Determining the importance of community-wide adult education needs. *Adult Education Quarterly, 33*(2), 201–214.

Kibler, R. J., Cegala, D. J. Watson, K. W., Barker, L. L., & Miles, D. T. (1981). *Objectives for instruction and evaluation* (2nd ed.). Boston: Allyn & Bacon.

Knowles, M. S. (1980). *The modern practice of adult education: From pedagogy to andragogy.* Chicago: Association Press/Follett.

Mager, R. F. (1962). *Preparing instructional objectives.* Palo Alto, CA: Fearon.

Mager, R. F. (1984). *Preparing instructional objectives.* (Rev. 2nd ed.). Belmont, CA: Fearon.

Millar, C., Morphet, T., & Saddington, T. (1986). Curriculum negotiation in professional adult education. *Journal of Curriculum Studies, 18*(4) 429–443.

Misanchuk, E. R., & Brack, R. E. (1988). A method for setting priorities for programming in university extension. *Canadian Journal of University Continuing Education, 14*(1), 60–73.

Queeney, D. S. (1995). *Assessing needs in continuing education.* San Francisco: Jossey-Bass.

Scissons, E. H. (1982). A typology of needs assessment definitions in adult education. *Adult Education, 33*(1), 20–28.

Sork, T. J., & Fielding, D. W. (1987). Identifying learning needs. In J. R. Arndt & S. J. Coons (Eds.), *Continuing education in pharmacy* (pp. 113–133). Alexandria, VA: American Association of Colleges of Pharmacy.

Sork, T. J. (1994). A factor analytic study of resource allocation criteria in adult education. *Proceedings of the 13th Annual Conference of the Canadian Association for the Study of Adult Education* (pp. 386–391). Vancouver: Simon Fraser University at Harbour Centre, Continuing Studies.

Tyler, R. W. (1949). *Basic principles of curriculum and instruction.* Chicago: University of Chicago Press.

Yelon, S. L. (1991). Writing and using instructional objectives. In L. J. Briggs, K. L. Gustafson, & M. H. Tillman (Eds.), *Instructional design: Principles and applications* (2nd ed.) (pp. 75–121). Englewood Cliffs, NJ: Educational Technology Publications.

Witkin, B. R., & Altschuld, J. W. (1995). *Planning and conducting needs assessments: A practical guide.* Thousand Oaks, CA: Sage.

12

Measurement and Appraisal of Program Success

David Deshler

ABSTRACT

This chapter provides an overview of program evaluation principles. The chapter begins with a consideration of several myths about evaluation. Following a question and answer format, I review what we know about the evaluation—how it differs from learning assessment, reasons for program and learning evaluation, the primary focus of program evaluation, selected methods and approaches to evaluation. I discuss reasons for involving learners and other stakeholders in conducting program evaluation. The review and discussion questions at the end of the chapter constitute key questions for planning program evaluation.

ASSESSMENT

Rating Scale: Please use the following scale in rating your present knowledge for each item.

1	2	3	4
No knowledge	Some knowledge	Adequate knowledge	Expert knowledge

A preliminary version of this chapter appeared in David Deshler (1996), Evaluating extension programmes. In Burton E. Swanson (Ed.), *Improving agricultural extension: A reference manual*. Rome: Food and Agricultural Organization of the United Nations.

1. Know several important books on program evaluation
   and assessment of learning.   _____
2. Am able to explain three or more approaches or
   models of evaluation.   _____
3. Am familiar with a broad range of questions that are
   likely to drive evaluation of programs.   _____
4. Am familiar with a broad range of questions that are
   likely to drive assessment of learning.   _____
5. Understand how to conduct many data-gathering
   methods for evaluation purposes.   _____
6. Am familiar with different reference points or perspectives in making evaluative judgments.   _____
7. Know how to manage a program evaluation effort.   _____

INTRODUCTION

Evaluation and appraisal of program success is both challenging and rewarding. It is challenging because adult and continuing
educators work with diverse learners, teach a variety of technical
and nontechnical subject matter, and employ a variety of methods
in many different program modes. In addition, educators are
subject to systems beyond their control that include organizational
rules, people in authority, rewards and incentives, plans and lack
of collective vision that often inhibit the effectiveness of even the
best educators. Therefore, standardized approaches to program
evaluation are not likely to be very informative or serve a wide
range of evaluative purposes. The chapter is organized around the
following questions: What are several evaluation myths? What are
some essential elements of evaluation? What is the difference
between program evaluation and assessment of learning? Why
evaluate programs? Why evaluate learning? What are alternative
approaches to program evaluation? What should be the focus of
program evaluation? What should be the focus for evaluation of
learning? What are methods for evaluation? What are reference
perspectives for making evaluative judgments? Why use participatory approaches to evaluation? What are key questions to ask
during evaluation planning?

WHAT ARE SEVERAL EVALUATION MYTHS?

Before considering definitions, purposes, types of approaches, and methods of evaluation, there are several myths that deserve comment, because they have often discouraged practitioners from engaging in useful evaluation. Most of us have memories of being evaluated and tested as children in school. Report card memories also come to mind. The idea of evaluation is often associated with apprehension, anxiety, and sometimes even fear if rejection and self-deprecation have resulted. These are genuine reasons why we, as adult and continuing educators are often reluctant to initiate evaluation of our own work as educators as well as that of our adult learners. Evaluation evokes ambivalence. Yes, the fear of knowing is a part of our past, but there is also the need to know how well we are doing either as learners or as educators. By avoiding evaluation we also deny ourselves and our learners the experience of appreciating accomplishments and achievements. It is a myth that evaluation is always a negative experience to be avoided. We need to overcome the following myths:

Myth #1: Evaluate only when mandated. It is a myth that evaluation should only occur if it is mandated. Many funded programs require evaluation as a form of accountability. This may be seen by funders as helpful both to them and to program administrators and educators. However, many educators have responded to this practice by saying to themselves that they do not need to evaluate unless it is mandated. On the contrary, evaluations that are self-initiated are more likely to address issues that can inform program improvement. In fact, self-initiated evaluation findings are more likely to be taken seriously for immediate improvement. Programs do not become responsible and excellent because they have mandated evaluation. They become responsible and excellent just as often through self-initiated evaluation.

Myth #2: Evaluation is an add-on. It is a myth that evaluation is an add-on activity or, at most, a pretest and a posttest. Yes, evaluation is by nature a reflective activity, but reflection on experience and accomplishments should not be an add-on, but fully integrated into program development, teaching, and learning activities. The evaluation activities can relate to the program development process through reflecting on program goals, assessment of social need, consideration of resources, and the assessment of alternative delivery systems and design of events and activities. It also can include the assessment of personnel, facilities, public relations, recruitment of volunteers, and program learners, as well as the evaluation of teaching methods, procedures, and processes of the program itself. Evaluation usually includes assessment of learner achievements and the extent to which learners experience benefits from the use of what they have learned. Evaluation also can assess the indirect effects of educational programs on the community in the form of changes in policies, services, and the economy. It is a myth that evaluation is an add-on. It is most meaningful when it is integrated into planning and operating programs (Patton, 1991).

Myth #3: Evaluation is an activity for experts. Another myth that should be challenged is that we have to be experts to engage in evaluation. Yes, complex methods can be used. However, we are constantly making informal judgments about our work and the work of others. Systematic evaluation can be undertaken by novice educators, and learners themselves can be helped to critique their own work. This chapter is intended to help novice educators and learners to do it themselves. It is a myth that evaluation should be undertaken only by technical experts.

Myth #4: Outside evaluators are best. It also is a myth that evaluation should only be done by external, outside, objective evaluators. Yes, external evaluators are often useful in providing an objective judgment especially to those who hold programs accountable. They can also challenge insiders to address what they have overlooked due to their nearsightedness. However, internal, self-initiated, and subjectively oriented evaluations can also be rigorous and valuable. In fact, because they often are participatory in generating, analyzing, and interpreting data, they may result in greater acceptability of the findings and recommendations. It is a myth that only external evaluations can be useful or valid.

Myth #5: There is one best evaluation approach. Still another myth is that there is a one best way to conduct an evaluation. Some approaches probably are better than others for addressing particular types of questions or concerns. However, the many types of evaluation approaches each have their strengths and limitations. Decisions concerning which approaches to use can be informed by knowing the choices and by determining which approaches provide the best fit for specific situation. Some situations require quantification and measurement, while others require qualitative, descriptive, and subjective data. It is a myth that there is only one best approach. Alternative approaches will be briefly described later in this chapter. Let us now consider the essential ingredients in evaluation.

WHAT ARE SOME ESSENTIAL FEATURES OF PROGRAM EVALUATION?

There are many definitions of evaluation. However, there are four common ingredients to them all: (1) An object, event, process, or the focus of evaluation that is often in the form of a question; (2) records or data regarding program and learner changes, procedures, and processes; (3) judgment reference points or perspectives, sometimes called criteria; and (4) judgments on the value or worth of what is being evaluated. As part of this chapter, we want to consider, along with program effectiveness (macro level), the importance of evaluation of adult learning achievements and processes on the part of both educators and learners themselves (micro level).

How Does Program Evaluation Differ from Assessment of Learning?

In adult and continuing education, evaluation usually means program evaluation, which includes concerns about accountability, program goals and philosophy, resources, planning and networking, program operation, recruitment of staff and training of volunteers, nature of educational events, and program impact, including changes to organizations, services, and public policies. Evaluation of learning is usually limited to a focus on learning experiences of learners, their experience of the process, their achievements and benefits, the quality and usefulness of the knowledge, and the relationship between learners and educational facilitators. While program evaluation focuses on the larger organizational questions and social contexts of the program (macro level), evaluation of learning focuses on what and how learners learn and how educators help or hinder the process of learning (micro level). Both levels of evaluation are essential, and most program evaluations include evaluation of learning achievements and their consequences on individuals, but also on the family, organization, or community.

Why Evaluate Programs?

Program evaluations (macro level) may serve one or more combinations of the following purposes.

Covert Purposes. This pseudo-evaluation purpose includes its use to postpone, buy time, or avoid threatening change; to evade administrative responsibility or provide a scapegoat for criticism; to avoid public embarrassment through a whitewash or cover-up evaluation; or to legitimate an external public image.

Mandated or Accountability Purposes. This purpose includes its use to satisfy those who demand accountability by providing requested or mandated evidence of performance; or to justify or advocate a position that supports continuation, proposed change, expansion, or reduction of a program.

Uncertainty-Reduction Purposes. This includes its use to increase credibility and support for unpopular decisions; to add or drop specific strategies, components, or techniques; to continue or discontinue a program; to install a similar program elsewhere; to allocate resources among competing programs; and to document a program's history.

Practice-Improvement Purposes. This purpose includes its use to increase efficiency and reduce waste; to identify and detect malfunctions and defects in procedures and program designs; to discover new approaches and alternative processes; to adjust programs to changing situations, clients, resources; and to understand a failure in order to prevent future failure.

Social Learning Purposes. This purpose includes the use of evaluation to stimulate informed political dialogue and challenge simplistic views; to resolve political conflicts intelligently; to address theoretical anomalies and add to the social science knowledge pool; and to fill in conceptual gaps and forge greater conceptual clarity concerning explanations and expectations (Deshler, 1984, pp. 8–9).

Why Evaluate Learning?

Why should adult and continuing educators be concerned about the evaluation of adult learning (micro level)? There are several reasons. The first is that we should want to know whether our efforts deter or motivate learning. Second, evaluation of learning can help educators and learners to understand learning dysfunctions, misconceptions, and miseducation. And third, evaluation can help the learners appreciate their own achievements, competencies, and benefits and improve the way they go about learning. In addition, sometimes evaluation results are used by outsiders to determine competence and skills for certification, classification, and comparison. Evaluation of learning is undertaken, first, to benefit learners, to enhance their appreciation of prior and acquired knowledge, and to increase their motivation and personal growth. Second, it is undertaken to improve the performance of educators (Beatty, Benefield, & Linhart, 1991). In addition, it is sometimes useful to outside certifiers or sponsors. Evaluation also can become the basis for communication between educators and learners (Moran, 1997).

What Are Some Alternative Approaches to Program Evaluation?

There are many ways of approaching the evaluation of programs in adult and continuing education. Choosing among these approaches is important because for each there are different assumptions about what data to collect, how to collect it, and how to make judgments about success. There are more than several dozen. However, the following seven major approaches will provide a sufficient choice for most evaluation situations: (1) Connoisseurship criticism model; (2) Goal-free model; (3) Attainment of objectives model; (4) Differential model; (5) Naturalistic model; (6) Experimental model; and (7) Participatory evaluation model.

Connoisseurship Criticism Model. This approach is best characterized by the use of expert judgment. Elementary, secondary, and higher education programs have used this model for many years in the form of visiting teams of educators who have been appointed by a state or national accreditation organization. Usually, the program (department, school, college, etc.) prepares documentation in advance of the visit. The experts then interview, analyze documents, and make judgments using their own judgment perspectives or those set as standards by the outside professional association that they are representing. Expert judgment is the key idea in this model (Eisner, 1983).

Goal-Free Model. This approach assumes that the outside evaluators do not know what the program has intended to accomplish, but that it is the task of the evaluators to uncover what is happening in terms of effects in relationship to needs of participants regardless of what goals the educators may have held. The focal point is to identify needs of learners and to then compare these needs with what people are actually experiencing as a result of the program. The gap is then viewed as a starting point for making changes in the program. This approach relies heavily on open-ended interviewing by persons who do not have a vested interest in the program (Scriven, 1972).

Attainment of Objectives Model. This approach assumes that the success of a program can be determined by measuring a program's outcomes against its own goals and objectives. This can be done either by outside evaluators or through internal self-evaluation. This type of evaluation begins with clarifying measurable objectives and then gathering data that validates the extent to which these objectives have been met. An addition to this model that is often necessary is the evaluation of the appropriateness of the goals and objectives given external circumstances and needs. This model has a limitation in that it tends to ignore the inputs and processes that go into producing outcomes (Provus, 1971).

Differential Model. The purpose of this model is to provide relevant information as a management tool to decision makers. It assumes that evaluation should be geared to decisions during program initiation, program contact, and program implementation stages in order to make results more relevant at each particular stage. Participation of stakeholders are central to the process since evaluation should serve their decisions. Sometimes cost effectiveness and operations monitoring are included (Stufflebeam, 1971; Tripodi, Fellin, & Epstein, 1971; Gold, 1988).

Naturalistic Model. This model assumes that a program is a natural experiment and that the purpose of evaluation is to understand how it is operating in its natural environment. It is also assumed that what is happening is due to multiple perspectives and values of both staff and participants. The design calls for data to be collected and analyzed from the multiple perspectives (funders, administrators, teachers, volunteers, learners, supervisors, employers, and other community organizations that may benefit from the program). The outcome of the evaluation is dialogue concerning disagreements about goals and objectives, nonmatching expectations, the identification of problems, unmet opportunities, new policies or procedures, and suggested changes in methods or activities. There is an assumption that programs are negotiated realities among the significant stake holders and that evaluation serves this value laden negotiation (Cronbach, 1980; Guba & Lincoln, 1989).

Experimental Model. The purpose of this approach is to determine whether changes in program outcomes (learning accomplishments) were due to the contributions of the program and not just to life's experiences or from other influences (Goldstein, 1986). This model asks the question, "Was there a difference in learning achievement that can be attributed to the program?" The simplest way to determine causality between the program inputs and program consequences is to make comparisons between at least two comparable groups, a group that received the educational treatment and a group that did not. This means that program accessibility, at least during the experiment, is withheld from those learners who serve as a control group. Because of the nature of human subjects, the ethics of withholding educational services, and the difficulty of controlling for external influences, it is extremely difficult and costly to operationalize this model. It is recommended that this model be used only when major changes are expected or when a major failure is anticipated in pilot efforts where causal claims are central to making major program investments (Rossi & Freeman, 1993).

Participatory Evaluation Model. The purpose of this model is for educators and learners themselves to initiate a critical reflection process focused on their own activities. This is done through identifying an anomaly of practice; subjecting it to critical reflection; explicating the underlying assumptions, habits of the mind, cause and effect expectations; and then, after creating new assumptions, current or change practices are then validated or invalidated through data collection and analysis. The model assumes a democratic participatory process along with autonomy on the part of educators and learners at the local level (Brunner & Guzman, 1989; Green, 1988). This is sometimes called participatory action research. The degree of participation of learners in evaluation will be discussed toward the end of this chapter.

What Should Be the Focus of Program Evaluation?

This question raises the specter of evaluating everything, which is an impossibility. For any evaluation effort, choices and priorities among many possible questions have to be made. A range of possibilities is represented in Table 12.1. This table dis-

Table 12.1 Focus for Program Evaluation (modified from Summers, 1997). Used by permission.

7.	Community Change	Change in public opinion, public policies, laws, allocation of resources, economic and social indicators, interorganizational relations.
6.	Organization Change	Change in employee performance management practice, service delivery, constituents served, methods used, facilities and equipment, cost/benefits improved.
5.	Individual Change	Changes in knowledge, attitudes, skills, aspirations, self-image, perspective, expenditure of effort and money; use of methods, services, production or tools; compliance or opposition to public policy; patterns of communication, career directions and family relationships.
4.	Reactions	Testimonials, opinions on instructional design; reactions to the relevance, helpfulness, perceived value of educational experience; reputation of the educational provider.
3.	Participation	Involvement of learners, staff, volunteers; attendance continuity, frequency, intensity of face-to-face contacts; extent of media assisted contacts; type of participate (planning, evaluation, recruiting); indicators of commitment.
2.	Activities	Planning; educational events (conferences, workshops, tutoring, distance education, on-the-job training, etc.); instructional methods; evaluation.
1.	Inputs/ Resources	Organizational sponsorship and networks; funds, facilities, equipment; philosophy, mission, goals objectives; staff, resource people, volunteers; cultural, economic, and political context.

plays in reverse order, seven major areas of focus for program evaluation: (1) Inputs/Resources; (2) Activities; (3) Participation; (4) Reactions; (5) Individual Change; (6) Organization Change; and (7) Community Change. Evaluations rarely cover all of these areas. Most limit themselves to combination of items that serve the evaluation model or the concerns of stakeholders.

Narrowing the focus usually begins during planning with the major stakeholders in a program effort (funders, administrators, teachers, learners, supervisors, employers). Interviews with these stakeholders are usually conducted at the outset of evaluation efforts, often during the program planning process, to identify the program model or approach and the questions that are central. When stakeholders do not agree negotiations about priorities, methods, and costs must occur so that the task can be reality based and doable. The key here is to determine the decisions stakeholders intend to make, based on the evaluation findings so that immediate use will be made of the information generated. Evaluation utilization is not based on quantity of data but on its timeliness and relevancy to decisions.

The seven evaluation models tend to place different emphases on the areas of focus shown in Table 12.1. For instance, the Connoisseurship Criticism Model most often concentrates on data from inputs, activities, and participation. The Goal-Free Model emphasizes individual change and organization change; it usually compares the philosophy, goals, and objectives of inputs to the extent of individual or organizational change outcomes. The Naturalistic Model places emphasis on understanding activities, participation, and reactions as processes that occur within cultural, economic, and political context inputs. The Experimental Model places emphasis on causal relationships between activities and individual or organizational change. The Participatory Evaluation Model places emphasis on specific anomalies in activities. It also emphasizes participation of learners themselves in the focus, data collection, interpretation, and implementation of action that emerges from the evaluation process.

What Should Be the Focus for Evaluation of Learning?

The evaluation of learning at the micro level can be considered from the perspective of the two most important stakeholders, the educators and the learners. When evaluating learning, there are many questions to answer. Central, of course, is how learners experience the learning process, and what they actually learn (the product of learning), their knowledge, attitudes, skills, and aspirations. The evaluation can also focus on the educator/learner transaction and the content, processes, and resources that are used. Since learning is always a social phenomenon, the evaluation can focus on the learning environment, organizational context, and the relevance of language, culture, and sometimes public policy to learning. These underlying cultural assumptions often explain resistance to learning as well as the way learning either reproduces existing racial, gender, and economic power relationships or challenges these existing relationships. Not all evaluations include all of these questions. Educators tend to focus on questions that serve their own perspectives. Learners likewise may be interested in questions that serve their perspectives. Often adult learners are eager to critically reflect on their past and present learning contexts in order to overcome socially constructed deterrents to their learning.

Evaluation of Learning: The Learner's Perspective

When learners consider evaluation of their own learning, they may ask themselves a broad range of questions. Have they, as learners:

- Gained factual knowledge that is useful to them?
- Made use of principles, concepts or theories in relationship to their real problems?
- Improved logical thinking, problem-solving and decision-making abilities?
- Developed specific psychomotor manual skills?
- Increased their interests in the subject or problem?
- Increased their hopes and aspirations regarding the future?
- Developed creative imaginative, inventive, or original skills?
- Recalled knowledge that is relevant to what they currently are doing?
- Learned how to learn better or gain access to more knowledge?
- Received guideposts for continuing their learning?
- Gained confidence and skill in presenting their ideas?
- Changed their assumptions, habits of the mind, priorities?

- Gained confidence in taking leadership?
- Overcome self-doubts, insecurities, and learning deterrents?
- Increased their commitment to take direct action?

These are the types of questions that learners can be encouraged to ask themselves throughout the learning process in discussions and interviews, as well as in questionnaires at the end of a learning session or unit.

Evaluation of Learning: The Educator's Perspective

When educators or learning facilitators consider evaluation of learning, they usually want to know how the learners perceive the process of learning, especially how they as educators have been helpful to it. The questions that educators ask themselves, and want judgments from learners to indicate whether the educators have been helpful, include the following. Have they, as educators:

- Shared up-to-date knowledge and methods?
- Related theory to practice?
- Showed concern about learners as human beings?
- Challenged learners to move beyond where they are now?
- Encouraged independent learning and responsibility?
- Pointed out what was important to learn?
- Given step-by-step instructions?
- Clarified goals and objectives?
- Promoted discussion and learner interaction?
- Encouraged silent learners to participate?
- Spoken with expressiveness and variety in tone of voice?
- Introduced a variety of useful teaching techniques and materials?
- Used understandable vocabulary?
- Encouraged the use of examples to illustrate concepts or practice?
- Summarized material presented?
- Respected racial, ethnic, and gender differences and their unique contributions to learning?
- Appreciated learning handicaps and disabilities?
- Praised learners during the learning activities?
- Helped learners critically reflect on how they learn?
- Appreciated prior knowledge of learners and made use of it during the activities to participants learn from each other?

Educators of adults do not need to wait until the end of all events and activities for learner responses to their teaching/facilitating behaviors. Asking learners these questions throughout the activities can create an openness to critical reflection and increase the possibilities that changes can be made during the course of activities. Asking learners to reflect on educator behaviors also encourages critical reflection on their own learning.

The purpose of listing all of these questions from both the learners' and educators' perspectives is not that one should ask them all, but to stimulate discussion about which are essential for a specific evaluation effort.

What Are Some Methods for Evaluation and Assessment?

The basic rule here is that the selection of methods follows the selection of focus, not the other way around. Each evaluation question must be examined in relationship to what would constitute data for answering it. The following brief descriptions of data collection methods, although by no means exhaustive, can be used as a tool kit for a variety of circumstances. The list includes interviews, observations, document analysis, feedback committees, group discussion assessment, peer review panels, snowball discussion technique, end-of-class analysis, testimonials and anecdotes, case studies, portfolios, rating scales and checklists, and pre-/posttests/quizzes.

Interviews

Interviews are probably the most widely used method for program evaluation including the evaluation of learning. Interviews are adaptable to a wide variety of programs, suited to an in-depth exploration of an issue. If the questions are standardized, responses can be tabulated numerically to indicate item strength. If questions are open-ended, in-depth unique responses can be generated that, in turn, can provide information regarding reasons why the activities are viewed differently by diverse groups of participants. Interviews may be conducted in person or by telephone. Conducting quality interviews requires training interviewers. The cost of time occurs not only during the interview process, but in the transcription of recorded data if a written form is not used at the time of the interview, or from data analysis especially from qualitative open-ended material. Interviews can be used prior to the beginning of educational experiences, during the activities, at the end, and sometime after a period of time to determine the extent that participants have used what they have learned.

Observations

Observers can be outsiders or persons who are involved in the learning activity and who take turns being observers. Observers are usually given a short list of items that may include extent of participation and personal interaction; nonverbal indicators of interest or inattention; leadership roles; performance levels; and conflict indicators, to name a few. Both qualitative data and quantitative data can be collected. Findings can be reported to the learners as a whole to start a reflective process about what may need to be changed or can be used as evidence of successful methods or learning outcomes (Worden & Neumaier, 1987). Another type of observation is through video or photodocumentation of both process and outcomes. These data are very powerful graphic ways of communicating the nature of a program and its outcomes to sponsors as well as to potential learners. Video records of learners' experiences also can be used to help them reflect on their own stories and learning outcomes.

Document Analysis

Many forms of adult and continuing education produce documents either in the course of their operation or as a result of their learners' activities. Examples include minutes of meetings, correspondence, budget records, lecture notes, participant papers, and newspaper reports, to name a few. These can be treated as data, content analyzed, and summarized in relationship to questions including the following: extent of inputs into the program; levels of participation, nature of goals and activities, and themes regarding problems, concerns, expectations, and new directions. These data are readily available and may be assessed on a continuing basis at a minimal cost and effort. Themes from documents can be a credible source of information. The sources are mostly limited to descriptive data that may be weakened if there are gaps in the records. These documents usually do not reveal participants' motivations or subjective experiences. However, documents often reveal difficulties of program operation.

Feedback Committees

When educational events last for more than eight hours or more than six sessions, learners can elect a feedback committee about one third of the way through the event or course. The duties of the feedback committee are to be open to any complaints participants may have about the event, ranging from the content, the facilities, or the leadership, to the involvement of learners in discussion or activities. The committee can bring items to the attention of the instructor or to the group as a whole (Apps, 1991). One way for the committee or an educator to gather feedback is to distribute 3×5 cards after units or segments of learning activities and encourage learners to write their responses to one or two questions. These can be collected and read aloud and discussed without identifying the source. Group members can then validate or invalidate the comments and recommend changes.

Group Discussion Assessment

This method can be incorporated into an ongoing group or meeting. It is relatively efficient in terms of costs and time use. The discussion is usually focused on several open-ended questions including educational expectations, learning resources, program design, strengths of activities, facilities, accessibility of program, costs, and identification of types of learning outcomes. These group discussions can be in the form of focus groups, created specifically for the evaluation and composed of a cross section of participants, or in the form of brainstorming sessions with participants in their regular groupings. Groups can create their own categories and then make priority choices about the importance of suggested changes. This is sometimes called the nominal group approach.

Peer Review Panels

Learners can become involved in evaluating one another's work through peer review panels. Panels can be taught to use standard referenced judgment perspectives. Their evaluative judgments can be made with or without identification of reviewers.

When using peer review panels, it is important to establish a positive climate of constructive criticism.

Snowball Discussion Technique

This calls for group members to alternate between written and oral discussion of a few short, open-ended questions. The written responses can be summarized by a committee while the discussion takes place, then reported to the group which then addresses a new set of questions that emerged out of the summarized responses. This snowball effect often cuts through initial superficial responses to more thoughtful ones. Another version of this involves first writing and then sharing what has been written in pairs who then form groups of four to summarize their consensus regarding questions. These summaries are then reported to the total group. The written statements can be collected and further analyzed along with tape recordings of the discussion (Harris & Bell, 1990).

End-of-Class Analysis

This can be done in several ways. The most frequently used is an evaluation form that is administered at the last class session. Another way is to have these forms distributed, collected, and summarized by the Feedback Committee. They can then report these findings and conduct a discussion on the overall strengths of the course, class, or educational event. After discussing what should not be changed, they can then discuss what specific modifications should be made (Apps, 1991).

Testimonials and Anecdotes

Testimonials and anecdotes can provide subjective records of educational experiences and activities from the perspective of the learners. They are a form of results data and can qualitatively describe the nature and process of educational change. These stories also can be easily understood by others outside the program as illustrations of the types of outcomes. The stories may lead to ideas for future programming. The disadvantages of this method include social desirability bias, nongeneralizability beyond the person giving the testimony, and difficulty in determining what happened as a result of the program variables other influences on the person. Stories can be either written by the learners or created as a result of an audiotaped interview.

Case Studies

In order to understand motivation of participants or potential participants, case studies of specific individual types of learners can be undertaken. The typology may be based on cultural, age, gender, and economic differences. Case studies are best constructed through repeated interviews over time and often include, in addition to self-report, data from persons who know the subject well. Diaries, logs, and journals can also contribute to case study data if participants can be persuaded to produce them, and if evaluators can guarantee the right to privacy and confidentiality of these sources. Case studies often reveal deterrents to participation as well as ways participants have overcome deterrents to learning through the program or otherwise.

Portfolios

Portfolios can be very useful to learners to document their own educational achievements and to educators to document that learners have demonstrated proficiencies. Portfolios contain resumes, work records, biographical material, descriptions of volunteer and field experiences, letters of recommendation, samples of written work, and photos of other products or achievements. For purposes of program evaluation, groups of portfolios can be summarized as documentation of proficiencies of individuals who have participated in specific educational experiences.

Rating Scales and Checklists

These are very useful in behavioral evaluations. Educators can use these in checking performance of learners. Learners can use these to check the performance of teachers. They can be administered in group settings and can be easily revised (Worden & Neumaier, 1987). Learners can use them to judge their own performance, current knowledge, or educational expectations. Rating scales and checklists are not very useful in measuring attitudes or consequences of performance.

Pretests/Posttests/Quizzes

The typical way that documentation of learning occurred during schooling was through testing, usually in the form of a pencil-paper examination. Adults have been socialized into expecting this and often have wanted to avoid it. However, they encounter this commonplace type of evaluation when they apply for a driver's license, when they register for taking the general education diploma (GED), or when they satisfy the requirements for licensure or certification for many occupations. In spite of the negative attitudes associated with tests and quizzes, they have useful evaluation purposes. A pretest or sample of prior knowledge is very useful for diagnosing learner proficiencies and projecting learning achievements, as well as understanding learner knowledge and attitudes. One of the basic tenets of adult education is that learners bring unique experience and competencies to the learning experience. Evaluating what they bring with them is essential to making good decisions about where to start and what methods might be relevant to improving the program. Asking learners to describe their expectations for learning and relevant past experiences on paper at the outset of a learning experience is one way of understanding their motivation and documenting what they already know. One form of a pretest is the construction of a concept map by either the learners themselves or by educators extrapolating concepts from interviews with learners (Deshler, 1990). These concept maps can be used to increase critical reflective evaluation on the part of learners about their underlying personal assumptions or about subject matter in their projected learning efforts. Posttests also can document learning achievement for certain types of learning. Collectively summarized tests and quizzes can provide a type of evidence that learners have achieved (Jacobs & Chase, 1992). Written work at the end of educational activities also can be content-analyzed for levels of achievement.

What Are Reference Perspectives for Making Evaluative Judgments?

After gathering, analyzing, and summarizing data, judgments must be made about the value and worth of a program (macro level) or individual achievements of learners (micro level). Judgments about value and worth are always determined from some judgment perspective. Judgments are always referenced to some anchor point. Differences of opinion regarding achievements often are the result of not only disagreeing on the facts, but also from how those facts are viewed from differing judgment perspectives regarding the same evidence.

There are at least five types of reference points or perspectives for making judgments about the value or worth of a program or of individuals' learning achievements. These types are

1. Standard-referenced judgment perspectives (sometimes called criterion referenced);
2. Cohort-referenced judgment perspectives (sometimes called norm referenced);
3. Difficulty-referenced judgment perspectives;
4. Progress-referenced judgment perspectives; and
5. Alternative-referenced judgment perspectives.

To illustrate the use of these judgment perspectives is the case of Maria Valenzuela's learning achievements in her efforts to learn English as a second language (ESL). It is customary for many who take ESL courses to take the Test of English for Speakers of Other Languages (TOFEL) exam. After three and six months, the teacher of the course selected a number of items from a typical TOFEL exam and gave them pre-tests to get the learners acquainted with the test. On the second pretest that had 100 possible points, Maria scored 65. Maria's instructor did not consider this to be a very good score since she had set 80 as the minimum score to be ready to take the TOFEL exam (standard referenced judgment point). However, Maria did not score too badly in comparison to others who were in the class. Some class members scored in the 50s while only four in a group of twelve scored better than Maria did (other-learner referenced judgment point). Maria probably felt much better about her achievement when she was compared on the "curve." When Maria found out about her score she was thrilled, because, in comparison to her first pretest score of 45, she had made considerable achievement (progress-referenced judgment point). Maria also felt good about her score since this was her first experience taking tests since she was in high school ten years ago. A score of 65 meant that she had overcome her fear of taking tests and had achieved even though it had been very difficult for her (difficulty-referenced judgment point). Maria thought about what she had given up to take on this ESL course. She had less time for her children. She was getting less sleep in order to do her studying and to get all the other family responsibilities accomplished. She wondered whether it was all worth it. She decided that her score of 65 meant that she was doing well enough to make the sacrifice for her family (alternative-referenced judgment perspective).

In grading systems of the past some teachers graded students in comparison to others in the class (other learner or norm-referenced basis) thus producing a general distribution of the class (so many "A" "B" "C" "D" and "Fs" distributed on a normal curve). Other teachers, however, used a standard-referenced basis. If 25 of the 30 members of the class reached the standard of an "A," then all those who achieved this standard would receive "As," even if this was not consistent with a normal "bell-shaped curve." Sometimes we thought that we should have been given a higher grade since for some subjects we had to work extra hard because the subject did not come easily to us (difficulty-referenced judgment perspective). Some teachers may have given us a higher grade rewarding our diligence and effort in spite of the fact that our achievement was not excellent in comparison to other students or her own standards. For some subjects we learned an enormous amount, given the fact that we knew very little at the outset of the course. Some of us reasoned to ourselves that such progress deserved recognition in our grade (progressed-referenced judgment perspective). This is sometimes referred to as "value added" achievement. Occasionally we regretted taking a particular course, since another course that we could have taken could possibly have yielded a better teacher, more interesting subject matter, and a higher grade (alternative-referenced judgment perspective).

Children became used to standard-referenced or other learner referenced achievement judgments from teachers. Occasionally some argued for progress or difficulty referenced judgments to be taken into consideration. Now as adults, all of these judgment points of reference come into play when they judge their own learning. Adults may even view the alternative-referenced judgment perspective to be the most important perspective to them. When they compare their achievements with what they have had to give up in order to learn, their feelings about these achievements may be quite different from the judgments of their instructors or educators who may still be using a standard or other learner-referenced approach to judging the value and worth of their learning achievements. The learners themselves usually bring the difficulty, progress, and alternative referenced judgments to their learning achievements. Adult and continuing educators will have only a partial notion of learning achievement unless they find out what these valuing perspectives are from their learners. After learners have achieved some learning, facilitators can use a variety of techniques that can bring to light the judgments of the learners. Questions like the following can be asked in questionnaires, or focus groups, or in the course of group discussions: (a) How much more do you know now than when you began this learning experience? (b) How difficult has it been for you to learn? and (c) Has it been worth learning this when you consider what you could have been doing with your time and energy?

These same points of reference or perspectives can be used at the macro or program evaluation level as well. Let us now consider making judgments using these perspectives in relationship to an Expanded Food and Nutrition Education Program (EFNEP) sponsored by the Cooperative Extension Service for low-income families. After gathering data at the county level on people involvement, on reactions to the program, and on individual change by low-income family members, it was determined that 182 families had been taught at least once a week by nine paraprofessional aids who were trained by a single extension educator. As a result of their efforts, the evaluation data indicated that approximately 40% of the families had increased fruits and vegetables in their diets and that 60% of the families had fewer colds during the year under evaluation. How significant is this educational achievement? When these achievements are compared with goals set by the Cooperative Extension agent, they fell short (standard-referenced judgment perspective). She wanted each of the nutrition education aids to reach at least twenty-five families per week instead of averaging about twenty. She also expected more than 40% of the families to increase fruits and vegetables in their diets based on a food-recall questionnaire. However, she compared notes with one of her colleagues in a nearby county and found that their achievements were well below those of her own aids (cohort-referenced judgment perspective). Some of the aids reminded her that it had been a very severe winter making family visits difficult, and that the aids also had to help their families with doctor visits (difficulty-referenced judgment perspective). In the light of this, the aids argued, they had been able to accomplish much more than they had expected. The aids asked their Extension educator to comment on what last year's nutrition aids had been able to do. The Extension educator reported that last year they had eight aids who had worked with 144 families and that they were able to achieve only a 35% increase in the use of fruits and vegetables. When the aids compared this year's achievements with last year's, they felt much better since they had increased both the number of families per aid and had increased the percentage of families who had increased the use of fruits and vegetables (progress-referenced judgment perspective). One of the aids, however, made the comment that the reason that more of her families could not increase their fruit and vegetable diets was due to price increases in the stores during the same period that family welfare checks had eroded due to inflation. Perhaps the government should have spent the food and nutrition program money by increasing the welfare checks (alternative-referenced judgment perspective). Another aid wondered whether an educational program that combined health education with nutrition education would be better than one that only concentrated on nutrition (alternative referenced judgment perspective). The Extension educator decided that, considering all of the perspectives overall, the program had been worth the effort even though it probably would not satisfy the expectations of the Congress and USDA.

In the two examples, a combination of judgment perspectives is required to provide a holistic picture of the success or lack of success of a particular effort. Sometimes standards are too high or too low for difficult or easy circumstances. Sometimes comparisons with other programs are unfair due to unequal resources. Often times only hindsight tells us that we should have tried something different. Evaluation is the art of judgment, not simply the use of sophisticated instrumentation.

Why Use Participatory Approaches to Evaluation?

How much involvement should the learners have in evaluating their own learning? Typically, in formal education, the teachers determine when evaluation is to occur, and by what instruments. They collect the data (tests, student work, observations, etc.) analyze and grade it and then pronounce their judgments, usually in the form of grades, sometimes with comments on student work. In nonformal education, the educator is often viewed as a facilitator, information provider, friend, and colleague. Learners are assumed to take responsibility for their own learning. Therefore, their being involved in the evaluation of their own learning and the evaluation of educators' effectiveness is consistent with the voluntary adult education tradition of sharing evaluation responsibilities. Learners, in many community based adult education programs, have participated in evaluation of learning through program committees. However, Arnstein (1969) has pointed out, in a much-quoted article regarding a ladder of participation, that there are various degrees of involvement and participation. In her model, the bottom rungs provide for merely token participation while the top rungs allow for citizen control. Table 12.2 depicts a ladder adapted from Arnstein that provides five levels or degrees of learner involvement in evaluation of learning. Adults are by nature involved in informal evaluation of their own learning using alternative-referenced judgments, difficulty-referenced judgments and progress-referenced judgments as individual learners. What is at issue is the degree to which we as adult and continuing educators will deliberately collaborate and share control with them in collecting, analyzing, and reflecting on evidence of their achievements and judgments in regard to the helpfulness of events, processes, and learning experiences provided through various programs. We encourage participatory approaches to the answering of these questions. Learners can be encouraged to take more responsibility for addressing these questions to themselves during learning activities and to engage in the analysis and interpretation of the evidence in groups or individually using the judgment perspectives that have been provided. Practice of Levels Three through Levels Five depicted in Table 12.2 is most desirable.

Table 12.2 Ladder of Participant Involvement in Evaluation of Learning

Level 5:	Participants plan and conduct their own evaluation of their learning, without assistance of educators.
Level 4:	Participants, in cooperation with educators, evaluate their learning.
Level 3:	Participants are invited to respond to the findings of the evaluation of their learning that has been prepared by educators.
Level 2:	Participants are informed of the results of the evaluation (conducted by educators) but are not asked to respond.
Level 1:	Participants provide information and outcomes of their learning to educators who have assumed the sole responsibility for the evaluation.

What Are Key Questions to Ask
During Evaluation Planning?

Evaluation and assessment of programs and of learning will occur informally on the part of both learners and continuing educators. The distinctions and approaches introduced in this chapter can make evaluating programs and learning more intentional, systematic, participatory, and relevant to both learners and educators. For this to occur, specific decisions have to be made at the outset as well as during and after learning activities and events. Asking key questions, such as those that follow below, can help focus planning decisions. Answering all these questions shapes an evaluation plan.

1. Which model of evaluation will be used?
2. How much participation from learners will be encouraged?
3. What will be the focus of the evaluation?
4. What questions do continuing educators seek to answer?
5. What questions do learners seek to answer?
6. How will records or documentation for each question be collected?
7. When will these procedures occur?
8. Who will collect, summarize, and interpret the records, documentation, or evidence?
9. Which reference points will be used to interpret and make judgments from the data?
10. How will the work be managed?
11. How will the findings of the evaluation be communicated?
12. How will evaluation be integral to learning as well as reporting?

Some evaluation questions can be determined at the outset by administrators educators and by learners. Other questions will emerge during learning activities. Still others can be determined at the end of learning activities while critically reflecting on what has happened and what has been learned. Making decisions about evaluation approaches; selecting high priority questions; determining specific methods for systematically collecting records and evidence at specific times prior to, during, and after major learning activities; and involving learners and educators together in critically reflecting on and interpreting the evidence will go a long way toward guaranteeing that evaluation itself is a major adult learning process.

QUESTIONS FOR STUDY AND DISCUSSION

1. To what extent do the myths about evaluation reviewed at the beginning of the chapter reflect attitudes about evaluation in your own organization? What might be done, and by whom, to dispel such myths?
2. Identify the reasons for which program evaluation can be justified in your organization?
3. This chapter describes seven approaches to program evaluation. Identify which, if any, of the elements named by the different models that could be applied to the programs for which you are responsible.
4. Table 12.1 identifies seven different program elements that can form the focus of program evaluation. Which elements are the current focus of most of your program planning efforts? What might be the likely results and/or benefits from adopting one or more additional elements on which to focus your program evaluation?
5. Which, if any, of the program evaluation methods mentioned could you add to those that you currently employ?
6. What is the utility of the concept of reference perspectives for making evaluative judgments? Critically assess the reference perspectives currently in use within your own organization. In light of the chapter discussion, which, if any, reference perspectives might be added or modified?
7. Critically assess the merits of involving your program participants and other stakeholders in planning evaluation of the programs for which you are responsible.
8. Assess the utility of the *key questions* offered as guidelines for the planning of program evaluation within your own organization.

REFERENCES

Apps, J. W. (1991). *Mastering the art of teaching of adults*. Malabar, FL: Krieger.

Arnstein, S. (1969). The Ladder of Citizen Participation. *Journal of American Institute of Planners, 35*, 221.

Beatty, P. T., Benefield, L. L., & Linhart, L. J. (1991). Evaluating the teaching and learning process. In Galbraith, M. W. (Ed.). *Facilitating adult learning: A transactional process.* Malabar, FL: Krieger.

Brunner, I., & Guzman, A. (1989). Participatory evaluation: A Tool to assess projects and empower people. In Conner, R. F. & Hendricks, M. (Eds.). *International innovations in evaluation methodology.* New Directions for Program Evaluation, *42*, 9–18. San Francisco: Jossey-Bass.

Cronbach, L. J. (1980). *Toward reform of program evaluation: Aims, methods, and institutional arrangements.* San Francisco, CA: Jossey-Bass.

Deshler, D. (Ed.) (1984). *Evaluation for program improvement.* New Directions for Continuing Education, *4.* San Francisco: Jossey-Bass.

Deshler, D. (1990). Concept mapping. In Mezirow, J. and Associates. *Fostering critical reflection in adulthood: A guide to transformative learning.* San Francisco: Jossey-Bass.

Deshler, D. (1996). "Evaluating Extension Programs" in B. Swanson (Ed), *Improving Agricultural Extension: A Reference Manual.* Rome: United Nations Food and Agriculture Organization.

Eisner, E. (1983). Educational connoisseurship and criticism: Their form and function in educational evaluation. In Madaus, G. F., Scriven, M., & Stufflebeam, D. (Eds.). *Evaluation models.* Boston: Kluwer-Nijhoff Publishing.

Gold, N. (1988). Stakeholders and program evaluation: characterizations and reflections. In A. S. Bryk (Ed.). *Stakeholder-based evaluation.* New Directions for Program Evaluation, *17*, 62–63. San Francisco: Jossey-Bass.

Goldstein, I. L. (1986). Evaluation procedures. In Goldstein, I. L., *Training in organizations: Needs assessment, development and evaluation* (2nd ed.). Monterey, CA: Brooks/Cole.

Guba, E. G., & Lincoln, Y. S. (1989). *Fourth-generation evaluation.* Newbury Park, CA: Sage.

Green, J. C. (1988). Stakeholder Participation and Utilization in Program Evaluation. *Evaluation Review, 12,* 91–116.

Harris, D., & Bell, C. (1990). *Evaluating and assessing for learning.* New York: Nichols/GP Publishing.

Jacobs, L. C., & Chase, C. I. (1992). *Developing and using tests effectively: A guide for faculty.* San Francisco: Jossey-Bass.

Moran, Joseph J. (1997). *Assessing adult learning: A guide for practitioners.* Malabar, FL: Krieger.

Patton, M. Q. (1991, October). Beyond Evaluation Myths. *Adult Learning,* 9–10, 28.

Provus, M. (1971). *Discrepancy evaluation.* Berkeley, CA: McCutchan.

Rossi, P. H., & Freeman, H. E. (1993). *Evaluation: A systematic approach* (5th ed.). Beverly Hills, CA: Sage.

Scriven, M. (1972). Pros and Cons about Goal-Free Evaluation. *Evaluation Comment, 3,* 1–5.

Stufflebeam, D. L. (1971). *Educational evaluation and decision making.* Itasca, IL: Peacock.

Summers, J. C. (1977). Dimensions of program effectiveness and accountability. Morgantown: West Virginia University, Office of Research and Development.

Tripodi, T., Fellin, P., & Epstein, I. (1971). *Social program evaluation: Guidelines for health education and welfare administration.* Itasca, IL: Peacock.

Worden, P. E., & Neumaier, P. A. (1987). *Source Book for Program Evaluation and Accountability.* Fort Collins: Colorado State Cooperative Extension, Colorado State University.

13

Designing Effective Instruction for Adults

Burton Sisco and John Cochenour

ABSTRACT

Some form of teaching-learning transaction is at the core of every education or training program. Although there is a considerable literature on instructional design, most of that literature has focused on teaching and learning in connection with children and adolescents in schools or with adults in worker roles. How that literature applies to the teaching and learning of adults, in a wide variety of settings—not just work settings—is the focus of this chapter. Following a review of major features of instructional design theory, the Individualizing Instructional Process Model (IIPM) is presented as a framework to planning the teaching-learning step of the education or training program. The IIPM is then applied to a particular educational activity. The chapter closes with a checklist that corresponds to the six steps of the IIPM.

ASSESSMENT

1. Define *instructional design*. To what extent do you consider program planning and instructional design parallel processes? How are they similar? How are they different?
2. To what extent do you incorporate principles of instructional design in your own education/training practice?
3. To what extent do you make provision for individualization of the learning experienced by those who participate in your education or training programs? What specific strategies for such individualization do you employ?

INTRODUCTION

Adult learning in formal settings is one of the fastest growing segments in all of education. Record numbers of adults are returning to the classroom for many reasons including skill improvement, job advancement, and personal understanding. At many colleges and universities, adults constitute a majority of the student body. In business and industry, training programs are expanding exponentially to help workers keep current and competitive. As we look to the future, more and more adults from all walks of life will be engaging in formal learning activities which present enormous opportunities for those individuals interested in the teaching and learning process—especially for adults. Yet, until recently, most efforts at organizing and designing effective instruction have focused on children, adolescents, or young adults. Although these efforts are laudable, they typically do not take into account the unique qualities and characteristics of adults. Thus, a void exists in uniting what we know about how to design effective instruction and what we know about how adults learn. The purpose of this chapter is to help close this gap. Specifically, we begin with a discussion of what instructional design means and offer an historical perspective of instructional design theory and associated theorists. We then focus attention on key principles of instructional design and how these principles can be used in the teaching and learning process. Next, we relate instructional design theory to adult learning situations by illustrating its use in a model for teaching adults. Finally, we offer a checklist for organizing adult instruction more effectively.

DEFINING INSTRUCTIONAL DESIGN

What is meant by instructional design? Instruction is defined in the *American Heritage Dictionary* (1985) as imparted knowledge and the art or practice of instructing. This definition can be amplified by comparing instruction with two related terms, instructions and teaching. Instructions are intended to assist in task accomplishment. For example, instructions are printed on a box to explain the proper procedures for efficiently opening the container. Such instructions can be discarded once the task is accomplished. There is no expectation that one remember such instructions or be able to replicate the task without the instructions. A key aspect of instruction, however, is the intent that some learning occur. This intent for learning to occur differentiates instruction from instructions (Ragan, 1985). In fact, Ragan insists that instruction should be considered to include all forms of intentioned learning activity. This would place teaching in a subcategory of instruction. Therefore, teaching is only one form of instruction characterized by face-to-face interaction between a teacher and student. Instruction is the umbrella under which many delivery methods fall: teaching, instructional video, computer-based, and so forth.

Design, again according to the *American Heritage Dictionary* (1985), refers to the invention and disposition of the forms, parts, or details of something according to a plan. Design activity is intended to promote the achievement of a stated goal in an effective and efficient manner. Instructional design then is the systematic application of a set of principles to achieve effective, efficient, and relevant instruction (Briggs, Gustafson, & Tillman, 1991). Instructional design is a process involving the analysis of learning needs and goals and the development of a delivery system to meet those needs. It includes the development of instructional materials, instructional activities, evaluation, and revision of learner activities. Instructional design focuses upon methods of instruction, including specific instructional method variables. In other words, instructional design acts as a blueprint that spells out the methods of instruction to apply.

HISTORICAL OVERVIEW

Instructional design has developed from contributions in several areas, but most important have been the contributions from (1) media and communications, (2) general systems theory, and (3) psychology and learning theory. Media and communications principles and strategies have played a role in the development of the science of instructional design, but this contribution has not been as significant as that of the other two fields (Reigeluth, 1983). Therefore, with this brief overview, we will discuss some contributions from the last two fields only. General systems theory provides much of the underlying process in instructional design.

Gustafson and Tillman (1991) suggest six principles from general systems theory that characterize the instructional design process:

1. The design process is dynamic and concerned with the whole; parts of the instructional package must be integrated and not dealt with piecemeal.
2. Coordination on the part of all participants is required.
3. The design process is intended to be orderly, but flexible.
4. The design process is research based.
5. Formative evaluation is required to ensure a stable and quality product.
6. Summative evaluation is also necessary where the final version of instruction is compared with alternatives or the original goals.

As these principles suggest, systems theory provides a logical process for the development and implementation of instruction. This process supports a framework for specifying the purpose of instruction, analyzing and selecting components, and continuously evaluating the system (Banathy, 1968).

The third major contributor to instructional design theory has been psychology and the learning theory tradition. Many authors trace the development of instructional design back to Edward Thorndike and his work on learning and instructional strategies (Gustafson & Tillman, 1991; Reigeluth, 1983). However, Reigeluth (1983) goes on to point out that the three theorists most responsible for the present development of instructional design are B. F. Skinner (1968, 1971, 1974); Jerome Bruner, and David Ausubel. Skinner and his behavioral approach to learning can be linked with Thorndike, while Bruner and Ausubel are more dependent upon cognitive psychology and its development dating back to John Dewey.

Although many others have contributed and continue to contribute to the development of instructional design theory, Skinner, Bruner, and Ausubel should be considered key in the initial developments of an attempt to link research in learning theory to the practical application of that theory to instructional delivery. There is not room in this chapter to review all of these contributions, but key principles can be drawn from several theories to be considered in developing instruction.

INSTRUCTIONAL DESIGN PRINCIPLES

There is a wide variety of instructional design theories that could be considered in a search for key principles. Andrews and Goodson (1980) listed 40 different theories or models in their analysis, Gagne and Dick (1983) review 12 different theories, and Reigeluth (1983) explores 8 theories in great detail. Additional theories and models continue to be developed, but there are common factors that most theories or models address.

Gropper (1977) identifies 10 common tasks in his synthesis of instructional models. Andrews and Goodson (1980) add another four for a total of 14 common tasks. Reigeluth (1983) proposes that all instructional theory deals with two broad concerns: methods and situations. Methods are described as the individual strategies employed, and situations are described as desired outcomes and existing conditions. Gropper (1983), in his proposal for a meta-theory of instruction, argues that every instructional theory or model should address two areas: conditions and treatments. Conditions are defined as being composed of learning requirements and learning obstacles which impose difficulty levels. Treatments are defined as levels of attention. This is further broken down to information quality and quantity, repetition, variety, and duration. The Gagne-Briggs theory (1979) of instruction proposes three major elements: outcomes, instructional events, and appropriate sequencing (Petry, Mouton, & Reigeluth, 1987). Merrill's (1973) component display theory also contains three major elements: outcomes, presentations, and prescriptions. Outcomes are two-dimensional, considering student performance and subject-matter content. Gustafson and Tillman (1991) present an instructional design model of 10 steps that includes analysis, organization, design, implementation, and evaluation.

Based upon these models and overviews, it can be determined that there are common activities or concerns that must be considered for effective instruction. We have selected a group of those common instructional elements to illustrate an instructional model, but it should be emphasized that many combinations of tasks could be determined based upon the variety of instructional models. It should also be noted that such lists can continually be expanded or simplified. For example, implementation or evaluation can be simply stated or expanded upon to develop many additional steps. This list is not organized in a specific order. The design process normally flows forward and backward, and might be better described by a spiraling or web-like chart than by a linear list. Figure 13.1 presents the common elements found in instructional theory.

Within these design elements one can find the outcomes, methods, and conditions that are part of every good model. However, the application of such components must still be tied to a particular philosophy of learning. If the learning philosophy is of a behavioral bent, behavioral objectives and assignments will of course be applied. A more cognitive approach might apply elaborative strategies. Our preference is to use these common principles as tied to a more cognitive learning approach that would stress learner control and individual differences.

APPLYING INSTRUCTIONAL DESIGN TO THE TEACHING OF ADULTS: THE INDIVIDUALIZING INSTRUCTIONAL PROCESS

Up to this point, we have discussed the foundations of instructional design and noted some of the pervasive design elements and

CONDITIONS

- Formulation of instructional goals
- Overall instructional organization
- Characterization of the learner population
- Describe system and environmental constraints

TREATMENTS

- Formulation of instructional strategy and methodology
- Implementation of instruction
- Instructional evaluation

Figure 13.1 Common instructional design elements

principles. We now turn our attention to a model of instruction that utilizes these elements of instructional design and what is known about adults as learners. The model is the "individualizing instructional process" developed by Hiemstra and Sisco (1990). It is rooted in much of the education and training literature of the past 20 years which stresses the importance of involving adults in the planning, implementation, and evaluation of the teaching and learning process. Additionally, the individualizing process is supported by research on self-directed learning and has been critically tested in numerous adult teaching and learning situations with consistent success (Sisco & Hiemstra, 1991).

Before describing the individualizing instructional process model (IIPM) and illustrating its use in a typical teaching and learning situation, it is important to explicate a number of assumptions upon which the model is based. These assumptions are predicated on the nature of adults, sound principles of learning and instruction, and how to organize instruction effectively. They also help guide our efforts as instructors of adults, regardless of setting, level, or background.

1. Adults can and do learn significant things throughout their lives.
2. Educational interventions ought to be organized so that growth and development are the ultimate outcome.
3. The potentiality of humans as learners can only be maximized when there is a deliberate interaction between three elements: the learning process, learning needs and interests, and available instructional resources.
4. When given the opportunity, adults prefer to be in charge of their own learning and actually thrive under such conditions.
5. Adults are capable of self-directed involvement in terms of personal commitment to and responsibility for learning, choice of learning approach, choice of learning resources, and choice of evaluation or validation techniques.
6. An instructor's role is multidimensional, including being a facilitator, manager, resource guide, expert, friend, advocate, authority, coach, and mentor.
7. Empowering learners to take responsibility for their own learning is the ultimate aim of education.
8. Educational interventions ought to promote a match between the needs of each learner and the needs of the instructor.

9. Teaching and learning excellence is the result of subject matter expertise, careful planning, a good deal of patience and flexibility, and a commitment to helping learners reach their potential.
10. The individualizing instructional process can be utilized in nearly every educational endeavor with commensurate success. (Sisco & Hiemstra, 1991, pp. 60–61)

THE INDIVIDUALIZING INSTRUCTIONAL PROCESS MODEL

The individualizing instructional process model (IIPM) consists of six specific steps as shown in Figure 13.2. In each step, considerable planning, analyzing, and decision-making must be made by an instructor as the model is implemented. The model is intended to serve as a framework for organizing instruction for adults, usually in a group setting such as a course, workshop, or training session, and should be used flexibly so that any individual or institutional constraints can be embraced and dealt with accordingly. It incorporates many of the instructional design elements discussed earlier and is tailored for use with adult students.

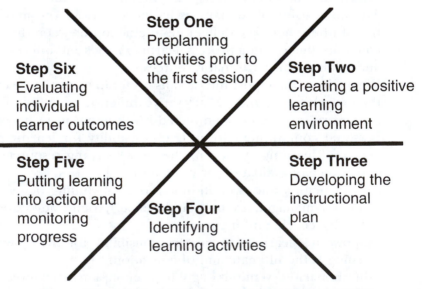

Figure 13.2 Individualizing instructional process model (IIPM)

Step One. Preplanning Activities Prior to the First Session. There are numerous activities to plan and decisions to be made before the first meeting of the learning event. For example, the instructor often starts by developing a rationale statement that describes the purpose of the learning experience and why learners should be interested in it, how it will help them professionally, and what competencies or outcomes they can expect to attain. Usually, some attention is given to the requirements of the learning experience, identifying any support materials such as books, articles, or audio/visual tapes, and locating outside speakers for guest presentations. Other preplanning activities often involve the preparation of a workbook or study guide that includes any necessary syllabus information, learning activity descriptions, bibliographic references, special readings, and other related materials. Some additional preplanning activities often include scheduling a meeting room where the learning event will take place, reserving any required audio/visual equipment, and making sure that the coordinating administrator has all the pertinent information for advertising the learning event.

Step Two. Creating a Positive Learning Environment. Once the learning experience is underway, there are a number of activities that can help ensure a positive learning environment. Some of these include paying attention to the physical layout of the meeting room, scheduling a break midway through the session for refreshments and a restroom visit if needed, creating a relaxed and trusting environment where participants are encouraged to meet each other and express their own opinions without risk of retribution. In addition, some thought should be given to introducing the course content, how each participant will get to know one another, and how the instructor will become acquainted with the participants. Sisco and Hiemstra (1991) call this the "Three Rs": relationship with the subject matter, relationship with each other, and relationship with the instructor.

Step Three. Developing the Instructional Plan. The next step in the individualizing instructional process involves spending time on such matters as potential learning topics, activities, and objectives. This is usually accomplished through a needs assessment procedure that is completed individually by participants according to their experience, interest level, and competence. Small groups are then formed for sharing and consensus building which the instructor uses to develop a learning plan that describes the topics to be studied, in what sequence, and through what kinds of instructional methods and techniques. This learning plan is then given to participants for final review and adoption.

Step Four. Identifying Learning Activities. This step is designed to help participants identify what it is they intend to learn, how they are going to learn it, what form the learning will take, when the learning activities are due, and what evaluation strategies will be used so as to demonstrate mastery of the subject(s) under investigation. A learning contract (O'Donnell & Caffarella, 1990; Knowles, 1986) is typically used here to document the various learning activities, to help participants personalize their learning objectives, and to foster greater control of their learning. Learning activities may take many forms including the interactive reading log, the theory log, and the personalized journal so that learners can synthesize, analyze, and reflect on their newly acquired knowledge.

Step Five. Putting Learning into Action and Monitoring Progress. Once the learning plan has been established, the next step in the individualizing instructional process is putting it into action and monitoring progress. A number of instructional techniques are typically used including lectures and mini-lectures, case studies, role playing, small and large group discussions, individual learning projects, field trips, and so forth. As the learning plan is implemented, the instructor monitors group and individual learner progress through formative evaluations which permit adjustments to be made as needed.

Step Six. Evaluating Individual Learner Outcomes. The sixth and final step in the individualizing instructional process involves evaluating individual learner outcomes. Here, the emphasis is on helping learners to demonstrate mastery of their learning objectives and activities as outlined in the personal learning contract. Through the use of the learning contract, each learner describes their intended learning activities and the criteria upon which each will be accomplished. This "criteria-referenced evaluation" process allows learners to document their learning outcomes in many ways while at the same time emphasizing content mastery, personal development, reflective thinking, and critical observation.

A key ingredient of the six-step IIPM is the promotion of effective educational practice through the creation of an instructional system that celebrates individual differences, experiences, and learning needs. By taking advantage of the resident expertise so common in older, more mature learners, the instructor can create optimum conditions for learning to occur. This is one of the guiding principles of instructional design and certainly is a hallmark of the individualizing instructional process. Understanding the instructional process, being flexible and supportive when the need arises, helping learners assume greater control of the learning process, varying the instructional methods and techniques so that active learning is emphasized, all add up to instructional success.

A CHECKLIST FOR IMPLEMENTING THE INDIVIDUALIZING INSTRUCTIONAL PROCESS

We have previously noted that the individualizing instructional process is anchored in good instructional design theory and proven knowledge about how adults learn. With proper care and preplanning, the system will work well for most any instructor of adults. In order to help instructors incorporate many of the ideas and design elements of the individualizing process into their own teaching, Figure 13.3 presents a checklist for reference. The checklist is divided into the six steps that constitute the individualizing instructional process. Simply use each item as a springboard to see if your instruction or curriculum package attends to the suggested element. The more each element is affirmatively checked, the greater the likelihood for success as an instructor of adults. That is the promise of the individualizing instructional process. Using this checklist, we will illustrate how the individualizing instructional process can be used in a typical teaching and learning situation with commensurate success.

USING THE INDIVIDUALIZING INSTRUCTIONAL PROCESS: AN EXAMPLE

The individualizing instructional process is designed for use in nearly every adult learning situation to optimize success. It has been used in a variety of instructional formats such as intensive summer courses, training workshops, conference presentations, laboratory-based activities, weekend courses, guided group discussions, and so forth. To show how the individualizing process works,

Step One: Preplanning Activities Prior to the First Session
☐ Learning rationale described?
☐ Potential learners understood?
☐ Instructional options considered?
☐ Necessary support materials and resources considered?
☐ Workbook or study guide materials collected and prepared?
☐ Organizational constraints discussed and approvals negotiated?

Step Two: Creating a Positive Learning Environment
☐ Physical environment examined?
☐ Icebreaker activities considered?
☐ Opening activities decided?
☐ How to make learners feel at ease decided?
☐ Personal comforts of learners considered?
☐ How will learning materials, contracting examples, learning resources, and so on be introduced?

Step Three: Developing the Instructional Plan
☐ Suggested learning activities determined?
☐ Appropriate needs assessment tools created and used?
☐ Responded to related questions and concerns about the learning experience?
☐ The role of experience emphasized?
☐ How learners will be helped to feel comfortable with the process determined?
☐ Learning plan laid out and matched with resources?

Step Four: Identifying Activities
☐ Self-directed learning concepts emphasized?
☐ Learning contract process understood?
☐ Learning objectives identified?
☐ Necessary time lines established?
☐ Needed learning resources and strategies discussed and located?
☐ Needed evidence to show achievement of learning objectives discussed?
☐ Necessary validation and evaluation strategies identified?

Step Five: Putting Learning into Action and Monitoring Progress
☐ Optimal instructional techniques decided?
☐ Variety of instructional techniques used?
☐ Conducting formative evaluations understood?
☐ Frequent feedback to the learners provided?
☐ Feedback from learners encouraged and received?
☐ Necessary validation and evaluation strategies identified?

Step Six: Evaluating Individual Learner Outcomes
☐ Appropriate summative techniques selected?
☐ Competency and transfer of learning skills emphasized?
☐ Various linkages from the learning activities and materials made to practice?
☐ Ensured that mastery of learning took place?
☐ Assessed that quality learning and critical thinking took place?
☐ Prepared for the next instructional situation?

Figure 13.3 Individualizing Instructional Process Checklist

we have selected a typical summer course meeting daily for 2 hours over a 4 week period. Because the individualizing instructional process is inherently flexible and responsive to learner needs, it can be used in almost any setting as long as appropriate adjustments are made; that is one of the strengths of the model.

Long before the initial meeting with potential students, the instructor begins the individualizing process with considerable preplanning and design work. Potential learning resources and text materials are located as well as the beginnings of a course workbook are assembled. The workbook is a tool that contains most of the essential material for the course. For example, a syllabus is included along with suggested course requirements and learning activities. Also included are bibliographic suggestions, a glossary, various supplemental readings, information about self-directed learning, a description of the teaching and learning process, and how the individualizing instructional process will be used to help learners' assume greater responsibility for their own learning.

The next activity involves arriving early before the first session so that the physical environment can be made more comfortable and conducive to learning. This typically involves rearranging chairs so that participants can see one another, adjusting the room temperature, checking the audio/visual equipment so it can be seen and heard at a distance, and preparing refreshments such as coffee, tea, and juice.

As participants begin arriving for the initial session, it is especially nice to greet them personally. Once everyone is seated, a few welcoming remarks are given along with a brief overview of the course. Participants are then asked to turn to their neighbor or count off in twos and work in dyads. A suggested interview format is given to participants for use in getting to know their partners. After about 15 to 20 minutes, participants are asked to introduce their dyadic partner to the entire group and vice versa. This introductory technique works especially well as it enables two people to become acquainted and for others in the group to learn something about the rest of the participants through subsequent introductions.

After the introduction exercise and a question and answer period about the course materials and suggested requirements, a brief break is taken so that participants can select a refreshment, go to the restroom, or simply revive the body. Then, an individual and group needs assessment exercise is introduced by the instructor. This involves a brief instructor-generated instrument of up to 20 items that usually have been covered in previous courses. The instrument is arranged according to four self-rating categories, "low competence," "medium competence," "high competence," and "don't know." The learners are informed that they are to rank each of the suggested topics according to the appropriate category response and that they may add additional items not indicated on the instrument. After each participant completes the needs assessment instrument, small groups of four or five are formed to discuss the individual ratings and see if they can come to consensus about which topics should be emphasized in the course and which should be eliminated or reduced in scope. Once this has been completed, small groups are asked to report their ratings to the reassembled large group. The instructor records the ratings and notes that a class plan or schedule of topics and accompanying assignments will be prepared for next class meeting based on the needs assessment results. The remaining class time is then given to discussion about the course content and some general remarks about the use of learning contracts which help personalize the course for participants.

During the following day, the instructor reviews the small group needs assessment results and prepares a class plan which lays out a daily schedule of learning topics, suggests appropriate learning goals and objectives, lists any required readings, and provides any required course deadlines. Even though the class plan details what will be learned over the coming weeks, there is plenty of "flex time" built in so that certain topics can be explored in depth as needs and interests dictate.

During the second class meeting, the class plan is presented to the group and discussed in detail. Questions and comments are encouraged so that everyone can develop a sense of ownership and comfort with the focus of the course. In most cases, participants quickly adopt the course plan because it reflects their needs and interests. However, in a few cases, learners may still disagree with portions of the plan. If this happens, individual meetings are scheduled with the instructor outside of class to work out an alternative plan. Once this is negotiated, most learners are satisfied with the direction of the course and become vested in it. The remaining time of the second session is spent on some learning activity that builds upon the learners' immediate needs and interests.

At the onset of the third session, learners are encouraged to start developing their personal learning contracts which specify what each participant intends to learn, what resources and strategies will be used, what form the learning will be presented in as evidence of accomplishment, how the evidence will be evaluated, and an expected time frame for completing the various activities. Participants are then asked to turn in a tentative learning contract by the end of the following week (midway through the four-week summer course) so that the instructor can provide feedback regarding how complete and realistic the plan is for meeting the course requirements and outcomes. The instructor also makes it clear that a learning contract is designed to be flexible and any changes may be negotiated up to the end of the course depending on the competency needs of the learner.

Over the remainder of the course, the instructor's role tends to parallel traditional instruction in many ways with one notable exception; extensive feedback is provided to participants as the learning experience unfolds so that individual and group progress is monitored. A variety of instructional techniques are used to keep learner interest high such as minilectures, small and large group discussions, simulations, case studies, videotapes, role playing, and debates. Learners are also encouraged to seek the instructor's assistance in securing needed learning resources so that they can complete their individually negotiated course requirements.

A number of evaluation techniques are used to assess the quality of the learning experience and individual learner progress. These include both formative and summative evaluation procedures. The formative evaluation procedure is used to gather feedback on the course as it unfolds. Here, special attention is paid to verbal and nonverbal feedback from the participants, employing a mid-term evaluation instrument on the course and the instructor, and occasionally soliciting written feedback on various aspects of the course. In addition, individual meetings are encouraged with learners outside of class if problems develop.

A summative evaluation approach is also used to solicit participant feedback about the instructor and the course which are administered at the conclusion of the summer class. Two instructor-generated instruments are used; one focusing on the performance of the instructor and the other focusing on the instructional process, course content, and resources used during the learning experience. To ensure quality feedback, participants are asked to not provide their names on any of the evaluation instruments unless they want to. Usually, participants take the various evaluation procedures very seriously, thus helping to improve the teaching and learning experience and the individualizing instructional process.

The individualizing instructional process offers a number of advantages to the instructor of adults. Chief among these are a proven system of instruction that works in nearly every adult learning setting, a system that incorporates the key elements of instructional design theory, and a system that takes into account the nascent needs and developmental rhythms of adults as learners. Yet, the individualizing process is not perfect and will need to be adjusted depending on such variables as institutional control, learner readiness for self-direction, and instructor willingness to help learners direct more of their own learning. At the same time, aspects of the individualizing process can be employed in even the most controlled environment by using a variety of instructional techniques, emphasizing a myriad of routes for competency mastery, and acknowledging the vast experiential base that adult learners possess. By employing a commitment to careful planning and creative problem solving, the individualizing instructional process can be successfully used to help learners reach their potential regardless of the impediments to the contrary. Our checklist (Figure 13.3) can help instructors organize their instructional efforts more effectively, thereby strengthening the teaching and learning outcomes for all.

CONCLUSION

This chapter sought to unite what we know about how to design effective instruction with what we know about how adults learn. Specifically, we began by defining instruction and design, noting how the two terms when combined, enable a more effective and systematic approach to teaching and learning. We then provided a brief historical overview of how the discipline of instructional design developed, followed by an explication of some key instructional design principles. We then introduced a model—the individualizing instructional process—that incorporates the foundations of instructional design with knowledge of how adults learn. Finally, we illustrated how the individualizing instructional process might be used in a typical classroom setting and offered a checklist for instructors to use in designing and implementing their own instructional efforts more effectively.

As we look to the future, it is clear that more and more adults will be continuing their education in a variety of formal educational settings. Some will enroll to upgrade skills, others to seek new career opportunities, and still others to increase their levels of personal understanding. The opportunity to serve these diversely motivated learners will be immense as long as individuals and institutions are up to the task. One way of ensuring a positive response is to organize instruction so that effective teaching and learning occur. It is our hope that the ideas expressed in this chapter will provide a blueprint for designing instruction that is both effective and up to the task of serving those adults who richly deserve our attention.

QUESTIONS FOR STUDY AND DISCUSSION

1. How can elements of instructional design contribute to the effective teaching and learning in your organization?
2. To what extent does the IIPM offer "added value" to those elements of instructional design you identified in connection with the previous question? Explain your response.
3. Assess the utility of the checklist in Figure 13.3 for planning instruction within your own organization. Are there questions on the checklist that you would modify? Are there questions you could add?
4. Having reviewed the principles of instructional design presented in this chapter, detail the instructional phase for a specific unit of instruction in connection with a specific education or training program within your own organization.

REFERENCES

American Heritage Dictionary (2nd ed.) (1985). Boston: Houghton Mifflin.

Andrews, D. H., & Goodson, L. A. (1980). A comparative analysis of models of instructional design. *Journal of Instructional Development, 3*(4), 2–16.

Ausubel, D. P. (1978). *Educational psychology: A cognitive view.* New York: Holt, Rinehart and Winston.

Banathy, B. H. (1968). *Instructional Systems.* Belmont, CA: Fearon.

Briggs, L. J., Gustafson, K. L., & Tillman, M. H. (Eds.). (1991). *Instructional design: Principles and applications.* Englewood Cliffs, NJ: Educational Technology Publications.

Bruner, J. S. (1966). *Toward a theory of instruction.* New York: Norton.

Bruner, J. S. (1973). *Beyond the information given: Studies in the psychology of knowing.* New York: Norton.

Bruner, J. S. (1977). *The process of education.* Cambridge, MA: Harvard University Press.

Bruner, J. S. (1996). *The culture of education.* Cambridge, MA: Harvard University Press.

Gagne, R. M., & Briggs, L. J. (1979). *Principles of instructional design* (2nd ed.). New York: Holt, Rinehart & Winston.

Gagne, R. M., & Dick, W. (1983). Instructional psychology. *Annual Review of Psychology, 34,* 261–295.

Gropper, G. L. (1977). On gaining acceptance for instructional design in a university setting. *Educational Technology, 17*(12), 7–12.

Gropper, G. L. (1983). A metatheory of instruction. In C. M. Reigeluth, (Ed.), *Instructional theories in action: Lessons illustrating selected theories and models* (pp. 11–44). Hillsdale, NJ: Erlbaum.

Gustafson, K. L., & Tillman, M. H. (1991). Introduction. In L. J. Briggs, K. L. Gustafson, & M. H. Tillman, (Eds.), *Instructional design: Principles and applications.* Englewood Cliffs, NJ: Educational Technology Publications.

Hiemstra, R., & Sisco, B. (1990). *Individualizing instruction: Making learning personal, empowering, and successful.* San Francisco: Jossey-Bass.

Knowles, M. S. (1986). *Using learning contracts.* San Francisco: Jossey-Bass.

Merrill, M. D. (1973). Component display theory. In C. M. Reigeluth, (Ed.), *Instructional-design theories and models: An overview of their current status* (pp. 279–334). Hillsdale, NJ: Erlbaum.

O'Donnell, J., & Caffarella, R. (1990). Learning contracts. In M. W. Galbraith (Ed.), *Adult learning methods: A guide for effective instruction* (pp. 133–160). Malabar, FL: Krieger.

Petry, B. , Mouton, H., & Reigeluth, C. M. (1987). A lesson based on the Gagne-Briggs theory of instruction. In C. M. Reigeluth, (Ed.), *Instructional theories in action: Lessons Illustrating selected theories and models* (pp. 11–44). Hillsdale, NJ: Erlbaum.

Ragan, T. J. (1985). Never done: Define instruction. *Educational Technology, 25*(7), 26–27.

Reigeluth, C. M. (Ed.). (1983). *Instructional-design theories and models: an overview of their current status.* Hillsdale, NJ: Erlbaum.

Sisco, B., & Hiemstra, R. (1991). Individualizing the teaching and learning process. In M. W. Galbraith (Ed.), *Facilitating adult learning: A transactional process* (pp. 57–73). Malabar, FL: Krieger.

Skinner, B. F. (1968). *The technology of teaching.* New York: Appleton-Century-Crofts.

Skinner, B. F. (1971). *Beyond freedom and dignity.* New York: Alfred A. Knopf.

Skinner, B. F. (1974). *About behaviorism.* New York: Alfred A. Knopf.

14

Selecting Formats for Learning

Robert A. Fellenz

ABSTRACT

Formats for learning refer to the manner in which programs are organized. In the literature of adult education they often have been referred to as "methods" and primarily relate to the way adults are organized for learning. This chapter examines the growing literature base on this topic and offers suggestions for selecting formats for learning. It reviews methods of organizing learners as individuals, groups, or communities. Individual methods are categorized according to amount of contact between learner and teacher and range from self-directed learning to tutoring. Group formats are divided into those used to promote action and those used for content delivery. Each segment is subdivided into methods useful with small, moderate, and large groups. Community formats are treated as individual, group, and total community approaches to the education of a community of people who have some common element which unifies them. The influence of teachers, content, and situations on format selection is also examined.

ASSESSMENT

1. Have you developed a conceptual basis or set of procedures for selecting formats for learning?
2. Are you familiar with Verner's distinction between methods, techniques, and devices and Houle's four categories of educational settings?

3. Do you understand Boyd, Apps and associates' (1980) program model which is based on a three-fold distinction among individuals, groups, and communities?
4. Do you appreciate the variety of formats that might be used to organize adult learners as individuals?
5. Are you aware of the many other options there are for organizing learners in addition to classes and workshops?
6. Do you understand the ways adult learners might be organized as individuals, groups, or total communities for the purpose of community education?
7. Do you see how teachers, content, or situations might affect the manner in which formats for learning might be selected?

INTRODUCTION

A vital step in the planning of a training or educational program for adults is the selection of an appropriate format for learning. In this chapter a "format for learning" will refer to the manner in which people are organized for learning experiences. In the traditional literature of adult education this concept is frequently referred to the "method" of instruction and is recognized as a fundamental decision in the program planning process. Paradoxically this step is frequently given little consideration by program planners. The typical approach too often is simply: "These people need training. How can we put together a workshop or class for them?" And planning for the class goes on with little or no thought given to other, perhaps more appropriate ways, of organizing the people for the educational experience.

There are basically four criteria that can be used either singularly or in conjunction to select effective formats for learning, namely characteristics of the learner, the teacher, the content, or the situation. In accord with traditional emphasis by adult educators on the adult *learner*, the individuals for whom the program is designed are the common basis for such decisions. Formats can be designed for individuals, for specific groups, or for total communities. However, at times the *instructional leader* can be the rationale for formatting decisions. For example, a consultant, a special team, or a distant learning format might be essential to program success.

At other times the *content* of a training program might be the leading determinant of format. In this case learning might be organized according to desired outcomes or objectives, theoretical or on-the-job training, or according to the content to be mastered by experienced or less experienced groups. Finally, specific *situations* within an organization might suggest other criteria for format selection. In specific situations organizing programs to promote individual versus staff versus organizational development may be appropriate. At other times preference might be given to formal, informal, or nonformal approaches.

This chapter is structured to provide first theoretical frameworks which several authors have offered that can enhance understanding and practice regarding selection of formats for learning. These ideas will be examined briefly to provide a conceptual background useful to readers who wish to adapt suggested practices to their personal situation. However, the major section of the chapter will present discussion of the various formats that can be used to organize learners and will offer suggestions for practice. Major attention in this section will be given to methods of organizing learners as individuals, groups, or communities. Discussion of formatting according to teacher characteristics or availability, according to requirements of specific content, or according to special situations or organizational needs will also be considered. The chapter will conclude with some thoughts on how proper selection of learning formats can improve overall programming.

THEORETICAL BACKGROUND

Verner (1962) recognized the importance of considering formats for organizing learners as well as strategies for dealing with the instructional materials as early as 1962. To enable adult educators to discuss these issues Verner set up a classification system consisting of "methods," "techniques," and "devices" that has remained useful through the decades. Methods are the ways in which educational programs are conducted "the decision being made on the basis of the nature of the educational task and the situation controlling the availability of the adult whom the program is intended to serve" (1964, p. 36). It has commonly come to refer to the way learners are organized by the instructional agency. As such it is an administrative task usually the responsibility of the programmer. Techniques are the ways in which the instructional agent arranges the interaction between the learners and the content or material to be learned. This lies within the province of the teacher. Devices are aids that add to the effectiveness of methods or techniques but do not instruct by themselves. Verner categorized devices in four groups: illustrative devices, extension devices, environmental devices, and manipulative devices.

In addition to providing a framework for discussion of the teaching/learning interaction, Verner (1964) intended to push those engaged in the instruction of adults to give more thought to methods or formats for organizing learners. It was his hope that through precise distinctions and careful study "we can even learn which methods or techniques are most appropriate for which type of learning task under what circumstances" (p. 37). However, it is questionable how many instructional agents have paid much attention to Verner's concern for the manner in which programs are organized. Even today the majority of learning activities organized for adults are structured through some form of lecture, class, or group training session.

Houle (1972) presented an even broader view of program planning. His model includes individual, group, and community approaches to learning as does Verner's but also identifies institutional situations. Houle's analytical scheme allows for 11 types of educational situations that fall within four major categories: individual, group, institutional, and mass. Individual subcategories comprise: (1) an activity planned by an individual learner engaged in self-directed study and (2) an activity planned by an individual for another. Group subcategories comprise (3) an activity a group plans for itself, (4) an activity designed by a designated instructor for, and sometimes with, a group of learners, (5) an activity planned for a group by a committee, and (6) an activity two or more groups plan in order to experience mutual improvement in their combined service. Institutional subcategories comprise (7) an activity to design a new institution, (8) an existing activity is planned in a new format, (9) a new activity is planned in an existing format, and (10) a new activity is planned cooperatively by two institutions in order to improve their combined programs of service. A mass activity comprises (11) an activity planned by an individual, group, or institution for a mass audience. In these categories Houle provides a comprehensive program planning model and an overview of the various formats in which any learning activity can be organized.

In this model Houle takes Verner's model a step further. He demonstrates that it is not only important to consider *for whom* the instructional program is intended but also *by whom* it is designed. This raises at least three interesting issues for program planners. For example, in category 1 there is no instructional agent. Does Houle's inclusion of such self-directed learning situations suggest that program planners have some responsibility for preparing or assisting individuals to be more adept at designing learning activities for themselves? Similarly, do the references to planning by two or more groups or institutions in several categories suggest that program planning might be enhanced by such collaboration?

The significance of Houle's inclusion of four separate categories of institutional situations should not escape notice. Paging through a local telephone directory noting all the institutions offering educational programs can be a revelation. Many such groups have primary goals other than education. Directors of such programs tend to be experts in areas other than educational programming. This provides the experienced programmer opportunities for collaboration as suggested in Houle's category 10. Another institutional approach worth noting here is the residential center. Although not a new institution, residential centers of adult education, such as Highlander or Chautauqua, have proven the value of their distinctive approaches. Their approaches to selecting formats for learning may provide ideas for other program directors.

Boyd, Apps, and associates (1980) designed an entire book around a program model based on a three-fold distinction among individuals, groups, and communities. They argued the need to determine the mode, the client, and the system in which a program was to be offered. By transactional mode they meant "to characterize the nature of the learner's situation: are adults working individually, in groups or classes, or as members of a community" (p. 5). In doing so they moved beyond Verner's distinction between methods and techniques for specific strategies, such as lectures, to consider to whom the educational effort might be directed. This client focus in their model simply meant "ascertaining who primarily benefit from the educational activity—the individual, the group, or the community" (p. 7). An additional third dimension of the Boyd, Apps, and associates (1980) model designated the personal, social, and cultural systems in which the program operated. In various situations one or the other of these systems might dominate.

Throughout the remainder of their book, Boyd, Apps, and associates (1980) distinguished educational activities primarily based on whether they were conducted in the individual, group, or community transactional mode. This model puts additional emphasis on the client for whom the program is designed as well as the ultimate purpose of the program. For example, even though a program might be designed to reach out to individuals, its ultimate purpose might be community development. An example used by Boyd, Apps, and associates points to an individual who enrolls in an independent study course to help his community better understand alcoholism. An individual might use the same mode of individual study for his personal benefit or with the intent of helping some group improve its operation. Their model certainly raises the question: Is it important to consider not only the mode in which a program is to be offered but also the purpose of those who will be participating in it?

Seaman and Fellenz (1989) added another component worthy of consideration here. Although their book described effective teaching strategies rather than program design, their approach also relates to programming. Essentially their model insists that people (learners and teachers), content, and situation must be considered in every instructional decision. Each of these four factors and their interrelationships must be taken into account. In varied situations or with different groups any one of these factors may demand dominant consideration. The experience level of the group, the teaching style of the instructor, the intended outcomes regarding the topic, the time available for the program are all examples of components that must be considered in planning a program.

These four factors of learner, teacher, content, and situation provide a program designer with another perspective from which to analyze a teaching/learning interaction. A program evaluation, for example, that neglects one of these factors might provide a skewed view of what really occurred. But perhaps even more important is the analysis of the interactions among the four factors. For example, can a content-centered instructor interact well with an independent group of learners? Can a specific topic be covered adequately in the same time frame for both an experienced and a novice group of learners? Ultimately, this model raises the issue of how static program design can remain.

These four models demonstrate the importance theorists have given through the decades to the thoughtful selection of instructional formats in program design for adult learners. But what specific help do they provide program designers? Two concerns seem to dominate these models. One is that of the transactional mode or the method of organizing learners. Is the program best designed for individuals, for groups, or for a broader community? All models implicitly state that when all things are considered the method in which the learners are organized will have a major impact on whether program objectives are achieved. The second principle that can be derived from the above discussion is that the interaction among the various factors involved must also be considered if program planning is to be effective. The multiple variables involved in instructional planning make the programmer's task a challenging one. But certainly the talents of the teacher(s), the level and objectives of the content, the situational factors, and varied personal, social, and cultural systems in which learners are operating must be taken into account if the right format for learning is to be selected.

PRINCIPLES FOR SELECTING FORMATS

Consideration of the above concepts provides seven general principles useful in the selection of formats for learning.

1. Analysis of the learners, the teacher(s), the content, and the situation are all essential to proper selection of formats for learning.
2. Before selecting a format for learning the major goals of the program must be clear.
3. Although methods of organizing learners as individuals, groups, and communities depends on program intent, characteristics of teachers, content level, and situations affect proper selection of formats for learning.
4. A program director who is aware of various individual, group,

and community formats and proper uses of each is more capable of proper selection of formats for learning.

5. Resources of the program affecting format selection include instructors' competencies, participants' abilities, physical and financial assets, and time available.
6. Collaboration with other institutions or programs could affect a program's long-term effect.
7. Formats selected for specific learning situations can have an effect on a total program's effectiveness.

Because awareness of potentially useful formats for learning is essential to insightful selection, the rest of this chapter will examine possible formats and offer suggestions for their use.

APPROPRIATE FORMATS

Learner-Based Formats

Learner-based formats for instructional activities have most frequently been distinguished by whether they are intended for individuals learning alone, in groups, as a total community (Boyd, Apps, & Associates, 1980; Seaman & Fellenz, 1989; Verner, 1962). Individuals learn alone through such formats as self-directed study, prepackaged learning, correspondence study, apprenticeship programs, or tutoring. Learning groups are usually organized for information acquisition or for planning action. Content acquisition is usually accomplished through small group teams, formal courses, or large group presentations. Action groups similarly are organized on small or large group approaches. Community approaches are accomplished through individual, group, or total community approaches. Characteristics as well as suggestions for use of each format will be described below.

Individual Approaches

Adults engage in more learning activities as individuals than in groups; however, more learning activities are planned for groups than for individuals. This apparent contradiction flows from the fact that, as Tough (1971) discovered, most adult learning projects are self initiated and self planned. Less than 20% of adult learning efforts rely on programs planned by others. Yet programs planned for individuals do play a significant role among formal approaches.

In the early history of our country, for example, much vocational training, be it for doctors or lawyers or for blacksmiths or boat builders, was conducted through apprenticeship training. Although the individualized approach has great advantages in serving individual learners, program directors may ignore such approaches because they think they will find the cost prohibitive. Others like the distinct social and cultural benefits that learning in group situations often adds.

Under individual approaches the following formats can be included: self-directed study, prepackaged learning, correspondence study, apprenticeship programs, and tutoring. In this order they move from formats with little to much contact with a teacher.

Self-directed Study

Although program planners are not directly involved in self-directed study, it is important for them to be knowledgeable about this format for learning. First of all, it reveals much about learner preferences for learning. The convenience and flexibility of choosing the time, place, and other incidentals of learning are often more important to adults than the assistance of a teacher or formal program. In addition there is little threat experienced in attempting to learn when no one else is aware of one's difficulties or failures. Two lessons flow from this: (1) design programs to be convenient, flexible, and nonthreatening, and (2) discover and use the needs, goals, and preferences of adult learners as the basis for programming. In addition, the related area of learning-how-to-learn can provide content ideas for future programming. Self-directed materials or even courses on how to be a better learner can build clientele for other programs.

Good programs for helping adults direct their own learning are marked by four characteristics according to Smith (1982), an authority on the subject. The first is positive attitudes about learning such as adulthood is the prime time for learning; there are many opportunities for learning around us; and we *can* take responsibility for our own learning. The second is possession of the basic literacy skills essential to learning. The third refers to understanding our personal learning processes, such as the blocks we raise to learning as well as the preferences and strengths we have. Finally there is an understanding of the processes essential to what Smith calls the three modes of learning, i.e., self-directed, collaborative, and institutional learning. In self-directed learning these essential processes are basically the processes needed by a program planner. One needs to be able to plan learning activities, to set goals, to find and assess resources, to evaluate results.

Prepackaged Learning

This category includes a growing number of approaches utilizing computers, videodiscs, or combinations of print, audio, and video devices. Complex packages, sometimes called modules or kits, may even include models on which to practice or list of other resources or practices to try. Prepackaged approaches to learning differ from self-directed formats in that some one has structured the learning in order for the person to accomplish specific learning outcomes. Apart from having specified learning objectives, such packaged learning kits maintain much of the flexibility and security of self-directed learning. The absence of a teacher or other learners to question or interact with makes this approach to learning less interesting to some adults. However, when such kits are professionally prepared they can be powerful learning aids.

Program planners can make previously prepared materials available to their clientele, incorporate such prepared kits into their courses or develop prepackaged materials of their own. The major drawback of such materials is the necessity of putting them together with little knowledge of who the learners will be. Somehow provision for diverse entry and exit levels must be built into the package. Besides being user friendly, good kits also provide alternative strategies for reaching learning goals in order to allow for varied learning styles and preferences. But perhaps the trait most desired by adults are avenues for obtaining feedback or getting questions answered. Complete indexes, lists of references, help segments, or even 800 numbers are almost a necessity today.

Correspondence Study

"Theoretically, correspondence study can be viewed as a compromise. It attempts to preserve the independent study of the learner and yet provide some personal relationship with a teacher" (Seaman & Fellenz, 1989, p. 30). This approach supplies instructional material to the home or office but maintains some contact with an instructor. Such personal interaction and feedback is relied on to maintain motivation needed to complete the course. Generally, it works well for some adults but fails miserably for many others.

Successes of modern communication devices, for example, multimedia computer programs and computer-conferencing via the Internet, offer suggestions for improvement of this format for programming. Modern communication devices make it possible to personalize such programs and direct them to learner interests and preferred styles. Feedback can be provided almost instantaneously through such devices as computer mediated communication or at the convenience of the learner through electronic mail. Other media, such as tapes, phones, videos can be used to make correspondence study more than print communication.

Apprenticeships or Internships

Both these approaches have had long histories of successful use in the training of adults. The term apprenticeship has generally been applied to training for mastery of a craft while internship has been applied to professional training. Essentially they follow the same process—that of learning through working with someone who models the behavior to be mastered. The practice implied in such a process usually guarantees successful development of appropriate skills. Although imitation of a competent model is a natural way of learning, apprenticeships can cause some problems with adults who like to maintain their independence. This may be true especially when "masters" are younger than learners or when they are reluctant to turn over responsibility.

Developing apprenticeship programs takes much preparation and interaction with community resource people but it can add greatly to a program's reputation. Such programs can be even more effective when training is provided for both masters and students. The master, for example, needs to realize that treating the adult apprentice as a partner or collaborator rather than an observer or "gofer" will lead to a better learning experience. So will admission of uncertainty and difficulty at times. It is much easier learning from a model who is open, sharing, and human than from one who is remote and inimitable. The apprentices must be assured that it is vital to participate, i.e., ask questions, try out ideas, apply practices to their own situations. Apprenticeships and internships are not designed to develop imitators but collaborators.

Tutoring or Directed Individual Study

One on one learning is an excellent way to design instruction. It is the natural way that much learning occurs when one person spontaneously shows another how to do something. Much of its success is due to the relationship that readily develops between someone who wants to learn and another who wants to teach that same content. It also relieves the programmer of many responsibilities; finding adequate facilities, developing varied levels of curricula, and adjusting times for meetings. However, competent tutors can be hard to find so training sessions designed to provide training in basic teaching skills may be necessary.

There are a number of ways in which a tutoring approach could be developed by a community or organizational programmer. A famous model is that of the Literacy Volunteers of America. Using community volunteers as tutors this program tackles the very difficult task of teaching less literate citizens to read and calculate. Some schools and communities have developed similar programs to teach various hobbies, skills, or other subjects. Another popular approach to tutoring uses more of a directed study or learning center approach. In this model a few highly trained resource people having access to a variety of resources direct the learning of individuals with a variety of needs. The director of such types of programs must be aware that success depends on the two major strengths of tutoring; i.e., a supportive relationship between the tutor and learner and true individualization of the teaching according to the needs of the learner.

Houle (1972) suggested four ways in which the educational leader can be involved in directed study. They seem to be relevant to many formats for learning and both to teachers and program directors. The first approach is the *teacher* model in which the leader lays out a program, prepares the students, directs progress, and follows up as needed. The second model is more of a *programmer* approach. Here the leader specifies goals, assesses learner entry skills, presents alternative learning strategies, and monitors and evaluates the system. An alternative pattern is that of the *coach*, who guides members through new experiences, challenges assumptions, and encourages new behavior. Finally, the *therapist* leader rejects dependency and encourages growth and independence in clients. Because these models can be transferred to the roles programmers might adopt in many learning formats, they are presented here.

Organizing Learners as Groups

For most adult learning activities, the learners are organized as groups. There are a number of very legitimate reasons for this. In many ways learning is a social activity. This is especially true for adults who use educational activities as a means of "getting out of the house," meeting interesting people, or influencing and being influenced by other people. Group approaches to learning are also usually more economical for one person can teach a whole group of learners. Besides, learning in groups is so traditional that most adults expect to be taught that way. But even though formal education uses group formats almost exclusively does not mean that such formats result in better programs. People vary in their learning needs, readiness levels, and educational goals. Treating them as homogeneous parts of a group may be a major reason why many formal programs lose nearly half of their participants before the completion of courses of study.

The principles of program planning for adults treated in other chapters of this book are relevant to selecting group formats for learning activities. Traditional concerns such as knowing potential program participants, determining program needs, determining program priorities, purposes, and objectives, appraising program successes, and designing instructional components of programs are vital components of group approaches. However, before automatically selecting a group format for a learning activity several questions should be asked. Is a group approach the best way to serve this clientele? Can this content be better taught through individual or community-wide formats? Will another group format best advance the overall mission of my organization?

Group formats use the class, workshop, or lecture so consistently that it is difficult to divide group methods into any logical order. The teaching of small groups differs greatly from large groups yet classes are organized for two or three participants or for many hundreds with the lecture being the major instructional technique regardless of size. Similarly, not all learning groups have information acquisition as their major objective. Many are convened primarily for noneducational objectives such as action planning, social objectives, or specific organizational goals. To provide some logical order to the following section the selection of possible group formats will be divided into groups with primary goals of action versus those of information acquisition. Each of these two categories will be considered according to size—small gatherings, moderate-sized groups, and large assemblies.

Small Action Groups

Most communities have dozens of action groups, groups formed out of concern for the schools, for some political cause, for environmental issues, or for the improved organization of a business. Most of these embody an educational component. Some are organized by a trained program developer but many are born of a cause and only later see a need to organize a learning agenda. Thus a program planner has a role to play in such organizations whether they operate in an educational, business, political, or community arena.

Because such groups operate on a problem-solving basis, they need to be organized differently from instructional groups. All problem-solving schemes consist of at least three basic components, information gathering, critical consideration, and action planning. These three steps must be structured into action group formats; neglect of any of these three components will lead to failure and quick dissolution of the group. Because change is the ultimate objective of such groups it is important for members to be aware of change strategies and processes and at the same time maintain the spirit necessary to persevere until change occurs. This spirit or enthusiasm is usually dependent on two factors, interpersonal communication and group cohesiveness. Thus the role of the educational leader becomes one of process facilitator reminding members of processes involved and pointing out blocks to interpersonal cooperation.

I would be extremely neglectful here not to mention a uniquely successful method for organizing small action groups. Myles Horton's success at Highlander in affecting civil rights, labor organization, environmental issues, and general community problem solving testifies to the method used. Groups of community members were brought together in a simple residential setting. They were encouraged to define their major concerns, to examine potential ways to resolve these issues, and to plan an effective strategy. Horton and his cohorts provided support, not answers. Music, humor, and other "cultural" activities plus the identification of potential resources and especially the mutual encouragement of all present were the essence of this support (Adams, 1975; Fellenz & Conti, 1990).

Moderate-sized Action Groups

The groups envisioned here are businesses, churches, leagues, associations, or other such groups that have a major purpose other than education. An educator frequently has little or no control over the format chosen for learning. However when programmers can select the format, they should do so in view of the organization's major objective and with a clear understanding of who will be in attendance. For example, if a church group wants an informational program on some religious topic, a lecture and discussion format may suffice; however, if it is a business group looking to improve the critical thinking strategies of staff, a more involving, practice-oriented approach is needed.

A serious concern when working with such groups is that of setting a learning atmosphere. Frequently members are accustomed to gather for purposes other than learning. If customary attitudes prevail, the educator may be shown respect but given little credibility. In such cases, action will seldom follow from the learning experience.

Workshops

Under this title are grouped all those large group gatherings that are intended to result in action rather than in information sharing. They may be as short as an hour or two, may last several days, or may be spread out over a long period. Because they are directed toward a large number of participants, a substantial number of resources are usually available. Thoughtful use of such resources can result in a well orchestrated program satisfying the intellectual, social, physical, and psychological needs crucial to bringing about change.

The very name, workshop, implies that people work together. This can satisfy two conditions usually conducive to action leading to change—mutual support and practice of essential skills. Support is so essential for change to occur that many organizations have used a "retreat" setting for workshops. Physically removing participants from all support for "the old way," such as fellow workers, friends, family, and usual physical environs and duties, and surrounding them with enthusiastic supporters of the new system is a great way to produce change. All that is needed in addition is continued support for the new way of doing things back in the home or work situation.

Small Learning Teams

There is a significant difference in format for small groups that gather for learning from those that gather to promote action. The Great Books discussion groups, Bible study groups, and issues groups of various kinds have been quite popular. Some have formed on their own but many have done so only when encouraged by some program developer. While some adults prefer organized classes in which responsibility can be turned over to the teacher, many others prefer the informality and personalized nature of the informal gathering. Such small group discussions promote learning yet leave much opportunity for socializing.

When promoting such groups, a programmer needs to balance the adults' appreciation for self-direction with the group's need for some kind of system to follow. Knowles (1970) suggests the following six-phase process for small learning teams: (1) Set a climate and identify resources. (2) Diagnose needs for learning through a collaborative process and with the assistance of a leader. (3) Set learning objectives. (4) Plan and conduct learning activities. (5) Present learning outcomes. (6) Evaluate the learning activities. He actually broke many of his classes and conference presentations into small groups and used some version of this process.

Courses

Traditional courses or "short course" are the most frequently used format for group learning activities. Everyone has experienced them; everyone knows what to expect. Consequently programmers find them easy to organize. They are flexible in that they can run for a semester or just a few days, they can be offered for credit or not, and they can serve a few or a few hundred. They are readily quantifiable and thus easy to administer. All in all they are cost effective approaches for disseminating information.

The traditional nature of courses can cause difficulties for administrators. Courses tend to be teacher controlled and one poor teacher can cast misgivings over a whole program. Careful selection and training of teachers is as important as careful selection of course topics. Because they are so traditionally taught through lectures, they tend to lack the flexibility essential to meeting diverse interests of people or advanced levels of content. Clear program descriptions or flexible teachers may help.

Large Group Presentations

Some believe that the size of the audience makes little difference when organizing adults for content delivery. While there is some truth to this, increasing the size of the group decreases the flexibility, especially the possibility of involving the learners. More attention is usually given to physical facilities and less to the individual learner. However the cost effectiveness of dealing with large groups can justify the allocation of more funds to more effective presenters and presentation devices. The feeling of being part of something successful when part of a large group is balanced by the difficulty of getting personal feedback in such situations.

When selecting a large group format a programmer should be aware of the importance of advanced publicity. Accurate information is important for several reasons. Adults are turned off by inaccurate descriptions of presentations; wasting time and money on a topic in which they are not interested or doing background study on irrelevant subjects frustrates them. So does the inability to voice disagreement with a presenter or to share their own insights on the topic. Question and answer sessions, punch and cookie periods, discussion or buzz groups can help. So can the involvement of multiple presenters through panels, committee hearings, dialogues, or other formats, provided they are well moderated. In some situations input from participants can be gathered before hand.

Organizing Learners as Total Communities

The design of community-wide approaches to education can be exciting. Imagine, turning a community into a learning society or engendering a community problem-solving agenda among citizens! This may seem far beyond the goal of a program developer but such approaches are being given more and more consideration by adult educators today. Boyd, Apps, and associates (1980) devoted five chapters of their book to community formats and Brookfield (1984) frequently analyzed the influence the community has upon the adult learner. Communities can be of all types and sizes according to Wright's (1980) definition as "a collectivity of people differentiated from the total population by a common interest" (p. 101). In this sense management personnel of a company, inhabitants of a trailer park, patrons of a library, or widely scattered members of a professional group could all be considered communities.

Designing formats for adult learners as communities means that a holistic approach will be taken to that community. Economic, geographic, political considerations must be taken into account as well as other educational opportunities and community activities. On the other hand community approaches do not have to involve all members of the community at the same time or place. Formats involving individuals, groups, or the total community are possible as long as the goal is to benefit the total community. A community that has become a learning community, that values and enjoys learning together is a wonderful place for an educator to work.

Organizing the Community as Individuals

Museums, libraries, and resource centers are examples of institutions organized to serve the learning needs of the total community, but to serve them through service to individuals. The fact that not all members of the community participate in learning activities of such institutions does not negate the fact that they exist to serve the learning needs of the community as a whole. Educational brokerage programs, or "learning exchanges" as they are sometimes called, are basically designed to match the learning needs of individuals to teaching resources available in the community. For example, a person who wishes to learn about Chile might be matched with another member of the community who lived in Chile for some time. The "teacher" might be compensated by some exchange of services, an agreed upon cash compensation, or credit for a reciprocal learning service. The program director facilitates contact between those desiring to learn and those willing to teach. Exhibits follow a similar format in that they are designed as a learning occasion for all the individuals of a specific community. The advent of computerized, multimedia technology has expanded tremendously the teaching potential of various exhibits.

Although adults like to learn in an individualized mode, they tend to do so through resources that are readily available. The educator who chooses to program through an individualized format must not only sell community members on the educational value of such learning programs but must also make them readily available and easy to use. Obviously, the needs and potential interests of the people must be recognized. But these are true of all formats. When designing community formats, programmers must also develop insight into the deeper needs of the community. Freire (1970) insisted that members of a community must become conscious of the underlying forces at work within the environment and be convinced that change is both good and possible if they are to be liberated. Various other adult educators, such as Coggins (1980), presented schemas for the personal growth of individuals believing a community's growth is dependent upon the growth of the members of that community. Thus, clarity regarding one's philosophy of education is important when choosing to work through community education formats.

Organizing the Community as Groups

Forums or town meetings are one format that can be used to educate a community through groups. In rural areas these approaches might reach the majority of a community but in most situations several meetings, such as neighborhood forums, would be needed to keep crowds small enough to get representative discussion. Another group approach to community-wide education is advisory groups or cadres representing different aspects of the community. Members of these groups would be expected to spread out and influence others in the community. A popular program in many communities today is what is commonly referred to as "Community Education." Most frequently organized through the public school system, this program offers a variety of educational experiences according to the needs and wants of local citizens.

Education of any community through group formats demands facility in group processes and community development skills. The development of process skills is often more important than the content taught. A revisit of the Montana Study by Counter, Paul, and Conti (1990) indicated what a powerful and enduring effect a leadership training program could have on a community even 40 years later. Campbell (1980) argued that community problem-solving groups are a good way to teach democracy through action and at the same time build an adult education program. The process skills learned by participants in such groups is often transferred to other situations spreading like ripples through a community.

Organizing the Community as a Whole

Community development efforts often take a holistic approach to the population. Depending on the size and complexity of the community, the organization of an educational program in such a format can be a task too complex for a single person. A team of professionals may be needed to give leadership to tasks such as clarifying problems and informing citizens, for as Wright (1980) said: "If planning is a process for determining appropriate future action through a sequence of choices, then it is clearly a learning task" (p. 123).

The choice of specific strategies for organizing learners as a total community often calls for expertise in communication, sociology, politics, and economics as well as education. See Moore and Brooks (1996) and Moore and Feldt (1993). Modern technology provides powerful tools for reaching out to communities through such vehicles as local cable channels, computer data banks, and mechanized bulletin boards. A festival approach is taken by the community in which this author lives. Each August a "Sweet Pea Festival" is held to celebrate culture and the arts. Regular activities include a truck load of wood scraps for children to use to build things, juried art and craft booths, outdoor plays, and musical performances by groups from varied cultures. Through this celebration the community is indeed educating its members for as Boyle (1980) reasoned "A culture influences the value judgments of all its members. Judgments are based upon value structures that have evolved out of the experiences of the individuals and groups concerned" (p. 93).

Teacher-Based Formats

Instructional leaders can at certain times and in certain situations be so important to the goals of a program that format selection must be adapted to them. Examples of this are consultants, team teaching, or the need for teachers to be at a distance from the learners.

Because consultants are people unique in knowledge of content or in presentation ability, programs may need to be modified to accommodate them. For example, a teacher who is part of the local staff can be used in individual or group formats, but the time a consultant is available is usually limited. Thus, group or total community formats become more logical, although the goals or content of the program might be so demanding that it is worth the added time of the consultant to work with selected individuals. Regardless, when adapting formats to a consultant, it is vital that the local director collaborate closely in program planning with any outside consultant. Excellent consultants can perform poorly when misinformed about number of participants, content knowledge level of the learners, physical environment, or specific goals of the program. Based on personal experience I know that a major fear of consultants is that they will be unable to establish rapport with a group because they have been misinformed about learners or situations. It is the task of the local director to set a proper atmosphere so that participants expect to relish what the consultant will deliver.

The decision to use a team to deliver an educational message can also influence format decisions. Teams make it much easier to facilitate implementation of total community formats. But again they call for careful planning and coordination in consultation with the program director both before and during the program.

Distance separating teachers from learners definitely impacts program formats. A recent experience teaching a course through computer conferencing moves this writer to make the following comments. Many adults expect some level of social interaction in a group learning experience. The formation of small learning teams, exchange of personal information with other group members, and face to face interaction with the teacher can enhance distance learning. Integrating some form of individual interaction between each learner and the teacher via e-mail or a toll free phone number is essential; between learners it is quite helpful. Education of both learners and teachers in how to learn through distance approaches produces a much better learning atmosphere. Such learning-how-to-learn instruction includes direction in being a self-directed learner, in time and resource management, and in wise use of learning strategies.

Because of the increased use and potential for ever greater use of distance learning formats, it is appropriate here to add a few additional thoughts about them. One important way of analyzing such formats is in terms of the communication between teacher and adult learners. When physical proximity is removed, oral and visual communication can continue through the use of technology. Various televised methodologies can preserve full-motion, two-way visual and audio interaction. Many years of research of such practices indicate that the learning of factual content in such situations is no different than in face-to-face instruction. Some people have voiced concern about the informal interaction between teacher and learner before or after class that is eliminated in such situations, but use of other technology such as e-mail may compensate for that lack of interaction.

One-way audio/visual communication, through the use of videotapes for example, has also been proven to be an effective format for distance learning. Much of what has been written earlier in this chapter about prepackaged formats is applicable here. Feedback to the learner and continued motivation may become problems when using this technology. This writer's experience indicates that the use of tapes, especially audiotapes, can be less effective with group audiences than with individuals.

The personal computer has made possible interesting additional formats for learning. Computer conferencing using modems or direct connections is becoming increasingly popular. Communication can be carried out in real or simulated time. Interactive conferencing systems seem to work quite well with those who have skills and patience with such technology. The low cost of communicating at vast distances and the atmosphere of intimacy generated through such communication can be quite motivating. However, problems do seem to increase as number of participants, time lapses between communications, or lack of technological expertise increases. Well planned orientation programs may alleviate some of these problems.

One approach that has been found effective in some situations is the integration of various technologies in distance learning formats. For example, the teacher may meet face to face with learners at times, use videotapes at other times and connect learners with one another through two-way audio/visual methods or computer conferencing at other times. The abilities and needs of teachers and learners, the type and level of content objectives, and numerous situational factors must be considered in the use of the technologies available for distance learning.

Content-Based Formats

Content objectives definitely influence the selection of program formats. This is obvious from traditional practices of teaching some content in classes, others in labs, and still others through on-the-job approaches. Such decisions should be influenced by specific objectives of the program, characteristics of learner groups, and unique features of teachers or situations. For example, having available a master performer in the content area would suggest some form of apprenticeship, perhaps creatively done with small groups of learners.

Different formats are useful in working with varied groups of learners. Novice groups usually need basic information about the content. This may be readily done through content oriented group formats which incorporate experiences with content relevant situations. Field trips, movies, and computer simulations could promote such familiarity with content practice situations. Experienced or expert practitioners need different approaches. Discussions of patterns of experience or creative approaches might be better expedited through action oriented group formats.

Overviews or awareness approaches to content areas generally call for group formats. Especially effective in such situations is the use of experienced personnel through panels, interviews, or approaches to increase experience with the content. When objectives call for the development of higher levels of thinking, such interactive approaches as discussions or case studies may be more effective. The development of attitudes almost always calls for small group approaches. Such content concerns definitely influence format selection.

Situation-Based Formats

Situational factors often stem from the organization sponsoring the learning. The philosophy of the organization and the physical and human resources available are two major factors influencing choice of format. Time provided must also be considered. Too often too much is attempted in too short a time. For example, a significant change in practice might call for awareness of advantages of the new practice, conviction that the new approach will work, and practice with the new to the point of facility. Attempting to accomplish this through a single format in a short time, such as a one-day workshop, is unrealistic.

Some institutions are designed to operate in a *formal* manner. This usually means that the educational agency has decisional power over both the objectives for learning and the methods by which these objectives will be sought. *Informal* organizations are designed to deliver specific content but allow diversity in methods of delivery. In both these situations the programmer has some decisional power regarding format for learning, but is likely to be affected by the traditions of the organization. In *nonformal* programs, however, both the content and format are determined by the learners. Learning centers are often organized nonformally. Here a programmer can only suggest formats, but the situation is open to creative approaches.

The philosophy of an organization definitely impacts choice of format. One way an organization's philosophy is implemented is through emphasis on personal development versus staff development versus organizational development. Choices regarding formats for learning are more flexible when directed toward personal development; content has more influence over format selection when emphasizing organizational development.

SUMMARY AND CONCLUSION

A format for learning, or "method" of adult education, refers to the manner in which a learning program is organized. Most frequently it concerns the organization of adult learners as individuals, groups, or communities. Formats for individuals can be categorized according to the amount of contact between the learner and the teacher and vary from the indirect contact of self-directed learning to the intimate contact of tutoring. Individual formats are most frequently chosen by adult learners but less often selected by programmers. They allow for a great deal of flexibility in meeting the needs, preferences, and learning styles of individual learners.

However they often call for more time, planning, and instructional resources.

Group formats dominate adult education programs. They can be organized to promote action or to deliver content and vary when directed to the needs of small, moderate, or large groups. Their popularity is due to several factors. They are such traditional formats for programs that both adult learners and programmers have come to expect them. Many adults like them because they can provide social interaction as well as intellectual stimulation. Programmers find them easy to organize and administer. However they are not always the most efficient way of learning and can serve the needs, level of expertise, and learning preferences of only part of any group.

Formats organizing learners as total communities have great potential. They can be structured to serve communities by working with individuals, with selected groups, or with all members of the community simultaneously. However community approaches often call for collaboration with other professionals and demand careful planning. Much time and many resources can be invested in community formats with little timely evidence of results.

The selection of formats for learning can also be influenced by teacher, content, or situational considerations. Time and financial considerations when using consultants as instructional leaders usually demand group or community formats although in some situations individual approaches can be quite efficient. Team teaching approaches are effective in many large group or community formats while situations in which learners and instructional staff cannot be brought together physically can be organized according to various distance learning formats. Content objectives emphasizing critical thinking or advanced levels of cognition may be best served though interactive small group formats while skill development objectives often demand individualized approaches. When simple awareness or overview of a content area is desired, community approaches may be both economical and effective. Specialized groups, such as novices or experts, need to have content treated differently and may be best organized according to different formats. Situational factors usually develop from the sponsoring institution's philosophy or resources. Those valuing content delivery may see traditional group approaches as the only legitimate format. Others encourage programmers or teachers to try formats they believe effective. Still others are dedicated to community development and approve of community-wide methods. Time, physical, and financial resources of the sponsoring institution can also make possible or limit choices of formats for learning.

The choice of the format in which a learning activity is offered can have a tremendous impact on the success of that learning activity. Yet in many situations little or no thought is given to the method used. The tradition of using classes or workshops is so strong that other options often are not even considered. Programmers, learners, and institutions expect group formats and go with group formats. Thus colleges traditionally use classes, literacy programs tutoring approaches, companies on-the-job training, and community developers advisory groups composed of influential leaders.

But think of what could happen if program directors put time and effort into considering other formats. Colleges might use total community formats to pull students and faculty with common interests together. Imagine the innovative and creative results that could come from such a holistic approach. Literacy programs might organize participants into problem solving groups that could act on some of the underlying problems leading to adult illiteracy. Companies might try alternative group formats such as quality circles or integrated management/worker discussion groups. Improved quality of operation of that company could readily result. And program developers might use more community formats that bring community members together to define their needs and organize strategies to attack their problems. At times the method is the message.

QUESTIONS FOR STUDY AND DISCUSSION

1. What formats for learning or methods of organizing learners do you find most useful? Least useful?
2. What formats for organizing learners as individuals could you incorporate into your program?
3. Do you distinguish between small group formats directed toward action verses such groupings directed toward content delivery?

4. With what other groups or organizations in your community could you collaborate to organize learners as a community in order to promote community problem solving?
5. What types of program formats does the philosophy of your organization promote? Could it be changed?

REFERENCES

Adams, Frank (1975). *Unearthing seeds of fire: The idea of Highlanded.* Winston-Salem, NC: John F. Blair.

Boyd, Robert D., Apps, Jerold W., & Associates (1980). *Redefining the discipline of adult education.* San Francisco: Jossey-Bass.

Boyle, Patrick G. (1980). Adult educators and community analysis. In R. D. Boyd, J. W. Apps, & Associates, *Redefining the discipline of adult education.* San Francisco: Jossey-Bass.

Brookfield, Stephen D. (1984). *Adult learners, adult education, and the community.* New York: Teachers College Press.

Campbell, M. Donald (1980). Community education for group growth. In R. D. Boyd, J. W. Apps & Associates, *Redefining the discipline of adult education.* San Francisco: Jossey-Bass.

Coggins, Chere C. (1980). Individual growth through community problem solving. In R. D. Boyd, J. W. Apps & Associates, *Redefining the discipline of adult education.* San Francisco: Jossey-Bass.

Counter, Janice E., Paul, Lynn C., & Conti, Gary J. (1990). Conrad, Montana: A community of memories. In G. J. Conti & R. A. Fellenz (Eds.), *Cultural influences on adult education.* Bozeman, MT: Center for Adult Learning Research, Montana State University.

Fellenz, Robert A., & Conti, Gary J. (1990). *Social environment and adult learning.* Bozeman, MT: Center for Adult Learning Research, Montana State University.

Freire, Paulo (1970). The adult literacy process as cultural action for freedom. *Harvard Educational Review, 40*(2).

Houle, Cyril O. (1972). *The design of education.* San Francisco: Jossey-Bass.

Knowles, Malcolm (1970). *The modern practice of adult education.* New York: Association Press.

Moore, A. B., & Brooks, R. (1996). *Transforming your community: Empowering for change.* Malabar, FL: Krieger.

Moore, A. B., & Feldt, J. A. (1993). *Facilitating community and decision-making groups.* Malabar, FL: Krieger.

Seaman, Don F., & Fellenz, Robert A. (1989). *Effective strategies for teaching adults.* Columbus, OH: Merrill.

Smith, Robert M. (1982). *Learning how to learn.* Chicago: Follet.

Tough, Alan (1971). *The adult's learning projects: A fresh approach to theory and practice in adult learning.* Toronto: Ontario Institute for Studies in Education.

Verner, Coolie (1962). *A conceptual scheme for the identification and classification of processes for adult education.* Chicago: Adult Education Association of the U.S.A.

Verner, Coolie (1964). Definition of terms. In G. Jensen, A. A. Liveright, & W. Hallenbeck (Eds.), *Adult education: Outlines of an emerging field of university study.* Washington, DC: Adult Education Association of the U.S.A.

Wright, Joan W. (1980). Community learning: A frontier for adult education. In R. D. Boyd, & J. W. Apps (eds), *Redefining the discipline of adult education.* San Francisco: Jossey-Bass.

15

Program Promotion and Marketing

Michael J. Havercamp

ABSTRACT

This chapter begins with a discussion of the conceptual underpinnings of program promotion and marketing. Four marketing principles are then elucidated to provide guidelines to programmers. A variety of promotional activities may be used. Programmers can be aided by an overall vision of the program that will match the desired quality and customer satisfaction. Inventiveness or creativity can also enhance the effectiveness of promotion of a specific education or training program in different settings.

ASSESSMENT

1. In terms of marketing, what do education, training, organizational development, and social change have in common?
2. What value should be placed on the issue of *quality* in marketing and how does this issue impact on organizations engaged in the marketing of training and organizational development programs?
3. What are some techniques for assessing wants and needs of target groups?
4. What are some approaches for involving target group participants in the planning and decision-making process of marketing programs?
5. In what ways does a *vision* influence the marketing process?
6. What are some creative approaches for promoting training, education, organizational development and social change programs?
7. In what ways is a marketer a facilitator?

SETTING THE CONCEPTUAL STAGE

Whether the focus is on education, training, organizational development or social change, certain strategies are needed to market these programs. It could be an adult literacy program through a public school district, a management program in strategic planning at a major corporation or a continuing education course on administrative law by a national nonprofit organization. It may be a televised program on behavior modification through a community college, a personal enrichment class by the YWCA, a public policy workshop through cooperative extension, or a population control program through an international organization. The list goes on. Educators are challenged to find, sometimes very creatively, marketing campaigns to match these programs.

My conception of marketing programs in education and training settings includes organization development and social change programs. Why organizational development and social change? might you ask, since there appears to be no consensus in the education and training field about including these topics (Merriam & Caffarella, 1991; Griffith & Cristarella, 1979; Freire, 1974; Hall, 1981). Actually, the lack of consensus is the point for requiring the inclusion of organizational development and social change in a marketing discussion. The education and training field is composed of varying epistomological perspectives about what is the essence and meaning of this evolving field. Is learning neutral? Is it an end in itself? Is it a means to an end? The beauty and often the frustration with conceptualizing the education and training field is its diversity and ambiguity.

Educators and trainers perform many traditional and non-traditional roles: professors, continuing education administrators, trainers and consultants (internal and external to organizations), teachers, community organizers, researchers, change agents, and the list continues. Some of these roles are complementary while others may be in conflict with each other, depending on one's values. The field of education and training isn't neatly defined. It can be seen as a colorful and unfinished mosaic. Its beauty is its whole, not its attractive parts. Some parts are similar and others are strikingly different. These parts however are interconnected and share a common purpose. Educators are all intrinsically involved in the development of individuals, groups, organizations, and communities. Learning may be considered as a core element for acquiring knowledge and skills. Some view learning for "its own sake" while others are predisposed to seeing it as an acceptable avenue to making change at the individual, organization, community, or societal level. But, despite orientation to training and development, *change* is about to occur; and, in my view, human development and change are intrinsically tied together. In the fourth edition of the *Strategic Marketing for Nonprofit Organizations*, Kotler and Andreasen (1991) suggest that "While marketing may use the tools of the educator or the propagandist, its critical distinguishing feature is that its ultimate goal is to influence behavior (either changing it or keeping it the same in the face of other pressures)" (p. 404).

This mosaic, a metaphor for the training and education, reflects differences and variations. Education and training as a conceptual field is elastic and moving, offering through time new and emerging images of what it is. Promotion and marketing strategies should be planned with this understanding.

Marketing must be customer-centered (Kotler & Andreasen, 1991; Fischer, 1987). According to Kotler and Andreasen (1991), "... all marketing analysis and planning begins and ends with the *customer*" (p. 53). Beder (1986) suggests that, besides being a strategy for attracting learners to a program, marketing is a methodology for guiding the educational design and implementation process, which includes promotion, pricing, and distribution (p. 3). Emphasizing the benefits to society, Griffith (1989) stresses the importance of effective program development to society. He says, "... program development that is sensitive to the felt needs of intended audiences and that openly communicates the full story about the programs being offered will enjoy satisfactory recruitment and retention and play a socially worthwhile role by improving the quality of life for all" (p. 32).

Simerly (1989) provides us with a useful analysis of approaches to marketing in continuing education, conceptualizing them as *traditional*, *exchange*, and *adaptive* models. Each model, according to Simerly, has a specific orientation. The traditional approach, focused on the organization, tends to be less responsive to the environment. Marketing is viewed as a tool for changing consumer beliefs in order to accept the organization's products. The focus of the exchange model is on finding a balance between consumer and organization needs, and in exchanging products and services each values. The adaptive approach is more responsive to the consumer, when compared to the other models, as the organization appears willing to change its program, products, and services to match consumer needs and wants (p. 5).

The program development literature on marketing emphasizes promotion of open-market programs. In-house training programs, however, particularly those suited to business and industry, often need agreement from employees at various levels of the organization to have a training program. Baker (1990) argues that in designing a training program, questions should address the level of *management support* and the level of *consensus* among participants for a proposed training project (pp. 2–13). These questions underscore the importance of getting "buy-in and commitment" from the organization's leadership and employees to in-house training and development programs.

When assessing how to market in-house programs, marketers should consider using employee involvement and teambuilding strategies: quality circles, survey feedback, suggestion systems, quality work-life teams, and focus groups. A major challenge of these efforts is to keep training and marketing questions focused on *quality improvement*, an increasingly dominant theme in business and industry in North America. A major outcome of successful training and organizational development programs is on continuously improving product quality. To show the importance of the *quality* movement, the Malcolm Baldrige National Quality Improvement Act was signed into law on August 20, 1987, and, according to Garvin (1991), "in just four years, the Malcolm Baldrige National Quality Award has become the most important catalyst for transforming American business … it provides companies with a comprehensive framework for assessing their progress toward the new paradigm of management and such commonly acknowledged goals as customer satisfaction and increased employee involvement" (p. 80).

Geber (1991) reports, based on a survey of company leaders, that the "… biggest challenge these executives see in the coming decade is not foreign competition but building and keeping a qualified work force" (p. 28). The futurist Drucker (1992) believes that *knowledge* is the primary resource for building the new society of organizations. "For managers the dynamics of knowledge impose one clear imperative: every organization has to build the management of change into its very structure" (Drucker, 1992, p. 97). Education and training products, in my view, must be reflective of this orientation to change.

Marketing should be initiated and planned based on the identification of specific learning settings. As summarized in Chapter 2, Houle's (1972) categories of educational design situations provide a conceptual framework for identifying these settings. They include eleven situations related to the individual, group, institution, and mass (p. 44). These settings, which Houle described two decades ago, remain a solid benchmark for raising specific marketing questions for determining learning episodes. The extent of a marketing plan (the type of questions asked) depends on an educational situation. For example, issues about organizational "buy-in" for a marketing plan are not needed in situations where an institution or organization is not involved in the activity. But, when an organization designs a training program in a new format (Houle's C-8 category), marketers are challenged to raise questions suitable to the organizational culture of the institution initiating and offering the learning activity.

Many books, articles, and pamphlets have been written on marketing, especially generic marketing. However, material on education and social marketing is comparatively recent. During the past 20 years, Kotler and Andreason (1991), Beder (1986), Fischer (1987), Griffith (1989) and many others have written on this topic. Their ideas, to a large extent, define the conceptual stage for more discussion, debate and invention around effective marketing. A discussion of specific elements associated with effective marketing builds on the work of these people. However, what follows is a slightly different characterization of marketing which considers marketing for training and education as well as marketing for organizational development and social change.

Kotler and Andreasen (1991) provide excellent planning guidelines for marketers who are designing, organizing and implementing marketing campaigns for nonprofit organizations. They include the following:

1. Analyze the organization wide mission, objectives, goals, and culture to which the marketing strategy must contribute.
2. Assess organization strengths and weaknesses to respond to threats and challenges presented by the external environment.
3. Analyze the *future* environment the marketer is likely to face with respect to
    a. Publics to be served
    b. Competition
    c. Social, political, technological, and economic development.
4. Determine the marketing mission, objectives, and specific goals for the relevant planning period.
5. Formulate the core marketing strategy to achieve the specified goals.
6. Put in place the necessary organizational structure and systems within the marketing function to ensure implementation of the designed strategy.
7. Establish detailed programs and tactics to carry out the core strategy for the planning period, including a timetable of activities and assignments of specific responsibilities.
8. Establish benchmarks to measure interim and final achievements of the program.
9. Implement the planned program.
10. Measure performance and adjust the core strategy, tactical details, or both as needed. (pp. 68–70).

When designing and implementing a marketing campaign, the marketer can be aided by four sets of specific *guiding principles*, represented by the following imperatives:

1. Be customer oriented
2. Be visionary
3. Be inventive
4. Be facilitative

In the following discussion, examples are drawn from a variety of related training, education, organizational change, and social change programs. These examples demonstrate the applicability of these principles in the formulation of a comprehensive plan which incorporates the "five Ps" of marketing: product, price, place, promotion, and people (Fischer, 1987).

MARKETING PRINCIPLES

Be Customer Oriented

Know the felt and perceived needs of the target audience. Morstain and Smart (1974) suggest that adults' participation in learning can be grouped consisting of six factors: social relationships, external expectations, social welfare, professional advancement, escape/stimulation, and cognitive interest (Merriam & Caffarella, 1991, p. 85).

When possible involve target groups, colleagues, and community representatives in the planning and implementation of a marketing campaign. Use traditional and nontraditional strategies to understand customers, clients, and users of programs and services. Consider the following suggestions.

Personal contacts and networking. If you were planning a training program on participatory management in a business setting, you could begin by asking 10 colleagues in your organization what they think are the most effective ways to promote the new training program and who might be interested in this program if it were offered. You could then use this information to design a survey and send it to targeted employees in the organization to thus solicit their perceptions on participatory management and what they think they would need to learn during a training program on this topic for it to be successful.

Interviews. If you were setting up a training program on small-scale business cooperatives, you could begin by interviewing 20 opinion leaders in a community regarding their views of the impact of such a program. You could follow-up by inviting them to a meeting to discuss the results of the interviews and determine if a training program would be beneficial to the community.

Delphi technique. If you were offering an interactive satellite program on sexual harassment in the work place, you could randomly choose 50 managers from a national training association and give them two questionnaires. The results of the first questionnaire could be summarized, and based on the results, a second questionnaire could then be sent to the same respondents. This would allow them to reevaluate their original answers based on the total group response.

Nominal group procedure. If you were preparing a continuing professional education for physicians, you could ask your education coordinators the following open-ended questions in a three-hour meeting: What do physicians feel are the most important issues facing their practice? Have each person in silence brainstorm the possible answers and write them down on paper. Next, have groups of three people record their individual responses on a piece on paper (maybe on a flipchart if appropriate), one at a time. Each person then evaluates and ranks the responses, giving points for the best five ideas. The best idea gets 10 points, the next best 9, and so on. Each group tabulates points and prepares a group report. Group reports are given and points from all the groups are tabulated. The results should suggest a preference of ideas or answers. These preferences can be used for discussing a possible second question: What educational programs might appropriately address the priority issues identified? The nominal group technique, as discussed, can be repeated to process the responses to the second question.

Focus groups. If you were planning a major social action campaign in the United States to deal with the increase of infant mortality, you could conduct four focus groups with each group representing a different region of the country. In each focus group, eight randomly selected women are brought together for a two-hour group interview. Four open-ended questions are asked, one at a time, of each person. The questions attempt to discern group members' understanding of the reasons for infant mortality and the possible strategies for tackling this program. Interview responses from the focus groups are summarized and assessed for content analysis. Themes emerging from group interviews are recorded and used to design intervention programs for reducing infant mortality.

Task force and advisory groups. If you were a governing board of a community organization and wanted to raise money, you could establish a 10-person task force made up of people who are known for raising money for nonprofit organizations. During the first task force meeting, members develop lists of their ideas for fundraising. After each idea is discussed for clarity, the group selects from this list those ideas most likely to receive funding. Before the meeting ends, task force members brainstorm the names of persons who could help in a fund raising campaign.

Community forums. If you were a public school district and wanted to determine the need for a new literacy program, you could conduct a community forum. During this forum, small groups of eight people could meet to brainstorm (a) the advantages of a literacy program, (b) potential participants, and (c) which agencies and community organizations might be interested in co-sponsoring the program. Following the meeting, the agencies and community organizations could be invited to a meeting to design the literacy program.

Simulation and gaming. If you wanted to help a group of church leaders examine their interest in community development issues, you could have them take part in a simulation game. The game could include three rounds of play where participants identify and score the importance of issues in their community. When the game ends, participants could discuss whether the church leadership should take the needed steps for becoming involved.

These strategies are but a few that marketers can consider for obtaining information on the wants and needs of target groups. Some of these approaches are at the same time suited for involving customers, clients and co-workers in the planning and decision-making process. The next principle to be discussed is importance of creating vision.

Be Visionary

Create the best image of what you would like to see occur in your marketing campaign. Let your vision drive the design and implementation of the marketing product. A vision is a conceptual roadmap which provides direction for where you are going.

Kotler and Andreasen (1991) propose that a characteristic of an effective core marketing strategy is to be visionary. "It (the strategy) will articulate a future for the organization that offers a clear sense of where the organization is going ..." (p. 165). As leaders in organizations and communities, program designers or marketers need to know where they are headed. This later point is underscored by Blanchard, Carew, and Parisi-Carew (1990) in *The One Minute Manager*. They quote a One Minute Manager who says, "A vision inspires performance and commitment" (p. 27).

Vision has many purposes. It provides direction for a new product or service and can be a motivational factor for those providing leadership.

The notion of *quality* and *customer satisfaction* should be benchmarks for building a meaningful vision. Create a vision for a product which meets these standards, and attempt to make the educational product the best for the target audiences.

A visionary conception of the future demands realism. While we first must stretch ourselves to create our best image (vision) for a marketing campaign, we must then carefully evaluate and assess it for its realizability. A question might be asked, "Is the vision achievable and manageable?

In organizations and communities, try to make the creation of a vision an enjoyable and challenging process. Encourage others, especially intuitive-type people (Agor, 1989), to take part in this important step. Consider using brainstorming techniques, such as picture drawing, to facilitate creativity. For example, 15 community leaders in a metropolitan community gather to discuss a low-income housing program. These leaders represent a diversity of language, ethnic, and cultural backgrounds. Perceived conflict exists among some leaders. A person known to be neutral to the parties serves as the facilitator for the meeting. Using metaphors and symbols, the facilitator asks each person to draw a picture of her or his ideal image for a low-income housing program. Participants use large paper, crayons, and color pens to create their pictures. (They may find searching through magazines useful for generating ideas. They can cut and paste pictures on their drawing.) When each picture is done, it is studied by the other participants who in turn give their interpretation of the drawing. At this time, the person who drew the picture stays silent. After interpretations have been given, the author of the drawing gives her or his comments. Following a discussion of all pictures, the facilitator asks the participants to identify any general themes that emerged from the discussions. The themes, presented in words or metaphors, are written or drawn on another sheet of paper for all participants to see.

The picture drawing process builds on participants' intuitions and helps them assess their level of agreement, in this case about low-income housing. The process is collaborative and can diffuse needless conflict.

Be Inventive

Assume you have identified an educational program and a target population. Your vision is clear and you now want to look at ways to promote a specific education and training program. As with the preceding principle on being visionary, try to be creative and involve appropriate others in the identification, assessment, and selection of promotional strategies. Promotional strategies may include any of the following:

Press release. A public school adult education program sends a one-page press release on a new community recreation program to newspapers in a targeted population area.

Brochure. A community college community services program sends a trifolded, one-page brochure on a series of small business seminars to business owners from a mailing list.

Teachers/staff. Volunteer teachers in an adult literacy program provide information to their students on a new literacy program.

Past participants. A national judicial continuing education program sends a letter to past participants informing them of a new one-week course and asks them to let others know about the course.

Direct mail. A university continuing education program sends a letter and brochure to city managers on a national mailing list telling them about a three-day conference on working effectively with community groups.

Television. A public health agency informs residents through a local television public service announcement that free blood pressure and blood cholesterol checks will be provided as part of a community health workshop.

Radio. A neighborhood organizer from a community organization is a guest on a local radio talk show to discuss an upcoming economic development training program for small business leaders.

Newspapers. A community college's environmental impact program is featured in a local newspaper.

Print ads. An international manufacturing organization buys ads in trade journals announcing a new conference on employee involvement strategies.

Tracking. A university conference center codes and tracks a mass mailing to hotel and restaurant executives in order to know who responded to the brochure.

Database marketing. A community college community services program, through its computerized registration system, identifies past registrants from financial management courses who may be interested in a new course on this topic.

Fliers. A training and development department in a financial services organization provides an attractive flier about a new video on customer relations which is available to all employees in the video library.

Posters. A public library places posters in public facility locations throughout the community announcing a new volunteer bilingual tutoring program, available free of charge to those wanting to improve their reading skills.

Special events. A university cooperative extension office has a display booth at a county fair providing brochures and other information about programs and services available on sustainable agriculture, water, human nutrition, family well-being, and community development.

Networking and personal contacts. A local YMCA asked each of its members to contact three people and let them know of an upcoming AIDS prevention workshop.

Product sampling. An educational television program gives a one-minute preview of a course on Native American history.

Coupons. A national association of trainers gives coupons to its members that allow them to receive savings on the purchase of specific training films.

Let us not forget one important strategy which is to build on success. People will talk with others about products and services with which they have had success.

There are no "right" or "wrong" answers to promotion. Strategies vary; each has its strengths and limitations. They should be assessed for their overriding purpose. For example, marketing campaigns involving social change often need intensive interactions and communications among target populations and the marketer or change agent (Kotler & Roberto, 1989); to motivate target adopters to undertake a desired action, networking and personal contacts may be a priority marketing technique. Marketers interested in generating inquiries and registrations may find other techniques most beneficial, such as direct mail. Falk (1986) says that many promotion strategies should be evaluated based on their "pulling power." He raises these helpful questions when making this assessment:

- Does one category of the media "pull" better than another?
- Does one newspaper or broadcast outlet "pull" better than another?

- Do promotions in one geographical area generate more registrations and inquiries than similar efforts in other geographical areas?
- Do promotional efforts occurring at a particular time of day, on a particular day of the week, or within a particular time frame before an event have measurable effects on the numbers of registrations?
- Is the sum of publicity efforts attracting the type of registrants and participants we seek? (p. 68)

As a marketer, think of yourself as a potential buyer of a specific product you are planning to sell. Ask yourself, to buy this product what do I need to know about it? How will I benefit from receiving it? What does it cost? If there is a price, is it appropriate to my wants and needs? Where do I acquire the product? Is this product intended for someone like me? These questions call for insight into the targeted groups and will help the marketer develop important and sometimes inventive promotion strategies for marketing.

Be Facilitative

Create a marketing vision, think target groups, and be inventive. Successful marketing invariably requires facilitation and working with others. Teamwork is a core element for building an effective marketing campaign. "None of us is as smart as all of us," boast Blanchard, Carew, and Parisi-Carew (1990, p. 25). As marketers performing many roles, from program coordinators to external consultants, we are challenged to creatively and effectively make use of others who can contribute insights and interests in a problem or new idea, influence and connectiveness with others, and knowledge and skills.

Building a marketing campaign requires leadership. Knowing marketing as a technical and logical strategy (moving from an understanding of target groups to selecting promotional techniques) is only one important part of effective marketing. Another component that is often neglected in books and articles on marketing, in my view, is the marketer as a leader. For Lawler (1986), he believes that a leader inspires loyalty, commitment, and motivation through his or her personal style and behavior (p. 208). He suggests that leaders need to build trust and openness and empower others (p. 211). The collaborative leader, which is what I am advocating here, is one who "… tap(s) into the synergistic power of teams and welcome(s) those who challenge the old ways of doing things" (Hennecke, 1991, p. 57).

Communication is a key to the marketer's success in working with individuals and groups. In a recent reprint of an article which first appeared in 1952, Carl Rogers (Rogers & Roethlisberger, 1991) observed that real communication involves "listening with understanding," which may be called active listening today. Working with others and gaining their insights, ideas, and thoughts require the marketer-facilitator to listen without judging. According to Rogers, "… I've found there is one main obstacle to communication: people's tendency to *evaluate*. Fortunately, I've discovered that if people can learn to *listen* with understanding, they can mitigate their impulses to be judgmental and thus greatly improve their communication with others" (p. 106). Listening effectively requires empathy which is more than paying attention to what someone is saying. According to Zalenznic (1992), empathy is "… the capacity to take in emotional signals and make them meaningful in a relationship" (p. 131). Being highly involved in teamwork and working with others, the marketer-facilitator is in the business of building and fostering relationships.

QUESTIONS FOR STUDY AND DISCUSSION

1. A multicounty economic development commission has decided to put on 10 one-day seminars for small business representatives. To design a comprehensive marketing campaign for these seminars, what questions need to be discussed at a planning meeting?

2. A university medical school continuing education division wishes to expand its programming to 5,000 physicians in rural settings who have been in family practice 0–3 years. What strategies should program marketers use to promote a three-day intensive educational conference on setting up a business management plan?

3. A community college has been asked by an automotive manufacturing company to help design a promotion campaign for an in-house training program on effective employee communications. During their first meeting with the company's train-

ing department, what questions should the college representatives try to have answered?

4. A cooperative extension office is designing a promotion strategy for a three-day institute on conflict resolution. What five promotion techniques should be considered to attract public agency and community leaders?

5. A neighborhood organization wants to get its community members to attend a meeting on health care issues. A planning meeting with 30 community members is set. What items should be on the agenda for this planning meeting?

6. A public school adult education center is threatened with closure resulting from insufficient enrollments in their community education program. What collaborative strategies should the center personnel consider to get community members to assess if the center should stay open?

REFERENCES

Agor, W. H. (1989). *Intuition in organizations: Leading and managing productively.* Newbury Park, CA: Sage.

Baker, G. (1990). A checklist for training programs. In Frantzreb, R. (Ed.), *Training and Development Yearbook 1990* (p. 2.13). Englewood Cliffs, NJ: Prentice Hall.

Beder, H. (1986). Basic concepts and principles of marketing. In Beder, H. (Ed.), *Marketing Continuing Education* (pp. 3–17). San Francisco: Jossey-Bass.

Blanchard, K., Carew, D., & Parisi-Carew, E. (1990). *The One Minute Manager. Builds High Performing Teams.* Escondido, CA.: Blanchard Training and Development.

Drucker, P. (1992, September-October). The new society of organizations. *Harvard Business Review*, 95–104.

Falk, C. (1986). Promoting continuing education programs. In H. Beder (Ed.), *Marketing Continuing Education* (pp. 49–71). San Francisco: Jossey-Bass.

Fischer, R. (1987). Successful marketing strategies and techniques. In Gessner, Q. (Ed.), *Handbook on Continuing Higher Education* (pp. 167–187). New York: Macmillan.

Freire, P. (1974). *Education for critical consciousness.* New York: Seabury Press.

Garvin, D. (1991, November-December). How the Baldrige award really works. *Harvard Business Review*, 80–93.

Geber, B. (1991). The recession squeezes training. *Training, 28*(4), 27–34.

Griffith, W. S. (1989). Recruiting and retaining adult students: A marketing perspective. In Cookson, P. (Ed.), *Recruiting and Retaining Adult Students.* San Francisco: Jossey-Bass, pp. 23–33.

Griffith, W. S., & Cristarella, M. (1979). Participatory research: Should it be a new methodology for adult educators? In J. Niemi (Ed.), *Viewpoints on Adult*

Education Research (pp. 43–70). Columbus, OH: ERIC Clearinghouse on Adult, Career and Vocational Education.

Hall, B. (1981). Participatory research, popular knowledge and power: A personal reflection. *Convergence, 14,* 6–19.

Hennecke, M. (1991). Toward the change-sensitive organization. *Training, 28*(5), 54–59.

Houle, C. (1972). *The Design of Education.* San Francisco: Jossey-Bass.

Kotler, P., & Roberto, E. (1989). *Social Marketing. Strategies for Changing Public Behavior.* New York: Free Press.

Kotler, P., & Andreasen, A. (1991). *Strategic marketing for nonprofit organizations* (4th ed.). Englewood Cliffs, NJ: Prentice Hall.

Lawler, E. (1986). *High-involvement management.* San Francisco: Jossey-Bass.

Merriam, S., & Caffarella, R. (1991). *Learning in adulthood.* San Francisco: Jossey-Bass.

Morstain, B. R., & Smart, J.C. (1974). Reasons for participation in adult education courses: A multivariate analysis of group differences. *Adult Education, 24*(2). In S. Merriam & R. Caffarella (1991). *Learning in adulthood* (p. 85). San Francisco: Jossey-Bass.

Rogers, C., & Roethlisberger, F. J. (1991, November-December). Barriers and gateways to communication. *Harvard Business Review,* 105–111. (Reprinted from *Harvard Business Review* July-August 1952).

Simerly, R. (1989). The strategic role of marketing for organizational success. In R. Simerly & Associates (Eds.), *Handbook on Marketing for Continuing Education* (pp. 3–29). San Francisco: Jossey-Bass.

Zaleznic, A. (1992, March-April). Managers and leaders: Are they different? *Harvard Business Review,* 126–135.

16

Reinventing Recruitment and Retention

B. Allan Quigley

ABSTRACT

Recruiting and retaining adults is typically seen as the single most unmanageable and frustrating dimension of program planning. Among administrators, programmers, and instructors, the semester-to-semester question is: "How can we develop better systems and better strategies to recruit and retain more students?" This chapter discusses how limiting such questions are and how we should try to gain a deeper understanding of the participation/nonpartici-pation issues involved. If viewed through the lens of combined theory and experience, recruitment and retention not only present opportunities for institutional and professional growth, but also can be an area of great social and educational opportunity for our entire field. Theoretical models and experience-based case studies are analyzed in terms of three demand levels: high-to medium demand, low-latent-no demand, and negative demand. Moving across demand areas, program planners are encouraged to reinvent recruitment and retention as issues become more complex in daily practice.

ASSESSMENT

1. To what extent do the adults for whom you plan education or training programs respond to the invitation to participate? How do you account for their positive response to your programs?

2. To what extent do the adults for whom you plan education or training programs resist or reject the invitation to participate? How do you account for their negative response to your programs?

3. Of those adults who begin their participation in your programs, what percentage persist and complete the program? How do you account for the ability of the program to retain these persisters?

4. Of those adults who begin their participation in your programs, what percentage discontinue their participation? Analyze the characteristics of these adults who drop out. Analyze the characteristics of your programs that contribute to the patterns of attrition.

PLANNING IN THE "REAL WORLD"

"Unfortunately, it is usually even harder to find out why people do not do something than why they do" (Cross, 1981, p. 97). It is here, in the murky world of why people do some things and not others, and why they begin something, then quit, that our applied field of adult education is truly tested. The more light adult education practitioners and researchers can shed on the two interlinked program areas of recruitment and retention, the better chance we will have of guiding our educational institutions and building a learning society into the next century. In fact, if the field which claims authority on behalf of adults and their learning cannot take the lead on recruiting and retaining adult learners, one wonders who should, and who will? At the institutional level, if we cannot guide our institutions on reaching and retaining students, our teaching methods, materials design, evaluation instruments, and carefully constructed mission statements will be for nothing.

However, unlike the nation's public schools, with few exceptions, adults ultimately are voluntary learners. They decide what, where, when, and how long they will spend with us. And, unlike other points along the program planning delivery process where educators can physically see students and talk with them, the people I am focusing on here for purposes of recruitment and retention have either not yet come, or have left and are all too often "unavailable for comment." To exacerbate the problem, educa-

tors need to ask if the learner comments they (occasionally) receive before and after the program give sufficient accuracy to really
interpret the past or plan with certainty into the future. So, they
struggle to guess and plan and revise courses on clumsy, often
unrepresentative needs sampling. Educators are often left wondering if they were perhaps just told what they wanted to hear through
"polite feedback." Given the importance of these issues touching
on the very survival of the adult education enterprise—on what
basis can a more satisfactory approach to recruitment and retention be built?

There has been no lack of suggestions. Strother and Klus
(1982) asserted some years ago that "An enterprise survives in
large part by satisfying the needs of several groups of people ...
[first among them, the] consumer" (p. 17). Building on the paradigm of student-as-consumer, the Total Quality Management literature has given us valuable marketing systems and consumer strategies. However, recruitment and retention holds much more complex
issues than a simplistic consumer-driven paradigm permits. On the
other hand, a number of important theoretical models and theories exist in the literature. But, if theory were the issue, it should be
possible to synthesize what exists and move ahead. Neither reductionist "strategies" nor erudite theory are enough.

Adult education is a field of research *and* practice and these
worlds must be pulled closer together and have one inform the
other on an every day basis. In a practice-based field, theory must
be able to be applied, observed, retested, and, ultimately, be able to
become an internalized part of lived experience. All too often
programmers and administrators will dismiss theory in favor of
personal experience. This is dangerous. As Kerlinger put it, the
common sense-driven naive realist: "tests his 'hypotheses,' ... but
he tests them in what might be called a selective fashion. He often
'selects' evidence simply because it is consistent with his hypoth-
esis" (Kerlinger, 1973, p. 3). Further, in the daily chaos of budgetary and political pressures—often referred to as the "the real
world"—there is the danger that an anti-intellectualism can surface which wants to scoff at theory. This may be because many
practitioners will say that adult education theory in this critical area
is, at best, unusable; at worst, irrelevant. It may also be that absence
of theory and research opens the door to those who can take
control by asserting that their own experiences have the greatest

validity. Thus, without theory or research taken seriously, the most vocal garner the greatest "authority."

What can be learned from all this? The position taken here is that the most significant person in the recruitment and retention arena is neither the learner, nor the employer, nor even the tax payer. Over the long term, programming success depends on the professional growth of the programmer and how well he or she can understand and influence planning realities.

CREATING AND RE-CREATING KNOWLEDGE

How can programmers be helped to do a better job? I believe there should be a better way to learn by doing, and do by learning. I believe a better inquiry process is needed to form, test, reflect upon, and continuously challenge both the world of experience and of theoretical knowledge. Although there is literature on such concepts as "theory-in-use" and "double loop learning" (e.g., Argyris, Putnam & Smith, 1985), as well as important discussions on reflective practice (Schön, 1983; and Chapter 6 in this text) and on praxis (Freire, 1970), the point that needs to be made here is that the development of a reflexive process often requires aspects of a paradigm shift. Or, as more fully discussed by Mezirow, elements of a personal "perspective transformation" (1990). Since recruiting and retaining adults happens in a social-cultural context of institutional values, cultural beliefs, and political power struggles, educators may end up challenging their own paradigms, along with those of others around them. However, to place programmers at the center of the program planning universe is to place self-challenge at the very heart of professional growth.

REFLEXIVE TURN

In this discussion, it is helpful to understand this self-challenge process as a "reflexive turn" (Stanage, 1987, p. 26). Grounded in the experiential work of Dewey (1938) and phenomenology, (Husserl, 1964; Speigelberg, 1964; Stanage, 1987), reflexive turn parallels "bracketing," the sixth step of Speigelberg's phenomenological method (Spiegelberg, 1960, p. 672). It is what Stanage describes as, "Suspending our believing in the 'existence' and 'causes(s)' of phenomena" (Stanage, 1989)—the step in the interpreting of events where we set aside all that we have come to believe about a phenomenon. It is where we step back and radically reconsider the knowledge and the beliefs gained thus far, including our own place in the interpretation. Reflexive turn is ultimately to think about our own thinking, as depicted in Figure 16.1.

In reflexive turn, experience-based common sense and received theory are separate yet, as depicted, are brought together to both inform each other and challenge each other. They shape our reality yet neither side can embrace all of reality. And, as shown below, there is a point where one needs to stop and hold everything in abeyance—to look back and turn thinking "back upon itself as

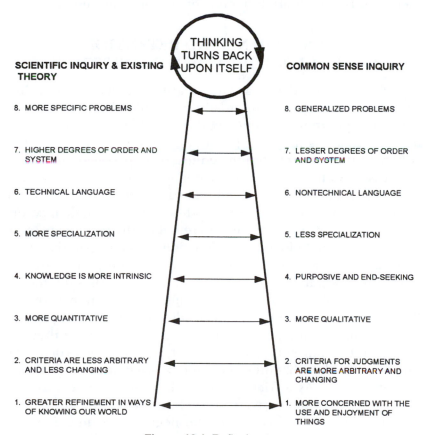

Figure 16.1 Reflexive turn

a self-critical process" (Stanage, 1987, p. 26). As is now discussed, this often happens in moments of self-doubt.

MODELS AND CASE STUDIES FOR REFLEXIVE PROFESSIONAL DEVELOPMENT

Recruitment and retention are discussed here in terms of three demand situations: (1) High-to-medium demand, (2) low-latent-to-no demand, and (3) negative demand (Beder & Quigley, 1990). A linkage between recruitment and retention is made in the sense that learner involvement or non-involvement in programs is manifested either by participation or nonparticipation; by persistence or dropout. In other words, adults "vote with their feet" either before or during programs. From this vantage point, recruitment and retention are functions on a time continuum.

RECRUITMENT AND RETENTION IN HIGH-TO-MEDIUM DEMAND SETTINGS

If demand is defined as "the degree to which an individual actually wants to participate in adult education" (Beder, 1991, p. 51), some program planners work with "high-to-medium" demand. This arena might be found, for instance, in a community college or university continuing education department, in a training division within a health or corporate setting, or in an agriculture outreach program. Here, adults actively request courses, register and stay in most courses as offered. In this high medium demand situation, recruitment and retention discussions are often based out of psychological and functional systems paradigms. Issues here are less concerned with "why" students participate and more with "when," "where," and "how" programs should be delivered. While much of our training and program planning literature insists that a thorough needs assessment must precede programming, many planners in these settings simply draw together a list of courses that went last year, include courses of topical interest, consider what other institutions are doing, and make an educated guess. As a friend of mine in a university continuing education department used to say, "The most one can lose is a few lines in a newspaper." However, he neglected to mention that neither those who rearranged their lives to take the classes, nor the staff who had to issue multiple refunds each term, nor the instructors who had prepared the classes in good faith saw recruitment as being quite this "simple." Thus, recruitment in high-to-medium settings is often equated with marketing proficiency (Griffith, 1989).

However, we can gain some insights into what is happening in this arena and inform both ourselves and our institution more effectively by combining a number of theoretical and research based models to help explain why adults participate in structured education in the first place (Courtney, 1993). In his application of Kurt Lewin's famous Force Field Analysis (1938), Miller (1967) understood adults as compelled/impelled to satisfy their needs through education—needs which, for Miller, were explainable through Maslow's needs hierarchy. Miller also saw adults as highly influenced by their socioeconomic class: lower lower, working class, lower middle, upper middle, and upper class. According to Miller, the likelihood of participation increases as learners' social status increases. As for the lower end of the social class scale, Miller concluded: "The lower lowers ... are the only group which is actually hostile to education because it conflicts with basic values arising out of their class position at the bottom of the heap ... education is inimical because it requires a strong enough belief in a future payoff to give up present gratifications" (p. 9). This latter statement will be challenged later, but these psychological concepts have been widely referenced over the past two decades to explain why adults join and remain in classes (Carp, Peterson, & Roelfs, 1974; Johnstone & Rivera, 1965; Reissman, 1962).

From Maslow and Miller, Cross developed a Chain of Response Model (Cross, 1981) which can serve as a lens to view the three demand areas being discussed. This model is especially useful since it allows a beginning point "self-evaluation" in the decision to participate. This beginning point is immediately followed directly by, "Attitudes about education" (Cross, 1981, p. 124), as shown in Figure 16.2.

As Cross says, her Chain of Response Model "assumes that participation is a learning activity, whether organized in classes or self-directed, is not a single act but the result of a chain of responses, each based on an evaluation of a position of the individual in his or her environment" (1981, p. 125). Following the model from self-evaluation through to the ultimate decision to participate

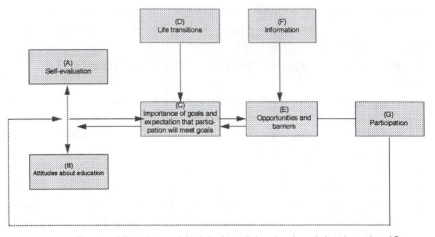

Figure 16.2 Chain of Response Model of participation in adult education (Cross, 1981, p. 124). Copyright 1981 by Jossey-Bass. Used by permission.

(or remain) reveals a process fraught with barriers (Cross, 1981). According to Cross, the categories of barriers which may interfere with the decision to join are: (1) "institutional" (e.g., barriers created by the educational institution, such as physical/geographic inaccessibility or inconvenient scheduling), (2) "situational" (e.g., barriers created in the lives of students such as a lack of day care, transportation, or time), and (3) barriers to participation and retention created by their own disposition (e.g., student attitudes about education itself) (Cross, 1981, pp. 98–108).

For the three demand areas here, the Chain of Response and the three categories of barriers can be framed as a series of decision phases where the preponderance of barriers arises at different moments for each of the three demand groups, shown in Figure 16.3. The greatest barriers to potential and enrolled students from the high-medium demand area typically do not arise in the first stage of decision making. For reasons of cultural, social, and economic experience, past education and past schooling experiences here, as well as their perception of self, are not stumbling blocks to "fitting back in to" education (Bourdieu, 1984; Giroux, 1983). As Courtney puts it, adult education can be seen as "membership ... occasioned by the desire to associate with others of like mind, interest and taste" (1993, p. 146). In this respect, self-evaluation is

Decision Phase I	Decision Phase II	Decision Phase III
ASSESSMENT OF SELF	ASSESSMENT OF LIFE SITUATIONS	ASSESSMENT OF INSTITUTION
Includes: • Perception of self • Attitude towards education • Experiences of schooling	Includes: • Finances • Family • Transportation • Health • Time available	Includes: • Goal relevance • Appropriateness • Geographic access • Course scheduling
ASSESSMENT OF SELF arises especially within: • negative demand • low-latent-no demand	ASSESSMENT OF LIFE SITUATIONS arises especially within: • negative demand • low-latent-no demand • high-medium demand	ASSESSMENT OF INSTITUTION arises especially within: • low-latent-no demand • high-medium demand

Figure 16.3 Chain of Response and barriers across demand areas

not an issue for programmers working in the high-medium demand area.

Instead, barriers typically arise here in Phases Two or Three, when adults assess their life situations and the nature/accessibility of the educational institution. By contrast, for the low-latent-no demand area, a preponderance of barriers can arise out of any of the three groupings of barriers and the decision to join or quit can take place at any of the three phases. The negative demand area becomes more complex in the sense that self-assessment and experiences with school can be very negative. As positive and rewarding as school may have been for adults in the medium-high demand area, school can have had an equally negative value for those in the negative demand area. The first two phases of the Chain of Response Model, therefore, have very different meaning across the groups.

Unfortunately, there has been a tendency in adult education practice and in the participation literature to see most adults through high-medium demand lenses. In fact, as the following case study reveals, recruitment and retention issues become increasingly complex as we move from high to negative demand, and the interpretation of the different "realities" involved can force reflexive turn.

Case Study 1: High-Medium in Conflict With Medium-Latent-No Demand

I was a community college programmer in an oil-rich Northern Alberta, Canadian community where almost any course offered was well attended. From typing, to welding, to cooking, to first-year college transfer classes, out of some 40 courses per semester over a 3 year period, I cannot recall canceling more than 5 for lack of enrollment. Attrition in these classes was relatively uncommon and usually was explainable through situational barriers. Using experience and "common sense," we had successful marketing strategies by using every media available, we guided learners "into learning activities with pre-enrollment information, information sessions, appropriate admissions procedures, counseling and advising" (Cookson, 1989, p. 108). We did (almost) everything right.

Had the college been familiar with the Chain of Response Model (Cross, 1981) or the barriers arising among different target populations, (and had we been prepared to integrate them) we might have avoided the following fiasco. At this same college, it was clear that Natives, one of Canada's visible minorities, were not well represented in courses. Nor were they well represented in the employment or oil rich economic future of the region itself. The community had a high population of Natives. No topic was of greater interest in the city than oil production; therefore, what better topic than "The Role of Natives and the Northern Oil Industry?" Using what our common sense told us, this course was marketed using standard advertising methods. Native students participating in our trades courses were also informed.

Despite our marketing, what do you think the turnout was like for this course? Aside from the VIP panel of invited guest speakers who dutifully sat at a raised set of tables at the front of the large classroom, the audience consisted of myself, my wife (who stayed because I needed a ride home), and the janitor who came into the room looking for his mop. I had an unmitigated failure. I was sure I had embarrassed the college and, as a young programmer, I remember how afraid I was of what the college management would say. However, I had underestimated the power of "reality adjustment" by those whose entire framework was "common sense." The next day, selected data and pure prejudice were elevated to "fact" as a senior manager shrugged the incident off, observing: "Natives are lazy and won't come to such courses anyway." My misreading of the demand and the course was never revisited in the college, except by me.

Considering this incident in light of Cross's Chain of Response Model, the first and second steps—learner self-evaluation and attitudes about education—would have suggested that voluntary participation in "any form of competitive education" (Cross, 1981, p. 125) which may be "considered achievement motivated" (p. 125) may be avoided by those who are not comfortable in such settings (also see Boshier's Congruence Model (Boshier, 1977). A simple needs assessment and consideration of the non-competitive nature of Cree and Chipweyan Native cultures might have told us that cultural differences would mitigate against attendance at a public forum like this. Or, even brief consideration of this group's attitudes towards "white" education in either the Lewin Force Field Analysis or the Cross Chain of Response Model might have warned us. Simple realization that we were seeing all students out of a "high demand" set of assumptions would have said that we needed a different approach here.

While it is relatively easy to conduct "public relations to inform and ... impress relevant publics," as Cookson (1989, p. 108) suggests in his first recruitment guideline, to do it well with awareness of who the audience is, and what *their* self-assessment and attitude toward the educational system are, is far more difficult. As a young programmer, it was here that a reflexive turn became possible. I had to "bracket" the institutional assumptions which fit what we did and ask if our thinking was founded on assumptions of homogeneous socioeconomic class, even to the point of racism for some on staff. I had to ask if culture needed to challenge aspects of our entire delivery system. More broadly, moving beyond high demand programming which fits normative patterns, I had to ask how, and "if," an institution such as ours could ever successfully launch such a course.

For many programmers working in established systems and in high-medium demand, it may be helpful to map differing needs on the Chain of Response Model. Try asking fundamental questions: What is the self-assessment of the intended audience? What are the attitudes of the intended audience towards education/adult education courses/and my institution in particular? To what extent does the intended audience believe these courses will lead to *their* goals—instead of those of my institution?

This reflexive turn, and similar experiences in other colleges, universities, employer settings, and government, led me to concentrate much of my future work on the "least heard"—the nonparticipants of adult education. It is here, I believe, that our field can make a much larger contribution to education and society by raising issues of nonparticipation above common sense hypotheses and beyond instrumental "strategies."

RECRUITMENT AND RETENTION
IN LOW-LATENT–NO DEMAND SETTINGS

After the publication of Miller's (1967) and Cross's (1981) work, Scanlan (1986) provided an extensive review of the deterrents literature. He concluding that "Deterrents to participation is a multidimensional concept, subsuming several logical groupings of psychological, social, and environmental variables" (p. 35). Whereas single explanations used to dominate our literature, more recently, multiple questions of prior schooling, culture, and gender have turned the field to look more closely at social and environmental variables (Courtney, 1993).

This trend is particularly significant for recruiting and retaining adults in low demand, latent demand areas where "Potential learners want an educational offering which does not exist" (Beder, 1991, p. 51, also see Kotler, 1975) and when there is "no demand" (Beder, 1991, p. 51)—meaning learners neither avoid nor seek structured learning courses. In no demand, "The educator needs ... to identify the demand and create the offering to meet it" (Beder, 1991, p. 51).

Now the issue begins to shift from participation to nonparticipation. And, as noted above, in the low-latent-no demand area, it is difficult to predict needs since one is typically not able to build on a participation track record. Here, it is unclear which assessment tool(s) are best, what "access" may mean, what level of program cost should be justified, or even what a successful rate of recruitment and/or retention might be among those who typically are not part of our programs. There is a growing body of literature to help us conduct needs assessments to more precisely differentiate between felt, perceived and real (or actual) needs (e.g., Boone, 1985; Boyle, 1981; Pratt, 1988; and see Chapter 10). There is a growing body of literature to help us interpret more diverse populations areas where low latent-no need may exist (e.g., Cookson,

1989; Sork & Caffarella, 1989). However, on nonparticipation, much of the most significant recent literature has arisen out of literacy education (Beder, 1991; Fingeret, 1984; Hayes, 1988; Quigley, 1992, 1993; Ziegahn, 1992).

As discussed, the early participation literature (e.g., Johnstone & Rivera, 1965; Carp, Peterson & Roelfs, 1974) tended to see participation from the vantage point of the high-medium demand institution—rather like the view from the management offices of the Northern college I have just described. Further, "The early literature was highly descriptive and almost divorced from theory" (Beder, 1991, p. 76). A third point, much of the early literature and, I would add, much of the current, is based on *participants* in programs. These are the wrong people upon which to build a nonparticipation research base. We learn little and run serious generalizability risks by asking questions of the committed and converted. More nonparticipation research based on nonpartici-pants is needed if we are to be more successful in the low-latent-no and negative demand areas.

The recent literacy literature is highly revealing in areas of culture and socioeconomic difference (Beder, 1989; Fingeret, 1983, 1985; Hayes, 1988). Beder, in a state-wide survey among adults who had never chosen to participate in adult basic education (ABE), found four basic reasons for nonparticipation: low perception of need ("I don't think I could use the things I would learn in school," Beder, 1991, p. 90); perceived effort ("School is too hard," Beder, 1991, p. 90); dislike for school; and situational barriers. Based on nonparticipants, situational factors always prevail, but negative attitudes towards programs and dislike for school were a prominent theme: "Many of the most powerful reasons for non-participation stem from attitudes towards adult literacy education" (Beder, 1991, p. 91).

The negative impact of schooling was again powerfully re-vealed by Baldwin (1991) who found lifelong negative effects on 7,800 school dropouts in a national GED follow up study. Negative attitudes accounted for over 2/3 of the response in study among 3,600 adults on why they had chosen not to complete school as young adults (Kirsch & Jungeblut, 1986). And, in one of the few national longitudinal studies in our field on this topic, 18,000 students were followed up and, once again, the decision to avoid "schooling" was a major outcome (Cervero & Fitzpatrick, 1990). It was Cervero and Fitzpatrick's conclusion that "schooling provides a powerful set of social circumstances that ... shape the individual" (1990, p. 92) and greatly influences the decision to return to education.

These types of findings point increasingly towards learner attitudes as a key in their decision to participate or not to participate. Thus, as we move from high-medium demand to low-latent-no-demand, the pendulum swings from institutional barriers, to situational, and over to dispositional, as was seen in Figure 16.1. It is suggested, therefore, that when working in the low-latent-no demand area, attitudes of adults cannot be ignored or assumed to be the same as those in high-medium demand areas of programming, as the following case study indicates.

Case Study 2: Working in Low-Latent–No Demand Areas

I was involved in establishing an adult basic education class in Northern Saskatchewan, Canada in 1972 for adults with less than a grade 12 education. Recruitment for the class was conducted with the help of referral agencies such as a federal employment agency and the local Indian Affairs office. Fifteen adults were referred to the ABE class: eight white adults, five Metis adults, and two treaty Indian adults. Only four were male, the rest were female. The Metis came from a nearby town, the white students came from the local town and nearby farms, and the two treaty Indian students came from the reservation by school bus. Our program was held in the town's modern high school with the standard ABE curriculum and many of the latest materials.

We practiced andragogical techniques (Knowles, 1980) from the outset and a nonthreatening classroom environment was soon created—at least so it seemed to the "common sense" of most in the classroom. There is no doubt in my mind that the principles of retention discussed by Cookson (1989, pp. 108-109) were being adhered to. We ensured "high-quality educational programming," we continued at least some student support services, included "hassle-free registration and admissions," and encouraged peer support. I gave what most in the field would consider "high-quality instruction that provided effective and personable learning experiences and positive group experiences" (Cookson, 1989, p. 109).

And, I tried to link "the program to prerequisite and succeeding programs" in many ways (Cookson, 1989, p. 108). We all tried to create "rituals and symbols that help to form a sense of shared meaning and connectedness among students, their important others, and program faculty and staff" (Cookson, 1989, p. 109). I did not perhaps "engage adult students in program governance" (Cookson, 1989, p. 109) as much as I now wish I had but this was not the way I had been trained and not the way others conducted ABE. I nevertheless did everything I could to "demonstrate that the program [was] responsive to formative, summative, and impact evaluations of and by adult students," (Cookson, 1989, p. 109). What I did not realize, however, was that I had less than 2 weeks to achieve all this.

Despite "common sense," I lacked the theoretical tools to anticipate what would happen. Had I known about participation models which provide closer analyses of the attitudinal side of nonparticipation—such as the Expectancy-Valence Motivational Model (Rubenson, 1978; Van Tilburg & DuBois, 1989), I might have had the tools to predict that two students would drop out in the first 3 weeks. Can you guess which ones they were?

The two female Native students who were being bused in from the Indian reservation were uncomfortable in this environment from the beginning. They kept their heads down. Whispered back and forth. Avoided speaking. Despite the academic promise demonstrated in their placement testing, after about a week they began to be absent from class. The common sense of the other students was that they were "unmotivated." After 3 weeks, I heard they had officially dropped the class. The local Indian Affairs counselor told me: "Those two have always been trouble."

Here was an example of viewing nonparticipation and drop-out on a selected data and reality-adjusted "common sense" basis. Here is a case study of stakeholders wanting to assume that their system of delivery and teaching was not culpable. That all cultures, beliefs, past experiences—perspectives of self and education/ schooling—are somehow the same, all normative. Basically, the common sense said: "If you are 'motivated,' you will succeed—in school as well as in life." After this incident, I began to reflect on what it means to be, "motivated?" The two students had been highly self-conscious, aloof, and never "engaged" in the class by adding comments or speaking up. Were they just "lazy"—as I had been told in the earlier case study?

As I later learned, making eye contact with "superiors" is considered disrespectful in many Indian cultures. Being expected to discuss issues and ideas in what would have been to them a competitive public setting—especially among a "white" dominant group—was a formula for failure. In fact, (like so many students labeled "poor self-image") they exhibited a solid self-image outside the classroom. As I later learned, they were neither lazy nor trouble on the reservation (Ziegahn, 1992). I had to ask if the problem was a cultural clash created by the andragogical setting which served the instructor and dominant culture students well, but utterly failed in this cross-cultural setting. The institutional, systemic barrier I had helped create was explainable through the first steps of Cross's (1981) Chain of Response Model on self-assessment and attitudes towards education/schooling. The dispositional barrier at work would have actually been measurable had I known about the Expectancy-Valence Motivational Model. As will be discussed, it would have been possible to assess these learners' individual beliefs, or valence, about education and schooling as well as their expectancy on their ability to succeed and their expectancy of the program. It may have happened that the two Native students' expectancy-valence was as high as any other student. We will never know. We were rich in self-legitimating common sense but bankrupt in theory.

For my part, I was forced to assess the "one size fits all" andragogical approach to adult teaching. Such experiences also force one to see how "common sense" can protect the majority by dismissing the minority—and, ironically, how our personal as well as institutional mission can be compromised at the same time. In dealing with low-latent-no demand audiences, then, the first step of Cross's Chain of Response Model, self-evaluation, takes on greater meaning. We need to ask how past schooling experiences may have shaped the expectancy of self and program, and what learners' beliefs and valence are towards schooling and education? We need to assess our own teaching and delivery assumptions through improved analyses and interpretations of how the world appears through the eyes of potential learners—even if it means challenging self-protective rationalizations.

Discussion

Such findings are important across the wide spectrum of adult education since adults are known to be greatly influenced by their past (Brookfield, 1991; Wlodkowski, 1985). They form much of their adult behavior and educational decision making around the expectancy and valence/belief that certain programs, courses or degrees will usher them to their goals. Further, in all walks of adult education, we are dealing with emotions—both positive and negative (Wlodkowski, 1985). As planners and instructors, we often contribute to the emotionally charged issues in the low-latent-no area of programming.

It is clear that the impact of schooling is lifelong—both positive and negative. But, how does the learner's past actually interact with a decision to re-enter and to persist in our programs? A recent study I conducted on this issue (Quigley, 1987, 1992) using expectancy/valence and the practice implications derived give some insight to the views of some in this group. We compared adult basic education (ABE) students who dropped out in the first three weeks in two major ABE centers in a northeastern U.S. city, with persisters who stayed in the ABE program for over six months. The dropouts were termed "reluctant learners"—virtually invisible students who had left within the first three weeks for no identifiable reason other than "low motivation," as assessed by the two institution's counselors and teachers. Like the two Native students, the reluctant learners in this study were assessed as being aloof; skeptical to hostile; shy to highly self-conscious and, from the beginning, disengaged, uncommitted and apparently "lacking in motivation." They were what public education would term "high risk students." Such adult students can be seen entering adult education programs every day across the workforce, on vocational education campuses, in military settings, in correctional centers, on college campuses. Much more work is needed on this question for purposes of this demand area.

However, in this recent study, with two highly trained interviewers: one white, one African American; one male, one female, we used expectancy valence theory as the theoretical frame to interview in-depth a total of 37 ABE students (17 Reluctant Learner dropouts and 20 in-program persisters). For the reluctant learner dropouts, interviews were conducted at neutral sites such as community centers or students' homes. Interviews were held at the two ABE centers for Persisters. Data were analyzed using ANOVA and Chi square. The study population was comprised of 73% African American, 23% white subjects; of whom 65% were female, 35% male; and the modal age group, 27%, was in the 28–33 year age bracket. The mean school grade attained was 9 years. This is a typical sample of urban ABE programs.

Statistical significance (p =. 05) was found in reluctant learners' response when asked if they liked their teachers back in school and, again, if they liked them in ABE. It seemed that reluctant learners may have "liked" their school teachers but felt they had not received adequate attention from them—a pattern they repeated in ABE (and holding implications for many other arenas of adult education). By contrast, significance was found (p = .05) when reluctant learner dropouts reported having received adequate attention from school counselors and, again, from ABE counselors—another pattern repeated (and again a finding holding implications for other arenas of adult education).

In sharp contrast, persisters did not need seek or feel strongly about either their past school or present ABE counselors. And, persisters did not complain of a lack of attention from either school or ABE teachers. It was found that reluctant learners had fewer friends than persisters back in school and again in ABE. Thus, the research team found relatively consistent behavior patterns in past school and ABE in both groups—an important retention finding for the entire field. Significantly, through expectancy-valence multivariate analysis we found that the expectancy of what the reluctant learners believed they could achieve upon entering the program had been slightly higher than persisters. And, we found that their valence and belief in the ABE program they were entering was again slightly higher than persisters' at the point of entry. They were not "unmotivated" at the beginning of the program. After dropping out, the valence towards ABE among the reluctant learners had decreased but their valence and belief in education had not diminished. After quitting, reluctant learners said they were willing to return to the program if asked, but many had already enrolled in alternative programs such as tutoring.

Why did these reluctant learners quit school before and why did they return to formal learning only to quit again? This study suggests that the lack of challenge and attention the reluctant learners felt they were given in school helped "push" them into quitting. Yet, they returned to ABE with a high belief in education. This finding contradicts much of the early literature discussed above. "Working class subjects," so called, were not hostile to education in this case because they were "at the bottom of the heap" (Miller, 1967, p. 9)—the exact reverse. In fact, in this and in a previous study on resistance to literacy (Quigley, 1987), these adults never devalued the dream of obtaining an education. "Education" was an absolute goal for all of the subjects. They dropped out of "school"—and repeated this pattern in "adult school." From their perspective, school had failed them again but education was still their life's goal. Mezirow (1990) says we are locked in our own histories and we tend to repeat them unless we experience a perspective transformation—a poignant observation for these students, and for practitioners and researchers alike. In short, what learners believe and what they see are key to how they will perform.

How can we improve recruitment in this area of demand? Ask how our program, institution, and professional goals are being perceived by the target audience. Try to find out what learner past experiences may mitigate against certain delivery and teaching models. To enhance recruitment and retention in the low-latent-no demand area we need to learn all we can about the possible dispositional barriers. We may then see new institutional barriers which we were previously blind to. In general, we need to "de-school" our adult education recruitment in this demand area by avoiding images or goals which potential learners may associate with past schooling. We may need to de-school our programs once learners enter, based on their perceptions. Since education is the absolute goal for so many here, it may be useful to aim our recruitment at educational outcomes—relevance, intangible value, recognition, immediate benefits, success rates and the true nature of our program.

Thus, the first step is to see self-evaluation and attitudes towards education/schooling in the Chain-of-response model as two separate issues through the eyes of the learner and to use these eyes to take a more critical look at what we are offering, and why. How can we enhance retention in this demand area? Again, there is much to be understood if we can see our programs through the lived experiences of our learners. In general, since the counselor in this study was a trusted confidant back in school and the one clear bridge to literacy in this study, strengthening the first-point-of-contact at intake is the first recommendation for reluctant learners, whether we are discussing literacy or other areas of adult education. Gaining more information about past schooling experiences, past friends, past teachers, learners' interactions with past counselors, past support levels in and out of school, ascertaining the perceived relevance and challenge-level potential learners hold of our programs, and applying this information to develop and support options for the "at-risk" reluctant learner, are all a critical part of enhancing retention in this demand area. For reluctant learners, a more recent study I conducted (1993), to be discussed next, indicated that in-program options such as smaller classes, team supported (counselor and teachers working together) and one-on-one tutoring with tutors or peers can all be effective classroom practices.

Where do under-resourced programs get the time to mount team approaches, create small group teaching, or develop one-on-one tutoring systems? The premise is that potential dropouts often require more attention than those who will persist. Rather than allot time equally, realign resource time according to need. Persisters may well respond to peer teaching or group projects—freeing teacher time for the more intensive attention the at-risk require. Persisters need very little counselor time. Perhaps focus more follow-up time on reluctant learners from the beginning. As for adding small group and one-on-one tutoring supplements, one of the centers mentioned here added one-on-one tutoring using volunteers in the evening. These are suggestions which hold potential for virtually any structured program in adult education. Are such approaches more expensive? Compared to the cost of attrition, smaller classes may look attractive as part of your program's next budget submission. Accountability sometimes argues for options.

If we fail in our retention and recruitment efforts, is there any point in trying again? Despite the prevailing tendency to assume that dropouts have "no motivation"—73% in this study said they would go back to ABE if asked. The majority were already registered in one-on-one tutoring or were pursing this option actively. The dropouts were disappointed because ABE lacked challenge but the notion that they are "lost" is incorrect. There is a strong desire for education among adults, even if it sometimes means ambivalence toward school.

Thus, when dealing with either recruitment or retention among those who come from low-latent-no demand areas, it might be the case that the "unmotivated" hold a higher belief in education and higher self-expectancy than those who get more of the teacher/peer attention and persist. Common sense together with a growing body of new models/analytical typologies, such as expectancy-valence, and discussions on the issue of factors impacting culturally diverse groups (e.g., Briscoe & Ross, 1989) can give us the tools to conduct more effective recruitment and retention in this more difficult setting.

However, what if students are clearly negative towards our programs? The reflexive turn which leads to the negative area of demand has convinced me that some potential learners avoid, indeed resist, programs. There are many adults (Beder & Quigley, 1990) who constitute this area of negative demand—an area many say is the most difficult to work in and, sadly, an area where many institutions apparently believe it is not worth the effort or investment.

RECRUITMENT AND RETENTION IN AREAS OF NEGATIVE DEMAND

According to Beder (1991), in the "negative" demand area, "potential learners actually avoid participation" (p. 51). Here, it becomes essential to "analyze the sources of the market's resistance; whether they lie largely in the area of *beliefs* about the offering, in the *values* touched upon by the offering, in the raw *feelings* engendered by the offering, or in the cost of acquiring the offering" (Kotler, 1975, p. 82). Almost anyone who has tried to work with learners who evidently avoid participation—from community based education, to corrections education, to groups who choose not to attend higher education, to small and large groups in work place settings—he or she will readily identify with this recruitment and retention issue. Few areas have more myths based out of "common sense" and less theoretical underpinning across the planning continuum.

A fuller understanding of negative resistance to education is being developed in the area of school education (e.g., Willis, 1977; Giroux, 1983; Fine, 1982; Stuckey, 1991). In adult education, Beder (1989), Fingeret (1983, 1985), Zeigahn, (1992); and Gowen (1992) are a few who have dealt with this area. The work I have conducted (Quigley, 1987, 1990, 1992, 1993) has also attempted to add findings and bridge theory from the sociology of education into the field of adult literacy education, and adult education more generally (Beder, 1991). The topic of resistance to education and now, adult education, is an emerging area of research which is important across the adult research and practice span. It helps explain why, for instance, professionals may choose not to participate in their own continuing professional development (Cervero, 1988; Murphy, 1986), why minorities may avoid or be singularly unsuccessful in higher education (Briscoe and Ross, 1989), why the incarcerated may reject training designed for their "own" benefit (Collins, 1987), and why some undereducated adults in work settings may conduct themselves in tacitly hostile ways to offered programs (Gowen, 1992). On a larger scale, it helps explain why, after over a decade of media campaigning, it is estimated that a mere 8% of those eligible participate in adult literacy education (Pugsley, 1990). It begins to give us some insight as to why figures of low literacy are now estimated to be as high as 90 million (Kirsch & Jungeblut, 1986). And, theory growing up in the negative demand area opens a window where we can gain a new, critical perspective on our programs, assumptions and, as discussed above, a reflexive turn for ourselves and our institutions. Studied as a rich source of critical discourse, the field itself can become more constructively self-critical and reinvent itself in this critical area.

It is in negative demand, I would argue, that "common sense" and much of our participation research fails to help in books such as this because both are typically founded on a framework and experiences involving participants—those already in programs. If we are to understand resistance and reluctance to remain in programs, it is essential that we build more research on resisters and those who have chosen to leave. As Murphy states: "The range of truth is wider than what the dominant voices say, and excluded voices may be among the most creative and important voices in any social setting" (1986, p. 173).

As an illustration of how researcher/practitioner frameworks can affect outcomes, it was seen above how earlier literature on participation viewed "The lower-lowers ... [as] actually hostile to education because it conflicts with basic values arising out of their class position at the bottom of the heap" (p. 9). But, consider another interpretation from early *literacy* literature on the same issue. In a meta-analysis, Anderson and Niemi (1970) cited the many anecdotal reports on who illiterates are and what various programs had done to reach the target population. They concluded not that illiterates are "hostile to education," but that ABE programs can actually preserve "the values of the middle class, [and] lack sufficient flexibility to function effectively with the disadvantaged" (p. 60). This observation on imposed values and program inflexibility was dramatically reported when Willis (1977) published his ethnomethodological studies on the "lads" in English schools. Throughout their young lives, these school students had seen "valued reality" as the factory floor labor of their uncles, brothers, sisters and parents. The pretentious middle class world advocated in school was simply worthy of a "laff." With work in the United States on schooling (e.g., Apple, 1982) and a growing body of literature on resistance in the sociology of education (e.g., Fine, 1982; Giroux, 1983), new insight into student resistance to normative school education has begun to arise.

Bringing this closer to reflexive turn on an individual level, while most of us will respond with some level of resistance to mandated or coercive educational activities—especially when we are expected to be part of a "majority view" which is in conflict with our own values, experiences or beliefs—it is important to note that some nonparticipating adults have experienced strong "moral and political indignation" (Giroux, 1983, p. 289) towards the very values assumed by schooling. From the perspective of dispositional barriers, they rejected the entire system of schooling earlier and are not ready as adults to buy into "schooling" again (Cervero & Fitzpatrick, 1990). The discussion of critical pedagogy and Resistance Theory (Bourdieu, 1984; Willis, 1977; Giroux, 1983) provides a fuller theoretical frame of resistance as cultural, political and economic hegemony, but my own recent research suggests that resistant adults are not always angry at school systems. They value education highly and demonstrate both "hard" and "soft" resistance to schooling, as discussed below. Our challenge in negative demand is to engage resistant adults on the basis of their perceptions about us, as will now be discussed.

RELUCTANCE AND RESISTANCE TO PROGRAMS

For purposes of this part of the discussion, dispositions which arise within negative demand will be presented as either a "soft" or "hard" resistance to what appears to be a return to unacceptable "schooling." A "soft" reaction here means reentry to adult education with reluctance, skepticism, and an anticipation one will quit. For retention, there is too often an unrecognized gap between what the programmers/instructors perceive and seek and what their learners perceive and seek from the same program. An example is found in a study of ABE programs across North Carolina (Fingeret & Danin, 1991). It was found that the goals held by learners—such as the ability to read and work with their own children—were widely different from the goals their teachers—such as creating better parents or workers or citizens (Fingeret, 1985). Thus, part of the explanation for attrition in an adult program can be a "soft" resistance, or demonstrated "reluctance" to stay. It is estimated that this group may be as large as one-third of the entire dropout population for adult basic education (Quigley, 1993). "Hard" resistance is closer to flat refusal to attend, as seen in the work of Willis (1977) and work I have done (Quigley, 1987, 1990). Taken in a larger sense, hard and soft resistance may be endemic across an entire workplace, creating a virtual culture of refusal or high dropout in certain factories, hospitals, prisons, military units or community colleges.

Regardless of the setting or level of education, for those whose quitting is not satisfactorily explained by either situational or institutional barriers, it becomes necessary to consider the complexities of dispositional barriers. Dropouts may in fact be signaling what is unacceptable in a program. One example of this is research on a nontraditional literacy program in New York where it was found that learners had previously left traditional ABE programs to join this new, nontraditional one because they were "bored and unable to learn from commercial workbooks and large classes" (Fingeret & Danin, 1991, p. 8). Again, in literacy programs in cities such as Pittsburgh, as many as 80 percent of literacy students have been reported dropping out of tutoring programs in the first eight months because of reactions such as, "a problem with the instructor" (Staff, 1991, p. 4). Other factors remain to be explored in resistance to our programs. In a recent study conducted by Quigley and Holsinger (1993), it was found that commonly used reading texts in literacy and ABE programs across the United States contained numerous examples of sexism, racism and socioeconomic stereotyping. In fact, they were the ones who suggested the study be done. This is one of the few studies of content of adult texts in our field and we need to examine other texts in other areas of the field if schooling and its inherent values is such a deterrent to resisters.

Despite advocacy for program and classroom change in the recent literacy literature (e.g., Fingeret & Jurmo, 1989) and calls in the mainstream adult education literature to "Engage adult students in program governance [and] establish and use structures for mutual planning" (Cookson, 1989, p. 108), it would seem that adult educators often want to gravitate to the very schooling models which were used to teach them. Despite the desire to enhance critical thinking and self-reliance in learners (Brookfield, 1991), there is a gravitational pull away from a critical examination of texts, methods and mutual decision making. This pull frequently occurs despite the irony that, through hard and soft resistance, nonparticipants and dropouts may be telling us (with their feet) what is still unacceptable, inappropriate or irrelevant.

TOWARD A FRAMEWORK FOR NEGATIVE DEMAND RESEARCH AND PRACTICE

How can we understand and work with those who are hard resisters to our programs? In the recent studies which I conducted in Pittsburgh (Quigley, 1992, 1993) involving adults who knew they were eligible to attend ABE programs but refused to do so, we began the work wondering if interviewees would be hostile toward education and ourselves. We also expected to hear: "no transportation," "no child care," "poverty" and similar situational problems as reasons for not attending programs since it is so common in the literacy literature. However, through in-depth interviewing, it was found that beneath situational/institutional problems lay levels of deep anger and profound guilt. We saw a world highly influenced by past schooling in conflict with the education promises we make.

Like the earlier study, every subject stated education was important. Many claimed they "should" go to ABE or literacy centers. However, none said they wanted to "return to school." Interviewers explored resisters' views of both ABE and past experiences with (1) teachers, (2) peers, (3) course content and (4) school/ ABE environments. It was found that course material was never singled out as particularly difficult by subjects themselves. Most considered this the "best part" of school and ABE. The single point where subject content was identified as problematic was when it was perceived as prejudiced or when culture, in this case black culture, was omitted. In this study, three groups emerged which may form a framework for negative demand research and practice.

Personal/Emotive Resisters

Here, teachers and students' peers (respectively) back in school were the most significant variables in the decision to quit school. The later resistance to literacy programs was highly influenced by personal trauma back in school. They felt betrayed by individuals within systems—not by systems themselves. They did not see themselves as victims of systems but as the scapegoat for individuals. As adults, they now live with a deep resentment towards certain teachers and peers, firm in their decision not to experience "school" again. They saw school as "too big" and lacking personal teacher/administrator attention. Although course content was considered "interesting"—teachers were not. Despite much of the resistance theory mentioned earlier, here, neither the macro-system nor the actual acquisition of knowledge were real issues. Lack of consideration, attention, and empathy were the real issues. An awareness and sensitivity both to the adult and to their culture, their values, their aspirations, were being asked for. Rebuilding trust denied in school was more important to personal resisters than any technology, access, or ideology.

It is suggested if we are to work in what is a negative demand area of programming, we need to ask what learners' past experiences have been and, if potential learners are perceived of as emotive/personal resisters, we need small classes, culturally sensitive teachers, peers whom they can trust to treat them with respect, and teachers and staff who will be willing to lend support. The atmosphere needs to be nonthreatening, low competitive and informed by learners' past experiences. However, not all who resist were of this sub-group.

Ideological/Cultural Resisters

A second group emerged which was also indelibly affected by past schooling. Here, both males and females resisted programs primarily out of an ideological clash between values and culture. Trust in "the system" was lost. For the African Americans in this group, school was recalled as a "white man's world." The curricula "taught me a philosophy of another man's society," said one interviewee. Consistent with research by Fine (1982), both black and white subjects were exceptionally sensitive to perceived systemic injustice. A White interviewee described how she had to change schools: "I hated the new school and quit after three months. Who gave them the authority to ruin my education?"

Looking back in anger, the issues for programmers working in negative demand areas may mean learning if the audience is resistant to our systems as representative symbols. If they are, as another interviewee put it, we must assure potential learners that opportunities will have "Something to do with my life." For ideological/cultural resisters, programs need to contain a high degree of learner input into the content and structure of the program. One-on-one meetings or advisory groups may help. Continuous formative evaluations of the program and teacher should be implemented. Dropouts need to be followed up. Here, the challenge is to rebuild a trust in the delivery system itself, not merely in the individuals involved. But, above all, success in delivering the kind of educational experience which all in this study dreamt of will mean recognizing adults have valuable opinions and experiences to share, if skillfully asked.

Older Resisters and Irrelevance of Schooling

For respondents in this study over the age of 50, ABE classes were of little interest. For this group, learning was not immediately associated with negative schooling; actually, most felt nostalgia for past schooling. "Listening and doing a lot of things" was described as "the best teacher" by one 55-year-old subject. These interviewees felt that they had learned for survival throughout their lives and there was now little point in returning to school: "I'm never going to go any place else or do anything else" said one older interviewee. For many older learners, the focus now is to "Push my daughter ... and my youngest son ... to complete school," as one put it. Yet, as with all respondents, education remained of vital importance.

If nonparticipating adults make choices based on their lived experiences like any other adult, we must allow the possibility that hard and soft resistance may be at work among those who do not participate and are choosing to quit programs once enrolled. Fingeret (1984) has observed, "If we do not learn to work with them, many illiterate adults will continue to refuse to work with us" (p. 145). In the negative demand area, whether it be corporate training settings, continuing professional education settings, community-based settings, corrections, or literacy, the issue is not whether potential learners want an "education" or not. In these studies, resisters and reluctant learners neither opposed education nor learning. The primary issue was the construct of "schooling."

CONCLUSION

Educators use the terms "lifelong education" and "lifelong learning" in this field a great deal. However, they often seem to be referring to those in the high-medium demand area when we use this term. The fresh hope which arises as we move across demand areas to resistance and the negative demand area is the overwhelming evidence that adults exhibiting soft and hard resistance to our programs actually value education, seek learning opportunities, and sincerely want to share their ideas and feelings for improving adult programs. We in this field constantly use terms such as "andragogy," "self directed," "critical pedagogy" and "critical reflectivity." We seek new models and say adults have the right to be involved in the determination of their own learning and—through this involvement—in the more resolute determination of their own future. The conflict between schooling and education which grows out of the Cross Chain of Response Model forces us to consider, reconsider, and, through reflexive turn, it can ultimately bring us to continually reinvent policies, systems, curricula, delivery models and educational methods. Moving from high-medium demand, to low-latent-no demand, to negative demand, it is clear that the views and dispositions of learners become increasingly important in the search for more effective approaches to our programming. And, in pursuing such a path, the common sense/

experiential side of judgement needs to be informed by theory and research. When we self-critically examine our personal and professional beliefs and values through reflexive development and thereby make informed new choices, it not only becomes possible for us to advance in our own professional growth and development, but also to advance our entire field.

As we enter a turbulent post-modern era it is suggested that the negative demand area is where our most meaningful feedback can be found and the frontier where our most significant contributions to educational knowledge and society can be made. As a student of mine expressed it, "Adult education is like a staircase. With every step up, I can see further."

QUESTIONS FOR STUDY AND DISCUSSION

1. The concept of *reflexive turn* has been presented in this chapter. Assess its theoretical significance in terms of what it adds to your understanding of the complexities of the recruitment and retention process. Assess the value of this concept with respect to your own professional development. Assess its practical significance in terms of your own programming efforts to help prospective participants to learn about your programs, to decide to participate, and to decide to persist until the programs have completed.
2. How would you describe the perceptions, beliefs, and motivations of the prospective participants you would like to have participate in your programs? To what extent does your description reflect an awareness of the three demand situations (high-to-medium demand, low-latent to no demand, and negative demand) described in this chapter?
3. To what extent do your current programming practices (including specific recruitment and retention strategies) represent, for your prospective program participants, a "clash between ideology and culture"? How might you change these strategies to more effectively serve the types of adults whom your programs currently serve? How might you change these strategies to more effectively serve the types of adults whom your programs could be designed to serve?

ENDNOTES

1. This generic term was used in Canada to describe treaty, nontreaty, nonstatus Indians and Metis people who are of Indian and white ancestry. Today, the terms "aboriginal" and "indigenous" people would also be used.
2. Metis refers to mixed ancestry.

REFERENCES

Anderson, D., & Niemi, J. (1970). *Adult education and the disadvantaged adult.* Syracuse University, NY: ERIC Clearinghouse on Adult Education.

Apple, M. (1982). *Education and power.* Boston: Routledge and Kegan Paul.

Argyris, C., Putman, R., & Smith, D. (1985). *Action science.* San Francisco: Jossey-Bass.

Baldwin, J. (1991, November). Why did they drop out? *GED profiles: Adults in transition, 4,* 1–7.

Beder, H. (1989). *Reasons for nonparticipation among Iowa adults who are eligible for ABE.* Des Moines, IA: Dept. of Education.

Beder, H. (1991). *Adult literacy: Issues for policy and practice.* Malabar, FL: Krieger.

Beder, H., & Quigley, A. (1990). Beyond the classroom. *Adult Learning, 1*(5), 19–21.

Boshier, R. (1977). Motivational orientations revisited: Life space motives and the educational participation scale. *Adult Education, 27,* 89–115.

Brookfield, S. (1991). *The skillful teacher.* San Francisco: Jossey-Bass.

Boone, E. (1985). *Developing programs in adult education.* Englewood Cliffs, NJ: Prentice-Hall.

Bourdieu, P. (1984). *Distinction: A social critique of the judgement of taste.* Cambridge: Harvard University Press.

Boyle, P. (1981). *Planning better programs.* New York: McGraw-Hill.

Briscoe, D., & Ross, J. (1989). Racial and ethnic minorities and adult education. In S. B. Merriam & P. M. Cunningham (Eds.). *Handbook of adult and continuing education.* San Francisco: Jossey-Bass.

Carp, A., Peterson, R., & Roelfs, P. (1974). Adult learning interests and experiences. In K. P. Cross, J. R. Valley, and Associates (Eds.). *Planning non-traditional programs.* San Francisco: Jossey-Bass.

Cervero, R. (1988). *Effective practice in continuing professional education.* San Francisco: Jossey-Bass.

Cervero, R., & Fitzpatrick, T. (1990). The enduring effects of family role and schooling on participation in adult education. *American Journal of Education, 99*(1), 77–94.

Collins, M. (1987). *Competence in adult education: A new perspective.* Lanham, MD: University Press of America.

Cookson P. (1989). (Ed.). *Recruiting and retaining adult students.* San Francisco: Jossey-Bass.

Courtney, S. (1993). *Why adults learn: Towards a theory of participation in adult education.* New York: Routledge.

Cross, P. (1981). *Adults as learners.* San Francisco: Jossey-Bass.

Dewey, J. (1938). *Experience and Education.* New York: Macmillan.

Fine, M. (1982). *Examining inequity: View from urban schools.* Unpublished manu-script, University of Pennsylvania, Philadelphia.

Fingeret, A. (1984). *Adult literacy education: Current and future directions.* (Contract No. NIE-C-40081-0035). Ohio: The Ohio State University National Center for Research in Vocational Education.

Fingeret, A. (1985). *North Carolina adult basic education instructional program evalua-tion.* Raleigh, NC.: Department of Adult and Community Education, North Carolina State University.

Fingeret, A. (1983). Social network: A new perspective on independence and illiterate adults. *Adult Education Quarterly, 33*(3), 133–146.

Fingeret, A., & Danin, S. (1991). "They really put a hurtin' on my brain": *Learning and literacy volunteers of New York City. Executive Summary.* Durham, NC: Literacy South.

Fingeret, A., & Jurmo, P. (Eds.). (1989). *Participatory literacy education.* San Fran-cisco: Jossey-Bass.

Freire, P. (1970). *Pedagogy of the oppressed.* New York: Seabury Press.

Giroux, H. (1983). *Theory and resistance in education.* South Hadley, MA: Bergin and Garvey.

Gowen, S. G. (1992). *The politics of workplace literacy: A case study.* New York: Teachers College Press.

Griffith, W. S. (1989). Recruiting and retaining adult students: A marketing perspective. In P. S. Cookson (Ed.), *Recruiting and retaining adult students.* San Francisco: Jossey-Bass.

Hayes, E. (1988). A typology of low literate adults based on perceptions of deterrents to participation in Adult Basic Education. *Adult Education Quar-terly, 39*(1), 1–10.

Husserl, E. (1964). *The idea of phenomenology.* (W. Alston & G. Nakhnikan, Trans.). The Hague: Matinus Nijoff.

Johnstone, J., & Rivera, R. (1965). *Volunteers for learning.* Chicago: Aldine.

Kerlinger, F. (1973). *Foundations of behavioral research.* New York: Holt, Rinehart and Winston.

Kirsch, I. S., & Jungeblut, A. J. (1986). *Literacy: Profiles of America's young adults.* Princeton, NJ: Educational Testing Service.

Knowles, M. (1980). *The modern practice of adult education.* (2nd Ed.). New York: Cambridge Books.

Kotler, P. (1975). *Marketing for non-profit organizations.* Englewood Cliffs, NJ: Prentice-Hall.

Lewin, K. (1938). *The conceptual representation of the measurement of psychological forces.* Durham, NC: Duke University Press.

Mezirow, J. (Ed.). (1990). *Fostering critical reflection in adulthood: A guide to transfor-mative and anticipatory learning.* San Francisco: Jossey-Bass.

Miller, H. (1967). *Participation of adults in education: A forcefield analysis.* Chicago: Center for the Study of Liberal Education for Adults.

Murphy, S. (1986). Resistance in the professions: Adult education and new paradigms of power. Unpublished doctoral dissertation. Department of Leadership and Education Policy Studies, De Kalb, Il: Northern Illinois University.

Pratt, D. (1988). Andragogy as a relational construct. *Adult Education Quarterly*, *38*(3), 160–181.

Pugsley, R. (1990). *Vital statistics: Who is served by the adult education program?* Washington, DC: Division of Adult Education and Literacy, United States Department of Education.

Quigley, A. (1987). Learning to work with them: Analyzing nonparticipation in adult basic education through resistance theory. *Adult Literacy and Basic Education*, *11*(2), 63–70.

Quigley, A. (1990). Hidden logic: Reproduction and resistance in adult literacy and adult basic education. *Adult Education Quarterly*, *40*(2), 103–115.

Quigley, A. (1992). *Understanding and overcoming resistance to adult literacy education.* Institute for the Study of Adult Literacy: Pennsylvania State University.

Quigley, A. (1993). *Retaining reluctant adults in adult literacy programs: A multivariate analysis.* Institute for the Study of Adult Literacy: Pennsylvania State University.

Quigley, A., & Holsinger, E. (1993). "Happy consciousness": Ideology and hidden curricula in literacy education. *Adult Education Quarterly*, *44*(1), 17–34.

Reissman, F. (1962). *The culturally deprived child.* New York: Harper and Row.

Rubenson, K. (1978). Participation in recurrent education: Problems relating to the undereducated and underprivileged. In C. Stalford (Ed.), *Adult learning needs and the demand for lifelong learning.* National Institute for Education, Washington, DC.

Scanlan, C. (1986). *Deterrents to participation: An adult education dilemma.* Columbus, OH: ERIC Clearinghouse on Adult, Career, and Vocational Education.

Schön, D. (1983). *The reflective practitioner.* New York: Basic Books.

Sork, T., & Caffarella, R. (1989). Planning programs for adults. In S. B. Merriam & P. M. Cunningham (Eds.). *Handbook of adult and continuing education.* San Francisco: Jossey-Bass.

Spiegelberg, H. (1960). *The essentials of the phenomenological method.* The Hague: Matinus Nijhoff.

Stanage, S. (1987). *Adult education and phenomenological research.* Malabar, FL: Kreiger.

Stanage, S. (1989, April). *Phenomenological methods.* Paper presented at the Critical Theory Preconference to the Adult Education Research Conference, University of Wisconsin, Madison, WI.

Staff. (1991). Yet, on the more dismal side. *PAACE News*, *15*(2), p. 5.

Strother, G., & Klus, J. (1982). *Administration of continuing education.* Belmont, CA: Wadsworth.

Stuckey, J. (1991). *The violence of literacy.* Portsmouth, NH: Boynton/Cook.

Van Tilburg, E., & DuBois, J. (1989). Literacy students' perceptions of successful participation in adult education: A cross cultural approach through expectancy valence. Paper presented at the Adult Education Research Conference, University of Wisconsin, Madison.

Willis, P. (1977). *Learning to labor: How working class kids get working class jobs.* New York: Columbia University Press.

Wlodkowski, R. J. (1985). *Enhancing adult motivation to learn.* San Francisco: Jossey-Bass.

Zeigahn, L., (1992). Learning, literacy, and participation: Sorting out Priorities. *Adult Education Quarterly*, *1*(43), 30–50.

17

Adding Value:
Program Financing
for Program Planners

Karen E. Watkins and Thomas L. Sechrest

ABSTRACT

Although few individuals enter the field of adult education and training because they love to prepare budgets, all need to do so at one time or another. Whether it is a proposed budget as part of a grant, a request for funding for a voluntary literacy program, or a formal budget process in a community education or corporate training department; the budgeting and financing of adult education requires careful planning. The ability to mount a strong defense for a program requires accurate analyses of both the costs and the benefits of that program. Ultimately, the goal of these programs is to add value. In this chapter, adult educators and trainers learn how to determine the value-added of their programs in financial terms.

ASSESSMENT

1. Do you now prepare budgets for an adult education or training program?
2. Do you defend these programs using cost-benefit analysis, break even analysis, or cost effectiveness analysis?
3. Can you identify direct costs? indirect costs? fixed costs? return on investment?
4. What are six sources of financing for your education or training program?

KEY TERMS

Cost   The amount of money required to develop, deliver, and evaluate a specific training and education program or activity. Costs are usually classified as direct or indirect.

Direct costs   Direct costs are expenses which are actually paid to support specific programs or activities. They include educator salaries, participant salaries in some cases, travel and per diem, consultant fees, materials, classroom and facility rentals, and any other charges which are *associated* with a program or activity. (Salaries are usually calculated on an hourly or daily basis and often are averaged to determine costs.)

Indirect costs   Indirect costs are expenses which are necessary for a program or activity but which cannot be directly associated with it. Indirect costs include *overhead*, such as management and administrative support, use of copying machines, payroll and accounting services, payments for office space, furniture, utilities and telephone charges, and *fringe benefits*, like vacation and sick leave, health insurance, pension coverage, child care and other nonattributable employee compensation. NOTE: Some accounting systems consider fringe benefits to be part of direct costs. Check your organization's system so that all of your calculations are consistent with its design. Indirect costs are often calculated as a percentage of direct costs.

Fixed costs   Expenses charged to a program or activity which would occur whether or not the program or activity takes place (e.g., salaries, office rental).

Variable costs   Expenses that change depending on the specific requirements of a program or activity (e.g., travel, materials, consultants).

Total cost   The sum of direct and indirect costs (also called *Full cost*).

Unit cost   The total cost divided by the number of participants, or the number of participant hours, or any other measure utilized by the accounting system under which the program or activity takes place.

Benefits   Benefits are the net *results* of a specific program or activity, usually quantified in monetary terms for accounting or analysis purposes.

Cost-benefit analysis A procedure in which the total cost of developing, delivering, and evaluating a specific training and education program or activity is compared with the net results of that program or activity quantified in monetary terms, to determine its economic efficiency.

Cost-effectiveness analysis A cost-benefit analysis without monetary quantification of results. This process enables a decision-maker to compare specific programs and activities with others in relation to overall goals and objectives. It is helpful when the monetary value of results is difficult to measure.

Break-even analysis A calculation through which the point where total revenues equal total expenses can be determined. It is helpful in making a decision about conducting a program or activity in which a significant investment may have been made but where potential enrollment does not appear sufficient to conduct the program or activity.

Return on investment (ROI) Though not usually thought of in terms of training and education programs and activities, the ROI is simply the benefits (or savings) attributable to a specific program or activity divided by that program's total costs. For a thorough assessment of this concept with case examples of how ROI has been determined, see Philips (1994).

Budget A plan for income and expenses for a specific program or activity (as well as for the entire organization) for a given period of time, usually a fiscal year or academic year.

INTRODUCTION

Roger Cameron was excited. He had completed his first quarter as the training manager for Abcon Industries, and the evaluations showed that his courses were well received and helpful to the managers in this growing technology firm. He had scheduled a meeting with Charise Evans, the executive vice president for human resources, to lay out his plans for a series of new seminars which would provide dynamic skills enhancement to managers, helping them to respond to the quickly changing issues they faced. Ms. Evans had given him the go-ahead to develop his strategy after having read his initial proposal. Roger had drawn on all of his creative skills to design seminars which would meet specific objectives and address the unique way in which the management team interacted. He had also planned a presentation about the seminars which was both entertaining and informative, using computer graphics and actual videotape footage from previous training sessions. Here was his first chance to really impress his new employer, and he had pulled out all the stops!

When Roger turned up the lights at the end of his presentation, he was delighted to see that Ms. Evans had a broad smile on her face. She was going to approve the proposal! "Tell me, Roger, what is all of this going to cost?" she asked. "Well," Roger replied, "I figure that we can probably find a hotel meeting room right here in town for a reasonable rate. If you add the cost of coffee and any incidental expenses, I would guess that these seminars would cost Abcon about $300 a day." Ms. Evans's smile turned into an executive chuckle. "I'll tell you what, Mr. Cameron," she said as she rose and quickly walked out of the conference room, "you come back to me when you can talk about the business side of training as well as you do the education side of training and then I'll try to decide whether or not I can support your proposal."

For many involved in the training and education of adults, this scenario is not far from the reality of daily professional life. Steeped in theoretical constructs about how people learn, the business pressures so critical to managers seem to escape even the most aware educators. The financial aspects of educational activities are often dealt with only superficially. Proposed annual budgets are "worked up" and submitted, and what survives from closed-door negotiations in which educators are frequently not included, is routinely accepted. We've heard it said: "The real task is to work within the resources given and to provide meaningful learning experiences for those who need our services! Financial planning and record keeping are to be endured as a burden required by the organization which is ancillary to our special mission. It should be patently obvious that educational activities are worth whatever it takes to pay for them. Why does the organization make us beg every year for a pittance when a greater need is being met? And why are our budgets the first victims of cost cutting?"

Yet, think of it this way. Training and education are big business. The American Society for Training and Development estimates that more than one hundred billion dollars is spent every year to support training and education activities for adults. Figures like these make even the most diehard supporter realize that the eye of business management will look most acutely at such expenditures. The role of practitioners should include being able to recognize and communicate that training and education exist primarily to contribute to the accomplishment of someone's goals and objectives. Whatever the environment, public or private, profit or nonprofit, open or closed, training and education in any organization must produce results. And results include financial aspects as well as programmatic ones. "Finance is the universal language of business, and Human Resources managers must learn to speak it" (Tracy, 1990). Even when adult educators seek to meet the needs of individuals, those individuals hope to get their money's worth.

Although many educators are comfortable working with somewhat loosely defined concepts such as needs assessment, employee development, empowerment, values and so forth, they blanch at the specificity of cost-benefit analysis, return on investment, and program planning and budgeting systems. Direct costs, indirect costs, overhead, and fiscal management represent concepts that are thought best left to the accountants. "Just tell me the bottom line: how much money do I have? I will work within those figures." This simplistic view denies any real comprehension of the financial impact of education and training activities. Educators must be able to do more than stay abreast of the latest tips and techniques for use in the classroom. They have to know business basics. The process of analyzing how educational activities can contribute to individual and organizational success and how much they cost can be completed only by taking the time to weigh the financial impact of offering adult education or training versus not offering it. Results may need to be quantified in financial as well as in educational or performance terms before funding may be granted. Knowing how to find and make efficient use of financial resources will enable us to more effectively serve adult learners.

To begin with, this chapter will define common terms used in financial systems. Then we will look at how educators can better comprehend and use such concepts as budgeting and cost-benefit analysis; how they can evaluate performance from a financial perspective; and how they can develop financial policies for the training and education of adults.

SOURCES OF FINANCIAL SUPPORT

Almost as important to financial awareness as the precise terms which serve as the framework for understanding are the sources of funds which provide the necessary support to programs and activities. Regardless of the nature of the organization, sources of funding can be classified into about six categories (Dahl, 1980; Knowles, 1980; Strother & Klus, 1982). They are known as (1) parent organization subsidy, (2) participant fees, (3) auxiliary enterprises and sales, (4) grants and contracts and gifts, (5) federal, state and local government tax funds, and (6) miscellaneous income.

Parent Organization Subsidy. Here, funding for training and education activities is received from the parent organization as part of an internal budget mechanism by which all its activities are funded. For example, employees who attend internal training classes or public seminars have their educational expenses supported by their employer, either through funding of an internal training operation or through paying the invoice for externally procured training. This is one of the most common sources of support for training and education programs. Usually, specific training needs are indicated and estimated costs are proposed and requested. During the internal budget planning and allocating process, these requests are considered and certain dollar amounts allocated for a specific budget cycle.

Participant Support. Participants are charged tuition or fees for attending programs or receiving services. Some companies even assess a fee for services provided internally, which is "charged back" to the requesting unit. Most participant tuition and fees are generated by programs which are available to a large population, such as public seminars, or courses at a community college. Organizations make these programs and services available, often marketing them through catalogs or brochures, and persons who attend those programs pay a charge for attending. Tuition and fees must cover all expenses and provide a profit margin for some organizations. For others, additional funding is necessary to augment the income from tuition and fees.

Auxiliary Enterprises and Sales. Funds can be generated in various ways to support training and education activities. Often, internally produced programs have wider application and, if successfully marketed, can be a source of income for an organization. Likewise, books, videotapes, support materials, or consulting and training services can be marketed to others for a negotiated fee. For those facilities with food services or room accommodations, additional income may be generated. An organization may even be able to underwrite its internal costs by making its programs and services available to others. Additionally, if internal capabilities are recognized as a potential source of income, management can plan for the developmental costs of programs and services to be recaptured after internal needs are met. An example might be a study course for a certification examination conducted by a professional association. The course is developed and presented for a fee. In addition to course fees, income may also be generated by selling guides and review materials for self-study.

Grants and Contracts and Gifts. These are available from businesses, foundations, trade and professional associations, labor unions, interest groups, philanthropic organizations, and individuals for specialized purposes. Some venture capitalists may also help underwrite developmental costs for materials, programs, and services which have potential for generating profitable income. In addition, some businesses will seek short-term project assistance from external sources. Individuals or organizations may make gifts, e.g., alumni donations or support for public television. In the case of gifts from individuals, "matching support" is sometimes available from their employers. Gifts from organizations can be used in a number of ways, some requiring recognition of the sponsor, others available with no restrictions.

Grants for training and education activities are available primarily to nonprofit organizations. The grant procedure is similar in most cases. A "request for proposal" for programs or services or some other notice will be widely circulated, and individuals and organizations interested in providing such programs and services will submit an application. After a selection process which varies with each requesting organization, a contract or grant document is executed which provides for specific payments when services are provided.

Federal, State and Local Government Tax Funds. These funds are used to support training and education activities for employees of those entities, and are often awarded for specific programs developed for the public good. These include job training programs, vocational and industrial education, consulting, research and development, formula and discretionary projects, and both broad-scale and specific endeavors solicited by individual units of government and paid for with tax funds. Again, notice of availability of funds is usually given in any one of a number of ways by the sponsoring unit of government, and "requests for proposals" are disseminated to potential grant recipients. Upon review and selection, programs and activities are conducted and providers are paid according to the terms of their agreement. One major source of such funds is the Job Training Partnership Act administered by the U.S. Department of Labor, which provides funds to states for training and retraining of displaced or unemployed workers. Vigilance is a key factor for identifying, applying for, and receiving support from government sources.

Miscellaneous Income. This category covers all other possible sources. Miscellaneous sources include endowments, royalty income, in-kind contributions (such as free use of classroom space), and other income-generating possibilities not classifiable above.

Education and training activities are supported in a number of different ways. With creativity, adult educators are able to piece together sources of support and to identify financial support from a broad array of contributors. One national conference we know of was financed through participant fees; corporations which underwrote meals, receptions, and speakers; a foundation which underwrote financial rewards for a recognition ceremony; three foundations which provided overall conference support; and an airline which offered discount travel! Any individual involved in the training and education of adults should be aware of all these types of sources, and responsive to the requirements of each when funding opportunities are available.

UNDERSTANDING FINANCIAL CONCEPTS

In this chapter, a simple approach to financial matters will be taken, involving common terms, suggesting methods that can be easily used, and encouraging broad understanding of financial concepts. Additional resources are suggested in the reference section which can serve individual readers who desire a more detailed discussion of financial matters, especially as they relate to the training and education of adults.

Essential to conceptual understanding is that planning and budgeting are inseparable. Even if the extent of planning you may have done in the past is limited to "lesson plans," you must recognize that there is cost involved every minute in which training and education activities are taking place. Further, because financial success is measured in terms of results, planning must be carefully executed both to specify the results expected or intended and to determine the appropriate financial support necessary. This integration of programmatic and financial thought will help provide answers to a plethora of recurring questions: What kinds of programs and activities should this organization offer or procure? Should educators attempt to develop and present these programs or activities in-house, or should they use consultants? How can they prioritize programs and activities for final decision making? To whom should programs or services be marketed or provided? What will each program or activity cost? What is the best price to charge, or how much should be paid? At what locations should the programs or activities be offered? How can practitioners allocate limited resources so that the most important training and education needs are met? Are there alternative methods for accomplishing results that are more cost-effective? If financial cutbacks occur in the middle of a planning period, can training and education activity plans be modified or is there a measurable way to assert that these programs and activities should be spared the budget ax? The list could go on and on.

To help answer these questions, there are some common financial tools which are used to help translate educational needs and accomplishments into financial terms.

A budget is, quite simply, a plan for income and expenses for a given period of time, usually a "fiscal year" or "school year" or "planning period." It is derived from a strategic planning process in which integrated and discrete organizational activities are proposed and agreed upon. Strategic planning is more fully described elsewhere in this book. "A budget helps translate plans into action by communicating plans to those responsible for carrying them out and by promoting financial accountability by providing a standard against which actual performance can be compared" (Holmberg-Wright, 1982). Budgets are used in the initial decision-making process to allocate funds for specific programs and activities. Likewise, they can be used if financial conditions change to determine which programs must be curtailed or discontinued. Budgets serve a communication function in which plans, activities and expected results are standardized, a coordination function, which allows each of the organizational units to systemically contribute its products and services to overall performance, and a control function, through which management can determine whether or not a program or activity is proceeding toward its intended results within monetary constraints.

There are several familiar approaches to budgeting. (In this chapter we concentrate on the ones which are most familiar to educational practitioners.) Those who work within different systems or who desire to know more about budgeting are encouraged to review the sources listed in the references at the end of this chapter. Quite often, two or more types of approaches to budgeting are in existence in an organization, depending on the nature of the organization and the sources of funds for its operations and the complexity of its financial system.

One approach which has been widely used in training and education is called the Program Planning and Budgeting System (PPBS). It attempts to integrate narrative and financial concepts into a detailed document which can be used in a variety of ways, predominantly to prioritize and assign value to the goals and objectives of programs and activities so that informed decisions can be made about them. The basic elements of a PPBS system are similar to those in instructional development. First, there is the definition of needs which a particular program or activity is expected to fulfill. Then there is the statement of objectives articulating how those needs will be met. The third step is the identification of resources and the specification of costs necessary to meet the stated objectives. Then the program or activity is conducted. In the final step, evaluation of the actual results and comparison with objectives and budgeted funds is conducted. The PPBS system answers the what?, why?, and how do we do it? questions, as well as how much money do we need to do it? and how do we know if we have accomplished our objectives?

Another approach is known as zero-based budgeting. It gained popularity during the 1970s as the federal government encouraged its use. It is still seen by some as a comprehensive way to plan for a dynamic and ever-changing future. In zero-based budgeting, it is assumed that each budget category or each program must be fully justified during certain budget preparation cycles. This means not just new programs, but everything. Each staff position, each business trip, each objective must be justified. Some governmental organizations use similar "sunset" provisions to require that tax-funded programs justify their continued existence.

Formula budgets are also common and use an approach based on standardized costs, assuming that each participant or organization or location or project needs just as much support as the next. Formulas, or mathematical algorithms, are used to allocate resources. Although certainly justifiable from a macro or equity perspective, some say that formula budgets do not allow the flexibility or creativity that may be necessary to respond dynamically in diverse markets or environments.

Discretionary budgets are those that are proposed for activities desired by an organization. Governmental entities will often seek proposals for specific activities which support program plans. A corporation may set aside a certain percentage of funds to pay for particular training and education activities above and beyond those for routine activities. Some maintain a contingency fund so that activities not enumerated during the planning process can be realized if management gives approval.

Incremental budgets are probably the easiest and most comfortable budgets for practitioners to use. For each line item in the budget base, adjustments are proposed based on inflation, expansion, profitability or other factors. An across-the-board increase is then applied to the budget base. It is the traditional "take last year's budget and add x% to get this year's budget." The major weakness of such an approach is its tenuous relationship to organizational goals and objectives. Some line items may need greater increases and some may not be needed at all but are being used instead to pad a budget. On the other hand, sometimes that padding is a major contributing factor to accomplishing unforeseen or under-budgeted goals and objectives.

Commonly, budgets used by those providing training and education services for adults can be classified as general and categorical.

General budgets enable those who control the funding to specify how monies will be spent. Priorities are set by management, by government, or by participants themselves; the expectation is that such priorities will be accomplished within the financial resources also provided.

Categorical budgets are usually found in larger organizations in which financial authority must be delegated to the lowest operational level possible. *Program budgets* are developed based on the results that are expected from identified subdivisions of the organization. Because results often cross organizational boundaries, program budgeting is often the approach used during the planning cycle. *Line item budgets* are developed based on specific expected costs, such as travel, personnel, supplies and equipment, etc. More often than not, program budgets include line item specifications, though they are developed from a larger perspective.

Both of these approaches leave room for changes based on newly identified needs and circumstances. In addition, limited modifications to budgets, within prescribed guidelines, are often allowed if justification for such changes are provided.

DEVELOPING A BUDGET

In its most direct form, and the one with which training and education practitioners will have the most opportunity to interact, a budget is an expense plan based on identified objectives that meet organizational and individual needs, and an income plan that details the amount of money available with which to operate. Or, more simply, it describes intended activities in monetary terms. For many, part of the reason for planning and developing a budget is to have an impact on the amount of money actually received. For others, it is expected that their operation will pay all expenses and even make a profit. Either way, you have to have a plan. "The budgeting process would be improved if those removed from the immediate understanding of program objectives and priorities could temper their enthusiasm for trying to make judgments with quantitative data in isolation from the value judgments and program qualities, which must be primary" (Gambino, 1979).

Communication is an integral part of budget development. Everyone should provide input and try to understand the limitations established by policy. Cooperative analysis of data from marketing or some other department, contingency planning, and the ability to respond rapidly to changing conditions are examples of the coordination that should be done during the overall planning process, paying special attention to overlaps or anticipating and preparing to overcome possible financial impediments. Performance data yields information which can be used to evaluate programs, activities, units and individuals, thus satisfying organizational control requirements.

Foremost in every case is the need for organizational goals and objectives to be specified and agreed upon. This may take place independently from the budget preparation. But make no mistake about it, the budget must be derived from a plan which is congruent with organizational reality and specific as regards its costs. When planning a continuing education program, budgets may be developed in concert with an advisory committee selected from the target audience for the program. Again, individual needs, the needs of the profession involved, or of participating agencies will drive the budget planning process. Budgets become a concrete manifestation of actual priorities, irrespective of those stated. Effective budgets achieve congruence between intended and financed priorities.

Budgets are usually established for a short time period, though objectives may be proposed which will take several budget periods to accomplish. Budgets must specify both income and expenditures. Income may be projected or actual. The budget should clearly detail the costs which are required by the organization's budget planning and by the objectives which have been established. Fixed costs, such as personnel, rent, etc. should be subtotaled, and then variable costs, such as travel, etc., factored in. The actual format of the budget will vary according to the specific procedural requirements of each organization. The five Worksheets provided at the end of this chapter are intended to help you to consider the actual costs and financial needs and to develop an expense budget. You may wish to expand the categories listed to incorporate the types of expenditures you commonly have.

Using these worksheets, a simple expense budget for a program or activity can be planned. Incorporate the specific forms and processes used in your organization so that all of the elements involved in costing programs and activities can be included.

DETERMINING COSTS

There are times when the costs for participants must be determined for your programs or activities, either for inclusion in the total budget or as a separate item. Laird (1985) has developed a simple process by which participant costs can be measured. Some of the items are included on the expense budget worksheet (Worksheet 1). Please note that the "replacement cost" or "lost time cost" Laird recommends for participants is not included here. Your organization may require such computations.

The participant cost is one factor that is often left out when calculating the total cost of an internal training and education program or activity (Worksheet 2). Given that there are usually more participants than instructors, the total amount can be staggering. If you sponsor public seminars, there is usually no need for such calculations. Besides, participants may be reluctant to share this information.

Consider an example using this approach, depicted in Worksheet 3. Roger Cameron, the trainer from Abcon Industries in the opening vignette, has been doing some homework and has gathered data which will help him prepare a budget that he can resubmit to Charise Evans. Here are some of the details: Cameron makes $30,000 per year. The Training Department secretary makes $18,000 per year. Fringe benefits at Abcon are calculated at 35% of salary. General overhead is calculated at 18% of salaries. Cameron has already spent approximately 10 days in preparing his seminars. Administrative support has consumed 5 days. He anticipates that he will spend 4 more days in development. Approximately 3 more days of administrative support will be necessary for development of the seminars. Cameron will be the lead trainer in the sessions. Secretarial support will not be necessary during the sessions. He plans to have a motivational speaker come in for 1 day to each of the eight sessions he has planned. The cost for the speaker is $750 per day plus expenses. Since the speaker is local, expenses are estimated at $20 per day for mileage, parking, etc. Twenty participants, each also earning an average of $30,000 per year, will attend each of the eight sessions. They will arrive on Sunday evening when there will be a cocktail reception (total cost for each: $500). The class will begin Monday morning and end in the early afternoon on Friday. All participants will return to their base locations at that time. The course will be conducted at a hotel in the headquarters town, which offers a free meeting room. There is a $50 per day additional charge for a breakout room. Refreshments are $12 per person per day, tax and gratuity included. Individuals will pay for their own meals and hotel rooms as well as travel, which is estimated at $500 per participant. The hotel will charge $75 per lodging room per day, tax included, and the per diem reimbursement is $50 per day, for a total of $125 per person per day. Each participant will stay for 5 days and nights. Cameron will receive $10 per day for incidental expenses. Each participant will receive a text which costs $20. Handout materials will cost another $10 per person. Approximately 100 overhead transparencies will be used, at $5 each. One commercial videotape must be purchased at $750. Rental of audiovisual equipment will cost $250 per session. Each participant will be mailed a general notice of the training as well as a packet of materials before the session. Total mailing cost will be $3.50. Evaluation will consist of a post-session form handed out to participants for them to mail back. Total evaluation cost for each person will be $1. Cameron expects to spend 3 days analyzing evaluation results.

Estimate the total cost of the eight sessions, including trainee costs, and then the unit cost, or cost per participant. You may use the sample Worksheet 3 provided at the end of the chapter. There may even be other costs you could consider in this example, or, depending on how your organization classifies costs, they may be categorized differently. You can also separate the participant costs by isolating the factors listed in Worksheet 4 at the end of the chapter.

By breaking down costs in this manner, you can see that training and education activities are expensive. Further, you can begin to understand why many educators avoid such calculations. Even with a relatively simple breakdown, there are a lot of issues and potential conflicts involved. One thing is certain: the total cost is a lot more than the $300 per day Roger Cameron first estimated.

This type of cost budgeting also allows you to make better decisions about training and education programs and activities, including looking for areas in which costs must be trimmed and deciding upon instructional alternatives, among others. Three of the processes used in such decisions are known as cost-benefit analysis, cost-effectiveness analysis and break-even analysis.

COST–BENEFIT ANALYSIS

A cost-benefit analysis is a procedure in which the total cost of developing, delivering, and evaluating a specific training and education program or activity is compared with the net results or benefits of that program or activity, quantified in monetary terms, to determine its economic efficiency. A number of authors have detailed the process of cost benefit analysis (see references), and many organizations use permutations of this approach. In this chapter, we will forego the complicated mathematical formulas and just deal with the basics.

In its simplest terms, you evolve a cost to benefit ratio:

$$\frac{\underline{BENEFIT}}{COST} \geq 1$$

Using a reality-based approach, the benefits of participating in a training and education program should be quantified. Some examples include reduced number of hours spent on unproductive work, increased profit margins, less processing time, greater personal confidence and competence, greater personal marketability, or any of a number of different such indicators, all related to increasing revenues or productivity and/or decreasing time or expenses. For an example of how to calculate potential benefits from adult education and training activities, see Worksheet 5 at the end of the chapter.

The example we have been using can illustrate a very simple and elementary cost-benefit analysis. Roger Cameron has designed seminars for managers in a high-tech firm that will help them to respond more rapidly to changes in their market. He believes that the total time from acknowledgment of a need for change in process to implementation can be reduced by 10%. Without involved calculating or a sophisticated approach, Cameron feels justified in stating that if their attendance at his seminar accomplishes the objectives, each manager will potentially save Abcon Industries $3,000 the first year (10% of a $30,000 salary). Since the total cost per participant for the training is $2,377, a simple cost-benefit analysis would indicate that this program should be conducted. Attendance at the course could be even more profitable if the savings were projected over more than one year. If this decreased response time also increases market share, more jobs could result, again making the program both individually and organizationally valuable.

COST-EFFECTIVENESS ANALYSIS

A cost-effectiveness analysis is similar to a cost-benefit analysis, but without the monetary quantification. It is useful when it is difficult to assign a monetary value to benefits. It includes such things as psychological factors, increased awareness, community good will, a change in attitudes, and other things that can be associated with participation in training and education programs and activities. It may appear that such things are positively impacted by participation, or there may be compelling sociopolitical reasons for participation, but they can't be proven financially.

Consider, for example, a voluntary organization to promote adult literacy. Although there are plenty of economic reasons why individuals might want to enhance literacy skills, there are equally compelling personal reasons: a father wants to read to his children, a retired person wants to read the Bible, an elderly individual wants to write her life story. Further, who could place an economic value on the satisfaction literacy volunteers experience in helping someone learn to read to meet goals like these? A cost-effectiveness analysis might break down actual costs and compare them to outcomes in anecdotal fashion: "Mary Jones, hospital kitchen staff—learned to read well enough to read the dietitian's daily instructions—cost of materials $25, instructor's time donated." Although we might be able to argue that Mary has also saved her job which could be expressed in economic terms, in instances like these, to do so may actually devalue the activity.

BREAK-EVEN ANALYSIS

Because every aspect of training and education programs and activities involves cost, some educators worry about costs which have been expended for programs and activities which may not be carried out. A good example is when a public seminar is developed and marketed, but enrollments do not meet expectations. Should the seminar be conducted, or should it be canceled and money refunded to those who have registered?

The simplest way to make such a determination is to estimate the total cost necessary to conduct the seminar. You may calculate that developing the seminar has already cost your organization $3,000. Each time that it is to be conducted, there will be an additional $1,000 in expenses. Assuming that each participant would pay $500 to attend the seminar, some calculations can be made. The first time that such a seminar is conducted, your organization has spent $4,000. Consequently, eight participants would enable you to "break even." If only six have registered, you are looking at a loss of $1,000. If nine register, you've made a profit. Whether or not you proceed in either of these cases is not solely determined by this break-even analysis, but it is a means by which your costs and your potential income can be compared. (For a more detailed explanation of break-even analysis, see Matkin, 1985 and 1997.)

HOW MUCH SHOULD WE CHARGE?
HOW MUCH SHOULD THEY PAY?

When it comes to comparing costs and expenses, whether in a profit or nonprofit operation, there comes a time when you must decide how much to charge for your services and, conversely, how much to pay for those you need. This is a time when budgeting and financial analysis skills will be of optimum benefit.

Many fees are market driven. The amount an organization is able to subsidize, what participants are willing to pay, and what needs are to be addressed will ultimately be the determining factors in how much is charged or paid for participation in a training activity. Some fees are established by policy or regulation, and institutional parameters are applied uniformly. In those cases, qualitative factors may have greater significance. Some organizations in the public sector such as community colleges take in tuition and fees which are returned to a general fund rather than to a specific programmatic entity. Then a legislative appropriation, most likely formula based, will return some amount of funding, though it may be more or less than the amount generated through the fees. Regardless, solid financial planning will enable you to maximize the potential for results, simply by providing data in terms that are widely standardized and understood.

When considering the factors related to establishing a competitive fee, it is systemically critical to recognize that all income will be related to enrollment. Enrollments are based on adjusted historical data, forecasts backed by market projection analyses, organizational requirements, and often instinctive hunches. And certainly, enrollments are affected by the fees charged. Sometimes it may be better to set a lower fee, managing the budget through the cost attrition that occurs as a course is repeated. A higher fee for an intensive activity may help to maintain a low student-teacher ratio.

The budget will serve as one baseline from which to make decisions. When the total cost of a program or activity is determined and then an enrollment estimation made, dividing the enrollment into the cost will provide a bottom line figure from which to operate. Adding profit margins and "fudge factors" can help you to arrive at a range of amounts. Factoring in historical data, market analyses, etc., will help you to set a fee that will attract sufficient enrollment to cover all costs and make a profit if desired.

What participants are willing to pay (for example, when an employee is to attend a public seminar) will be related to the need which the activity is intended to fulfill, the type of position the employee occupies, the nature of the seminar and the instructor, and the amount of money available to support the activity. Some organizations are willing to pay more for certain employees than for others and for certain types of programs than for others. The ability to function consistently with facts and figures will help you to analyze, criticize, and/or defend proposed participation in training and education activities.

SUMMARY

This is a time of burgeoning technology, job expansion, corporate mergers and buyouts, and highly specific training and education needs with reduced resources. The ability to plan, communicate, and effectively function with accurate financial data is paramount. Proving that training and education activities contribute to profitability is an important aspect of program planning and management. Deciding how much to charge or to pay for programs and activities helps to stretch limited budgets. Ensuring that well-thought-out goals and objectives can be accomplished cost-effectively is a mark of a training and education professional.

Simple concepts and common sense rule in most cases. Sure, some financial considerations are complex and far beyond our ability or desire to understand. But basic awareness and ability will enable you to communicate, coordinate, control and evaluate effectiveness so that obtaining the necessary funding, providing the required return on investment, and even justifying the existence of your programs and activities can be done forcefully, knowledgeably, in solid financial terms. In effect, you will be able to demonstrate that highly valued educational activities add value of a different kind.

QUESTIONS FOR STUDY AND DISCUSSION

1. What would it cost to offer the ideal program in your area of adult education and training?
2. How could you finance it?
3. What are some ethical issues of settling for less?
4. What are some ethical issues surrounding placing an economic value on human learning?
5. Do these issues vary by context (i.e., in business, nonprofit or government agencies, etc.)?
6. Should who pays determine who has a say in program planning?
7. Ideally, who should be involved in budgeting for adult education and training in our area of practice?

REFERENCES

Anderson, R. E., & Kasl, E. S. (1982). *The costs and financing of adult education and training.* Lexington, MA: D. C. Heath.

Bell, C. R. (1983). How training departments win budget battles. *Training and Development Journal,* September, *37,* 9, 42–49.

Cafarella, R. S. (1988). *Program development and evaluation resource book for trainers.* New York: Wiley.

Droms, W. G. (1982). *Finance and accounting for non-financial managers.* Reading, MA: Addison-Wesley.

Dahl, D. A. (1980). Resources. In A. B. Knox (Ed.), *Developing, administering and evaluating adult education.* San Francisco: Jossey-Bass.

Finkel, C. L. (1987). The true cost of a training program. *Training and Development Journal,* September, *41,* 9, 74–76.

Fitz-Enz, J. (1990). *Human value management: the value-adding human resource management strategy for the 1990s.* San Francisco: Jossey-Bass.

Flamholtz, E. G. (1985). *Human resource accounting: advances in concepts, methods and applications* (2nd Ed.). San Francisco: Jossey-Bass.

Gambino, A. J. (1979). *Planning and control in higher education.* New York: National Association of Accountants.

Head, G. E. (1985). *Training cost analysis: A practical guide.* Washington, DC: Marlin Press.

Holmberg-Wright, K. (1982). The budget as a planning instrument. In T. Shipp (Ed.), *Creative financing and budgeting.* San Francisco: Jossey-Bass.

Kearsley, G. (1982). *Costs, benefits and productivity in training systems.* Reading, MA: Addison-Wesley.

Kidd, J. R. (1962). *Financing continuing education.* New York: Scarecrow Press.

Knowles, M. S. (1980). *The modern practice of adult education.* New York: Cambridge.

Laird, D. S. (1985). *Approaches to training and development* (2nd Ed.). Reading, MA: Addison-Wesley.

Lloyd, T. (1989). Winning the budget battle. *Training, 26,* 5, May, 57–62.

Matkin, G. W. (1985). *Effective budgeting in continuing education.* San Francisco: Jossey-Bass.

Matkin, G. W. (1997). *Using financial information in continuing education: accepted methods and new approaches.* Phoenix: Oryx Press.

Nadler, L., & Nadler, Z. (1990). *The Handbook of human resource development* (2nd Ed.). New York: Wiley.

Nadler, L., & Wiggs, G. D. (1986). *Managing human resource development: a practical guide.* San Francisco: Jossey-Bass.

Nilson, C. (1989). *Training program workbook and kit.* Englewood Cliffs, NJ: Prentice-Hall.

Philips, J. (1994). *In action: Return on investment.* Alexandria, VA: ASTD Press.

Spencer, Jr., L. M. (1986). *Calculating human resource costs and benefits.* New York: Wiley.

Strother, G. B., & Klus, J. P. (1982). *Administration of continuing education.* Belmont, CA: Wadsworth.

Swanson, R. A., & Gradous, D. B. (1988). *Forecasting financial benefits of human resource development.* San Francisco: Jossey-Bass.

Tracy, W. R. (1990). *Leadership skills: standout performance of human resources managers.* New York: American Management Association.

Welsch, G. A. (1988). *Budgeting: profit, planning and control* (5th Ed.). Englewood Cliffs, NJ: Prentice-Hall.

Worksheet 1 Expense Budgeting for Programs and Activities

GOAL OR OBJECTIVE TO BE MET THROUGH THIS ACTIVITY:

Budget Items	Phases			
	Development	Delivery	Evaluation	Subtotal
DIRECT COSTS				
Staff Salaries				
Professional				
Administrative				
Other				
Consultants				
Instructional Materials				
Books				
Articles				
Handouts				
Manuals				
Transparencies				
Slides				
Videotapes				
Videodiscs				
Audiotapes/CDs				
Computer materials/charges				
Satellites uplink/downlink				

Telephone charges
Video-conferencing charges
Supplies
Other

Equipment (Rental/Purchase)
Media playback
Media record
Computers
Specialized support services
Equipment maintenance

Facility Costs
Function room charges
Breakout room(s) charges
Refreshment breaks
Tips
Telephone/Fax
Parking
Social/Entertainment
Catered meals (specify)
Services
Miscellaneous
Incidental
Other

Promotional/Evaluation Materials
Design
Purchase
Printing
Distribution/Mailing
Return processing

Worksheet 1 (*Continued*)

Budget Items	Phases			
	Development	Delivery	Evaluation	Subtotal
INDIRECT COSTS				
Staff fringe benefits				
Participant fringe benefits				
General overhead				
Other				
OTHER COSTS				
SUBTOTAL FOR EACH PHASE				
GRAND TOTAL				

Worksheet 2 Participant Costs (adapted from Laird, 1985)

Participant Costs	Total
NUMBER OF PARTICIPANTS × median salary × training hours OR NUMBER OF PARTICIPANTS × daily median salary × number of days	
FRINGE BENEFITS: Number of participants × your organization's fringe benefits rate	
OVERHEAD: Number of participants × your organization's overhead rate	
TRAVEL: Total from participant expense reports, or median cost × number of participants	
PER DIEM: Total from participant expense reports, or median daily allowance × number of participants × number of days	
MATERIALS: Unit cost × number of participants	
GRAND TOTAL	

Worksheet 3 Expenses Budgeting for a Sample Program

GOAL OR OBJECTIVE TO BE MET THROUGH THIS ACTIVITY:

Budget Items	Phases			Subtotal
	Development	Delivery	Evaluation	
DIRECT COSTS				
Staff Salaries				
Professional				
($30,000/year = $125/day)	1250	5000	375	6625
(Each session = 5 days; 8 sessions are planned)				
Administrative	600			600
($18,000/year = $75/day)				
Other (including participants)				
($30,000/year = $125/day)		37500		37500
(5 days × $125/day × 60 participants)				
Consultants				
Honoraria		6000		6000
(8 days × $750/day)				
Lodging/meals and incidental		160		160
($20/day × 8 days)				

Instructional Materials		
Books	3200	3200
Articles	1600	1600
Handouts	500	500
Manuals	750	750
Transparencies		
Slides		
Videotapes		
Videodiscs		
Audiotapes/CDs		
Computer materials/charges		
Satellites uplink/downlink		
Telephone charges		
Video-conferencing charges		
Supplies		
Other		
Equipment (Rental/Purchase)		
Media playback	2000	2000
(8 sessions × $250/session)		
Media record		
Computers		
Specialized support services		
Equipment maintenance		

Worksheet 3 (*Continued*)

	Phases			
Budget Items	Development	Delivery	Evaluation	Subtotal
Facility Costs				
Function room charges				
Breakout room(s) charges		2000		2000
($50/day × 5 days × 8 sessions)				
Refreshment breaks		9600		9600
($12 per person per day × 5 days × 8 sessions × 20 participants)				
Tips				
Telephone/Fax				
Parking, social/entertainment		4000		4000
(Estimated: $500 per session × 8 sessions)				
Catered meals (Specify)				
Services				
Miscellaneous				
Staff incidental		4000		4000
($10/day × 5 days × 8 sessions)				
Other				
Promotional/Evaluation Materials				
Design				
Purchase				
Printing/Distribution/Mailing		560		560
($3.50 × 160 participants)				
Return processing		160		160
($1 × 160 participants)				

Participants' Costs				
Transportation				80000
(Average: $500)				
Lodging/Meals				100000
($125/day × 5 days × $160)				
INDIRECT COSTS				
Staff fringe benefits				2546
(35% × total staff salaries)				
Participant fringe benefits				1312
(35% × total participant salaries)				
General overhead				1984
(18% × total salaries)				
Other				
OTHER COSTS				
SUBTOTAL FOR EACH PHASE	1850	252920	375	227747
GRAND TOTAL				$277,645

WORKSHEET 4 Participant Costs for Sample Program

Participant Costs	Total
Number of participants × median salary × training hours OR Number of participants × daily median salary × number of days	20,000
Fringe benefits	7,000
Overhead	3,600
TRAVEL: Total from participant expense reports, or median cost × number of participants	80,000
PER DIEM: Total from participant expense reports, or median daily allowance × number of participants × number of days	40,000
LODGING: Total from participant expense reports OR median daily allowance × number of participants × number of days	60,000
MATERIALS: Unit cost × number of participants	4,800
GRAND TOTAL	$215,400

Worksheet 5 Calculating Benefits

Monetary Benefits	Calculation	Estimated Financial Benefit
• Productivity increases	Calculated by taking the median salary of participants and multiplying by the actual or expected % increase in performance	$
• Savings from reduced errors	Calculated by multiplying the total error costs times the actual or expected % of errors reduced	$
• Increased profit from reduced cycle times		$
○ in manufacturing	Cost per day times # of days eliminated in the manufacturing process	$
○ in marketing	Earnings per day times # of days eliminated in the marketing cycle	$
○ in product development	Earnings per day from new products plus savings per day in development costs times # of days eliminated in the product development cycle	$

Nonmonetary Benefits	Calculation	Estimated Benefit Value
• Increased employee satisfaction	% increase in overall climate survey ratings, reduced absenteeism or turnover	Payoff may lead to increased productivity gains which can be assigned an expected financial gain
• Increased customer goodwill	% increase in overall sales, especially repeat or referral business	Payoff may lead to increased sales which can be assigned an expected financial gain
• Increased employee knowledge and skills	% increase in overall long term performance	Payoff may lead to increased productivity gains which can be assigned an expected financial gain
• Enhanced employee creativity	% increase in employee suggestions, new product ideas	Possible increase in profits

18

Staffing

Daniele D. Flannery

ABSTRACT

This chapter provides an overview of different aspects of staffing in connection with planning, conducting, and evaluating education and training programs. The planner must first identify which job functions are needed and second to determine how many people are required and whether they should be part-time or fulltime and whether they should come from inside or outside the organization. The planner should consider alternative criteria for selection of staff. Once staff has been selected, they must be nurtured through orientation, encouragement and support. Additionally, staff performance has to be appraised. Each of these aspects entails deciding among various alternatives, many of which are discussed in this chapter. The aim of all of these staffing activities is well-qualified and up-to-date program administrators, program designers, and program instructors.

ASSESSMENT

Directions: If you possess the knowledge and/or skill for each competency of the staffing function, check *A* and/or *B*. If you need knowledge and/or skill for each competency, check *C* and/or *D*.

Staffing Function Competency	Possess		Need	
	Knowl-edge A	Skill B	Knowl-edge C	Skill D
1. Able to determine needed role functions.				
2. Able to determine needed personnel, number of positions, part or full time, hiring from inside or outside the organization.				
3. Able to operationalize specific skills needed.				
4. Able to characterize the organizational culture.				
5. Able to match future employees' values with the organizational culture.				
6. Able to write job descriptions.				
7. Able to solicit evidence of possession of needed skills in interviews.				
8. Able to oversee staff development including creation of individual development plans.				
9. Able to develop initial performance appraisal documents.				
10. Able to conduct positive staff evaluation.				

KEY TERMS AND CONCEPTS

Staffing   A job responsibility which includes supplying employees to meet the needs of an organization, developing their work-related skills, and evaluating performance.

Program administrator   The person who manages or supervises the program effort.

Program designer   The person responsible for the content and design of the program.

Program instructor   The person responsible for delivering the instruction.

Organizational culture   A pattern of basic assumptions about ways
   of perceiving, thinking, feeling, and acting in a given group
   that are considered correct and valid (Schein, 1985).

Job description   A document developed for the hiring process to
   clearly state the parameters of a position open in an organization.

Staff evaluation   Measurement and appraisal of useful information on how the employees are perceiving and performing
   their jobs.

INTRODUCTION

This chapter on staffing is written for persons who do program
planning in any setting where education is a primary or secondary
purpose of the programming. Included, but not limited to these
settings, are the following: community education, training and
development, literacy education, continuing higher education,
continuing professional education, and patient education. While
there may be unique aspects to a setting, such as no paid full-time
staff, or a hierarchical organizational structure which strongly
influences the program planning efforts, this chapter provides
information that can be adapted to all education and training
settings. Where feasible, specific note will be made of aspects
unique to particular situations. The chapter consists of four major
sections: (1) knowing what is needed in staffing, (2) selecting the
staff, (3) caring for the staff, and (4) evaluating the staff.

KNOWING WHAT IS NEEDED

Staffing involves knowing what job functions are needed and
such specifics as number of personnel required, whether they
should be full or part-time, whether they should come from within
or outside of the agency.

What Functions Are Needed?

The first step in staffing is to know what functions you want
people to fill. There are varieties of roles and role functions discussed in the literature on program planning. Although the titles

or functions under a title may vary, there is agreement on the functions to be performed in the program planning endeavor. The roles most frequently mentioned in the literature are program administrator, program designer, and instructor (Caffarella, 1994; Lauffer, 1978; Laird, 1985; Nadler, 1984).

The Program Administrator

The program administrator manages or supervises the entire effort. In program planning the administrative function may be a macro or a micro one. A macro administrative function is one where the administrator is the supervisor of an entire agency, such as the YWCA or the head of a training and development department. This individual is clearly responsible for what occurs on a large scale. The individual most often oversees all employees, all programs, all budgets, etc. An administrative function on a micro level is one where the individual is responsible for coordinating the program, such as facilitating a teleconference on adult returning students or developing a self-esteem workshop for low income women. Whereas the micro administrative function may include the same responsibilities as the macro administrative function, the micro administrative function is focused on particular aspects of the work of the agency, college, or training department. It is not responsible for the entire operation. Functions of the administrator may include the following

Personnel: selects staff, hires, manages, supervises, develops, and evaluates all staff, paid and volunteer;
Facilities: sets facilities standards, secures facilities, equipment, materials, and makes physical arrangements.
Programs: coordinates, schedules, and promotes programs, attends to enrollments, arranges for instructors, supervises on-going programs, develops new ideas for programs, conducts needs analysis, sets overall program objectives, establishes program priorities and evaluates programs;
Finance: develops budgets, monitors expenditures, and accounts for expenditures;
Public Relations: liaises and maintains relations with the staff, the organization and the community;
Policy: sets, communicates, enforces and evaluates policy.

The Program Designer

The program designer is responsible for the content and process design of the program. Functions include:

Knowledge: is knowledgeable about subject matter;

Curriculum: establishes the instructional objectives, determines the precise content to be learned, analyzes the tasks or information to be taught, determines the sequence in which the content should be delivered, and organizes units of learning;

Methods and Materials: knows and uses psychological, social and learning implications of different kinds of materials being employed, creatively chooses the instructional format which includes selection of methods and media, keeps informed of forms of educational technology, develops the instructional plans for an integrated program, and provides all materials to implement the program (Nadler, 1979);

Evaluation: pretests the program and makes adjustments based on data from pretest, in consultation with the instructor and program administrator, conducts formative evaluations of the program design throughout the program, and conducts a summative evaluation of the program design at the end of the program.

The Instructor or Facilitator

Along with delivering the instruction, the instructor or facilitator is responsible for assisting the learners to achieve the learning objectives. Functions of the instructor include

Instruction: delivers learning design;

Attention to Learner: analyzes and responds to individual learner needs, adapts design to meet learner needs, and encourages learners;

Instructional Feedback and Evaluation: provides ongoing feedback and evaluation to the learners in order to facilitate learning, and provides feedback to the designers about the strengths and weaknesses of the curriculum design.

Having dealt with the major program planning functions, it must be acknowledged that in a training and development context, some authors (Munson, 1984; Nadler, 1979) include a research function. Some of the tasks of this function may include: training needs analysis, program follow-up, and program development or adaptation. Other aspects not usually mentioned, often because of time or other constraints, include vendor research, training methods research, keeping in touch with other companies' activities, and determining availability of off-the-shelf training programs and outside consulting services. Indeed, these are important functions to program planning and can be included under the appropriate staff functions, if the agency resources permit.

Exercise One

In order to consider the necessity of each of the program planning functions, select a real or hypothetical program. Check those functions cited earlier which you need in your particular organization in order to carry out the development, administration and production of this program. (Add any functions which may be missing.)

Personnel Specifics

Now that the necessary program planning functions have been selected, three questions must be asked: How many persons are needed to perform the functions? Will they work part- or full-time on the program? Will they be from inside or outside the agency? Depending on the organization or the particular program, the titles and functions in an institution may not be discrete ones. In some cases one or two persons may perform all of the functions. In other cases, the functions may be spread among four or five people. The decisions regarding number of persons, part- or full-time, and from inside or outside the organization are made in light of the scope of the proposed program, estimated time to carry out the program planning functions, availability of funding and other needed resources, and availability of persons with appropriate expertise to work part or full-time at particular tasks.

Although the issues of staffing from "inside" or "outside" the organization are often discussed in the training sector, these concepts have relevance for any adult education setting where program planning is being considered. Staffing from inside most typically refers to using personnel already hired from within the organization, institution, or agency. In training this could mean delegating several already-employed trainers to develop a program on workplace literacy. In continuing education, the need for developing a certificate program which stresses basic principles of management for line supervisors could be met by instructors who already teach in credit programs on campus. But staffing from inside may also refer to using persons who are integrally part of an agency or movement such as board members or volunteers. These individuals most often are committed to the purposes of the agency, have been part of its efforts for some time, and often have engaged in participating in and planning much of what has been carried out. Examples include persons who have served on the boards of YWCAs, the many people who have been part of Alzheimer's caregiver groups or of Educators for Social Responsibility.

"Going outside" to hire refers to the practice of hiring a consultant to fulfill a particular program planning role for a specific time or event. Munson (1984) suggests outside persons should be hired (or solicited) when there is no person in the agency to perform the tasks, there is need for specific expertise, the current staff is overworked, the person hired has already developed the program the organization wants to offer, or when an outsider may have greater stature or be more credible than an insider. While there are benefits to going outside, there are risks too. The work of someone not connected with the organization may conflict with the philosophy, goals, and organizational culture of the agency. An outsider may not understand the agency's clientele or may not be accepted. This approach can be costly. A rule of thumb for business concerning cost is that the "cost advantage per participant increases as the trainee population passes and exceeds roughly thirty to forty people in number" (Munson, 1984, p. 53).

In many adult education and training settings, there is often a need to go outside and to hire one or more permanent persons, part or full-time, to do program planning. A local hospital hires an RN to administer a "Resource Mother's Program" to train women in the community to mentor low-income women during pregnancy and for the first year of the infant's life. The ABC Poultry Company hires a person to develop and conduct a workplace literacy program.

Exercise Two

Look at a real or hypothetical program. Consider the scope of your program; your budget; how many people you need and whether each one will be part or full time; whether you will select someone from inside, a new permanent employee, or an outside consultant; and how the tasks will be divided.

SELECTING THE STAFF

Seven aspects should be considered in selecting the staff: the particular skills required for each position, the characteristics of organization's culture in which the person will work, matching of these two aspects with the person being sought, determining the salary, establishing additional qualifications, writing the job description, and advertising for and recruiting the staff.

Particular Skills Required

What are the particular skills needed to perform the tasks? Some required skills pertain to all of the tasks. Competencies generally agreed to be demanded by all of the role areas include industry understanding; questioning, listening, writing and organizing ideas; design and implementation of feedback and evaluation systems (ASTD, 1983; Laird, 1985), and "ability to respond appropriately and ability to apply human motivation and reinforcement theory" (Laird, 1985, p. 32). A sound understanding of the learning process is also essential. While this may be apparent for the program designer and the instructor, the administrator too must understand the learning process. The administrator oversees the educational functions (Nadler, 1979) and must therefore create a climate for learning from the organizational perspective (Caffarella, 1988). All persons must be credible. For Knowles (1980) credibility is based on the person's position, background and/or personal impact. I speak specifically of the credibility of the instructor, suggesting that high credibility predisposes the trainee to more readily accept the material presented. In reality, each of the persons must be credible in order to be effective within the organization, the community and with the learners. All persons must understand the cultural and sociological factors which influence the organization, the community and the learner (Flannery, 1991a). Nadler (1984) stresses that the program designer must communicate with everyone who is related to the learning situation. In HRD this includes the learner and the instructor, the person (supervisor) to whom the learner has a responsibility, and the learner's own peer group. This communication is not just an informing, but may often be, a seeking of relevant ideas, materials and approaches. All persons must communicate their specific program planning endeavors to others. Not only is this necessary for informing boards, funding sources, and superiors of progress, but it is also an important way to continue to legitimate the program and their respective parts of the program planning process. All personnel must have a genuine interest in the learners' learning. This, rather than the technical aspects of their roles, must be foremost. The person in each position must be able to deal as effectively with groups as with individuals.

Skills Specific to Particular Areas of Expertise

For each of the three roles of program planning (program administrator, program designer and instructor), the particular role competencies were detailed earlier. As practiced in Exercise One, each agency must personalize its needs by analyzing the listed competencies for its own unique needs.

Exercise Three

Select one real or hypothetical position your agency must fill. Keeping in mind the original functions for the position listed in Exercise One and the skills for each position cited above, operationalize the competencies for the position which you will fill.

Organizational Culture

The second step in selecting the staff is to review and make explicit the organizational culture. Organizational culture is "a pattern of basic assumptions—invented, discovered, or developed by a given group as it learns to cope with its problems of external adaptation and internal integration—that has worked well enough to be considered valid and, therefore, to be taught to new members as the correct way to perceive, think, and feel in relation to those problems" (Schein, 1985, p. 9). These assumptions and beliefs may not be spoken, and may operate subconsciously, but they do "determine the behavior patterns and the visible artifacts such as architecture, office layout, dress codes and so on" (Schein, 1985, p.

9). (See Morgan [1986] and Chapter 7 in this volume for dominant metaphors of organizational culture.)

Organizational culture manifests itself in behavior of the organizations' individuals and groups in five ways:

1. *Corporate values.* Values include the beliefs about what is good for the organization and why it should happen as expressed by the ends (goals) and means (action plans for achieving goals) (Armstrong, 1988). These may include values regarding job security, pay and benefits, the relationship of work and family, autonomy and control, norms regarding work level and quality, and ethical behavior (London, Bassman, & Fernandez, 1990).

2. *Organizational climate.* The organizational climate is the working atmosphere of the organization, the expression of how the corporate culture and its values are perceived, experienced and reacted to by its members (Armstrong, 1988).

3. *Management style.* The organization may support managerial behavior and the exercise of authority in certain ways (Armstrong, 1988). Managers' beliefs about the nature of people are reflected in the leadership style(s) supported and chosen. These beliefs have implications for the way decisions are made, for the nature of interpersonal relationships (Ilsley & Niemi, 1981), and for the way control is exercised and autonomy is viewed. Ilsley and Niemi (1981) use the following example. According to McGregor's theory X of management (1960), if persons are believed to be unmotivated and unable to be responsible for their own work behaviors, the manager will perceive the way to achieve the organization's goals is by tight control of the worker through specific task instruction and strict supervision. If, on the other hand, workers are believed to be highly motivated and capable of sharing in the decision-making responsibilities, managers allow more control and more decision-making responsibility by the worker (theory Y). With reference to participation in a volunteer setting, Ilsley and Niemi (1981) add a third approach to management. In this approach the manager believes persons are "self-actualized." These persons may be highly motivated, able to assume more responsibility for decision making regarding their work. Clearly, the organizational climate mentioned in the previous point

cannot be separated from the managerial style. The working climate is strongly related to the beliefs about management which are operationalized by managerial performance.

4. *Program planning.* The status of the program planning function varies from organization to organization. For business, it may serve to support the organization's objectives. For continuing education, program planning is an essential function of the organization. Regardless of the status of program planning, programmatic emphases are related to the emphases of the parent organization's values and expectations (Simerly, et al., 1987). Without the tacit support of the organization, program planning departments and personnel will not have significant influence in the organization. Votruba (1981) specifically cautions those in continuing education that program planning will not become strategically important to the university unless they attend to the traditions, distinctive faculty and curricular strengths of the institution. Further, without support, programs will simply not be allowed.

5. *Teaching/learning exchange.* The organizational culture influences the teaching/learning exchange much the same way it influences managerial style. Organizational beliefs and values drive the beliefs about learning and teaching.

These beliefs concern adult learners, the psychological theories that best explain adult learning, curriculum building, and teaching methods (Nadler, 1979). Within the organization's value system learners may be viewed as unmotivated, unable to determine their own learning needs, requiring specific direction as to what and how to learn, and incapable of evaluating their own learning. When such views prevail, program planners see themselves as experts who determine the specifics of the content, structure the sequencing of the material, and predetermine the logic and style of the presentation. Instructors who adhere to such views emphasize the lecture as the way to impart knowledge or skills which can be clearly and specifically evaluated. There is little input from learners and little consideration that they may differ in their needs or in how they learn.

In an alternative organizational value system learners may be viewed as knowing what they need to learn, motivated to learn and capable of engaging in dialogue with the program designer or instructor about how they might best learn. When these alternative views prevail, program planners see themselves as consultants who work with the learners to bring about educational change. Instructors who adhere to this alternative view emphasize action projects and discussion that enable adults to articulate what they feel they need, to determine their own goals, and to select how best to achieve them.

In this model, the instructor creates a learning environment and enables rather than determines the learning process. Contrary to the first scenario, this set of beliefs promotes reflection on experience, includes the place of the affect in learning and teaching, and incorporates the roles of continued negotiation and renegotiation in the teaching/learning practice (Brookfield, 1986).

Most often, there must be a fit between the organizational culture and the person(s) to be hired. The exception may be when an organization has reviewed its present culture and seeks to change that culture, perhaps to adapt the organizational culture to meet perceptions of needs of a changing workforce (London, et al., 1990). For example, employees who are better educated may expect greater participation in decision making. Perceiving this, the organization may want to gradually change to encourage greater participation in decision making and thus begin to hire persons who represent the future directions or the organizational culture rather than the present ones.

Exercise Four
Using the five ways organizational culture manifests itself, as discussed above, analyze your real or hypothetical organization's culture. Detail the specific culture and required behaviors, using each of the categories above that are dominant in your organization.

Matching Organizational Culture and Prospective Employees

The third step in selecting staff is to match the organizational culture, which includes the values, attitudes, expectations, norms and behaviors, with those of prospective employees (London, et al., 1990). As Knox (1981) states, program planning is a series of connected decisions that are personal, situational and value based. Not only does the organization have a system of beliefs, values and attitudes, but those being hired also have systems of beliefs, values and attitudes. If the individual's culture diverges too much from the organizational culture, the hiree will not remain with the organization or will be unhappy. Too, given the importance of a working relationship between the program planners and the organization, there must be a degree of similarity to the operational beliefs which underlie the program planning endeavors and personnel. The match between the hiree's work-related values with those of the organization is not only important for paid staff roles, but also for volunteer roles. (See Ilsley and Niemi, 1981, ch. 4 for more on the importance of climates for volunteer participation.) If the organizational culture cannot support the motivations of the volunteer, there is little likelihood that the volunteer will remain with the agency.

Exercise Five

Imagine a hypothetical interviewee for one of the positions you have determined you need. Decide how you will identify the interviewee's work-related values. Compare these with those of the organization that you ascertained in Exercise Four. Determine if there is a match between your hypothetical interviewee and the organizational culture.

Determining the Salary

In a broad sense salary includes both the amount of money the person will be paid for the position and the benefits which supplement the salary. Benefits may include such items as health coverage, unemployment compensation, life insurance, retirement, child care, and compensatory time for overtime work. The amount of money the person is paid as well as the additional benefits offered are determined by considering the institution's existing salary structure, company and area compensation for similar tasks, and by weighing the monetary resources available to accomplish the desired program. It must be noted that the voluntary sector should not be left out of these salary considerations. Although there may not be monetary remuneration, the organization may still offer benefits to volunteers (e.g., child care, and educational benefits).

Additional Qualifications Needed

Examples of additional requirements which may be particular to your organization may include experience performing the tasks required (e.g., a specified number of years of experience in program design or experience in instruction via audioconference); a record of successful instruction (as indicated by participant and supervisor evaluations of instruction); or the ability to use certain equipment (e.g., computer for instructional design).

Exercise Six

Determine the salary range for the open position, the benefits available as a salary supplement and any additional qualifications required for the position.

Writing the Job Description

The job description includes information about the position itself, background requirements, and information about the working conditions such as hours and benefits. The position description should be brief, yet clear. The first part of the job description is concerned with the details of the position. It should include the job title, a one or two sentence description of the position, five or six of the specific responsibilities and the persons to whom the new employee will report. Each specific responsibility should be expressed briefly and clearly and should start with an active functional verb (e.g., instructs students with reading difficulties on an individual basis). The second part of the job description is concerned with supporting details. These may include the background requirements for the position such as education, experience, particular expertise, working conditions including work hours, vacations and holidays, location, salary, benefits, listing of available training opportunities, and available ancillary services such as child care, transportation, food service (Ilsley & Niemi, 1981). In screening a volunteer for a position, Ilsley and Niemi (1981) urge that the statement of working conditions include "opportunities to learn new skills, a volunteer's degree of responsibility (including decision-making responsibility), and degree of job flexibility in terms of time" (p. 53).

In job detailing, some organizations, particularly in the business community, may have a more detailed format description that reflects an organizational culture and stresses strict measurable accountability. Such a description must include (a) the objectives or overall results to be accomplished by the position and the dimensions or scope of the position: (b) measurable standards to be used to determine when the objectives or results have been successfully achieved; (c) any management or supervisory duties; (d) primary technical duties and responsibilities; and (e) necessary significant working relationships within the organization (Munson, 1984, p. 43).

Exercise Seven

Using the information put together in Exercises Three, Five and Six, and the information provided above, write a job description for the position vacancy.

Advertising, Recruiting, and Interviewing Staff

Once the job description has been written, it is used as the basis for drafting the position advertisement. Supply enough information in the advertisement to solicit responses from persons who fit the requirements. Those who are interested can formally request the full job description.

Persons interested in program planning positions may be recruited from teacher-training institutions (if the person's experience has been supplemented with actual program planning experience from the business sector), from instructors in the armed forces, and educational technologists in schools or training settings (Nadler, 1979). From a business sector point or view, the hirer may wish to look first within the organization for candidates, and then to extend the search to government employment agencies, private employment bureaus, and recruitment consultants to external sources. In addition to the above sectors, recruitment of volunteers can also include looking at community organizations such as YWCA and YMCA, Head Start Programs, VISTA, service clubs, retired citizen organizations, parent-teacher associations, religious organizations and voluntary bureaus (Ilsley & Niemi, 1981).

The job description specifies criteria against which all prospective candidates will be assessed. The description may provide a broad framework for the committee or individual doing the hiring to consider and appraise each candidate. Each criterion in the job description may be given a rating of importance. This rating may be numerical, such as (1) first, (2) second, etc., or it may be a percentage of importance the item carries, such as 10% or 25% of what the job entails. Set up a score review sheet for each candidate. On each item rate the individual from (1) high to (5) low. (At the bottom of the rating sheet write any notes you wish on why you assigned a particular score.) Multiply each individual item score by the numerical or percentage rating of importance. The lower the score, the closer the individual is to the qualifications that were desired. These separate scores can provide a basis for discussion of the relative merits of each candidate. The scores also may be totaled for each candidate. Again, the lower the total score, the closer the candidate would be to the desired qualifications.

Identifying specific job description competencies in the interview should be planned ahead of time. A detailed example of the process for hiring instructors can he found in Flannery (1991b) and is briefly described here. One function of the instructor is to deliver the learning design. In so doing, the instructor is expected to be knowledgeable about the topic at hand and to communicate about the topic effectively. A hypothetical topic might be basic managerial skills. In the interview one way to look for the two competencies is to engage the individual in a discussion of one session the individual teaches about basic managerial skills. The committee should ask itself the following questions: "Does the person relate a cohesive topic?" "Does the individual give concrete examples as part of the explanation?" "How well does the individual clearly and completely answer the committee's questions about the topic?" "Does the individual reframe explanations so the content can be understood from the questioner's learning style?"

Exercise Eight

First, determine the importance of each of the parts of the job description by assigning a percentage of importance to each item. Second, determine specifically what questions in the interview will be asked to determine if the interviewee possesses the required competencies.

CARING FOR STAFF

Once the staff has been hired, staffing responsibilities do not end. Rather, the staff must be nurtured. Staff nurturing consists of orientation, development, support, and encouragement. This is a responsibility of the administrator.

Orientation

New staff must initially be oriented to the policies, procedures and requirements of the organization. This orientation is often provided at the beginning of one's tenure in an agency. Its purpose is to generally inform, to introduce the most important people and their functions, and to alleviate initial anxiety (Ilsley & Niemi, 1981). Although this first orientation is necessary to introduce people to the overall climate and expectations of the agency, it is usually not enough. As the person experiences the various "firsts" of the position, questions arise as to policies, pertinent contacts, and methods of operating. Too, the administrator needs to know the employee's concerns and needs. Subsequent orientations may be held or a resource person may be appointed to give the new employee/volunteer the information or assistance needed.

Development

"Professional development is a process of keeping current in the state of the art, keeping competent in the state of practice, and keeping open to new theories, techniques and values" (Chalofsky & Lincoln, 1983, p. 13). To offer staff development is to offer opportunities for improvement and updating. Laird (1985) urges the establishment of a "development plan" for each of the program planning staff. This plan lists the particular needs the individual has in order to perform the assigned tasks well and to remain current with state of the art information. The development plan can be designed jointly by the administrator and the individual, or developed by the individual and presented to the administrator for any additional input. When and how the individual will obtain the skills or new learning are detailed in the development plan. Drawing on employee development plans, the administrator sees that opportunities for the needed in-service training are available.

Exercise Nine

The new employee has been hired for the open position. Become the new employee. Consider the strengths and weaknesses you bring to this position. Create a plan for your own professional development in this specific position.

Support and Encouragement

Motivation theories offer insight into staff persons' initial and continued performance. Even though this chapter will not go into detail about theories of motivation, it is necessary to raise the topic because in understanding personal motives the administrator can find ways to support and encourage employees.

Motives have been conceptualized as intrinsic and extrinsic. Intrinsic motives are directed to some result internal to the individual. Enjoyment in designing a superb program and delight with an instructional segment which stimulated a high degree of learner involvement are examples of intrinsic motives. External motives are directed to some result outside the individual. Working to obtain an award for the superb program design or meeting company goals for learner involvement in the teaching/learning process are examples of extrinsic motives. Employees have different combinations of intrinsic and extrinsic factors which motivate them on the job. These factors may change over time and as circumstances change. It has been argued that when both extrinsic and intrinsic organizational rewards are high, the employee may devalue intrinsic rewards. Conversely, when organizational rewards are low, intrinsic rewards become more important for the employee (Straw, 1976). As the administrator understands the factors related to employee motivation, appropriate support and encouragement can be provided for each employee.

It must be noted that there is evidence that volunteer staff differ from employed staff in their motivations for work. In comparing paid staff and volunteer staff workers in similar settings, Pearce (1982) found that volunteers were much more variable in their work performance than employees. Volunteers were more enthusiastic about their work and did extra things that needed to be done. But they could not necessarily be relied on to arrive at work or to perform at a minimal level. Employees, by contrast, could be relied on to arrive at work and to perform at an acceptable level, but were less likely to approach their job with zeal. Second, volunteers ignored organizational leaders, employees did not. The organizational structures differ in methods of allocating formal authority. In volunteer organizations authority is vested in the membership as a whole. Leaders are more dependent on volunteers for their work efforts, and have to provide personal inducements other than wages to retain the volunteer. (See Ilsley & Niemi, 1981, for a discussion of ways to give recognition to the volunteer's accomplishments.) In the employing organization all authority is invested in the employer. Leaders are not as dependent on employees for their work efforts because salaries and inducements may be used as leverage for work. The motivations of these two groups clearly differ, challenging leaders to be knowledgeable and creative in their support and encouragement of workers.

EVALUATING THE STAFF

Although much has been written in the adult education and training literature about program evaluation (Guba & Lincoln, 1988; Kirkpatrick, 1994; Fink, 1995; and Moran, 1996), little has been written about the evaluation of persons who engage in the programming endeavor. Yet this is a vital component of the staffing process. Further, since program planning success is related in part to those persons who contribute to its design, it is integrally linked to the program planning process.

The aim of staff evaluation is management of performance. People are assessed for how they are performing in their jobs. The information that is obtained provides a basis for the planning of training, further on-the-job experience, self-development, or mentoring programs which will promote the professional development of the employee or volunteer.

The appraisal aspect of the staff evaluation is related to four aspects previously mentioned: (1) the job description, (2) the skills needed for the job, (3) how the skills were looked for in the interview, and (4) the developmental plan worked out once the employee was hired. Early in the individual's tenure with the agency, these aspects provide a framework for evaluating the staff member. The administrator and the employee should have a clear and common understanding of each point of the future evaluation. When the evaluation takes place, the purpose should be to provide feedback to the employee, the administrator, and the agency. First, the feedback will identify employee strengths and weakness. Next, it will be a catalyst for planning what development the employee needs to strengthen positive aspects and to improve the weak aspects. Finally, the process can include appraisal of those aspects of the agency or administrative style which cause problems for the employee. The employee and the administrator together can look at joint solutions, clarify expectations, causes of problems, and potential solutions (London et al., 1990). The administrator is responsible for following up on the assessment on an organizational as well as an individual level. This includes assigning responsibility, establishing a firm timetable for change, and establishing feedback procedures (London et al., 1990).

Questions about evaluations are often connected to the organizational culture of the agency. In many businesses, the goal of the process is to deal as far as possible with objectively observed facts. In this model, the material from the job description, specific skills needed for the tasks and developmental plan are concretized in terms of specific behaviors, standards of the behavior, time available for completion of the behavior, and the target results. For example, a safety training program for new employees of a poultry plant on how to handle equipment will be developed and piloted by August 1. There will be two criteria for success: (1) at the end of the training program 90% of the new employees will demonstrate proper usage of the equipment, and (2) the long-term target, after one year of employment, will be a 70% reduction of carpel tunnel-related work claims by this group.

The appraisal process for other agencies, often human service agencies, combines collection of both objectively observed facts and subjective material. The basis for collecting these data is the belief that "It is virtually impossible to imagine any human behavior that is not heavily mediated by the context in which it occurs" (Guba & Lincoln, 1981, p. 62). This latter process includes concern for understanding beliefs the employee has about the tasks performed, perceived influences in the agency environment, perception of ability to do the tasks, and importance of the tasks to the worker. It also links both extrinsic and intrinsic aspects of motivation to evaluation.

Exercise Ten

Prepare a brief initial appraisal document which draws on information contained in (a) the job description you wrote, (b) the list of skills needed for the job, (c) and the hypothetical employee development plan.

Approaches to Staff Evaluation

The processes for actually conducting the appraisal vary. Four particular aspects of conducting the staff evaluation will be considered here: (1) collecting objectively observed facts and subjective opinions, using quantitative and qualitative data; (2) self-assessment and other-assessment; (3) collecting data during the course or end of an employment year; (4) and proactive and reactive evaluations.

Using Quantitative and Qualitative Data

Collection of data may involve several approaches. (See Patton, 1990 for detailed methods.) A quantitative approach uses some sort of rating scale to determine and rate specific behavior. The rating scale might include the following: (1) superior, (2) well above standard, (3) above standard, (4) at standard, (5) below standard, and (6) unsatisfactory. Each of the behaviors an individual is expected to perform would be rated according to the scale. Specific comments could be added after the behaviors were rated.

A qualitative approach would seek to understand how workers perceive their assigned tasks, the circumstances of carrying them out, and their beliefs about the difficulty/ease or value of the tasks. Qualitative data would be collected through interviews, case studies or ethnographies. (See Kanter, 1977, for an ethnography in the business sector that demonstrates the material which can be collected through qualitative means.)

Self-Assessment and Other-Assessment

The question arises, "Who should do the evaluating, the employee or someone else?" Many performance appraisal systems call for employees to rate themselves and then compare their ratings to those of their administrators and supervisors. The problem with such an approach is that studies demonstrate little congruence between self-perceptions and evaluations by others (Shrauger & Schoeneman, 1979; Harris & Schaubroeck, 1988; Nowack, 1992). Self-responses by managers and professional personnel are more likely to be skewed toward the positive side (Nowack, 1992). Should the self-assessment process be discarded? I think not. First, the self-assessment and other ratings should be compared to other measures such as objective performance criteria. Second, those using self-ratings should expect some disagreement between the self-rating and that of others. Such disagreement can provide an opportunity for all to "explore the nature and meaning of these perceptual gaps and encourage discussion among all individuals providing ratings" (Nowack, 1992). In this way, individuals can begin to understand how others perceive them, and all parties involved can work at defining a common set of expectations for the position. Third, there are guidelines which can facilitate the accuracy of self-assessment ratings. (See Schrauger & Osberg, 1981.)

Time of Collecting Staff Evaluation Data

Staff evaluation should take place continuously in order for staff development to be an active process (Nadler, 1984). In other words, administrators should look at the work of individuals as it occurs. As Holt (1987) suggests, "creative evaluation sometimes includes impromptu interviewing during coffee breaks, during individual and group briefings, or while traveling to and from off-site programs with staff" (p. 178). In addition to ongoing evaluation, a six-month or yearly evaluation should be held. The purpose of such evaluation is to summarize the time frame, bring the employee's work together so it may be looked at as a whole, and make long range plans for improvement.

Proactive and Reactive Evaluation

Proactive evaluations are those which anticipate what will occur and help to prevent problems. Reactive evaluations are those which occur as a result of a problem arising and are usually too late to correct the problem (Holt, 1987). For example, from experience, a program administrator may perceive that a newly designed program will not be acceptable to the organization in its present form. If the administrator points this out to the program designer before the program is distributed, the designer will have the opportunity to remedy the situation. If the problem is not pointed out ahead of time, the leadership of the organization will find the program lacking and chastise the program designer.

Exercise Eleven

Design an overall evaluation procedure for a new employee. Specify how you will collect observable facts, subjective facts, quantitative and qualitative data, self-assessment and other-assessment. Decide when and how often you will collect such data (throughout or at the end of the year). Decide whether you will accept both reactive and proactive forms of evaluation. Determine what you will do and why.

SUMMARY

It should be clear from this chapter that staffing is much more than a quick and easy selection of new employees. Rather, it is a detailed function requiring skill to define clearly the tasks needed to be performed, to perceive the corporate culture in which the tasks will be done, and to match well an interviewee with the organization and the tasks to be performed. It includes development, support, encouragement and evaluation of the staff persons. Without well qualified and up-to-date persons filling the roles of program administrator, program designer and program instructor, one cannot expect quality, state-of-the-art programming. Hence, while often forgotten in the literature about program planning, the role of staffing programs is pivotal to the program planning process.

QUESTIONS FOR STUDY AND DISCUSSION

1. What are the major program planning functions in your organization?
2. On what bases are the number of needed program planning personnel determined? When hiring, how can it be determined if the applicant possesses the required skills?
3. How can the organizational culture of an institution he determined?
4. In the interview, how can it be determined if there is a match between the organizational culture and the work-related values of the interviewee?
5. What aspects might be considered in determining salary range and benefits?
6. What content should be included in writing a job description?
7. What ideas might be incorporated into creating a developmental plan with an employee?
8. What documents might be considered relevant for an initial performance appraisal?
9. What are the major considerations in the design and collection of the employee evaluation?

REFERENCES

American Society for Training and Development. (1983). *Workplace basics: The skills employers want.* Washington, DC.

Armstrong, M. (1988). *A handbook of human resource management.* New York: Nichols.

Brookfield, S. D. (1986). *Understanding and facilitating adult learning.* San Francisco: Jossey-Bass.

Caffarella, R. S. (1988). *Program development and evaluation resource hook for trainers.* New York: John Wiley.

Caffarella, R. S. (1994). *Planning programs for adult learners.* San Francisco: Jossey-Bass.

Chalofsky, N., & Lincoln, C. I. (1983). *Up the HRD ladder: A guide for professional growth.* Reading, MA: Addison-Wesley.

Fink, A. (1995). *Evaluation for education and psychology.* Thousand Oaks, CA: Sage.

Flannery, D. D. (1991a). Adults' expectations of instructors: criteria for hiring and evaluating instructors. *Continuing Higher Education Review,* 55(1 and 2), 34–46.

Flannery, D. D. (1991b). Adult learning: Little boxes all the same. *Adult Learning,* 3(3), 31.

Guba, E. G., & Lincoln, Y. S. (1981). *Effective evaluation: Improving the usefulness of evaluation through naturalistic approaches.* San Francisco: Jossey-Bass.

Harris, M., & Schaubroech, J. (1988). A meta-analysis of self-supervisor, self-peer and peer-supervisor ratings. *Personnel Psychology, 41,* 43–62.

Holt, M. E. (1987). Using evaluation to monitor plans and assess results. In R. C. Simerly and Associates (Ed.), *Strategic planning and leadership in continuing education.* San Francisco: Jossey-Bass (166–164).

Ilsley, P. J., & Niemi, J. (1981). *Recruiting and training volunteers.* New York: McGraw-Hill.

Kanter, R. M. (1977). *Men and women of the corporation.* New York: Basic Books.

Kirkpatrick, D. L. (1994). *Evaluating training programs: The four levels.* San Francisco: Berrett-Koehler.

Knowles, M. S. (1980). *The modern practice of adult education* (2nd ed.). New York: Cambridge.

Knox, A. B. (1981). The continuing education agency and its parent organization. In J. C. Votruba (Ed.), *Strengthening internal support for continuing education.* New Directions for Continuing Education, no. 9. San Francisco: Jossey-Bass.

Laird, D. (1985). *Approaches to training and development* (2nd ed.). Reading, MA: Addison-Wesley.

Lauffer, A. (1978). *Doing continuing education and staff development.* New York: McGraw-Hill.

London, M., Bassman, E. S., & Fernandez, J. P. (1990). *Human resource forecasting and strategy development: guidelines for analyzing and fulfilling organizational needs.* New York: Quorum Books.

McGregor, D. (1960). *The human side of enterprise.* New York: McGraw-Hill.

Moran, J. J. (1997). *Assessing adult learning: A guide for practitioners.* Malabar, FL: Krieger.

Morgan, G. (1986). *Images of organization.* Newbury Park, CA: Sage.

Munson, L. (1984). *How to conduct training seminars.* New York: McGraw-Hill.

Nadler, L. (1984). *Handbook of human resource development.* New York: John Wiley.

Nadler, L. (1979). *Developing human resources* (2nd ed). Austin, TX: Learning Concepts.

Nowack, K. M. (1992) Self-Assessment and later-assessment as a dimension of management development. In R. A. Swanson (Ed.). *Human Resource Development Quarterly,* 3(2), 141–155.

Patton, M. (1990). *Qualitative evaluation and research methods* (2nd ed.). Newbury Park, CA: Sage.

Pearce, J. L. (1982) Leading and following volunteers: Implications for a changing society. *The Journal of Applied Behavioral Science, 6*(3), 385–394.

Schein, E. H. (1985). *Organizational culture and leadership: A dynamic view.* San Francisco: Jossey-Bass.

Schrauger, J. S., & Osberg, T. (1981). The relative accuracy of self-predictions and judgments by others in psychological assessment. *Psychological Bulletin, 90,* 322–351.

Schrauger, J. S., & Schoeneman, T. 3. (1979). Symbolic interactionist view of self-concept: Through the looking glass darkly. *Psychological Bulletin, 86,* 549–572.

Simerly, R. C., & Associates (1987). *Strategic planning and leadership in continuing education.* San Francisco: Jossey-Bass.

Straw, B. M. (1976). *Intrinsic and extrinsic motivation.* Morristown, NJ: General Learning Press.

Votruba, J. C. (1981). A final note to continuing educators working as change agents. In J. C. Votruba (Ed.), *Strengthening internal support for continuing education.* New Directions for Continuing Education. 9. San Francisco: Jossey-Bass.

## 19

Program Planning in Retrospect

Peter S. Cookson

Program planning is a complex process that involves the bringing together of ideas, activities, and resources in order to achieve improvements in knowledge, skills, or sensitivity for individuals, groups, and organizations. The focus of the authors of this book has been the planning of programs that are primarily under organizational or institutional sponsorship. This chapter takes a retrospective look at the overall process. In stepping back to take in the "big picture," so to speak, a cohesive, interrelated, and unitary process becomes discernible. The first part of this final chapter reviews the process as it has been described in preceding chapters. The final section explores some of the implications of that process for the program planning profession.

THE PROGRAM PLANNING PROCESS REVIEWED

Chapter 1 presented the conceptual context not only for program planning, but also for the selection and organization of the contents of the chapters that followed. That context included Houle's (1972) definition of adult education as a comprehensive process that encompasses all forms of organized and systematic learning engaged in by adults, regardless of the organizational or institutional auspices or the purpose—as long as the intent is improvement of men and women (alone, in groups, or institutional settings). No distinction is made between the terms *education* and *training*. Given Houle's definition, both are instances of what

Houle (1972) refers to as *a basic unity of process* which all education and training programs have in common.

The second part of the conceptual framework constituted a typology of adult education organizational, technological, and programmatic elements. These elements, together with their sub-elements, enable distinctions not otherwise possible. They also enable discerning program planners to make comparisons across multiple organizational and program realities.

The third part of the conceptual framework delineated a comprehensive approach to program planning that builds on and attempts to go beyond a synthesis of prototypical and other program planning models presented in the literature. This framework provided the outline for the table of contents of the book and, at the same time, suggested some major amendments to the steps offered by program planning models described in the adult education and training literature.

To acquaint readers with the nature of the planning, Chapter 2 presented three prototypical models and Chapter 3 described a number of alternative program planning models. A useful exercise is to compare the underlying assumptions and planning elements named by all of these models. Out of such an exercise can come a heightened sensitivity to issues that otherwise go unnoticed in day-to-day planning practice.

Building on insights offered by both prototypical and alternative program planning models, programmers can themselves attend not only to the "how-to's," but also the "why's" of their own programming practice. Chapter 4 suggested a process of self-examination in terms of one's current or potential programming roles. Developing a philosophical and ethical orientation, as described in Chapter 5, can ensure a more self-directed and more confident posture toward one's own programming practice. As illustrated in Chapter 6 such self-reflection can be further reinforced by program planners seeking a realistic view of their own practice—not solely in terms of idealized practices embodied in program planning models, but also in terms of the political and strategic realities in the social context of the organizational sponsor, with its attendant sets of stakeholders and interests.

Once planners form a professional and realistic sense of self as program planners, their thoughts can turn to the planning context. Part of that context, covered in Chapter 7, comprises the situational context to which the organizational sponsor is continuously subject. Once programmers identify these economic, cultural, political forces, they can increase their awareness of not only their nature but also of the implications for their work.

Continuing a commitment to relevant and realistic programming leads the programmer to consider the organizational context for planning. Although this step blends into an assessment of specific learning needs, it can be regarded as qualitatively and conceptually separate. Chapter 8 presented specific metaphors programmers can use to analyze the organizational context of their training or continuing education programs. Informed about organizational parameters, as well as the attendant sets of realities held by various stakeholders within the organization, programmers can more knowledgeably focus on the details of any given program assignment.

Another essential part of the planning context is the nature of adult learners. Chapter 9 explained that the capacity and motivation of adults to participate and learn in education and training programs can vary as they experience physiological and psychological changes resulting from their movement through the life cycle. Behaviorist, cognitivist, humanistic, social learning, andragogical, transformative learning, and adult development theories of learning provide not only explanations of how adults learn, but also how that learning can be induced or facilitated.

With a strong understanding and orientation to the various contexts of planning work, the program planner can focus clearly on the contingencies attendant to specific program activities. One step that is filled with numerous possibilities for further planning activities is that of specification of specific learning needs. Chapter 10 explained that the functionalist (rational, technical, or positivist) approach to needs assessment assumes that needs can be objectively identified and measured. Based on the scientific approach, the functionalist approach enables the planner to focus on helping adults learn what they need to know to solve their problems.

The empowerment perspective, on the other hand, focuses on empowering individuals, communities, or societies in order to change the oppressive structures to which they are subjected. In this subjectivist view, needs assessment is integral to part of the whole educational process. Operating from either perspective, program planners can involve several sets of stakeholders in the determination of learning needs. In the decisions that surround this step, the core question, "What is my reason for doing this program?" calls for planners to activate their own beliefs and values, together with a sense of professional artistry.

If programs are to be effective, program planners must convey to others a clear sense of the desired outcomes. Hence, it is of vital importance that planners be familiar with a variety of approaches to determine program priorities, purposes, and objectives. As described in Chapter 11, program planners must possess not only the technical skills to arrive at clear sets of program priorities, but they must also be aware of and be able to reconcile the often conflicting sets of values of sometimes multiple sets of program stakeholders. Setting priorities inevitably involves engaging the active participation of others, setting and applying selection criteria, and tabulating the differential weightings. Trainers and continuing educators may determine program priorities by processing the various possibilities through a series of filters corresponding to specified values, different dimensions of importance, various feasibility criteria, or a combination of both importance and feasibility criteria. To go beyond program purposes, planners may elect to designate specific objectives. Alternatives to setting specific program objectives may include specification of program purposes, program processes, program content, and/or beneficial outcomes.

With the press of day-to-day responsibilities, programmers often overlook or dismiss the value of effective program evaluation. Yet programmers can benefit greatly from knowing whether their efforts deter or enable learning, identifying problem areas, and conveying to others the worth of their program activities. Chapter 12 indicated that evaluation methods vary substantially according to the evaluation approach adopted. Although the planner may assume at least seven kinds of evaluation focuses, they most often limit their evaluations by default to participant reactions. Yet at the micro level, evaluation can also take into account learners' perspectives, educators' perspectives, or a combination of both groups. Such information may be gathered via interviews, observations, documents, feedback committees, group discussions, peer review panels, snowball discussion techniques, end-of-class analyses, testimonials and anecdotes, case studies, portfolios, rating scales, and checklists, as well as by pretests, posttests, and quizzes.

The concept of evaluation *reference points,* or the standards with which actual performance can be compared, also suggests ways in which programmers may enlarge their repertoire of evaluation strategies.

Typically the culmination of program planning is marked by the step in which organized learning occurs—usually in connection with instruction. Design of the instructional component of education or training programs involves systematic application of instructional design principles. At the heart of the individualizing instructional process, as presented in Chapter 13, are specific assumptions about the adult learners, the roles of the instructor, and the centrality of individualizing the instructional process. A six-step individualizing instructional process model offered guidelines to the planning of this step. The checklist provided as part of the chapter constitutes an additional tool for programmers seeking to improve their overall program planning performance.

Determination of the formats for learning refers to the designation of the specific methods and techniques to take place when adults are organized for learning experiences. Chapter 14 explained that formats can vary according to the characteristics of the learner, the instructor, the content, and the situation. Vital to knowledgeable selection of suitable formats is an understanding of relevant theories, including Verner's (1964) tripartite distinction of method, technique and device, Houle's (1972) designation of 11 categories of learning situations, Boyd and Apps's (1980) distinction among individuals, groups, and communities, and Seaman and Fellenz's (1989) four aspects of teaching-learning interactions: learner, teacher, content, and situation. Each of these aspects may be viewed as points of reference in lessening programmers' overdependence upon classes and workshops and in broadening their options for specific formats for learning: individual formats, group formats, and formats for learners in total communities.

Participation in education and training programs is generally voluntary. Even when it is not, the cooperation and willingness of adults to participate are still dependent upon individual volition. Promotion and marketing are vital components to the program planning process for both training and education programs— even those that are conducted *in-house.* Programmers who have conducted analyses of the environment both internal and external to the organizational sponsor and who have entered into negotiations with participants and other stakeholders, will have already implemented many marketing principles. As suggested by Chapter 15, additional strategies will incorporate specification of marketing objectives, formulation of specific marketing strategies, establishment of benchmarks for evaluation, and measurement of performance. Implementation of marketing strategies can be facilitated via personal contacts and networking, interviews, the Delphi technique, nominal group procedure, focus groups, task forces and advisory groups, community forums, simulation, and gaming. Promotional strategies may involve such strategies as press releases, brochures, contacts with teachers, past participants, direct mail, television, radio, newspapers, ads in trade journals, tracking responses to mailings, data base marketing, fliers, posters, special events, networking and personal contacts, product sampling, and coupons.

Before programmers can effectively induce prospective participants to initiate their participation or subsequently to continue their participation until the completion of the program, they must understand why such adults do or do not typically participate in their programs. They must examine such participation through the eyes of their prospective participants. Such examination can be possible as programmers learn to critically examine aspects of their own practice and to question their own often facile explanations of the actions of reluctant and resistant participants. Reconsideration of their own and others' typical interpretations of what they observe can lead to new insights and more effective ways of responding to what was the formerly misunderstood performance of others. As elucidated in Chapter 16, adults exhibit one of three patterns of demand toward education and training programs: high-to-medium demand, low-latent-no demand, and negative demand. Adults with high-to-medium demand are quick to respond to whatever programs programmers offer. Adults with low-latent-no demand, however, perceive the education and training programs quite differently from adults in the first group. Certain adults' self-assessment, past schooling experiences, and culture can clash with the values inherent in education and training programming. Programmers who perceive how such conditions can exacerbate dispositional barriers to participation can take responsive measures to improve their recruitment and retention effectiveness. An understanding of the reluctance and resistance experienced by adults who experience subcategories of negative demand can assist programmers to arrive at insightful explanations closer to the reality of those whom they would recruit and retain in their programs.

In their work, programmers need to demonstrate "value added" to their supervisors, as well as to others with an interest in the "success" of the programs. Effective programmers can benefit from: awareness of potential sources of funding for their programs, understanding of financial concepts, ability to formulate a budget, and skills in conducting various forms of financial analysis. In determining the "value added" by their programs, programmers can draw on the tools of cost-benefit analysis, cost-effectiveness analysis, and break-even analysis to determine program pricing as well as to build a solid foundation of support for their programs with their respective stakeholders. These dimensions of program financing were discussed in Chapter 17.

Without well-qualified and up-to-date persons filling the roles of program administrator, program designer, and program instructor, quality, state-of-the-art programming cannot be expected. The role of staffing programs is pivotal to the program planning process. Effective program planners recognize staffing is much more than a quick and easy selection of new employees. Indeed, they recognize staffing as a detailed function requiring skill to define clearly the tasks needed to be performed, perceive the organizational culture in which the tasks will be done, and match interviewees with the organization and job requirements. As described in Chapter 18, staffing includes development, support, encouragement, and evaluation of the staff persons. It is a vital part of program planning.

FORGING A PROFESSIONAL IDENTITY

A question I have often asked the participants in my courses and workshops on program planning is, "What is the *so what* of this information?" My participants and I have then proceeded to explore the implications for their current practice of the principles learned. It has been most gratifying for me to see emerge from such explorations an increased understanding of the dynamics of their work, a heightened sense of appreciation of adult learners, an augmented desire to forge a professional trainer or continuing education identity, and a commitment to seek continuous movement toward mastery of the planner's craft.

Without exception, the authors of the chapters reviewed in the previous section have set the stage for continuing reflection and exploration of not only the *what* and the *how* of program planning practices, but also the *so what.* They have avoided *cookbook approaches* consisting of a predetermined number of steps to accomplish specific programming tasks. Although such prescriptions may work in specific situations described in train-the-trainer workshops, they do little to stimulate a lifelong pursuit of mastery of the program planning craft that I characterize as comprising the forging of a professional identity.

To optimize professional growth and development, the authors in this text have chosen to describe multiple approaches to accomplish the different program planning tasks. They have also placed these approaches within theoretical frameworks. Study of the chapters in this book can enable program planners to add to their repertoire of systematic responses to the problems that arise from their day-to-day practice. They can thus increase the opportunities for men and women to experience the learning required to meet their own learning and performance objectives as well as those set by their respective organizations and societies. As programmers experiment with both the familiar and the new approaches described in this book, as they reflect on how these approaches relate to their experience, as they engage in dialogue with program participants as well as colleagues and peers (both within and without their respective organizations), and as they take into account the results of before-during-and-after program evaluations, they can more competently and knowledgeably plan and implement effective training and educational programs. It is my hope that study of this book will be yet one step in what may be a lifelong journey toward program planning improvement and mastery.

A commitment to mastery can lead program planners to engage a growing body of literature on various aspects of program planning. Systematic reading of professional training and continuing education journals, and participation in professional meetings and other association activities are specific ways to increase awareness of program planning approaches.

One of the fundamental points that has found expression throughout this book is that, regardless of the setting in which adults are learning, "a basic unity of process" constitutes an integral component of the entire program planning process. Those who do not perceive program planning in this way may be limiting their vision to the specific concerns of program *x* or program *y* or to the need to satisfy the demands of their particular organization. Recognition of "a basic unity of process," however, enables program planners to transcend the particulars of the moment, to cultivate a sense of solidarity with practitioners across the training and education spectrum, and to exercise a greater commitment to their craft than would otherwise be possible. Such an enlarged vision can more adequately incorporate the interests of adult learners as well as the standards and ideals of their respective professional associations and the fields of training or education practice such associations represent. When shared by a critical mass of interacting individuals, these components of a "professional identity" make possible concerted actions to strengthen the fields of training and continuing education, as well as the more encompassing field of lifelong education.

The goal is for program planners to cultivate a sense of critical reflection about their practice, the organizational and external contexts in which they work, as well as the realities encountered by both current and prospective program participants and other stakeholders. By virtue of their increased discernment and a commitment to act responsibly and ethically, such program planners can come to recognize options not even imagined by no less well meaning, no less hard working, but less discerning program planners. To that end this book has been written.

REFERENCES

Boyd, R. D., & Apps, J. W. (1980). A conceptual model for adult education. In R. D. Boyd, J. W. Apps, & Associates, *Redefining the discipline of adult education.* San Francisco: Jossey-Bass.

Houle, C. O. (1972). *The design of education.* San Francisco: Jossey-Bass.

Seaman, D. F., & Fellenz, R. A. (1989). *Effective strategies for teaching adults.* Columbus, OH, Merrill.

Verner, C. M. (1964). Definition of terms. In G. Jensen, A. A. Liveright, & W. Hallenbeck (Eds.), *Adult education: Outlines of an emerging field of university study.* Washington, DC: Adult Education Association of the U.S.A.

Author Index

Subject Index